Principles of Geoarchaeology

Principles
of Geoarchaeology

A NORTH AMERICAN PERSPECTIVE

Michael R. Waters

The University of Arizona Press
TUCSON

First paperbound printing 1996
The University of Arizona Press
Copyright © 1992
The Arizona Board of Regents
All rights reserved
∞ This book is printed on acid-free, archival-quality paper.
Manufactured in the United States of America

97 96   6 5 4 3

Library of Congress Cataloging-in-Publication Data

Waters, Michael R.
    Principles of geoarchaeology : a North American perspective /
Michael R. Waters.
        p.   cm.
    Includes bibliographical references (p.   ) and index.
    ISBN 0-8165-0989-1 (cl : acid-free paper)
    ISBN 0-8165-1770-3 (pbk : acid-free paper)
    1. Archaeological geology.   2. Archaeological geology—North
America.   3. North America—Antiquities.   4. Indians of North
America—Antiquities.   5. Excavations (Archaeology)—North America.
I. Title.
CC77.5.W38   1992
970.01—dc20   92-13120
                                                                   CIP

British Cataloguing-in-Publication Data
A catalogue record for this book is available from the British Library.

Believe in your dreams.
If the road you're traveling seems
    all uphill, never quit.
For what's far will be near
    and your hopes will win out
        if you hold to your dreams and never doubt.

J. BERGSMA

For
My parents, John and Jane Waters, who encouraged and supported my dreams, and
My wife and daughter, Sue and Kate Waters, who help me attain my dreams and who continue to share them.

Contents

List of Figures   xi

List of Tables   xvii

Preface   xix

Acknowledgments   xxiii

1. Geoarchaeology   3
    Research Objectives of Geoarchaeology   7
    Conclusion   12

2. Geoarchaeological Foundations   15
    The Archaeological Site Matrix: Sediments and Soils   15
    Stratigraphy   60
    The Geoarchaeological Interpretation of Sediments, Soils,
       and Stratigraphy   88
    Conclusion   114

3. Alluvial Environments   115
    Streamflow   116
    Sediment Erosion, Transport, and Deposition   120
    Alluvial Environments: Rivers, Arroyos, Terraces, and Fans   123
    Alluvial Landscape Evolution and the Archaeological Record   157
    Alluvial Landscape Reconstruction   163
    Conclusion   183

4. Eolian Environments   185

    Sediment Erosion, Transport, and Deposition   185

    Sand Dunes   187

    Loess and Dust   202

    Stone Pavements   204

    Eolian Erosion   208

    Volcanic Ash (Tephra)   210

    Conclusion   213

5. Springs, Lakes, Rockshelters, and Other Terrestrial Environments   215

    Springs   215

    Lakes   220

    Slopes   230

    Glaciers   234

    Rockshelters and Caves   240

    Conclusion   247

6. Coastal Environments   249

    Coastal Processes   249

    Late Quaternary Sea Level Changes   251

    Coastal Environments: Erosional, Submerged, and
      Depositional Coastlines   254

    Coastal Landscape Evolution and the Archaeological Record   262

    Coastal Landscape Reconstruction   280

    Conclusion   290

7. The Postburial Disturbance of Archaeological Site Contexts   291

    Cryoturbation   292

    Argilliturbation   299

    Graviturbation   301

    Deformation   304

    Other Physical Disturbance Processes   306

    Floralturbation   306

    Faunalturbation   309

    Conclusion   316

8. Geoarchaeological Research   317

Appendix A. Geoarchaeological Studies Illustrating the Effects of Fluvial
    Landscape Evolution on the Archaeological Record   321
Appendix B. Geoarchaeological Studies Illustrating Site-Specific Synchronic
    and Diachronic Alluvial Landscape Reconstructions   323
Appendix C. Geoarchaeological Studies Illustrating Regional Synchronic
    and Diachronic Alluvial Landscape Reconstructions   325

References   327

Index   389

Figures

1.1   Generalized model of a human ecosystem   5

1.2   Kirk Bryan in southern Arizona, 1917   9

1.3   Ernst Antevs at the Double Adobe site in Arizona, ca. 1935   10

2.1   Compositional breakdown of the archaeological matrix   17

2.2   Physical and chemical weathering of granite bedrock   18

2.3   Physical and chemical weathering in different precipitation and temperature regimes   19

2.4   Textural classification of clastic sediments by Folk   22

2.5   USDA textural classification of soils   23

2.6   The range of sorting observable in clastic sediments   24

2.7   Well-sorted Pleistocene beach sand and gravel overlain by poorly sorted alluvium in the Salton Trough in Mexico   25

2.8   Classification of the shape of gravel-size particles   27

2.9   The range of rounding and sphericity of sand grains   28

2.10   Tufa-encrusted rocks along the shoreline of Paleolake Cahuilla in California   29

2.11   Mazama ash along Skull Creek in Oregon   32

2.12   Terminology for stratification and bedding structures   34

2.13   Subenvironments of a meandering river depositional environment   38

2.14   Lateral facies relationships between sediments in coexisting alluvial-fan and braided-stream environments   39

2.15   The transformation of an unaltered sediment into a soil profile   41

2.16   The four major processes of soil formation   42

2.17   Major soil structures   44

2.18   Differentiating and classifying the eleven soil orders   54

2.19   The relationship between time and diagnostic soil horizons   55

2.20   The relationship between soil orders and climate   56

2.21   Asa paleosol buried by overbank alluvium on the floodplain of the
       Brazos River in Texas   58

2.22   Stratigraphic and surficial relationships of buried, exhumed, and
       relict paleosols   59

2.23   Lithostratigraphic units of the San Xavier Bridge site in
       Arizona   64

2.24   The valley deposits of a meandering river   66

2.25   The stratigraphy of Whitewater Draw in Arizona   67

2.26   Types of conformable vertical contacts   69

2.27   A late Holocene alluvial section in Delaware Canyon in
       Oklahoma   72

2.28   Lateral relationships between lithostratigraphic units   73

2.29   The upper portion of the lithostratigraphy and pedostratigraphy at
       the Lubbock Lake site in Texas   75

2.30   Types of unconformable contacts   78

2.31   The landscape evolution of a hypothetical alluvial valley and the
       resultant stratigraphic and archaeological record   84

2.32   The correlation of alluvial sequences in Arizona   89

2.33   Landsat photograph of southern Arizona and northern
       Sonora   90

2.34   How archaeological remains become incorporated into sediments
       and soils   94

2.35   The effects of rapid and slow sedimentation rates on archaeological
       occupation surfaces   96

2.36   The black mat at the Murray Springs Clovis site in Arizona   101

2.37   The creation and physical modification of an archaeological site
       context by natural transformational processes   102

2.38   Stratigraphy at the Lubbock Lake site   106

2.39   Geological and cultural history of the Lubbock Lake site   108

2.40   Major lithostratigraphic and pedostratigraphic units at the Lubbock
       Lake site   109

2.41   Sedimentation rates at the Lubbock Lake site   113

3.1   A typical drainage basin   117

3.2   The sources of water for a stream channel   118

3.3   The relationship between stormflow, baseflow, and stream
        discharge   119

3.4   The streamflow velocity needed to entrain, transport, and deposit
        clastic sediments   121

3.5   The transport of clastic sediments within a channel   122

3.6   Map views of meandering, braided, straight, and anastomosing
        rivers   123

3.7   A cross section through a braided stream   124

3.8   Stratigraphy of the C. W. Harris site in California   129

3.9   Erosion and deposition on a meandering river   130

3.10   Cross section through a meandering river   131

3.11   Cross section through a coarse-grained meandering river   133

3.12   Meander loops, showing chute and neck cut-offs   136

3.13   The avulsion of a very sinuous meandering river   137

3.14   Stratigraphy of the Peace Point site in Canada   139

3.15   Textural data from the Pen Point site in South Carolina   141

3.16   Archaeological sites within a natural levee and adjacent
        deposits   142

3.17   Cross section through an anastomosing river   144

3.18   The morphology and deposits of a discontinuous gully and arroyo
        environment   145

3.19   The Santa Cruz River in Arizona   147

3.20   The formation of erosional and depositional stream terraces   150

3.21   The sequence of terraces along the central Des Moines River Valley
        in Iowa   152

3.22   Stratigraphy at the Cherokee Sewer site in Iowa   158

3.23   Landscape evolution and resultant stratigraphy in small drainages in
        the Loess Hills of Iowa   160

3.24   The temporal and spatial relationships of the DeForest
        formation   161

3.25   Cross section showing the modern and ancient topography at the
        Colby site in Wyoming   165

3.26   Geomorphic map of the Colby site in Wyoming   166

3.27   A pile of mammoth bones at the Colby site   167

3.28   Stratigraphy at the Coffey site in Kansas   168

3.29   Typical Ak-Chin fields in the Talahogan Valley in Arizona   172

3.30   Map of the distribution of Hohokam farming settlements on the
       bajada emanating from the Sierrita Mountains in Arizona   174

3.31   Landscape and settlement changes along the San Xavier reach of the
       Santa Cruz River in Arizona from A.D. 800 to 1450   176

3.32   Landscape and settlement changes around the Swan Lake meander
       of the Mississippi River during the last 2000 years   180

4.1   The relationship between particle size and wind velocity   187

4.2   The wind-borne transport of sediment particles   188

4.3   Cross section through a sand dune   189

4.4   Basic eolian dune forms   190

4.5   Topographic dune types   194

4.6   Stratigraphy of the Ake site in New Mexico   197

4.7   Stratigraphy of the Casper site in Wyoming   199

4.8   A parabolic dune near the Casper site in Wyoming   201

4.9   A stratigraphic section of the Dry Creek site in Alaska   204

4.10   Desert pavement near Cibola, Arizona   205

4.11   The formation of a desert pavement by deflation   206

4.12   Stages in the formation of a ventifact   209

4.13   The geographic distribution of the Mazama Ash   211

5.1   Cross section through a typical gravity spring   217

5.2   The stratigraphy of Boney Springs in Missouri   218

5.3   The sequential development of the Hot Springs mammoth locality in
       South Dakota   220

5.4   Cross section through a lake showing temperature stratification of
       the water   221

5.5   The Drinkwater Playa in the Mojave Desert in California   224

5.6   The distribution of pluvial lakes in the western United States during
       the late Pleistocene   226

5.7   A hearth interbedded between late Holocene lacustrine deposits of
       Paleolake Cahuilla   228

5.8   Types of mass movements on slopes   231

5.9   Paleogeographic map of North America during the glacial
       maximum   235

5.10   Landforms and deposits created by continental glaciers   236

5.11   Late Pleistocene glacial till in Montana   237

5.12   Stratigraphy of the Hidden Falls site in Alaska   238

5.13   Rockshelter morphology and characteristics   241

5.14   Landscape evolution of Thorne Cave in Utah   245

5.15   Evolution of a hypothetical rockshelter   246

6.1   Terminology associated with near-shore waves   250

6.2   Beach drift in the swash zone   251

6.3   Longshore and rip currents along a coastline   252

6.4   Eustatic sea-level curves documenting the rise in sea level during the
       last 12,000 years   253

6.5   Wave-cut features associated with an erosional coastline   255

6.6   The shoreface, foreshore, and backshore areas of a beach   257

6.7   Cross section through a typical barrier island   258

6.8   Cross section through a typical tidal flat   259

6.9   The formation of a chenier   260

6.10   A deltaic plain   261

6.11   Submerged sites off the coast of southern California   264

6.12   Shorelines at various times during the late Quaternary on the
       continental shelf of the Gulf Coast   265

6.13   Sea level and the Island Field site on Delaware Bay   267

6.14   Hypothetical changes in landscape and environment along a
       coastline as a result of sea level changes   268

6.15   The destruction of a midden by wave processes   271

6.16   Map and cross-section views of initial occupation sites on a
       prograding shoreline   273

6.17   Processes of marine transgression   276

6.18   Generalized cross section of a submerged portion of the Sabine
       River   279

6.19   Landscape evolution of a submerged segment of the Sabine River off
       the Louisiana coast   282

6.20   Landscape evolution around Cape Henlopen in Delaware   284

6.21   Environmental succession and periods of human occupation during
       an idealized cycle of delta lobe formation   286

6.22   Maps showing the evolution of the Mississippi Delta and the
       succession of occupation on each delta lobe   288

7.1   Refitting of artifacts from the Cave Springs site in Tennessee   293

7.2   Map of the maximum potential depth of soil freezing in the United
       States   294

7.3   Processes associated with freezing and thawing of the ground and
       the resultant movement of an object   296

7.4   Vertical distribution of artifacts at the Hungry Whistler site in
       Colorado   297

7.5   The upward movement of artifacts due to the expansion and
       contraction of a clay matrix   300

7.6   Downslope movement and redeposition of artifacts on slopes   301

7.7   Effects of gelifluction on the Denbigh culture layer at the Iyatayet
       site in Alaska   303

7.8   Human burial offset along a fault line at the Campbell site in
       Missouri   305

7.9   The disturbance of surface and subsurface zones by tree fall   308

7.10   The disturbance of artifacts by root growth and the formation of
       root casts   310

7.11   Calcium carbonate root cast developed in alluvium in the Salton
       Basin in California   311

7.12   Crayfish burrows at the Aubrey site in Texas   313

7.13   Vertical distribution of material at the Jasper Ridge site in
       California   315

Tables

2.1   Wentworth Grain-Size Classification for Sediments with Equivalent
      Phi (ϕ) Units and Sieve Numbers of U.S. Standard Sieves   20
2.2   Sorting Classes Based on Standard Deviation   26
2.3   Terms Used to Describe Bedding Thickness   35
2.4   Soil Horizon Nomenclature   46
2.5   Diagnostic Surface and Subsurface Soil Horizons   50
2.6   A Classification of Quaternary Dating Methods   80
3.1   Preservation Potentials for Buried Archaeological Sites in the
      Central Des Moines River Valley, Iowa   154

Preface

Geoarchaeology is the field of study that applies the concepts and methods of the geosciences to archaeological research. Geoarchaeological studies are important to archaeology because they can significantly enhance the interpretation of human prehistory. The objective of this book is to present the fundamentals of geoarchaeology and discuss their application to archaeology.

A number of books have already been written about geoarchaeology, such as *Environment and Archaeology* (Butzer 1971), *Archaeology as Human Ecology* (Butzer 1982), *Archaeological Geology* (Rapp and Gifford 1985), *Archaeological Sediments in Context* (Stein and Farrand, eds. 1985), *Archaeological Geology of North America* (Lasca and Donahue 1990), and *Geoarchaeology: Earth Science and the Past* (Davidson and Shackley 1976). These are all excellent volumes that provide broad geographical and temporal treatments of geoarchaeology. My book differs from these volumes by presenting a more geographically and temporally focused approach to the field of geoarchaeology that is aimed at the archaeological audience. Specifically, the book is different in three important ways.

First, it focuses on the field aspects of geoarchaeology—stratigraphy, site formation processes, and landscape reconstruction—which are the aspects of geoarchaeology that I believe are the most fundamental to archaeology. The laboratory aspects of geoarchaeology (e.g., techniques used to determine the texture or chemical composition of a stratigraphic unit quantitatively), although important to geoarchaeological interpretation, are not discussed here. These techniques have been thoroughly covered in other volumes by Courty, Goldberg, and Macphail (1989), Limbrey (1975), and Shackley (1975). Furthermore, it is not the intent of this book to cover all aspects of the connection between the geosciences and archaeology. Neither dating techniques nor the application of geophysics and geochemistry to archaeology (e.g., in determining the provenance of artifacts from a site or prospecting for sites or buried features on a site) are reviewed here, as these topics are often considered the domain of archaeometry, not geoarchaeology (Butzer 1982; Parkes 1987). Discussions of specific dating methods can be found in many volumes (e.g., Mahaney 1984; Rutter 1985; Taylor 1987). Reviews of geophysical and geochemical applications to archaeology are found in Butzer 1982, Leute 1987, Parkes 1987, and Rapp and Gifford 1985.

Second, this book focuses on the late Quaternary of North America. This temporal and geographical focus permits detailed discussions of those geoarchaeological methods and concepts that are directly applicable to archaeological research in North America. A broader geographical treatment would have necessitated the dilution of many of the discussions.

Third, this book is specifically tailored to the archaeological audience. I have written the text so that no prior knowledge of geology is required to understand the concepts presented. The text is organized so that basic geological concepts are reviewed at the beginning of each section, followed by discussions and examples of their application to archaeology. This structure is used because it is necessary to understand geological principles before one can understand their application. Furthermore, I have kept geological jargon to a minimum; when geological terms are used, they are defined in the text. Expanded definitions of any term used in this book can be found in the *Glossary of Geology* (Bates and Jackson 1987). Finally, references given in each chapter emphasize the primary geoarchaeological literature, while only secondary geological handbooks and texts are cited. These references will guide the reader to either more detailed summary discussions of geological processes and deposits or to specific geoarchaeological studies that amplify the concepts presented here.

The principles of geoarchaeology are covered in eight chapters. Chapter 1 presents an overview of geoarchaeology and its major research objectives. Chapter 2 introduces the essentials of sedimentology, stratigraphy, geomorphology, pedology, and geochronology, which are necessary to fully understand how the archaeological site matrix is created and dated, how the prehistoric landscape around an archaeological site is reconstructed, and how landscapes can and have changed through time. The next four chapters describe the alluvial, eolian, lacustrine, glacial, rockshelter, spring, and coastal depositional environments in which archaeological sites are buried and preserved. In each of these chapters, the physical processes, deposits, and landforms associated with each environment are reviewed first. These reviews are followed by discussions of natural site formation processes and landscape reconstructions illustrating relationships between people and the land. Chapter 7 discusses the geological and biological processes that operate to modify and destroy archaeological sites and their contexts after burial. The final chapter presents a review of geoarchaeological methodologies and discusses the importance of incorporating geoarchaeological investigations into all stages of an archaeological project from research design through field work to analysis.

One final note: this volume is not a cookbook that will allow anyone without geoarchaeological training to go out to a site and make his or her own interpretations about the origin of the site matrix and paleoenvironmental reconstructions, anymore than one could read a book about car repair and become a master mechanic. Because of the complexity and variability of geological processes, every site or region is geologically unique. To become a geoarchaeologist one must undergo extensive training in both the geosciences and anthropology. This book is intended to provide a background in the fundamentals of geoarchaeology, demonstrate the contributions that can be made by geoarchaeological investigations, and demonstrate the need to make geoarchaeological studies an integral part of archaeological research. In short, I hope this book helps to enhance the interdisciplinary cooperation between the geosciences and archaeology that was fostered over a century ago.

As Colin Renfrew has stated, "because archaeology recovers almost all of its basic data by excavation, every archaeological problem starts as a problem in geoarchaeology" (1976:2). Geoarchaeology is an indispensable part of modern archaeological research, which, in concert with the other archaeological subdisciplines of zooarchaeology, archaeobotany, and archaeometry, can sharpen the interpretation of traditional archaeological data and allow us to understand prehistory more fully. Based on the enthusiasm and response of my archaeological colleagues to the results of geoarchaeological studies at their sites, I am confident that geoarchaeology will continue to grow and will find its proper place in all future archaeological research.

Acknowledgments

I would like to thank the College of Liberal Arts of Texas A & M University, particularly Dean Daniel Fallon and then–Associate Dean Arnold Vedlitz, for their support, which enabled me to work on this book during the summers of 1987 and 1989.

An earlier draft of this manuscript was read by graduate students in my geoarchaeology class. Joy Aderholm, Shawn Carlson, Donald Corrick, Lain Ellis, Mark Gillespie, Norman Haywood, John Jacob, Gary Jones, Steve Lang, Floyd Largent, Cheryl Metz, Lee Nordt, Robyn Pearson, Cynthia Pope, Joe Powell, and Greg Schlenker provided helpful comments. Michelle L. White provided expert technical editing. The manuscript submitted to the University of Arizona Press was reviewed by Jack Donahue and Vance T. Holliday. Both provided valuable comments that improved the final version of the manuscript.

Dora Lopez and Becky Jobling assisted with the typing and printing of the manuscript. Drafted illustrations were prepared under the direction of Tim Davis at the Cartographics Laboratory of the Department of Geography at Texas A & M University. Jana Perry Long, Mike Mitchell, and John Maslonka all prepared the final illustrations in this book. I thank all of them for their care in the preparation of the manuscript and illustrations. Funding for the completion of the illustrations was provided by the College of Liberal Arts and the College of Geosciences, Texas A & M University. I thank Dean Daniel Fallon and Associate Dean Charles Johnson of the College of Liberal Arts and Dean Melvin Friedman and Associate Dean Earl Hoskins of the College of Geosciences for this support. I also thank Vaughn Bryant, head of the Department of Anthropology, and John R. Giardino, head of the Department of Geography, Texas A & M University, for their assistance in obtaining this funding. Joe Simmons provided helpful critiques of my illustrations. Photographs were provided by the Arizona State Museum and by John Albanese, Stan Davis, Reid Ferring, C. Vance Haynes, Eileen Johnson, Peter Mehringer, and W. Raymond Wood.

I also appreciate the support and encouragement of the University of Arizona Press and its staff for the production of this book. I would like to single out Jennifer Shopland, Barbara Beatty, Gregory McNamee, and Alan Schroder for their assistance.

Finally I would like to thank my mentors, C. Vance Haynes and Julian D. Hayden, who through the years encouraged my studies and gave me the tools I needed to pursue a career in geoarchaeology. It has been my good fortune to know and work with these two fine people. Also, I would like to thank all the archaeologists that I have worked with for their support of my geoarchaeological studies. These studies have given me the experience I needed to write this book.

Principles of Geoarchaeology

1

Geoarchaeology

For over a century, archaeologists have been investigating the prehistory of North America. At first they were busy with the task of describing the contents of sites and building regional cultural chronologies, but as the archaeological data base for North America became established, archaeologists began to ask more complex questions about the prehistoric cultures they were investigating. These questions, in turn, demanded more sophisticated interpretation of their field data. This need generated close relationships between archaeology and other scientific disciplines. As the interpretations generated by these outside disciplines became indispensable to archaeological research, subdisciplines of archaeology emerged. Archaeobotany and zooarchaeology are two subdisciplines that evolved from early interdisciplinary studies by botanists and zoologists. Both make a substantial contribution to archaeological research by reconstructing the prehistoric biological communities that surrounded a site and by providing data needed to interpret prehistoric subsistence and diet. Similarly, interdisciplinary cooperation between the physical sciences and archaeology gave rise to archaeometry, which is concerned with chronometric dating techniques, the provenance of materials from archaeological sites, and geophysical and geochemical prospecting for sites or buried features on a site (Butzer 1982; Leute 1987; Parkes 1987). Practitioners of zooarchaeology, archaeobotany, and archaeometry devote most of their effort to archaeological research and the development of new approaches to archaeological problems.

In this regard, one of the longest interdisciplinary relationships has existed between the geosciences and archaeology, and yet geoarchaeology has only recently emerged as a viable and distinct subdiscipline of archaeology. Geoarchaeology is the application of concepts and methods of the geosciences to archaeological research. More specifically, geoarchaeology uses techniques and approaches from geomorphology (the study of landform origin and morphology), sedimentology (the study of the characteristics and formation of deposits), pedology (the study of soil formation and morphology), stratigraphy (the study of the sequence and correlation of sediments and soils), and geochronology (the study of time in a stratigraphic sequence) to investigate and interpret the sediments, soils, and landforms at archaeological sites. An alternative label, archaeological geology, has also been proposed for this subdiscipline. Disagreement exists, however, as to the exact definition of these labels and how each describes the connection between the geosciences and archaeology (Farrand 1985a; Thorson and Holliday 1990).

Although numerous definitions exist for both geoarchaeology and archaeological geology (Gladfelter 1977, 1981; Hassan 1979; Renfrew 1976; Shackley 1979, 1981), the definitions proposed by Butzer (1980a, 1982) and Rapp and Gifford (1982; Gifford and Rapp 1985a) are the most widely quoted. Archaeological geology is defined by Butzer (1982:5) as "geology that is pursued with an archaeological bias or application," and Gifford and Rapp (1985a:19) define it as "the application of geologic principles and techniques to the solution of archaeological problems." Geoarchaeology, on the other hand, is defined by Butzer (1982:35) as "archaeological research using the methods and concepts of the earth sciences" and Gifford and Rapp (1985a:15) define it as "archaeology pursued with the help of geological methodology." While geoarchaeology and archaeological geology use the same techniques to investigate sites, and while they study the same data set, Butzer believes that archaeological geology and geoarchaeology are differentiated by their research objectives and theoretical frameworks. Butzer sees archaeological geology as the routine application of geological concepts and techniques to archaeological research, with little integration of the geological information into the final archaeological interpretations (e.g., simply characterizing and reporting on the attributes of the site matrix). In contrast, he notes, the results of geoarchaeological investigations are coherently integrated with archaeological interpretations because geoarchaeological research objectives are from the start archaeologically framed (e.g., characterizing the attributes of the site matrix to identify site formation processes, permit the reconstruction of the prehistoric landscape around the site, and identify the effects of environmental processes on the location of the site). Furthermore, geoarchaeology is a component of the paradigm Butzer (1978a, 1980a, 1982) and Schoenwetter (1981) call contextual archaeology.

Contextual archaeology is a systems approach in which the contextual components of the human ecosystem (flora, fauna, climate, landscape, and human culture) are reconstructed and the interactions between them are used to explain cultural stability and change (Fig. 1.1). People develop an adaptation that is in a state of dynamic equilibrium with the other compo-

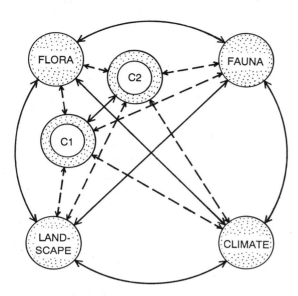

FIGURE 1.1. Generalized model of a human ecosystem, illustrating the relationship between a given culture (C1), a neighboring culture (C2), and the noncultural environment composed of flora, fauna, climate, and landscape subsystems. (Modified from Fedele 1976)

nents of the human ecosystem. This adaptation is maintained as long as the cultural subsystem is flexible enough to adjust itself to internal stresses and external changes in other parts of the ecosystem. However, if the intensity and duration of internal or external stresses caused by change in one or more components of the system is greater than the ability of the cultural subsystem to endure, the system will be sent into disequilibrium and will trigger changes in human behavior. For example, the appearance, reorganization, or abandonment of prehistoric settlements in a given region over time may have been triggered by changing landscape factors (e.g., a rise in a lake level, floodplain entrenchment, or channel meander abandonment), floral factors (e.g., changes in plant assemblages), faunal factors (e.g., animal extinctions or migrations), climatic factors (e.g., drought or increased rainfall), or cultural factors (e.g., conflict or change in the political structure or the level of technological achievement, mobility, or subsistence). Because these factors are part of the larger ecosystem, they may act alone or in combination to cause behavioral responses.

Bradfield's 1971 study of the historic Hopi village of Oraibi in northern Arizona provides an excellent example of this point. Oraibi was situated next to Oraibi Wash, where the conditions for floodwater farming were ideal. Fields were located on the wide and undissected floodplain. Small ditches diverted water out of the shallow channel, and dikes were used to spread the water over the fields. In 1905 and 1906 the floodplain of Oraibi Wash, which had been stable for hundreds of years, became entrenched; the shallow channel that traversed the floodplain was transformed almost overnight into a deep arroyo. This resulted in the loss of primary farmland because water could no longer be directed out of the channel to crops on the floodplain. The Hopi occupants of Oraibi, about 880 people, had already been divided by religious and social disagreements before the floodplain was entrenched (Bradfield 1971; Titiev 1944). The entrenchment of the floodplain intensified these conflicts, especially because older clan farmland was differentially lost and many people faced the threat of starvation. Over the next few years, most of the population abandoned the village of Oraibi and established new settlements or moved into nearby villages. A few people remained at Oraibi and farmed the small patches of irrigatable land that remained. Clearly, the combination of change in the landscape component (entrenchment of Oraibi Wash) and the cultural component (a factionalized and conflicting population) of the human ecosystem triggered settlement reorganization. During this time, however, the other components of the human ecosystem (climate, flora, and fauna) did not change and thus were not part of the stimuli that triggered the behavioral change.

For the human ecological or contextual approach to work at an archaeological site, the site must be investigated not only by the archaeologist but also by a team of specialists that includes a geoarchaeologist, archaeobotanist, and zooarchaeologist (Butzer 1982; Schoenwetter 1981). The geoarchaeologist reconstructs the geological factors of the human ecosystem from the sediments and soils. The archaeobotanist elucidates the floral elements from pollen, phytoliths, and plant macrofossils, and the zooarchaeologist derives the faunal components from the bone assemblages. Climate reconstructions are facilitated by combining the geological and biological data sets and additional studies by other specialists (e.g., a dendroclimatologist). The archaeologist reconstructs the cultural factors of the human ecosystem from the artifacts, features, and structures at the site. The simultaneous investigation and integration of the pertinent geological, biological, climatic, and cultural data sets are what constitute the contextual approach. Each specialist contributes an important part of the reconstruction of the total prehistoric human ecosystem in order to understand the dynamics of human behavior and the reasons for its change through time (Butzer 1982; Clarke 1968; Dincauze 1987; Fedele 1976; Schoenwetter 1981). For example, Gumerman and his colleagues (Gumerman 1988) used the human ecological approach in their study of the prehistoric Anasazi archaeology of Black Mesa in northern Arizona. They analyzed the interplay of environmental and human variables and developed hypotheses to explain prehistoric range expansion, population mobility, abandonment, migration, upland-lowland movements, interaction among different groups, subsistence activities, and territoriality.

Returning to the differences between geoarchaeology and archaeological geology, even though differences are defined by the proponents of these labels, it is clear that the ultimate objective of both is to pursue archaeological research using the principles and methodologies of the geosciences. Regardless of whether we call it archaeological geology or geoarchaeology, both ultimately have the same interdisciplinary objective: to gather and interpret relevant geological data that aid in archaeological interpretation. Like Butzer (1982) and Gladfelter (1981), I prefer the one-word label *geoarchaeology* because it highlights the "geo" data set of the archaeological record. Also, the *geo* prefix emphasizes and modifies the noun *archaeology*, which is the primary reason for studying the matrix of a site. Using this term also implies use of a human ecological systems approach to archaeological research.

Research Objectives of Geoarchaeology

The role of geoarchaeology in modern archaeological research has been shaped by the growth and development of American archaeology. I will not review in detail the emergence and development of geoarchaeology in North America, because general and regional reviews of this topic are presented in Bettis et al. 1985, Dixon and Smith 1990, Ferring 1990a, Gagliano 1984, Gifford and Rapp 1985a and 1985b, Haynes 1990, Rapp and Gifford 1982, and Wilson 1990. Instead, I will emphasize the major research objectives of geoarchaeology and briefly review their emergence.

The first and most fundamental objective of geoarchaeology is to place sites and their contents in a relative and absolute temporal context through the application of stratigraphic principles and absolute dating techniques (Renfrew 1976). This was the original contribution of geology to archaeology, which led to early cooperation between geologists and archaeologists.

During the late nineteenth and early twentieth centuries, geologists became involved in the debate concerning the first appearance of humans in the New World (Haynes 1990), just as they had become involved in a similar debate in Europe during the previous century (Lyell 1863). As in the European controversy, the role of geology in the American debate was to interpret the stratigraphy of early sites and estimate their age. Even though the timing of the arrival of humans to the Americas is still debated today, the first breakthrough concerning the antiquity of humans in North America came in 1927, when Figgins (1927) and Cook (1927) discovered fluted projectile points in direct association with extinct bison in undisturbed deposits near Folsom, New Mexico. Further excavations at the Folsom site by B. Brown confirmed their discovery. However, the association of artifacts with extinct bison was not enough evidence to assign a Pleistocene age to the site, because in the 1920s the age and taxonomy of extinct bison were ambiguous (Meltzer 1991a). To determine the age of the Folsom site unequivocally required stratigraphic studies by a geologist. The following summer, Kirk Bryan conducted geological fieldwork (1929a, 1937), and at the Geological Society of America meetings four months later, Bryan concluded that "the age of the material containing *B. taylori* [now *Bison antiquus*] and the implements must be late Pleistocene or perhaps early Recent [Holocene]" (1929a:129). Thus geology provided the necessary evidence (stratigraphy and dating) to demonstrate conclusively the Pleistocene antiquity of humans in North America. This relationship established the traditional role of geology in archaeology: documenting the stratigraphy and establishing the age of artifact-bearing strata.

Geology maintained a close relationship with archaeology for the next three to four decades as archaeology focused on constructing regional cultural chronologies. Two notable geologists, Kirk Bryan (Fig. 1.2) and Ernst Antevs (Fig. 1.3), dominated the field of geoarchaeology during this era (Haynes 1990) and may be considered the fathers of North American geoarchaeology. These geologists and their students studied the stratigraphy and geochronology at such important archaeological sites as the Lindenmeier Folsom site in Colorado (Bryan and Ray 1940), Sandia Cave in New Mexico (Bryan 1941), Ventana Cave in Arizona (Bryan 1950), Blackwater Draw in New Mexico (Antevs 1935, 1949), Lake Mojave in California (Antevs 1937), the Lehner and Naco Clovis sites in Arizona (Antevs 1953, 1959), and the Cochise Culture sites in Whitewater Draw in Arizona (Antevs 1941). The age of these and other archaeological sites was estimated by correlating the characteristics of the artifact-bearing stratum and the overall site stratigraphy with landforms and deposits thought to have been created during particular climatic episodes defined for the late Quaternary. Many of the ages estimated for archaeological sites were remarkably accurate. For example, Ernst Antevs (1935, 1955, 1959) estimated that the Clovis components at the Lehner site in Arizona and Blackwater Draw in New Mexico dated between 13,000 and 12,000 B.P., based on his geologic-climatic dating technique. Radiocarbon ages have subsequently shown that Clovis dates between 11,500 and 11,000 B.P. (Haynes 1982a, 1982b).

FIGURE 1.2. Kirk Bryan in southern Arizona in 1917. (Photograph courtesy
C. Vance Haynes)

Today, estimating the age of artifact-bearing deposits is no longer necessary in most cases. Instead, ages are assigned to artifact-bearing stratigraphic
units by the radiocarbon method or some other numerical dating technique.
However, correct interpretation of the ages generated from site samples still
requires precise knowledge of the stratigraphic and sedimentologic context
and the postdepositional history of the matrix in order to evaluate potential
avenues of mixing and contamination that might skew the dating of the
archaeological contexts. Even though radiometric methods of dating can
determine the numerical age of stratigraphic units, geoarchaeological investigations of the stratigraphy are still needed to determine the true age of the
site matrix. Microstratigraphic investigations and site dating are crucial to
archaeological interpretations because they provide the spatial framework,
as well as the relative and absolute temporal framework, on which all archaeological and other scientific data are referenced. Further, more sophisticated
geoarchaeological interpretations are predicated on the site and regional
stratigraphy as well as the geochronology of the area surrounding the site.

FIGURE 1.3. Ernst Antevs pointing to a Sulphur Spring stage handstone (mano) in a sand deposit in Whitewater Draw at the Double Adobe site in Arizona, ca. 1935. (Photograph courtesy the Arizona State Museum, University of Arizona)

The second research objective of geoarchaeology is to understand the natural processes of site formation (Renfrew 1976). Site formation has become a major research focus of archaeology in the past few decades as archaeological research has been redirected toward understanding prehistoric human behavior. Schiffer (1972, 1975, 1976, 1983, 1987) has pointed out that the reconstruction of human behavior must be drawn from the archaeological context, which he defines as the extant three-dimensional spatial patterning of individual artifacts, features, and other debris on a site. Before archaeologists can infer meaningful interpretations of human behavior from this existing context, they must know how it was created.

Schiffer has defined two processes that create a site and its associated context: cultural transformations and natural transformations. Cultural transformations are the human processes that created the intentional patterning of artifacts and features on a site. Beyond the site level, archaeologists attempt to reconstruct the regional spatial patterning of human behavior by studying the spatial configuration of a group of related sites. This patterning, which reflects human behavior, is called the systemic context. The analysis of the systemic context is the domain of archaeology.

But before human behavior can be meaningfully reconstructed, it is necessary to understand the natural transformations that have affected the systemic context of a site. The analysis of natural site-formation processes is concerned with understanding the physical, chemical, and biological factors responsible for the burial, alteration, and destruction of the systemic context at a site. On a regional level, the study of natural site-formation processes is important to the evaluation of whether the archaeological record of a region is representative of the type and density of sites that once existed in that area at a particular time and through time. The interpretation of natural site-formation processes and the evaluation of how these processes have affected the context of a site and the archaeological record is the realm of geoarchaeology.

The third research objective of geoarchaeology is to reconstruct the landscape that existed around a site or group of sites at the time of occupation. This is important because reconstructions of past human behavior are incomplete unless a site is placed in its noncultural environmental context (see Braidwood 1957; Butzer 1971, 1980a, 1982; Clarke 1968; Davidson 1985; Dincauze 1987; Evans 1978; Fedele 1976; Gladfelter 1977; Hassan 1985a; Renfrew 1976; Schoenwetter 1981; Shackley 1981; Vita-Finzi 1978).

The noncultural environment is composed of living and nonliving components (Butzer 1980a, 1982; Fedele 1976). The living aspect of the noncultural environment is the biological realm, the plant and animal resources that existed around the site during its occupation. Past biological communities are reconstructed from ecofacts (plant macrofossils, pollen, phytoliths, and faunal remains) recovered from a site and areas surrounding it. The reconstruction of the biological aspects of the noncultural environment is the domain of archaeobotany and zooarchaeology. Environmental archaeologists have long recognized that the biological environment is dynamic and that floral and faunal communities change through time. Understanding the changes that have occurred to the floral and faunal communities during the late Quaternary has led to more sophisticated reconstructions of past human interactions with the biological environment.

The nonliving component of the external environment is the geomorphic landscape, the platform on which all biological organisms (plants, humans, and other animals) have evolved, lived, and interacted through time. Until recently, landscape reconstruction has been neglected because of the erroneous belief that the physical processes and configuration of the landscape are constant aspects of the environment that have remained unchanged through time. Indeed, the landscape is a dynamic component of the environment that has changed through time and that consequently is important to reconstruct. Just as the modern floral and faunal assemblages of a region may not resemble those that existed at different times during the late Quaternary, the extant physical landscape may not resemble the prehistoric landscape (Renfrew 1976). It is essential to reconstruct the physical landscape at the time a site was occupied as well as before and after occupation. This places prehistoric human occupation in the context of a dynamic and evolving landscape to elucidate human–land interactions and perhaps in some cases to identify causal factors that may explain culture change.

Conclusion

In summary, geoarchaeology is concerned with context (Butzer 1980a, 1982; Stein and Farrand 1985). As Butzer (1982:4) succinctly states, context is the "four-dimensional spatial-temporal matrix that comprises both a cultural environment and a non-cultural environment and that can be applied to a single artifact or to a constellation of sites." Clearly, the three broad research objectives of geoarchaeology are concerned with context: (1) the temporal context of the site (stratigraphy and geochronology); (2) the spatial context and preservation of material on a site and between sites (natural site-formation processes); and (3) the prehistoric landscape context of a site. At a synthetic level, geoarchaeological reconstructions of the physical environment should be integrated with zooarchaeological and archaeobotanical reconstructions of the biological environment and with cultural reconstructions based on traditional archaeological data. This places archaeological sites in their cultural, biological, climatic, and landscape context. This approach is what Butzer (1980a, 1982) and Schoenwetter (1981) refer to as contextual archaeology. The basic premise of contextual archaeology is that the site was part of a prehistoric biological and physical environment that, together with cultural factors, made up the components of a complete human ecosystem. When human ecosystems are reconstructed and tracked through time using geoarchaeological, archaeobotanical, zooarchaeological, and traditional archaeological data, accurate and sophisticated interpretations of human behavior and prehistory emerge.

2

Geoarchaeological Foundations

Most archaeological information is obtained by excavating artifacts and other remains from a matrix composed of different layers and horizons that are often arranged in a complex vertical sequence. While the artifacts, ecofacts, and features collected and recorded during excavation provide much information about the prehistoric people who lived on a site, a proper understanding of the nature and origin of the site matrix and its stratigraphy is necessary to document a site fully and to provide new insights into the archaeological record. This chapter presents the essential concepts of sedimentology, pedology, stratigraphy, and geomorphology, and it lays the foundation for the succeeding chapters, which deal with natural site-formation processes and the landscape evolution of different environments.

The Archaeological Site Matrix: Sediments and Soils

The matrix of an archaeological site—the physical medium that surrounds all artifacts, features, and ecofacts—is composed of two major components: sediments and soils (Fig. 2.1). The terms *sediment* and *soil* are not synonymous, and they are often misused. It is important to know the difference between them because sediments and soils are created by different processes and each conveys different information about the prehistoric landscape.

Sediments

Sediments are the solid inorganic and organic particles accumulated or precipitated by natural or human processes. For example, the silt mechanically deposited on a floodplain during a flood, the marl chemically precipitated in a lake, the peat layer created by the accumulation of waterlogged vegetation in a marsh, and the layer of ash formed during a volcanic eruption are all sediments. Natural sedimentary deposits are created by four different pro-

cesses: (1) the mechanical accumulation of solid particles by processes such
as flowing water, wind, and gravity; (2) the chemical precipitation of layers
of crystals from constituents (e.g., ions and oxides) dissolved in water; (3) the
decomposition and accumulation of organic material; and (4) the production and deposition of material from volcanic eruptions. These processes
create the four corresponding types of natural sediments: (1) clastic sediments, (2) chemical sediments, (3) carbonaceous or organic sediments, and
(4) pyroclastic sediments (Fig. 2.1). These four types of sediments accumulate in what are called sedimentary or depositional environments. If artifacts
and features occur in the locus of deposition, they become buried by sediments. Humans also create sedimentary deposits such as middens, mounds,
and refuse heaps. These deposits are called archaeosediments (Fig. 2.1;
Butzer 1982). The matrix at an archaeological site can be composed of any
combination of natural sediments and archaeosediments.

Because sediments are formed in a variety of ways, they exhibit different
physical characteristics. The following discussion first summarizes the origin and characteristics of clastic and chemical sediments, which are often
the most abundant component of any site matrix, and then reviews carbonaceous sediments, pyroclastic sediments, archaeosediments, sedimentary
structures, and depositional environments. This review is based on the following summary geological volumes: Blatt et al. 1972; Boggs 1987; Bullard
1979; R. A. Davis 1983; Folk 1974; Krumbein and Sloss 1963; Leeder 1982;
Pettijohn 1975; Pettijohn et al. 1972; and Reineck and Singh 1980. Archaeological treatments of sediments include Butzer 1971, 1982; Cornwall 1958;
Evans 1978; Hassan 1978; Pyddoke 1961; Shackley 1975, 1981; Stein 1985,
1987; and Stein and Rapp 1985.

Physical and Chemical Weathering: The Source of Clastic and Chemical Sediments

Weathering is the surficial disintegration and decomposition of exposed
rocks by physical and chemical processes (Birkeland 1984; Ollier 1969; Ritter 1986). During physical and chemical weathering, solid rock is softened
and fragmented into particles of different sizes, and soluble chemical products are released from the minerals comprising the rocks (Fig. 2.2). These
weathering products ultimately accumulate as clastic and chemical sediments. Both the lithology of the source rocks and the weathering processes
determine the composition and size of the debris produced. The effects of
physical and chemical weathering are difficult to separate, and they usually
operate simultaneously.

Physical weathering is the process by which rocks are physically disintegrated into smaller fragments with no significant change in chemical or

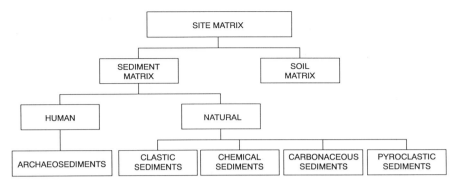

FIGURE 2.1. Compositional breakdown of the archaeological matrix.

mineralogical composition. A number of processes contribute to physical weathering, including repeated expansion and contraction of the rock by freezing and thawing of water in fractures; expansion of cracks as salt crystals grow and push the rock apart; surficial expansion and contraction of rock because of daily heating and cooling; wedging and prying of rock due to root growth; and fracturing of rock due to fire.

Chemical weathering is the process by which the chemical and mineralogical composition of a rock becomes altered by reactions with water, oxygen, and carbon dioxide. Chemical materials (primarily ions and oxides) are released from the minerals, become dissolved in water, and are then transported away from the mineral surface by groundwater or surface streamflow. In addition, the structurally altered minerals at the weathering site often recombine to form new secondary minerals, usually clays. Chemical weathering also promotes physical weathering by disrupting the rock fabric and producing a residue of weathered grains.

The relative importance of physical and chemical weathering in a region depends primarily on temperature and rainfall (Fig. 2.3). Chemical weathering is strongest where both temperature and precipitation are high, while strong mechanical weathering occurs where mean annual temperatures are between $-7°$ and $-18°C$ and precipitation is between 250 and 1,000 mm. Minimal weathering occurs where the precipitation is less than 250 mm.

Together, physical and chemical weathering processes create three types of weathering products: (1) individual solid mineral grains and larger fragments of the source rock; (2) secondary minerals, mostly clay minerals, created by the recrystallization of chemically altered mineral structures; and (3) soluble chemical constituents (ions and oxides) released from the parent

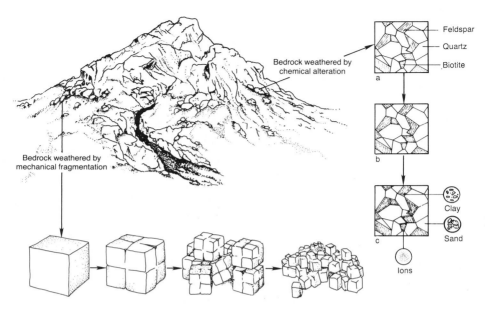

FIGURE 2.2. Physical and chemical weathering of granite bedrock. Physical weathering produces shattered rubble adjacent to the outcrop. As the cubes show, pure mechanical weathering breaks the rock down into smaller fragments with no chemical alteration of the rock. Note that as physical weathering progresses and smaller fragments are produced, the amount of exposed surface area increases. This provides more surface area for chemical weathering to occur. Chemical weathering attacks the weatherable minerals within the rock, in this case biotite and feldspar. Quartz is resistant to chemical weathering and will not decay. The three frames to the right provide magnified views of the granite (as seen using thin sections and a microscope) in three stages of chemical decay: (a) fresh, unaltered granite, (b) biotite and feldspar beginning to decay as water penetrates along crystal contacts, causing chemical reactions and mineral decomposition, (c) biotite and feldspar extensively decayed as chemical reactions continue, grain boundaries weaken, and the rock disintegrates into fragments. Soluble ions are released from the grains of biotite and feldspar, and clay minerals are created from their decay. Sand-size particles of unweathered quartz and weathered mineral grains are created as the rock falls apart. (Modified from Marsh 1987)

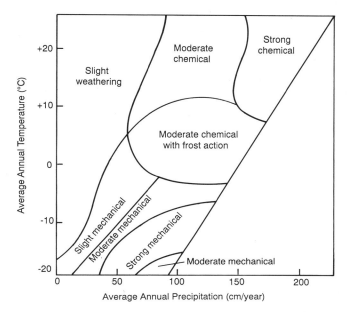

FIGURE 2.3. The relative importance of physical and chemical weathering in different precipitation and temperature regimes. (Modified from Marsh 1987)

rock. This weathering debris is the ultimate source of all clastic and chemical sediments.

Clastic Sediments

Clastic sediments often make up the most significant portion of the archaeological site matrix. Clastic sediments are the solid mineral grains (e.g., quartz, feldspar, mica, and hornblende) or rock fragments (e.g., basalt, granite, and schist) that vary in size from large, gravel-size clasts to small, clay-size grains. Clastic particles are mechanically transported by water, wind, ice, and gravity from their place of origin to environments such as river valleys, sand dune fields, and coastal barrier islands, where they accumulate to form sedimentary deposits.

These transport and depositional processes generate the distinctive textural properties of clastic sediments: (1) the size of particles, (2) the morphology of particles, and (3) the fabric of clastic deposits. Consequently, these textural properties yield valuable data on the mode of particle transport, the energy of the flow, and the depositional environment.

Table 2.1 Wentworth Grain-Size Classification for Sediments, Equivalent Phi (ϕ) Units, and Sieve Numbers of U.S. Standard Sieves

	U.S. Standard Sieve Mesh	Millimeters		Phi (ϕ) Units	Wentworth Size Class
		4096		−12	Boulder
		1024		−10	
		256———	256———	− 8	
					Cobble
Gravel		64———	64———	− 6	
		16		− 4	Pebble
	5———	4———	4———	− 2	
	6	3.36		− 1.75	
	7	2.83		− 1.5	Granule
	8	2.38		− 1.25	
	10———	2.00——	2———	− 1.0	
	12	1.68		− 0.75	
	14	1.41		− 0.5	Very coarse sand
	16	1.19		− 0.25	
	18———	1.00——	1———	0.0	
	20	0.84		0.25	
	25	0.71		0.5	Coarse sand
	30	0.59		0.75	
	35———	0.50——½		1.0	
	40	0.42		1.25	
Sand	45	0.35		1.5	Medium sand
	50	0.30		1.75	
	60———	0.25——¼		2.0	
	70	0.210		2.25	
	80	0.177		2.5	Fine sand
	100	0.149		2.75	
	120———	0.125——⅛		3.0	
	140	0.105		3.25	
	170	0.088		3.5	Very fine sand
	200	0.074		3.75	

Table 2.1 *(Continued)*

U.S. Standard Sieve Mesh	Millimeters	Phi (ϕ) Units	Wentworth Size Class
——————230——————	0.0625—1/16 ——————	4.0————————————	
270	0.053	4.25	
325	0.044	4.5	Coarse silt
	0.037	4.75	
Silt —————————	0.0312—1/32 —————	5.0————————————	
			Medium silt
—————————	0.0156—1/64 —————	6.0————————————	
			Fine silt
—————————	0.0078—1/128————	7.0————————————	
			Very fine silt
—————————————	0.0039—1/256————	8.0————————————	
	0.0020	9.0	
	0.00098	10.0	
Clay	0.00049	11.0	Clay
	0.00024	12.0	
	0.00012	13.0	
	0.00006	14.0	

Grain Size Nomenclature and Classification.   The size of clastic particles (regardless of lithology and mineralogy) varies from small, clay-size grains a few microns in diameter to boulders several meters across. This spectrum of particle sizes is divided into a number of size units, each with upper and lower limits. The almost universally accepted particle size units and nomenclature used to describe clastic particles is called the Wentworth scale (Table 2.1). This scale divides clastic particles into four major size categories: (1) gravel, particles with a diameter greater than 2 mm; (2) sand, particles with a diameter between 2 and 0.0625 mm; (3) silt, particles with a diameter between 0.0625 and 0.0039 mm; and (4) clay, particles with a diameter smaller than 0.0039 mm. These major size categories are further subdivided

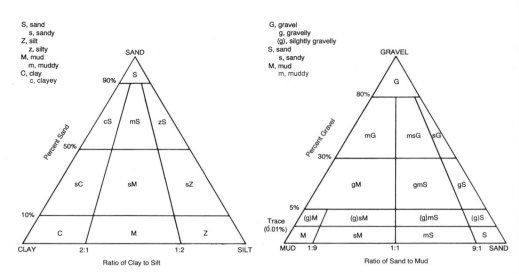

FIGURE 2.4. Textural classification of clastic sediments by Folk (1954, 1974).

into smaller particle categories. For example, based on grain diameter differences, sand is divided into very fine, fine, medium, coarse, and very coarse fractions. Another classification, known as the logarithmic phi (ϕ) scale is often used to describe the same grain size categories (Table 2.1). Phi values are assigned positive and negative designations, with 0.0 phi corresponding to a grain diameter of 1 mm. As phi values become more positive, grain size decreases; as phi values become more negative, grain size increases. These terms and designations are used to describe the size of individual clastic particles. However, the clastic sedimentary matrix at a site is made up of aggregates of individual particles that may be the same size (e.g., a layer of sand or silt) or a mixture of different sizes (e.g., a layer of mixed sand and silt). Sedimentologists have devised a number of classification schemes to describe sedimentary deposits consisting of combinations of gravel, sand, silt, and clay. Many of these classification systems are incomplete and omit entire ranges of possible combinations of the four sediment sizes by classifying only the sand and smaller-size grain fractions. The two most widely used and encompassing classifications are those of Folk (1954, 1974) and the Soil Conservation Service of the United States Department of Agriculture (USDA) (Soil Survey Staff 1951, 1975).

The Folk system for classifying the texture of sedimentary deposits uses two triangular diagrams (Fig. 2.4). One diagram is used when gravel is present, and the other when gravel is absent. When gravel is present in the sedimentary deposit, a name is assigned to the unit by determining the percentage of gravel and the ratio of the total amount of sand relative to silt and clay (defined as mud). If no gravel is present, the sediments are classified by the percentage of sand present and the ratio of clay to silt. Both scales produce descriptive names for sediments that are modified by adjectives. For example, if a deposit is composed of 60% sand, 30% silt, and 10% clay, it is designated a silty sand. In this classification, the last part of the name is the dominant constituent of the clastic matrix, and the preceding modifiers describe the secondary constituents of the sedimentary unit.

Another well-known and often-used system of classifying clastic sedimentary deposits is the USDA classification, which was originally developed to describe soils (Fig. 2.5). In this system, one triangular diagram is used to classify the nongravel fraction of sediments (sand, silt, and clay) into one of twelve textural categories. Standardized names are assigned to the sediment matrix based on the relative percentages of sand, silt, and clay in the sample. Most sediments are characterized as loams (sediments with roughly equivalent percentages of sand, silt, and clay) or a variant of a loam when one particle size dominates the sediment body, such as sandy loam or silt loam. Again, the major constituent of the sediment matrix occurs at the end of the name, and adjective modifiers provide supplementary information about the other, less dominant secondary constituents. If particles coarser than 2 mm (larger than sand size) make up 15 to 50% of the sediment volume, the

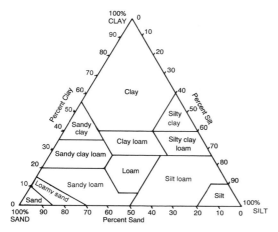

FIGURE 2.5. USDA textural classification of soils. (Soil Survey Staff 1951, 1975)

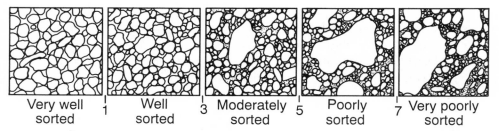

Very well | 1 | Well | 3 | Moderately | 5 | Poorly | 7 | Very poorly
sorted | | sorted | | sorted | | sorted | | sorted

FIGURE 2.6. The range of sorting observable in clastic sediments. The drawings represent a sand deposit as seen under a 10× hand lens. The large spars are sand-size grains, and the fine stipple represents silt- and clay-size material. The numbers indicate the number of particle size classes included in the great bulk (80%) of the deposit. For example, if a deposit has 60% medium sand and 40% fine sand, it is considered well sorted. This method can be used in the field to determine the degree of sorting of a deposit. (Modified from Compton 1962)

textural terms assigned from the textural triangle are modified by the terms *gravelly* (if the coarse material is between 2 mm and 7.6 cm in diameter), *cobbly* (if the coarse particles are between 7.6 and 25 cm in diameter), and *stony* or *bouldery* (if the coarse particles are more than 25 cm in diameter). The term *very* modifies any of these textural modifiers if the coarse fraction makes up 50 to 90% of the sediment volume.

Although the USDA classification scheme was originally devised to describe the texture of soils, it is also used to describe sedimentary deposits. This scheme provides adequate descriptions of sedimentary units composed of sand, silt, clay, or combinations of these particles, but it provides an inadequate description of gravelly deposits. Even when gravel is the dominant material, the finer-grained fraction is used to describe the sedimentary layer. In contrast, the Folk classification was designed specifically to characterize the texture of sedimentary deposits and therefore encompasses the complete range of sediment particle combinations and consistently emphasizes the dominant and genetically significant grain sizes of clastic sediments. Consequently, the Folk classification is preferred for characterizing natural clastic sediments.

Another important sediment characteristic is sorting, which refers to the degree to which the particles in a sedimentary unit are of similar size (Figs. 2.6 and 2.7). Specifically, sorting is a measure of the spread (standard deviation) of grain sizes around the mean grain size of the deposit. If 68% of the particles in a deposit fall within specified phi value limits around the mean grain size, they are classified into one of seven categories ranging from

Colluvium
———
Beach
sand and
gravel

FIGURE 2.7. Well-sorted Pleistocene beach sand and gravel of Paleolake Cahuilla unconformably overlain by poorly sorted alluvium and colluvium. This exposure is in the Salton Trough south of the U.S.–Mexico border.

very poorly sorted to very well sorted (Table 2.2). For example, if 68% of the particles lie within 1.00 to 2.00 phi units of the mean grain size (measured in phi units) the deposit is poorly sorted. However, if 68% of the grains from a single deposit lie within a standard deviation of 0.35 and 0.50 phi, the deposit is well sorted. Sorting reflects the mode of transport and degree of reworking of sediment, and consequently it is an important criterion for identifying depositional environments.

Particle Morphology.   Just as clastic particles are not the same size, they also vary in their morphology. Particle morphology concerns the shape, roundness, sphericity, and surface texture of grains. These particle characteristics are important to determining the mode of sediment transport and identifying depositional environments.

   Particle shape or form refers to the configuration of the particle. Gravel-size clasts can be placed into four shape categories (oblate, equant, bladed, and prolate; see Fig. 2.8), based on the ratios of the three mutually perpendicular axes that define the longest (a axis), intermediate (b axis), and shortest (c axis) dimensions of the particle. The shape of a sand-size particle is described by its degree of sphericity. Sphericity is a measure of how close the grain approximates a sphere and is determined by comparing the length of the three mutually perpendicular axes. As the length of the axes becomes more equal, the sand grain becomes more spherical (Fig. 2.9). Roundness is a measure of the sharpness or smoothness of the corners and edges of a

Table 2.2 Sorting Classes Based on Standard
                   Deviation

Standard Deviation (ϕ Units)	Sorting Class
< 0.35	Very well sorted
0.35–0.50	Well sorted
0.50–0.71	Moderately well sorted
0.71–1.00	Moderately sorted
1.00–2.00	Poorly sorted
2.00–4.00	Very poorly sorted
> 4.00	Extremely poorly sorted

SOURCE: Folk 1974

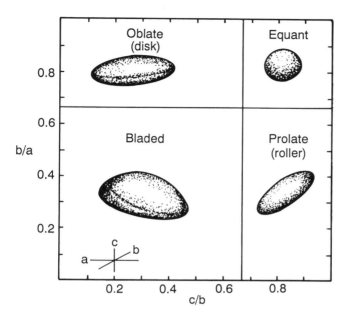

FIGURE 2.8. Classification of the shape of gravel-size particles. The *a* axis is the longest, the *b* axis is intermediate, and the *c* axis is shortest. The ratios of axes *b* to *a* and *c* to *b* divide gravels into four shape categories. (After Zingg 1935)

particle, and it is expressed by a hierarchy of six categories ranging from very angular to well rounded (Fig. 2.9). Surface texture refers to the micro-relief of the surface of the particle. Microrelief can include pits, scratches, polish, frosting, and other features.

Particle Fabric. The third important textural property of clastic sediments is the fabric, or overall arrangement of particles in the matrix. Two aspects of the sedimentary fabric are the orientation and packing of particles.

Orientation refers to the spatial position of the clastic particles in a deposit. Many grains, especially gravel-size particles, have their long axis oriented either parallel or perpendicular to the main direction of fluid flow. In addition, the long or intermediate axis of these particles may be inclined at an angle to the direction of flow. Gravel in stream channels, for instance, commonly displays what is called imbrication, a fabric in which the long axis of each particle is oriented either parallel or perpendicular to the flow and the particles are inclined or dip upstream.

Particle packing is the spacing or density of the particles in a deposit and

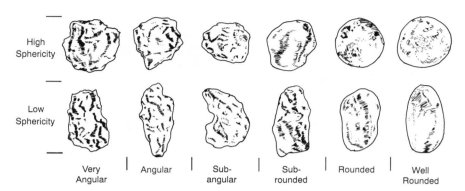

FIGURE 2.9. Sand grains, showing the range of rounding and sphericity as seen under a 10 × hand lens. (After Powers 1953)

their three-dimensional grain-to-grain relationships. Generally, clastic sedimentary deposits exhibit either a grain-supported fabric or a matrix-supported fabric. Grain-supported fabrics are found in deposits in which grains of the same size category are in contact with one another (e.g., gravel-size particles in contact with other gravel-size particles in the bed of a stream channel). Matrix-supported fabrics are found in poorly sorted deposits of mixed particle size in which grains of the same size category do not touch one another (e.g., debris flow and glacial deposits in which gravels are isolated from one another in a finer-grained matrix of sand or mud).

The fabric of a sedimentary deposit influences the size and number of pores or voids in the deposit. This has a significant influence on porosity (the total volume of void space in a mass of sediment) and permeability (the ability of water to pass through the sediment).

Mineralogy.   So far, only textural properties such as the size and arrangement of clastic particles have been considered. It is also important to identify the mineralogy and lithology of particles, because this information can determine the provenance, or ultimate source, of the clastic sediments. The mineralogy of any particular deposit depends on the mineralogy of the source area and the type of weathering that occurs there.

Chemical Sediments

In contrast to clastic sediments, which are solid particles that are physically transported and accumulated, chemical sediments are created at or near the site of final deposition. Soluble chemical products (e.g., ions and oxides) are released from rocks and minerals during subaerial weathering, become dissolved in water, and are transported from the weathered outcrop by surface runoff in streams or in the groundwater to environments such as freshwater lakes, springs, and caves. Here, inorganic chemical reactions and organic biological processes precipitate the dissolved chemical constituents out of solution to produce solid sedimentary deposits. There are a number of different types of chemical sediments, but only carbonates, evaporites, and siliceous chemical sediments are reviewed here. These are the most common chemical sedimentary deposits encountered at archaeological sites.

Carbonate sediments include all chemical sediments composed of calcium and magnesium carbonates. Sediments of this group include freshwater lacustrine marls, spring and lacustrine tufas, cave travertines, and coastal limestones. Tufas are porous coatings of calcium carbonate that are precipitated directly onto hard rock surfaces by algae (Fig. 2.10) or onto the leaves, stems, and roots of plants. Tufa typically accumulates along the margin of springs and lakes. Travertine is a more dense and layered calcium carbonate deposit common around lakes and in caves. In caves, travertine precipitates

FIGURE 2.10. Tufa-encrusted rocks below the high-water mark (12 m) of late Holocene Paleolake Cahuilla near the Santa Rosa Mountains in California. Tufa is the white, spongelike crust, and the rock is the darker material in the center (the steel head of the hammer rests on the rock and the rubber handle on the tufa).

as stalactites, stalagmites, and flowstones. Marls are more extensive deposits of calcium carbonate that are created in freshwater lakes through direct chemical precipitation or through the accumulation and cementation of sand-size and mud-size calcium carbonate particles (e.g., shell fragments, spherical nodules of calcium carbonate, and pellets).

Evaporites, commonly referred to as salts, are chemical sediments composed of minerals precipitated directly from saline solutions. This process typically occurs in closed or restricted basins, where evaporation exceeds the addition of fresh water, and salts dissolved in the water concentrate into a saline brine. Inorganic chemical reactions occur in the brine and cause salt crystals to precipitate. These crystals accumulate on the floor of the basin and form widespread layers. The composition of the resultant evaporite minerals depends on the chemical composition of the brine, but the most common evaporite minerals are gypsum, halite, and anhydrite. Evaporites commonly form in playa lakes in arid regions but can occur in any region where water circulation is restricted, such as a coastal lagoon.

Siliceous chemical sediments are those composed of silica. These sediments generally accumulate in lacustrine and spring environments. One of the most common siliceous sediments is diatomite, a light-colored deposit composed of the siliceous microscopic shells of diatoms. Diatoms are aquatic plants that remove dissolved silica from the water and secrete a siliceous shell. Upon the death of these organisms, their shells sink to the bottom of the water body, where they collect to form layers of diatomite. Another form of terrestrial siliceous sediment is sinter, a crustlike deposit that precipitates around hot springs.

Pyroclastic Sediments

Pyroclastic sediments, sometimes referred to as tephra, are solid particles explosively ejected from a volcanic vent. When present, tephra is generally a small but important component of the sedimentary matrix of a site. Pyroclastic sediments are more likely to be part of the matrix of sites in western North America, where volcanic activity has occurred during the late Quaternary (Péwé 1975; Sarna-Wojcicki et al. 1983; Sheets and Grayson 1979; Steen-McIntyre 1985).

Pyroclastic debris reflects the composition of the lava in the volcanic vent and is composed of any combination of (1) rock fragments of the vent rock or lava; (2) whole or fragmentary mineral grains derived from the solidifying lava; and (3) glass, which commonly occurs as curved fragments known as shards. A simple classification of pyroclastic materials is based on the size of the debris. Blocks are large, angular fragments with a diameter greater than

64 mm that accumulate near the base of the volcano. Bombs are particles of a similar size but with a rounded or oblate shape. They are created when a mass of lava is hurled from the crater and solidifies in flight. Smaller fragments, ranging between 2 and 64 mm in diameter, are called cinders or lapilli, and they accumulate to form tuffs. The smallest fragments, less than 2 mm in diameter, are called ash or volcanic dust. During a volcanic eruption, the coarsest particles (blocks, cinders, and bombs) accumulate around the crater, while finer particles (volcanic ash) are transported downwind over great distances in the atmosphere and are deposited over thousands of square kilometers.

Volcanic ash is one of the most common types of pyroclastic sediment that forms spatially widespread deposits that are distinctive time-equivalent layers in stratigraphic sections (Fig. 2.11). These deposits are generally well sorted and bedded, but they occasionally contain bombs and blocks.

Once deposited, pyroclastic sediments are susceptible to erosion. Pyroclastic sediments that accumulate in unstable situations, such as on hillslopes and uplands, are often eroded and mixed with nonvolcanic clastic sediments as they are transported downslope. If volcanic fragments still make up more than 50% of the resultant secondary deposit, it is called a volcaniclastic sediment.

Carbonaceous Sediments

Most sediments contain small amounts of organic matter derived from the decay of plant and animal tissue. However, when a sedimentary layer consists entirely of organic matter or contains large quantities of organic debris, it is referred to as a carbonaceous sediment. Large amounts of organic matter tend to accumulate in waterlogged environments such as lagoons, lakes, and bogs, in which oxygen-deficient (reducing) conditions exist, bacterial activity is minimal, and organic matter production (i.e., plant growth) is great. If the environment is well oxygenated and supports a large bacterial community, plant debris does not accumulate and carbonaceous sediments do not form. Peat and sapropel are the two most common carbonaceous sediments.

Peat is a deposit of plant remains that have accumulated in a water-saturated environment. Vegetal remains make up 70 to 90% of the total deposit, with mineral matter nearly absent. The vegetal remains show little decomposition, and the structure of the original plant material is still present.

Sapropel is an accumulation of fine organic matter that is commonly mixed with silt and clay. This mix forms an ooze or sludge at the bottom of lakes, bogs, and lagoons as organic remains decompose and putrefy under reducing conditions.

FIGURE 2.11. Mazama ash (the white layer at the level of the man's left hand) interbedded with alluvium along Skull Creek in the Catlow Valley in southeastern Oregon. The Mazama tephra is a marker horizon that dates to approximately 6900 B.P.
(Photograph by Peter W. Mehringer, Jr.)

Archaeosediments

Humans are also geomorphic agents that create sedimentary deposits and
chemically alter preexisting sediments (Rosen 1986; Stein 1985, 1987; Stein
and Rapp 1985). These sediments are different from naturally deposited
sediments because they are created as a result of human activity. They have
been labeled anthropogenic sediments (Hassan 1978), anthropogenic soils

(Eidt 1985), anthropic soils (Eidt 1985; Sjoberg 1976), anthropic sediments or deposits (Gasche and Tunca 1983), anthrogenic sediments (Whittlesey et al. 1982), and archaeosediments (Butzer 1982). Archaeosediments, the term used here for these deposits, are defined as those sediments created by intentional or unintentional human activities. Archaeosediments include mounds or earthworks composed of intentionally excavated natural sediments and soils, trash accumulated in pits, byproducts of construction such as the berms adjacent to canals, accumulations of shells in heaps, and middens, which are a combination of chemically altered natural sediments, accumulated organic and inorganic refuse, and sediment brought onto the site on the soles of feet and clothing.

Human activity may also accelerate sediment formation. For example, in a rockshelter the heat generated from repeated campfires may cause accelerated spalling of sediment and rock debris from the roof of the shelter (Farrand 1985b).

By some definitions, archaeosediments should include all human-altered sediments and soils. In my opinion, however, pithouses, fallen walls, mud bricks, and hearths should be considered features and artifacts, not archaeosediments.

Sedimentary Structures

Sediments that have accumulated in sedimentary environments, such as streams or beaches, commonly show layering and other structural features called sedimentary structures. Most structures, such as layering, cross-bedding, and ripples, form during sediment deposition. Other structures, such as mud cracks, folded bedding, and faults, develop after sediment accumulation. Each structure has a specific three-dimensional internal pattern that may have a surficial expression. Sedimentary structures are most common in clastic and pyroclastic sediments but are also present in nonclastic sediments. A great variety of sedimentary structures exists, but only the most common are discussed here. Detailed treatments of sedimentary structures are provided in Collinson and Thompson 1982, Pettijohn and Potter 1964, and Reineck and Singh 1980.

Stratification and Bedding Structures.   Layering, or stratification, is the most common primary structure of sediments. Layering, illustrated in Figure 2.12, is created incrementally by the repeated alternation between periods of sediment deposition and pauses in sediment accumulation. Each pulse of sedimentation, when followed by a period of nondeposition or erosion, creates a stratum. *Stratum* is a general term used to describe a single tabular or lenticular layer of sediment of any thickness that is lithologically, textur-

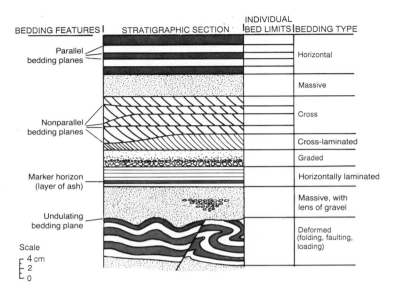

BEDDING FEATURES | STRATIGRAPHIC SECTION | INDIVIDUAL BED LIMITS | BEDDING TYPE

FIGURE 2.12. Terminology for stratification and bedding structures.

ally, or structurally distinguishable from overlying, underlying, or adjacent layers or strata. Otto (1938) considered a stratum to be deposited under essentially constant physical, chemical, and biological conditions, and he referred to these layers as sedimentation units. A sedimentation unit or stratum greater than 1 cm in thickness is called a bed. Although a bed may be several meters thick, the term is generally used to describe a layer no thicker than 1 to 2 m (Table 2.3). Beds may be created by a single rapid event such as flooding, lasting only a few hours or days, or they may represent sedimentation that took place very slowly, requiring several months, such as clay settling from suspension in a lake. The upper and lower surfaces of beds, distinguished by textural, mineralogical, or structural discontinuities, are known as bedding planes or boundary planes. Bedding planes are created during intervals of nondeposition or by minor episodes of erosion that occur between pulses of sedimentation. These short hiatuses in deposition are called diastems. Bedding plane surfaces may be either parallel, nonparallel, or undulatory.

A bed is deposited either horizontally or at an angle to the underlying bed. A flat-lying sequence of beds that lie parallel to the underlying bed is referred to as being horizontally bedded. In contrast, a sequence of beds that intersect the top of the underlying bed at an angle is referred to as being cross-bedded. Cross-bedding is created by the deposition of sediment on a sloping face, such as on the inclined surfaces of dunes, fans, bars, deltas, and beaches. Internally, beds may be (1) composed of smaller sediment units called laminae; (2) texturally homogeneous or massive; or (3) texturally gradational or graded.

Laminae are sediment layers that are less than 1 cm thick. In contrast to beds, laminae are uniform in composition and texture and show no internal structure. Thus, they cannot be divided into smaller units. Laminae may have lower and upper bounding surfaces that have the same lateral extent as the enclosing bed, or they may terminate in the bed. Laminae are created by short-lived fluctuations in the sedimentological conditions during the formation of the bed. These fluctuations create variations in grain size, mineral composition, and other characteristics. Laminae are deposited either parallel to or at an angle to the lower bounding surface of a bed. Those that are parallel to the lower bedding plane are referred to as horizontally laminated. Laminae that are inclined at an angle to a lower bounding surface of a bed are referred to as cross-laminated. Cross-lamination is usually created by the deposition of sediment on the lee side of small ripples.

Beds may also exhibit massive or graded structure. Massive or structureless bedding refers to beds in which internal structures, such as laminations, are absent and the sediments appear homogeneous. In some cases, laminations may be present but are only detectable with X-rays or in thin section with the aid of a microscope. In many cases, massive textures are secondary, having been created by bioturbation (mixing caused by plants and burrowing animals) that has destroyed the original bedding.

Table 2.3 Terms Used to Describe Bedding Thickness

Thickness (cm)	Descriptive Term
100+	Very thick bed
30–100	Thick bed
10–30	Medium bed
3–10	Thin bed
1–3	Very thin bed
0–1	Laminae: Thick laminae, 3–10 mm Thin laminae, 0–3 mm

SOURCES: Ingram 1954; McKee & Weir 1953

Beds that show grading are also devoid of internal laminations and instead show a vertical gradation in grain size. Normal grading is characterized by the progressive change in grain size upward through the bed, with coarse particles at the base becoming progressively finer at the top due to the differential settling of grains from suspension.

Informal designations are used to describe distinctive strata (beds and laminae) and their geometry. If a bed or lamination has conspicuous attributes that differentiate it from adjacent layers (e.g., color, composition, texture, fossil content, or cementation), this layer may be referred to as a marker horizon. If the bed or lamination is bounded by converging surfaces (i.e., it is thickest in the middle and thins to extinction at the edges), it is called a lens.

Other primary sedimentary structures that may occur in sediments include deformation structures and bedding-plane marks. Deformation structures are created by the deformation of soft or consolidated sediments and include faults, folds, and slumps. Distinctive marks such as grooves, flutes, load structures, mud cracks, and raindrop impressions may occur on bedding planes.

Growth Bedding.   Growth bedding is the stratification produced by the growth of organisms as opposed to layering created by mechanical sediment deposition. Growth bedding is most common in carbonate sediments. Laminae are created as carbonate grains adhere to the sticky surfaces of algae. Once the algae are covered with a thin layer of sediment, new algae grow upward through the sediment layer to create a fresh surface, which traps another thin layer of sediment. Successive periods of algal growth and deposition create a finely laminated deposit. Laminae can vary from flat to irregularly crinkled nodular masses or moundlike forms.

Sedimentary Environments

Through the action of various geomorphic agents and processes, clastic, chemical, carbonaceous, and pyroclastic sediments are produced, transported, and ultimately deposited. The locations where sediments accumulate are called depositional or sedimentary environments (Galloway and Hobday 1983; Lowe and Walker 1984; Reading 1986; Reineck and Singh 1980; Scholle and Spearing 1982; Walker, ed. 1984). These are discrete geomorphic settings characterized by a unique set of physical, chemical, and biological processes.

There are many ways to classify depositional environments. The approach taken here is a genetic classification, which differentiates among depositional environments based on the dominant agent or combination of agents of deposition. Using this criterion, eight major categories of depositional environments can be identified:

1. Alluvial environments, in which sediments are transported and deposited by flowing water in meandering, braided, anastomosing, and ephemeral rivers, and alluvial fans;

2. Eolian environments, in which sediments are transported and accumulated by wind into dunes and loess, and gravels are concentrated in source regions to form deflationary lag pavements;

3. Spring environments, in which sediments are accumulated at the point where groundwater emerges at the surface;

4. Lacustrine environments, in which sediments are deposited in and around standing bodies of water such as lakes, ponds, and bogs;

5. Colluvial environments, in which sediments are deposited primarily by gravitational forces on slopes;

6. Glacial environments, in which sediments are transported and accumulated by glacial ice;

7. Rockshelter environments, in which sediments transported by water, gravity, and wind are trapped in rock overhangs; and

8. Coastal environments, in which sediments are accumulated by wave and tidal processes along the coastline and in deltas.

These major sedimentary environments are actually a complex assemblage of many different subenvironments. The meandering river environment, for example, (Fig. 2.13) is composed of channel, point bar, levee, crevasse splay, oxbow lake, and floodbasin subenvironments. Each of these subenvironments is shaped by flowing water, but each is differentiated by a unique set of processes that generate characteristic deposits. The channel is characterized by high-velocity flowing water and is the locus of gravel and sand deposition. The floodbasin adjacent to the channel is characterized by lower-velocity flow and consequently is the locus of silt and clay deposition. Channel margins, influenced by intermediate water velocities, are the loci of sand and silt deposition in levees and crevasse splays. Thus the sediments deposited in each subenvironment have unique sets of characteristics that distinguish them from the deposits of other subenvironments. The sediment characteristics of each subenvironment are combined into an assemblage of deposits that identify the larger depositional environment.

By studying the texture, bedding, sedimentary structures, and other characteristics of a sedimentary deposit, it is possible to determine (1) the agent and process of sediment deposition (e.g., running water, glacial ice, wind, or gravity), and (2) the geomorphic setting or environment of deposi-

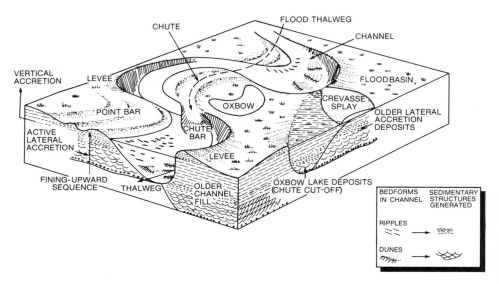

FIGURE 2.13. The various subenvironments of a meandering river depositional environment. Note that each subenvironment is characterized by a distinctive sequence of sediments (a facies) that distinguish it from other sediments (facies) deposited in adjacent subenvironments. These facies become interbedded where they come into contact with one another. (Modified from Walker and Cant 1984)

tion (e.g., beach, tidal flat, point bar, floodplain, or sand dune). The deposits associated with individual sedimentary environments are discussed in Chapters 3 through 6. Also, one should not get the impression that these depositional environments are spatially segregated from one another. Instead, different depositional environments commonly coexist in a region, and as a consequence of their dynamic nature, the deposits they create often overlap in the stratigraphy.

Facies

At any given time, sedimentation can be occurring concurrently in a number of different depositional environments and subenvironments. As described above, different types and sequences of sediments accumulate in each of the coexisting but distinct subenvironments of a meandering stream—gravel and sand accumulate in the channel, silt and clay on the floodplain, and sand and silt on the levees. These different sedimentary deposits, each associated with its specific subenvironment, are called facies. In this example, three facies are defined—a gravel facies, sand and silt facies, and silt and clay facies, which reflect deposition in the channel, channel margin, and flood-basin subenvironments respectively.

A facies is a spatially restricted sedimentary deposit that exhibits characteristics (e.g., lithology, texture, structure, and fossil content) that are significantly different from the characteristics of other deposits that are the same age (Hallam 1981; Moore 1949; Walker 1984). Facies interfinger or become interbedded where they come into contact with one another. This occurs at the interface of two adjacent subenvironments (Fig. 2.13) or two adjacent environments (Fig. 2.14). In short, facies are distinguishable sedimentary deposits of the same age that reflect lateral variations in sediment characteristics. These lateral relationships reflect deposition in different but coexisting adjacent depositional subenvironments and environments that in turn reflect lateral environmental relationships that are important to the reconstruction of prehistoric environments.

If the boundaries between depositional environments remain relatively stable or stationary, the resultant deposits maintain their geographic position except for small-scale intertonguing. However, laterally coexisting envi-

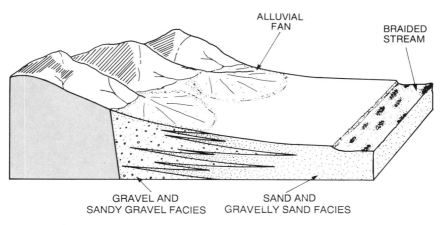

FIGURE 2.14. Lateral facies relationships between sediments deposited in coexisting alluvial-fan and braided-stream environments. In each environment, a unique assemblage of sediments has accumulated (gravel and sandy gravel in the alluvial fan, and sand and gravelly sand in the bed of the braided stream). Thus, on the basis of lithologic characteristics, two facies are defined (a gravel and sandy gravel facies, and a sand and gravelly sand facies). Through time, the valley has been aggrading, and the two environments have shifted position as either the braided stream or the alluvial fans became dominant. Thus the two facies became interbedded with one another.

ronments and subenvironments in a given region may be dynamic and may shift position through time. The position of sedimentary environments and subenvironments shifted repeatedly during the late Quaternary as a result of external stimuli, such as changes in climate, tectonic activity, glacial-interglacial cycles, sea level changes, or internal geomorphic responses in the environmental system. Lateral shifts occur on two different scales: (1) the small-scale spatial shift of subenvironments within a single broad environment (e.g., shifting of the channel, point bars, and levees on the floodplain), and (2) the large-scale spatial shift of environments (e.g., shifting of marine, shoreline, and land positions during the course of sea level changes). These shifts cause sedimentary environments and their associated deposits to become spatially displaced through time. As a result, the deposits of one subenvironment or environment come to overlie the deposits accumulated in another adjacent subenvironment or environment (Figs. 2.13 and 2.14). This concept is known as Walther's Law.

Soils

Soils are the weathering profiles developed by the in-place physical and chemical alteration of preexisting sediments. If a sediment mass is stable, weathering at the surface creates horizons with distinctive physical and chemical properties that become superimposed on the previously deposited sediments. These distinctive horizons and their arrangement in a vertical sequence make up the soil profile. Soil profiles extend from the surface downward to fresh, unaltered sediment, or what soil scientists call the parent material. For a soil profile to develop, the sedimentary deposit must be stable; that is, the surface must be undergoing minimal erosion and deposition. Soil profiles are laterally extensive, but their characteristics vary from place to place, depending on the duration of weathering, the climate during soil formation, the composition of the parent material, the overlying vegetation, and the topographic situation.

Soils are not sedimentary deposits, and the two must not be confused. Sediments are produced by weathering, are transported as solid particles or dissolved chemicals, and are accumulated or precipitated in sedimentary environments. Soils are vertical sequences of distinctive horizons created by *in situ* weathering of a stable sedimentary deposit at the surface (Fig. 2.15).

The discussion of the essential concepts of pedology (the study of soil genesis, morphology, and taxonomy) that follows is based largely on Birkeland 1984; Buol et al. 1989; and the Soil Survey Staff 1951, 1975, and 1990. Archaeological treatments of soils include Butzer 1971, 1982; Cornwall 1958; Courty et al. 1989; Evans 1978; Holliday 1989a, 1990, 1992; Limbrey 1975; and Shackley 1975, 1981.

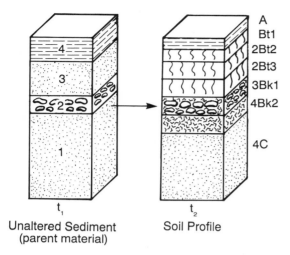

FIGURE 2.15. The transformation of an unaltered sediment (parent material) composed of four distinct units of sand (1 and 3), gravel (2), and silt (4) stabilized at time 1 (t_1) into a soil at time 2 (t_2). Hypothetical soil horizons and their designations are shown. Note that the soil horizons bear little resemblance to the original stratigraphy. The soil horizon designations at right are discussed below under Soil Profile Nomenclature and in Table 2.4.

Processes of Soil Formation

Soil formation is a surficial process during which the upper portion of a sedimentary deposit or rock layer on a stable surface is physically and chemically altered in place. Four general processes are responsible for transforming an unaltered sediment into a soil (Fig. 2.16): (1) the addition of material to the soil from the ground surface and atmosphere, (2) the transformation of substances in the soil, (3) the vertical transfer of material in the soil, and (4) the removal of constituents from the soil.

The process of addition includes the introduction of organic matter to the soil from the decay of surface vegetation and animals, and the introduction of dissolved and solid particles washed from the atmosphere during rainfall.

The second process, transformation, involves the decomposition and alteration of organic material and minerals in the soil. For example, leaves, roots, and stems of plants decompose into humus and other organic compounds, and minerals chemically alter into clays and dissolved chemical constituents (ions and oxides).

Transfer, the third process, primarily refers to the downward translocation of solid particles and soluble constituents in the soil. Fine, clay-size

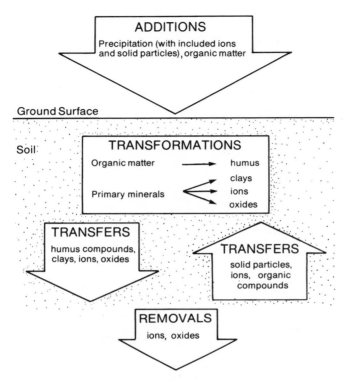

FIGURE 2.16. The four major processes of soil formation and the direction and specific reactions that take place within each. (Modified from Birkeland 1984)

particles, organic matter, and dissolved chemical constituents (especially calcium, iron, and aluminum) are carried by water downward through the voids between soil particles by gravity. Translocation stops and the transported material is accumulated or precipitated when the water is drawn or sucked onto the surface of soil voids or plant roots, or when there is a change in soil chemistry. This movement of dissolved and solid substances downward through the soil is called eluviation. The leached horizon created by the removal of materials is called the eluvial horizon. The accumulation of translocated soil material is referred to as illuviation, and the horizon formed is termed an illuvial horizon. Solid and dissolved constituents in soils may also be transferred upward by the capillary rise of groundwater to levels above the water table and by the biological activity of plants and animals.

The last process, removal, refers to the complete leaching of chemical constituents from the soil. If leaching is intense, ions and oxides that are dissolved in the percolating water do not accumulate in the soil. Instead, they are flushed through the soil and become part of the dissolved load of the groundwater.

During the process of soil formation, the original characteristics of the parent sediment are destroyed and are replaced by new soil textures and structures (Fig. 2.15). For instance, the translocation of clay alters a sedimentary layer of sand into a pedogenic horizon of sandy clay. Soil development also obscures the original layering and structure of the sedimentary units and the contacts separating different stratigraphic units.

The four processes of soil formation are responsible for the creation of the distinctive horizons that make up the soil profile. It is important to remember that soil formation is a surficial process; the weathering zone (the active zone of soil formation) extends only from the stable surface to the depth where water stops moving downward (i.e., the depth of maximum wetting). Soil formation most commonly occurs on stable surfaces that are undergoing no deposition or erosion.

In some instances, however, soil formation may take place while deposition is occurring if pedogenic alteration of the sediment keeps pace with deposition. This happens in situations in which the rate of deposition is slow. This process results in the formation of a cumulative or accretionary soil, which is generally characterized by a very thick surface organic horizon. Topographic situations favorable to the formation of cumulative soils include colluvial environments at the base of hillslopes, riverine floodplains, and eolian settings where loess is accumulating.

Soil Properties

A number of properties are used to distinguish soil profiles from the unaltered parent material or sediment. Pedogenically altered sediments display new colors, textures, structures, and chemical properties. These signatures of in-place weathering are used to identify the soil profile and to differentiate and subdivide the profile into horizons.

The color of the original sediment is altered during soil formation. The colors acquired by different soil horizons are indicators of their organic and chemical composition. For example, soil horizons that are black to dark brown are usually high in organic matter; a red or blue color indicates the presence of oxidized or reduced iron, respectively; and a light gray to white color may indicate the presence of calcium carbonate or an intensely leached horizon. Soil colors are assigned standardized names and shorthand letter and number designations using the Munsell soil color charts. Soil color notation is divided into three measurable parts: (1) hue (the dominant spectral color: red, yellow, blue, or green), designated by a number and letters;

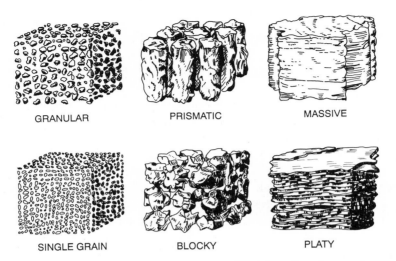

GRANULAR   PRISMATIC   MASSIVE

SINGLE GRAIN   BLOCKY   PLATY

FIGURE 2.17. Major soil structures. (Modified from Donahue et al. 1977)

(2) value (the relative darkness or lightness of the color), designated by a number; and (3) chroma (the purity of the color), designated by a number. The color dark reddish brown has the designation 5YR 3/3.

Soil texture refers to the relative proportion of sand, silt, and clay particles that make up the soil horizon. Standardized textural names are assigned to the horizon using the USDA textural classification shown in Figure 2.5. The name assigned to describe the texture of a soil horizon emphasizes that portion of the horizon made up of grains that are less than 2 mm in diameter. This is because soil scientists are primarily interested in soil fertility and the degree of translocation of clay-size and silt-size particles in the soil. If gravel is present, it is given a subordinate role in assigning a textural name regardless of the amount present.

Individual soil particles of sand, silt, and clay are commonly joined or bound together into lumps or aggregates called peds, which are separated from one another by cracks or planes of weakness. The characteristics of the peds constitute what is called the structure of the soil. Peds are classified into four primary types based on their morphology: (1) platy, (2) prismatic or columnar, (3) angular or subangular blocky, and (4) granular or crumb (Fig. 2.17).

Platy structure is characterized by particles arranged into flat horizontal planes that resemble laminations. Prismatic and columnar peds are long vertical columns bounded by flat sides. Peds with a prismatic structure have flat tops and bottoms, while those designated as columnar have rounded tops. Blocky structure resembles imperfect cubes or blocks with flattened sides that fit the shape of adjacent peds. Angular blocky peds have sharp edges and sides, while subangular blocky peds have rounded edges and sides. Granular or crumb structure refers to peds with irregular surfaces that resemble imperfect spheres.

These basic ped types are further subdivided into five size categories ranging from very fine to very coarse (Soil Survey Staff 1951, 1975). Finally, ped development is described as weak, moderate, or strong depending on how well formed or distinct the peds are in the soil horizon.

A soil horizon characterized by no aggregates or peds is called structureless. Structureless horizons are classified as either single-grained or massive (Fig. 2.17). Single-grained describes a horizon with unconsolidated particles such as loose sand, while the term massive describes a coherent or cohesive mass.

Other important characteristics of soils include soil moisture, acidity and alkalinity (pH), organic matter content, calcium carbonate content, and the type and amount of exchangeable or nonexchangeable ions. Most of these properties must be determined in the laboratory.

Soil Profile Nomenclature

The soil forming processes—addition, translocation, transformation, and removal—are responsible for physically, chemically, and biologically altering a previously deposited, stable sediment mass into a soil profile. In the zone of weathering, materials like organic matter, clay, and calcium carbonate accumulate at different depths below the surface. This creates a sequence of distinctive zones called horizons, which lie horizontal to one another and parallel to the surface (Fig. 2.15). These horizons have distinctive physical, chemical, and biological properties that are easily recognized in the field and that are used to subdivide the soil profile. Six major or master soil horizons are defined and designated by the capital letters O, A, E, B, C, and R (Table 2.4). Generally, only a few of these master horizons occur together in a typical soil profile.

A well-developed soil profile is commonly characterized by three main horizons, designated A, B, and C, from top to bottom (Fig. 2.15). However, in many cases in which the soil is less well developed, the A horizon may directly overlie the C horizon, with no intermediate B horizon. The A horizon is the zone where decomposed organic matter or humus accumulates. It is also the zone from which solid and soluble constituents are removed. As water passes through the A horizon, it picks up clay particles and ions and translocates them down into the B horizon, where they accumulate. The B horizon can be characterized by the accumulation of clay, iron compounds,

Table 2.4 Soil Horizon Nomenclature[a]

Master Horizons

ORGANIC HORIZONS[b]

O Horizon	Dark-colored surface accumulation of organic matter (from plants and animals) overlying mineral soil. Subdivided on the degree of decomposition of organic matter.
	Oi — Organic matter slightly decomposed. Distinct fresh to partly decomposed plant and faunal remains (e.g., leaves, needles, twigs, faunal excrement) visible to the naked eye.
	Oe — Organic matter in intermediate stage of decomposition.
	Oa — Organic matter highly decomposed. Organic debris (plant and faunal remains) is mostly decomposed and original form of most of it is not recognizable by the naked eye.

MINERAL HORIZONS[b]

A Horizon	Mineral horizon that formed at the surface or below an O horizon. Characterized by the accumulation of humified organic matter mixed with solid mineral grains. Mineral portion of the horizon dominates. Typically darker colored than underlying horizons.
	Ap — Horizon with properties resulting from cultivation, pasturing, or similar types of disturbance.
E Horizon	Light-colored horizon that underlies an O or A horizon. Characterized by the loss of clay, soluble iron, soluble aluminum, organic matter, or some combination of these. This results in the concentration of quartz and other weather-resistant minerals.

Table 2.4 *Continued*

Master Horizons	
B Horizon	Mineral horizon formed below an A, E, or O horizon that shows little or no evidence of the original sediment or rock structure and is primarily characterized by illuvial concentrations of clay, iron, aluminum, humus, carbonates, gypsum, or silica. Several kinds of B horizons are recognized.

	Bh	Accumulation of organic matter and minor aluminum.
	Bhs, Bs	Accumulation of organic matter and aluminum and iron compounds.
	Bk	Accumulation of calcium carbonate.
	Bo	Residual concentration of compounds of iron and aluminum. More soluble materials have been removed.
	Bq	Accumulation of silica.
	Bt	Accumulation of clay.
	Btn	Accumulation of clay and high sodium content.
	Bw	Development of redder color or structure, loss of carbonates, with no apparent illuvial accumulation of material.
	By	Accumulation of gypsum.
	Bz	Accumulation of salts more soluble than gypsum.

C Horizon	Subsurface mineral horizon, excluding hard bedrock, that is essentially unaltered or slightly altered parent material (sedimentary structures and textures are partly or totally preserved). This horizon may be unconsolidated or weakly consolidated and lack properties of O, A, E, or B horizons.

	Cr	Horizon of soft weathered bedrock between the soil and underlying unweathered rock.

R Horizon	Consolidated, hard bedrock underlying soil.

Table 2.4 *Continued*

b	Buried soil horizon.
c	Horizon contains concretions or hard nodules cemented by iron, aluminum, manganese, or titanium.
f	Horizon is frozen year-round.
g	Horizon in which gleying has occurred. Iron has been converted to a reduced state as a consequence of being saturated with water. Commonly, gleyed soils have a neutral color (grey) or are mottled. Strongly gleyed soils are blue to green.
k	Horizon characterized by the accumulation of alkaline earth carbonates, mostly calcium carbonate.
m	Horizon that is more than 90% cemented or indurated. Cementing material is designated (e.g., km, carbonate; ym, gypsum).
n	Horizon characterized by an accumulation of sodium.
v	Horizon characterized by the presence of iron-rich, humus-poor reddish material that hardens irreversibly when dried. This is called plinthite.
x	Horizon that is hard to very hard, with high hulk density, brittle, and seemingly cemented when dry (fragipan-like).
y	Horizon with an accumulation of gypsum.
z	Horizon with an accumulation of salts more soluble than gypsum.

SOURCES: Birkeland 1984, Bettis 1984, and Soil Survey Staff 1990.

[a]The designations and descriptions given here supersede the designations and descriptions given in *Soil Taxonomy* (Soil Survey Staff 1975) and the USDA *Soil Survey Manual* (Soil Survey Staff 1951). This classification is summarized in Birkeland 1984, Bettis 1984, and Soil Survey Staff 1990.

[b]A mineral horizon is a horizon consisting predominantly of, and having its properties determined predominantly by, mineral matter (i.e., clastic particles). It usually contains less than 20% organic matter. An organic horizon is a horizon whose properties are determined by the organic material that makes up the horizon (usually greater than 20%).

[c]Lowercase letters follow the master horizon designation. Those designations that are specific to a particular master horizon have deen described above. The designations that can be used for a variety of horizons are given here.

organic matter, aluminum, gypsum, calcium carbonate, silica, soluble salts, or combinations of these materials. The underlying C horizon is the zone of fresh, unconsolidated parent material (sediment) that is essentially unaltered by soil forming processes. The A and B horizons are commonly referred to as the solum, the zone created by soil forming processes. In short, the A and B horizons represent the pedogenically altered sediment matrix, while the C horizon represents the original, unaltered sediment matrix, or soil parent material.

Other master horizons, designated R, O, and E, may also be present in some soils. R horizons are zones of consolidated bedrock that occur close to the surface. In areas such as forests, where organic matter production is great, organic debris accumulates on the surface of the A horizon. Such accumulations of organic litter above the mineral soil are referred to as O horizons. In some soils, light-colored horizons composed of mineral grains resistant to chemical weathering, such as quartz, occur beneath the A horizon. These zones, designated E horizons, have been intensely leached by water and are devoid of iron and aluminum compounds, organic matter, and clay.

The master horizons of a soil profile are further subdivided on the basis of observable properties. Designations are assigned to soil horizons based on the type of material accumulated in the horizon or other soil properties. A lowercase letter following the master horizon designation is used to indicate the presence of a particular property in that horizon. For example, the accumulation of translocated clay in the B horizon is designated Bt, the accumulation of translocated calcium carbonate is designated Bk, and the designation Bg indicates that it formed under the influence of a fluctuating water table. A complete list of these suffixes is provided in Table 2.4. Further internal subdivisions based on color, structure, or other properties in a given horizon are indicated by arabic numerals that follow the letter designation. For example, if three subdivisions are possible in a Bt horizon, they are designated Bt1, Bt2, and Bt3 (Fig. 2.15). If significant changes in particle size or lithology are present in the soil profile—which usually reflects a soil developed on two or more different parent materials or sediment layers—arabic numerals are placed in front of the master horizon designations. For instance, four changes in lithology within a Bt horizon would be designated Bt, 2Bt, 3Bt, and 4Bt from top to bottom (for an illustration of this concept, see Fig. 2.15; note that no numeral is used for the first horizon). Prefix numerals are not used if the parent material is uniform from the top to the bottom of the soil profile.

The boundaries between horizons and subhorizons range from sharp to transitional. The microrelief between horizons also ranges from smooth to

Table 2.5 Diagnostic Surface and Subsurface Soil Horizons

Diagnostic Horizon	Defining Criteria	Possible Field Horizon Designation
DIAGNOSTIC SURFACE HORIZONS (EPIPEDONS):		
Mollic	Thick, dark-colored, humus-rich surface horizon, abundant calcium, magnesium, and potassium.	A, A & B
Umbric	Like Mollic epidedon, but depleted in calcium, magnesium, and potassium.	A, A & B
Histic	Very high in organic matter and water saturated for part of the year (essentially peat).	O
Anthropic	Like Mollic epidedon, but high phosphorous content (indicates continued use of surface by humans).	A, A & B
Plaggen	Human-made surface horizon created by long continued manuring.	A
Ochric	Light-colored horizon that does not meet the definitions of any other epidedon. Usually low organic matter content.	A
DIAGNOSTIC SUBSURFACE HORIZONS:		
Albic	Light-colored horizon characterized by removal of clay and iron oxides.	E
Argillic	Horizon of significant clay accumulation. Clay content greater than overlying or underlying horizons.	Bt
Natric	Like argillic horizon, but has columnar structure and high sodium content.	Btn
Spodic	Horizon with significant accumulation of aluminum and organic matter, with or without iron.	Bh, Bs, Bhs
Cambic	Slightly altered horizon that may exhibit reddening, soil structure development, or complete loss of carbonates.	Bw
Oxic	Thick, extremely weathered horizon with few weatherable minerals.	Bo

Table 2.5 *Continued*

Diagnostic Horizon	Defining Criteria	Possible Field Horizon Designation
Calcic	Horizon of significant accumulation of calcium carbonate.	Bk
Petrocalcic	Strongly cemented calcic horizon.	Bkm
Gypsic	Horizon of gypsum accumulation.	By
Petrogypsic	Strongly cemented gypsic horizon.	Bym
Salic	Horizon enriched in secondary salts.	Bz
Duripan	Dense, hard horizon cemented with silica.	Bqm
Fragipan	Dense, hard compacted horizon.	Bx, Cx

SOURCE: Soil Survey Staff 1975, 1990

undulatory. Various terms are used to describe and designate these boundary characteristics (see Soil Survey Staff 1951, 1975).

Diagnostic Surface and Subsurface Soil Horizons

As discussed above, organic matter accumulates primarily in the A horizon of soils, and solid and chemical constituents accumulate in the B horizon. Organic matter, solid materials, and chemical constituents accumulate in these soil horizons in different quantities, ranging from minor amounts that are barely observable to significant concentrations that dominate the appearance of the horizon. If the accumulated materials are present in any detectable quantities in a horizon, lowercase letter designations following the master horizon designations are used to identify these accumulations (Table 2.4). However, if significant concentrations of translocated material such as organic matter, clay, calcium carbonate, iron, or other materials are present, and if this accumulation dominates the physical and chemical properties of the horizon, diagnostic soil horizons are defined. Two types of diagnostic horizons are recognized: (1) diagnostic surface horizons, called epipedons, which roughly correspond to the A horizon; and (2) diagnostic subsurface horizons, which primarily correlate to the B horizon. Diagnostic surface and subsurface horizons are defined in *Soil Taxonomy* (Soil Survey Staff 1975) on the basis of specific measurable physical and chemical properties (Table 2.5).

All diagnostic surface and subsurface horizons are given names and shorthand designations. For example, a diagnostic soil horizon known as a calcic horizon is defined as having considerable amounts of calcium carbonate accumulated in the B horizon. The symbol Bk is used to designate this diagnostic subsurface soil horizon. However, the symbol Bk by itself may not indicate the presence of a calcic horizon, because the symbol Bk is used to designate the presence of *any* amount of calcium carbonate in the B horizon. Therefore, the presence of a calcic horizon must be specified. Not all Bk horizons are calcic horizons, but all calcic horizons are Bk horizons.

Soil Taxonomy (Soil Survey Staff 1975) recognizes six diagnostic surface horizons. These epipedons include the entire A horizon and sometimes the upper portion of the underlying B horizon. Three of the six epipedons—mollic, umbric, and ochric—are the most common. A mollic epipedon is a thick, dark-colored surface horizon that generally forms beneath grasslands. The dark color is due to the presence of abundant humus that is rich in calcium, magnesium, and potassium. Umbric epipedons are dark-colored, organic-rich surface horizons that generally develop under forests. They resemble mollic epipedons but are depleted in calcium, magnesium, and potassium. Ochric epipedons are light-colored A horizons that generally contain less than 1% organic matter. These generally develop in arid and semiarid regions. The other epipedons are anthropic (a mollic epipedon high in phosphorous), histic (an epipedon high in organic matter), and plaggen (a human-made surface layer created by manuring).

Diagnostic subsurface horizons are characterized by significant accumulations of clay, iron compounds with or without organic matter, aluminum, gypsum, calcium carbonate, silica, soluble salts, or combinations of these materials. These develop in horizons beneath the surficial A horizon. Specific names are used to designate each type of diagnostic subsurface horizon, depending on the materials present. Subsurface horizons in which substantial amounts of clay have accumulated are called argillic (Bt) horizons. These are commonly red to brown in color and exhibit soil structure. Natric horizons (Btn) are similar to argillic horizons but have columnar structure and a high sodium content. Natric horizons tend to form in saline regions, especially around playa lakes. Cambic horizons (Bw) are slightly altered and may exhibit reddening, soil structure development (destruction of original sediment bedding), or the complete absence of carbonates. Oxic horizons (Bo) are thick, extremely weathered, clay-rich horizons. Soils of this type are extremely old and generally do not occur in North America. Spodic horizons (Bh, Bs, or Bhs) are zones with significant accumulations of aluminum and organic matter, with or without iron, and they typically form beneath coniferous forests. Light-colored, intensively leached albic horizons (E) usually overlie a spodic horizon. Calcic horizons (Bk) are zones where translocated calcium carbonate accumulates. If calcium carbonate completely cements the soil horizon and becomes indurated, the term petrocalcic (Bkm) is used. If gypsum accumulates in the horizon, it is called a gypsic (By) horizon. If the horizon becomes strongly cemented by gypsum, the term petrogypsic (Bym) is used. If soluble salts (e.g., sodium chloride), are translocated into the horizon and precipitated, a salic (Bz) horizon is created. Subsurface horizons may also be characterized by duripans (dense, hard horizons cemented with silica; Bqm) or fragipans (dense, hard compacted horizons; Bx). Fragipans may also form in the C horizon (Cx).

Soil Classification

The presence or absence of diagnostic surface and subsurface horizons along with other criteria, such as climate, are used to classify soils into eleven major categories called soil orders (Fig. 2.18). These are further subdivided into suborders, great groups, and smaller categories. The names assigned to soils in *Soil Taxonomy* (Soil Survey Staff 1975), such as Haplargid, Paleustol, and Calciorthid, are based on a complicated scheme of assembling words by adding several prefixes to a base. The scheme is summarized in Birkeland 1984, Buol et al. 1989, and *Keys to Soil Taxonomy* (Soil Survey Staff 1990), and is fully described in *Soil Taxonomy.*

Factors of Soil Formation

The four primary soil forming processes already discussed are the processes responsible for transforming an unaltered sediment into a soil profile. Soil characteristics and the rate at which the soil forming processes operate are controlled by the interaction of five variables, known as the soil forming factors: (1) parent material, the initial texture and composition of the sedimentary deposit; (2) topography, the position of the soil in relation to elevation, slope angle, and aspect; (3) organisms, the floral and faunal assemblages that live or have lived on and in the soil; (4) climate, especially the temperature and precipitation regime during soil formation; and (5) time, the duration of soil formation. These factors determine (1) whether diagnostic soil horizons are present or absent; (2) which diagnostic soil horizons can potentially form; and (3) the degree of development and rate of formation of any diagnostic horizons.

Of the five soil forming variables, time and climate are the most important factors influencing soil properties and the rate at which soils form. Time refers to the number of years during which pedogenic processes have operated on a stabilized parent material. The passage of time is required for the soil forming processes to transform an unaltered sediment into a soil. In any

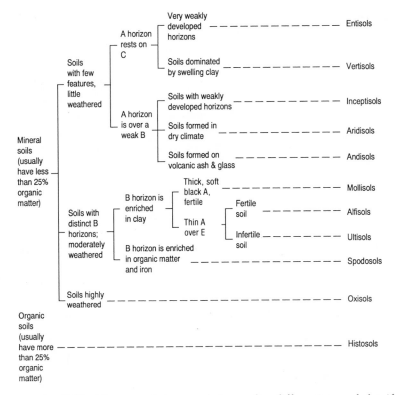

FIGURE 2.18. The general characteristics used to differentiate and classify the eleven major soil orders defined by the Soil Survey Staff (1975, 1990). (Modified from Ritter 1986)

given region, recognizable soil horizons are in general weakly developed or absent if the duration of pedogenesis has been short. In contrast, if the soil profile has been forming for a long period of time in the same region, diagnostic soil horizons are strongly developed in the soil profile. Soil properties and diagnostic surface and subsurface horizons form at different rates and therefore require different amounts of time to develop (Fig. 2.19). For example, organic matter can accumulate to form an organic-rich A horizon in less than a hundred years, while the formation of an argillic B horizon usually requires thousands of years of clay translocation. Calcic horizons progress through stages of development as greater volumes of calcium carbonate accumulate in the soil horizon. If the rate of diagnostic soil horizon formation is known, these horizons can be used to approximate the duration of soil formation.

The soil properties and diagnostic horizons associated with weakly to strongly developed soils in any given region can be ordered into a relative developmental sequence from youngest to oldest called a soil chronosequence. A soil chronosequence is useful for establishing the relative sequence of landform development in an area. If the absolute duration of soil formation can be determined, absolute ages can be assigned to the chronosequence. This chronosequence can be used to determine the approximate age of surficial landforms or archaeological sites in or under the soil profiles.

Climate, especially the properties of temperature and precipitation, influences the nature and intensity of soil forming processes. Climate directly affects the properties of a soil and the type of diagnostic horizons created (Fig. 2.20). For example, soluble salts and calcium carbonate are more likely to accumulate and form calcic and salic horizons in arid and semiarid climates, where the depth of leaching is shallow. In contrast, salts and calcium carbonate can be completely removed from the soil in humid climates, where leaching is intense. Climate also strongly influences the rate at which soil properties or diagnostic horizons form. Variations in climate from region to region can accelerate or slow the formation of the soil profile. For example, argillic B horizons form more rapidly in humid regions than in arid and semiarid ones because of the greater intensity of weathering, clay mineral production, and clay translocation in humid soils. Similarly, the rate of soil formation varies in a region if the climate changes over time. For example, soil formation in the American Southwest was accelerated during the wetter

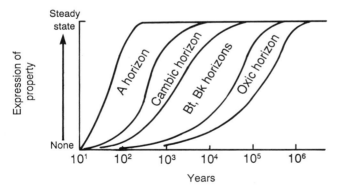

FIGURE 2.19. The amount of time needed for various soil diagnostic horizons to form. Differences in the time required to form the same diagnostic horizon reflects the effect of climate on soil horizon development. The same horizon will form rapidly in one climate but slowly in another. (Modified from Birkeland 1984)

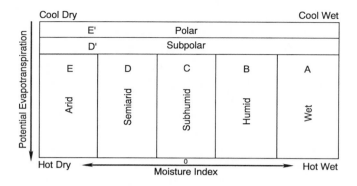

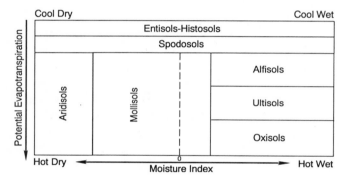

FIGURE 2.20. The relationship between soil orders and climate. The upper diagram shows the main climate types according to the Thornthwaite classification. The lower diagram shows the corresponding soil orders commonly found in each climate zone. (Modified from Miller 1985)

conditions of the Pleistocene, which promoted greater weathering and leaching, but has slowed during the drier conditions of the Holocene because these conditions promote reduced rates of weathering and leaching.

The other soil forming factors—parent material, soil organisms, and topography—also influence soil profile development. The texture and mineralogy of the parent material determine the initial conditions for soil formation and the ultimate types of chemical constituents and clay minerals formed. The texture of the parent material influences the translocation of water and the formation of illuvial horizons. For example, calcium carbonate accumulates more rapidly in highly permeable sandy parent material than in a less permeable silty sediment.

The presence and type of vegetation also influence soil formation because vegetation is the predominant source of organic matter accumulated in soils. Mollic epipedons, as noted above, are typically formed under grasslands, while umbric epipedons are created under forests. The distribution of albic and spodic horizons is determined by vegetation because they form only under coniferous forests.

Finally, topography also affects the development of soil profiles. Profiles of the same age that occur in the same region vary according to their position in the landscape. Those on hillslopes tend to be thinner because of continual erosion, while those at the base of slopes are generally thicker, forming cumulic profiles, because soil formation keeps pace with slow deposition. Soils formed in low-lying areas may become waterlogged, or gleyed, while those on higher ground will be well drained and oxidized. Soil development is also influenced by the aspect, the direction a hillslope faces. In the northern hemisphere, north-facing slopes are wetter and cooler and tend to have different soil characteristics than their warmer and drier south-facing counterparts.

Soil formation is a complex process that results from the interaction of all five soil forming factors: time, climate, parent material, organisms, and topography. These factors operate together so closely to influence the processes that shape the appearance of the resultant soil that it is difficult to distinguish among their effects.

Paleosols

Soils that formed in the past and that are no longer actively forming today are known as paleosols (see Bronger and Catt 1989; Kemp 1985; Morrison 1978; Retallack 1988; Valentine and Dalrymple 1976; Wright 1986; Yaalon 1971). Soils cease to form when they are buried to a depth that removes them from active soil forming processes (Fig. 2.21) or may change minimally if the climatic or biological regime under which they formed changes. Three types of paleosols are defined: buried, exhumed, and relict (Fig. 2.22).

A buried paleosol is a soil that is buried by sediment and is no longer subject to the processes that created it. Buried soils reflect former conditions of landscape stability during which pedogenic weathering occurred. A new soil will begin to form on the younger sediments that bury the soil if the surface again becomes stable. If the younger sediments that bury the soil are thicker than the zone of active pedogenesis, the buried soil will not undergo further pedogenic alteration; it is completely removed from the pedogenic agencies of the surficial environment. Buried soils are recognized in a stratigraphic sequence because they retain their soil textures, structures, and diagnostic horizons. However, the upper portions of buried soils are sometimes

FIGURE 2.21. Asa paleosol buried by 1.5 m of overbank alluvium on the floodplain of the Brazos River in Texas. The paleosol is a cumulative, overthickened A
horizon with an incipient argillic Bt horizon. This soil represents a period of relative
landscape stability and very slow vertical floodplain accretion from around 1300 to
500 B.P. Late prehistoric sites of the Toyah and Austin phases are incorporated into
its profile. The Asa paleosol is completely removed from modern surficial pedogenic
weathering, and a new soil has formed at the surface.

missing because they were eroded before they were buried. Also, the physical
and chemical properties of the soil may be altered by postburial processes
(e.g., by compaction and by the movement of groundwater). In some cases,
only a thin mantle of sediment buries the soil, so it is still in the zone of
active pedogenesis. Consequently, that portion of the buried soil in the zone
of active pedogenesis is subject to postburial soil formation that extends
from the surface through the overlying sediment and into the upper portion
of the buried soil. This results in what is called a welded soil profile. Buried
soils may subsequently be reexposed to the modern surface if erosion removes the sediment covering the soil. The reexposed soil is known as an
exhumed paleosol.

     Paleosols may also occur at the surface. These are called relict paleosols,
and they are found on ancient landforms that escaped destruction or burial.

Relict soils formed under a past pedologic regime when climatic and biological conditions were different from today. Because relict soils remain subaerially exposed after the pedologic regime changes, they are affected by later pedogenic conditions and as a result, younger pedogenic features are superimposed on those of the older, relict soil. These soils are also sometimes called polygenetic (or composite) soils.

A relict soil develops its diagnostic characteristics during the strongest period of soil development to which it was subjected. If the original soil on a surface was weakly developed, it would be altered and masked by subsequent stronger pedogenesis. However, once a strongly developed soil has formed, it will remain relatively unaffected by later, weaker pedogenesis. For example, in the American Southwest deeply leached soil profiles characterized by well-developed argillic and calcic horizons developed during the wetter conditions of the Pleistocene. Subsequent leaching during the drier conditions of the Holocene has been less intense and has led to the imprint of weaker and shallower calcic horizons in the relict argillic horizons (which are no longer forming).

Some soil scientists (Catt 1986; Holliday 1990; Kemp 1985) prefer not to use the term *paleosol*. Holliday has proposed that the term *soil* be used to designate both active surface and inactive buried pedogenic profiles. He suggests that the genetic history of the soil and its relationship to landforms, stratigraphy, and past environmental conditions can be discussed in the text of a report. This is a reasonable alternative to the somewhat complex and sometimes ambiguous paleosol terminology.

Paleosols are important for a variety of reasons. First, the presence of a paleosol indicates that an episode of landscape stability occurred in the past,

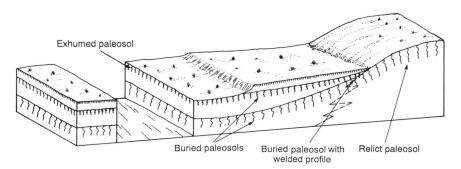

FIGURE 2.22. Stratigraphic and surficial relationships of buried, exhumed, and relict paleosols. The surfaces corresponding to the tops of the buried paleosols are unconformities.

during which there was minimal deposition and erosion. Second, because soils form at the surface, they mirror the surficial topography. While some landforms are never buried and have relict paleosols, some areas characterized by stability and soil formation are later buried by younger sediments. In this case, a buried paleosol can be used to reconstruct the paleotopography during the episode of landscape stability. Third, paleosols in a stratigraphic sequence can be used as stratigraphic markers to facilitate correlation. For example, in the floodplain stratigraphy of the Brazos River in Texas, the Asa paleosol is a useful stratigraphic marker that is used to differentiate late Holocene alluvium from early and middle Holocene sediments (Fig. 2.21). Fourth, the physical and chemical characteristics of a paleosol can be used to reconstruct the climatic conditions under which they formed (Birkeland 1984; Holliday 1989a, 1990). Reider (1982, 1983, 1990) used the physical and chemical characteristics of paleosols at numerous sites in the plains and mountains of Colorado and Wyoming to reconstruct climatic conditions during the late Quaternary. Similarly, Holliday (1985a, 1985b, 1985c, 1990) used variations in soil profile characteristics (morphology) from the five paleosols at the Lubbock Lake site in Texas to reconstruct increases and decreases in effective precipitation and temperature during the Holocene. Fifth, because vegetation affects soil profile development, the morphologic properties of paleosols can also sometimes be used to reconstruct the vegetation that was present during the period of soil formation (Birkeland 1984; Holliday 1990). By examining paleosols, Holliday (1987a) was able to demonstrate that the Southern High Plains during the late Pleistocene, the time of earliest human occupation of the region, was not covered with a boreal forest but instead with an open grassland. Sorenson and others (1971) reconstructed shifts in the forest-tundra boundary during the Holocene by mapping and dating buried and altered forest and tundra soils in southwest Keewatin in the Northwest Territories, Canada. In short, paleosols preserve information about past conditions of soil formation and episodes of landscape stability.

Stratigraphy

Stratigraphy is the study of the spatial and temporal relationships between sediments and soils. Stratigraphic sequences are created because depositional environments are dynamic and constantly changing. At any given time, sedimentary environments will be characterized by one of three potential conditions: (1) aggradation, when sediments are accumulating; (2) stability, when erosion and deposition are negligible and during which soil formation may occur; or (3) degradation, when previously deposited sediments and previously formed soils are removed by erosion. One of these conditions dominates the physical environment at any given time. If the environmental conditions change, an interbedded sequence of sediments, soils, and erosional contacts is created.

Understanding the microstratigraphy of a site and the regional stratigraphy adjacent to the site are essential to archaeological interpretation. First and foremost, stratigraphy provides the relative temporal and spatial framework on which to organize all archaeological data by separating temporally distinct assemblages of artifacts, ecofacts, and features that record the history of human activity at the site. Second, the vertical and horizontal relationships between sediments, soils, and the contacts between them preserve the temporal and spatial record of periods of deposition, erosion, and landscape stability that occurred before, during, and after the occupation of a site. These stratigraphic relationships are used to determine the nature of the physical environment around a site at the time it was occupied and to interpret changes that occurred in the environment through time. These reconstructions place archaeological sites in their regional landscape context.

Stratigraphic investigations at an archaeological site have four fundamental objectives: (1) to subdivide and group the sediments and soils at the site into meaningful packages or physical stratigraphic units based on observable characteristics and to record the nature of the contacts between these units; (2) to order these stratigraphic units into their proper relative sequence from oldest to youngest; (3) to determine the absolute age of the stratigraphic units and the amount of time represented by sediment accumulation, stability (soil development), and degradation using chronometric dating techniques; and (4) to correlate the stratigraphic units at a site with the regional stratigraphy adjacent to the site. In short, stratigraphic studies at archaeological sites must objectively define and categorize the sediments and soils (physical material units), the contacts between them, and the amount of time they represent. These aspects of the stratigraphy are characterized by using and modifying stratigraphic nomenclature from geology.

Geologists have defined a number of different types of stratigraphic units to describe and categorize their knowledge of 4.5 billion years of earth history. They divide and combine stratigraphic sequences of sediments and soils on the basis of such criteria as composition and texture, time, the presence of bounding disconformities, and the fossil content in order to categorize the sediments and soils into lithostratigraphic units, chronostratigraphic units, allostratigraphic units, biostratigraphic units, and eight other types of stratigraphic units. These units are defined in the *North American Stratigraphic Code* (NACOSN 1983).

Some of the defined stratigraphic categories and associated nomenclature are applicable to archaeological research, while others are not. This results from the differences in the span of time investigated by geologists compared to the time depth investigated by archaeologists. Geologists are concerned with events that occurred over millions of years during the last 4.5 billion years. In contrast, archaeologists working in North America are concerned with events that occurred over decades, centuries, or thousands of years during the last 12,000 to 30,000 years. Also, archaeologists obtain better time resolution than earth scientists because sites and Quaternary stratigraphic sections can be dated with greater accuracy and precision than is possible for rocks that are millions to billions of years old. Hence, fewer stratigraphic categories are needed in archaeology.

An archaeological stratigraphic code has been proposed by Gasche and Tunca (1983), but it has not been adopted. The value of a separate archaeological stratigraphic code and categorization of units has been debated (see De Meyer 1984, 1987; Farrand 1984a, 1984b; Stein 1987, 1990). Doubts have been raised concerning whether a separate archaeological stratigraphic code is necessary because the existing geological code defines units that are useful to archaeological research (Stein 1987, 1990). Separate geological and archaeological codes would hinder correlations between the site microstratigraphy and regional geologic stratigraphy and thus would interfere with the exchange of information between archaeology and the geosciences. Another stratigraphic classification system has also been proposed by Harris (1975, 1977, 1979a, 1979b), but it has limited utility outside western Europe (Farrand 1984a).

Three categories of stratigraphic units defined by the *North American Stratigraphic Code*—lithostratigraphic units, pedostratigraphic units, and chronostratigraphic units—can be modified to meet the needs of archaeological stratigraphy. The following discussion of the essential concepts, principles, and terminology of these three stratigraphic categories is based on Boggs 1987; Catt 1986, 1988; Flint 1971; the *International Stratigraphic Guide* (Hedberg 1976); Krumbein and Sloss 1963; Lowe and Walker 1984; the *North American Stratigraphic Code* (NACOSN 1983); Schoch 1989; and Wright 1986.

Lithostratigraphy

Lithostratigraphy is concerned with objectively dividing and combining the sequence of sediments at an archaeological site into meaningful, recognizable, and distinguishable packages (see Fig. 2.23). These objectively defined packages of strata are called lithostratigraphic units, which are defined as three-dimensional bodies of unaltered sediment that are compositionally, texturally, or structurally distinguishable from adjacent, overlying, and underlying lithostratigraphic units. Observable physical characteristics and properties of the sediments are the sole criteria used to subdivide the site stratigraphy into identifiable lithostratigraphic units. The archaeological, faunal, or floral content of the unit and its age, determined by chronometric means, are not considered in the definition of lithostratigraphic units.

The sediments comprising a lithostratigraphic unit were deposited over a given interval of time, but the specific amount of time represented by a single unit may vary from place to place. Consequently, lithostratigraphic units are usually time transgressive. Obviously, a lithostratigraphic unit is older at its base and becomes progressively younger upward, as governed by the law of superposition. Likewise, a lithostratigraphic unit may be time transgressive in its horizontal dimension; in other words, the same unit may be older in one location and younger in another. To illustrate this concept, consider the meandering river shown in Figure 2.24. As the channel and its associated point bars migrate across the valley, not only is a distinctive vertical sequence deposited at any one spot but this vertical sequence is also deposited as a continuous horizontal body or layer across the entire width of the floodplain. The lateral accretion deposits left as a result of river migration are lithologically distinctive and are grouped into a single lithostratigraphic unit. The time represented by this unit is not considered in its definition even though it may have taken two thousand years for the river to migrate from one side of the valley to the other. Consequently, radiocarbon ages from material in this unit and its archaeological, faunal, and floral contents would be relatively recent on one side of the valley and up to 2,000 years older on the other even though the remains occur in the same lithostratigraphic unit. In short, the upper and lower boundaries and the body of a lithostratigraphic unit are time transgressive; that is, they cut across time horizons.

The degree to which a lithostratigraphic unit is time transgressive depends on the total amount of time represented by its deposition. The time transgressive nature of the unit and its boundaries diminishes as the amount of time represented by the unit decreases. If deposition of the unit occurs over a very short period (days, weeks, months, or up to several years), the time transgressive nature of the unit is negligible. For example, the fine-grained ash and dust ejected during a volcanic eruption that lasts for only a few days or weeks creates a distinctive lithostratigraphic unit. This ash layer is not time transgressive but is instead time parallel, because the layer accumulated very rapidly. Conversely, the longer the duration of time represented by the formation of a unit, the greater will be the time transgressive nature of the unit, as illustrated in the hypothetical meandering river example.

Because archaeological contexts in North America date to the late Pleis-

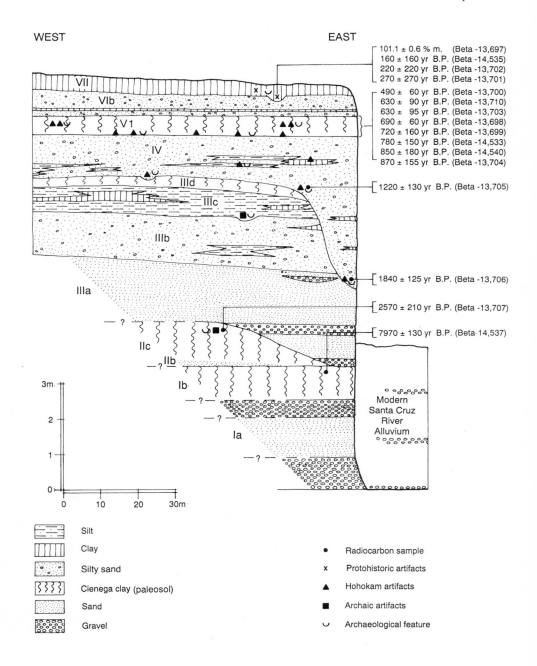

WEST   EAST

101.1 ± 0.6 % m. (Beta -13,697)
160 ± 160 yr B.P. (Beta -14,535)
220 ± 220 yr B.P. (Beta -13,702)
270 ± 270 yr B.P. (Beta -13,701)

490 ± 60 yr B.P. (Beta -13,700)
630 ± 90 yr B.P. (Beta -13,710)
630 ± 95 yr B.P. (Beta -13,703)
690 ± 60 yr B.P. (Beta -13,698)
720 ± 160 yr B.P. (Beta -13,699)
780 ± 150 yr B.P. (Beta -14,533)
850 ± 180 yr B.P. (Beta -14,540)
870 ± 155 yr B.P. (Beta -13,704)

1220 ± 130 yr B.P. (Beta -13,705)

1840 ± 125 yr B.P. (Beta -13,706)

2570 ± 210 yr B.P. (Beta -13,707)

7970 ± 130 yr B.P. (Beta-14,537)

VII
VIb
V 1
IV
IIId
IIIc
IIIb
IIIa
IIc
IIb
Ib
Ia

Modern
Santa Cruz
River
Alluvium

3m
2
1
0

0   10   20   30m

Silt
Clay
Silty sand
Cienega clay (paleosol)
Sand
Gravel

•   Radiocarbon sample
x   Protohistoric artifacts
▲   Hohokam artifacts
■   Archaic artifacts
◡   Archaeological feature

tocene and the Holocene, the time transgressive nature of a lithostratigraphic unit is recognized by directly dating samples from the lithostratigraphic unit and the overlying and underlying units at spatially separated localities. This determines the amount of time represented by a unit at any location and shows how it varies in time from place to place. For example, in the Sulphur Springs Valley in Arizona (Fig. 2.25), gravel and sand were deposited in a braided stream environment during the late Quaternary (Waters 1986a, 1986b, 1990). The gravel and sand layers are compositionally and texturally identical from place to place and are classified as a single major lithostratigraphic unit defined as unit D. Unit D is subdivided into subunits Da and Db to distinguish the gravel and sand facies. Radiocarbon ages from unit D vary from one exposure to the next. At one locality, radiocarbon ages from charcoal in the sand and gravel range from 15,000 to 12,000 B.P.; at another exposure, ages range from 10,400 to 8200 B.P.; and at yet another location, dates from this unit range from 9500 to 8000 B.P. These ages show that this lithostratigraphic unit was deposited between 15,000 and 8000 B.P. but that deposition occurred in separated locations at different times, creating lithostratigraphic sections that represent different time intervals (i.e., unit D is time transgressive from place to place). The realization that individual exposures of the same unit did not represent the same interval of time was important in interpreting the early Holocene archaeology of the region because both artifacts and extinct Pleistocene megafauna were found in this lithostratigraphic unit, which suggested a temporal association between the two

FIGURE 2.23. Lithostratigraphic units defined on the basis of observable physical characteristics at the San Xavier Bridge site in Arizona. Major units of formation rank are designated by Roman numerals, and units of member rank within each formation are designated by letters. Radiocarbon ages from each unit are given in years B.P. Unconformities separate units Ib and IIb, units IIc and IIIa, units IIId and IV, units IV and V1, and units V1 and VIb. The unconformity between units IIId and IV, where an erosional channel cuts deeply into the older units, is the most obvious, but this unconformable surface becomes almost undetectable to the west, where erosion was less prominent. Direct lateral tracing from the channel revealed this erosional contact, as well as the unconformities between IV and V1, and V1 and VIb (corresponding channels are not shown). The unconformity between units Ib and IIb was revealed by an abrupt discordance in radiocarbon ages. Conformable contacts separate the units of member rank. Note that Archaic remains are found in two lithostratigraphic units (IIc and IIIc) and that Hohokam culture artifacts are found in units IV and V1. Archaeological remains at the San Xavier Bridge site occurred within lithostratigraphic units, within paleosols, and on the contacts between lithostratigraphic and pedostratigraphic units. (From Waters 1988b)

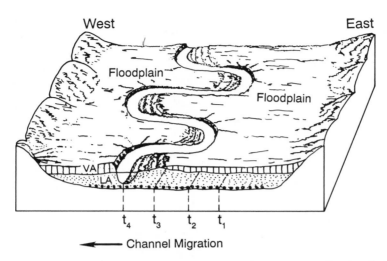

West   East

Floodplain

Floodplain

VA

LA

t_4 t_3 t_2 t_1

←——— Channel Migration

FIGURE 2.24. The valley deposits of a meandering river, indicating the lateral accretion deposits (LA) formed in the channel and point bars by lateral channel movement and the vertical accretion deposits (VA) formed on the floodplain by overbank flooding. As the river meandered from east to west over the last 2000 years, with no channel downcutting, a single laterally continuous lithostratigraphic unit of gravel and sand was constructed by lateral accretion (t_1 indicates the position of the stream at 2000 B.P., t_2 at 1500 B.P., t_3 at 500 B.P., and t_4 today). Consequently, because of the large time-transgressive nature of the lateral accretion deposits (LA), the artifacts and faunal remains at point t_1 are older than those at t_4 even though they occur within the same lithostratigraphic unit.

sets of remains (Sayles 1983; Sayles and Antevs 1941). However, it was found that *in situ* remains of extinct Pleistocene megafauna were confined to the older (15,000 to 11,000 B.P.) portions of the sand and gravel deposits, while *in situ* artifacts and reworked Pleistocene fossils were found in the younger (10,000 to 8000 B.P.) portions of the sand and gravels of the same lithostratigraphic unit (Waters 1986a, 1986b, 1990). Consequently, correlations between different exposures of this time transgressive lithostratigraphic unit led Sayles and Antevs (1941) to the erroneous conclusion that the artifacts and megafaunal remains were temporally associated.

The *North American Stratigraphic Code* (NACOSN 1983) defines four types of lithostratigraphic units: groups, formations, members, and beds. Of these, the formation is the fundamental lithostratigraphic unit. A formation is a distinctive body that may be a homogeneous stratum or an assemblage of heterogeneous strata that are differentiated from overlying, underlying, or

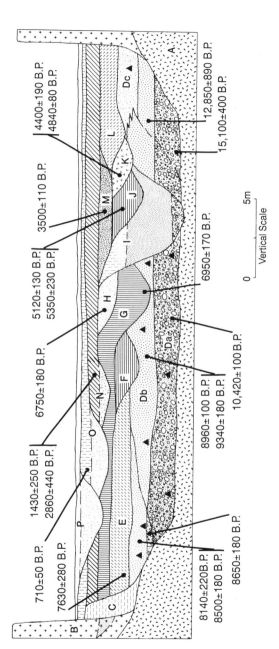

FIGURE 2.25. A generalized composite geologic cross section of Whitewater Draw in Arizona. Sulphur Spring stage artifacts (indicated by solid triangles) are found in lithostratigraphic units Da, Db, and Dc. Pleistocene megafaunal remains are
also found in the older portions of these units. Radiocarbon ages are reported in years B.P. Note the numerous erosional
unconformities represented by channels, especially unit I, which represents a period of arroyo cutting and filling during the
middle Holocene. (From Waters 1986b)

adjacent formations on the basis of physical appearance. Formation boundaries are defined by changes in the physical character of the strata. They can
vary in thickness and geographic extent but must be mappable or traceable
for long distances, usually beyond the boundaries of a site. Formations may
be internally subdivided into members if strata in the formation are compositionally or texturally distinguishable. For instance, in Whitewater Draw
(Fig. 2.25), unit D is of formation rank because it is easily recognized and
can be traced over many kilometers. Subunits Da and Db represent members
in the formation because they are texturally distinguishable. The subdivision
of lithostratigraphic units into units of formation and member rank is also
illustrated in Figure 2.23, the San Xavier Bridge site in Arizona.

   If a particular layer in a formation is unusually distinctive and serves as
a marker horizon that is easily recognized over great distances in the formation, it is called a bed. For example, a distinctive bed composed of clay that
was approximately 5 cm thick in unit VIb at the San Xavier Bridge site was
a marker horizon that could be traced over several kilometers. This clay bed
enhanced correlations between the deposits on the site and the stratigraphy
adjacent to it.

   A type section or locality is designated where the formation is well exposed and thoroughly described. Formations are assigned names following
the procedures described in the *North American Stratigraphic Code* (NACOSN
1983). Two or more formations may be combined to form a group.

   Less formal nomenclature is commonly used to designate this same hierarchy of lithostratigraphic units at archaeological sites. Commonly, informal
designations or symbols, such as Roman numerals, Arabic numerals, or letters, are assigned to the different lithostratigraphic units at a site (e.g., Figs.
2.23 and 2.25). For example, units of formation rank may be labeled A
through Z or 1 through 26, from oldest to youngest. Additional letter or
number subscripts are commonly used to designate units of member and bed
rank. By geologic convention, lithostratigraphic units should always be assigned designations from the base upward through the stratigraphic section.

Lithostratigraphic Contacts

Sediment accumulation is not a steady process. Instead, deposition is interrupted by (1) short intervals of stability, when neither erosion nor deposition
occurs; (2) long intervals of stability, when neither erosion nor deposition
occurs and during which that portion of a lithostratigraphic unit in the zone
of active pedogenesis is altered into a soil; or (3) intervals of erosion, when
older sediments and soils are removed. These breaks in deposition create the
boundaries or contacts between lithostratigraphic units. Physically, these
contacts are planar or irregular surfaces. The study of the boundaries be-

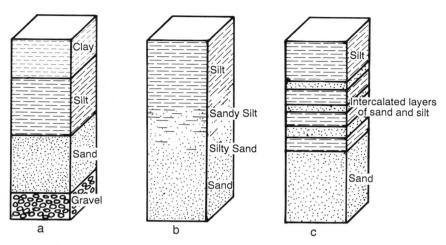

FIGURE 2.26. Conformable contacts: (a) abrupt contacts between discrete layers of gravel, sand, silt, and clay; (b) gradational contact between sand and silt; and (c) intercalated contact between sand and silt. (Modified from Boggs 1987)

tween lithostratigraphic units is as important as the study of the texture, composition, and structure of the units themselves. The contacts between a vertical sequence of lithostratigraphic units are defined as either conformable or unconformable, depending on whether deposition was relatively continuous (interrupted by only short intervals of nondeposition or minor erosion) or was interrupted by long periods of erosion or nondeposition. An interruption in deposition, regardless of duration or cause (nondeposition or erosion), is called a hiatus. The hiatus is physically represented by the surface or contact between the overlying and underlying lithostratigraphic units.

Conformable Contacts.   Conformable contacts between lithostratigraphic units are surfaces that represent no significant breaks, or hiatuses, in deposition due to erosion or nondeposition. The relatively unbroken sequence of deposits created as a result of the more or less uninterrupted accumulation of sediments is said to be conformable (Fig. 2.26).

Conformable stratigraphic sequences are created between laterally contiguous facies. For example, in Figure 2.24 three different facies are accumulating in each of the coexisting but different subenvironments of a meandering stream: gravel in the channel, sand and silt in the point bar, and clay on the floodplain. As the meandering stream migrated from one side of the valley to the other, the channel, point bar, and floodplain environments and their associated deposits were spatially displaced. As a result, the deposits of one subenvironment came to conformably overlie the deposits accumulated in the adjacent subenvironments. As shown in Figure 2.24, channel deposits at the base of the sequence are conformably overlain by point bar deposits, which are conformably overlain in turn by floodplain sediments. Figure 2.14 shows a facies relationship between alluvial fan and braided stream environments. The strata and contacts created are conformable because there has been no episode of erosion or stability. In each case, the change in lithologic character in the conformable sequence reflects a shift in the conditions of deposition. Conformable strata also develop where environmental conditions remain essentially constant. For example, continuous deposition in a lake basin creates a conformable stratigraphic sequence.

Conformable contacts are classified as abrupt, gradational, or intercalated. Abrupt contacts are characterized by a sudden and distinct change in sediment composition, texture, or structure (Fig. 2.26a). Abrupt contacts coincide with depositional bedding planes that formed as a result of changes in local depositional conditions. Bedding planes represent minor hiatuses in sedimentation during a relatively constant period of deposition. These pauses in sedimentation, lasting from a few hours to several years, during which little or no erosion occurs before deposition resumes, are called diastems. Diastems are important because they represent intervals of time that are unrecorded by material strata. The time elapsed during a pause in sedimentation is represented by the contact between conformable lithostratigraphic units. It is important to recognize that in most stratigraphic sequences, more time is represented by the diastems than by the sediments deposited between them (Sadler 1981). However, even though strata deposited in a single depositional environment have abrupt contacts between strata representing numerous hiatuses, these strata are still considered conformable. The alluvial sequence of Whitewater Draw and the San Xavier Bridge site, both in Arizona, provide examples of abrupt conformable contacts. In Whitewater Draw an abrupt conformable contact separates lithostratigraphic units Da (gravel) from Db (sand). Both were deposited in the channels and bars of a braided river that once flowed through the region. Changes in the location of active channels and the migration of bars resulted in sand deposits conformably overlying gravel deposits and in places gravel conformably overlying sand (Fig. 2.25). Radiocarbon ages and stratigraphic investigations show that no significant surface of erosion or stability separates these units; the abrupt contacts were created solely by the shifting subenvironments in the braided streambed. Major erosional breaks occur above and below unit D. Therefore no conformable contact exists between units A and D and units D and E. Instead, these are unconformable contacts.

Likewise, at the San Xavier Bridge site there are numerous conformable vertical sequences with abrupt contacts. In each, gravel occurs at the base, followed by an abrupt conformable contact, then sand, abrupt contact, silty sand, abrupt contact, and clay (Fig. 2.23). Each of these conformable sequences lies between unconformable surfaces.

The vertical relationships between conformable strata may also be characterized by gradational or intercalated contacts. Gradational contacts are characterized by a vertical transition zone between two different superposed lithostratigraphic units. In this zone the characteristics of underlying and overlying units become mixed and difficult to separate. Consequently, a clear boundary between the two units is difficult to define. For example, the transition zone between a lithostratigraphic unit dominated by sand and an overlying lithostratigraphic unit dominated by silt is represented by a progressive upward change from sand to silty sand, to sandy silt, and then to silt (Fig. 2.26b). Intercalated conformable contacts are marked by transition zones of interstratified discrete layers of the overlying and underlying units. The proportion and thickness of the layers change upward through the transition zone. For example, the transition between an underlying sand unit and an overlying silt unit is characterized by alternating thin sand and silt beds, with the silt layers becoming more dominant and thicker toward the top of the transition zone (Fig. 2.26c).

Unconformable Contacts.   In contrast to conformable contacts, unconformable contacts between lithostratigraphic units are surfaces of erosion or nondeposition that represent significant breaks in sediment deposition of greater duration than diastems. Unconformable contacts usually represent hundreds or thousands of years of nondeposition and/or erosion. Unconformable contacts, or unconformities, are created during periods of either landscape stability or landscape degradation.

During periods of landscape stability, deposition and erosion cease and soil formation occurs on the stabilized surface. When deposition resumes, the soil is buried. The surface defined by the top of the buried soil and the base of the overlying deposits is an unconformity (Fig. 2.22). This unconformable surface represents the time elapsed during landscape stability before the next period of deposition. This concept is further elaborated in the discussion of pedostratigraphy below.

Unconformable surfaces in a stratigraphic sequence are also the result of erosion of the landscape by flowing water, wind, ice, and other geomorphic agents (Fig. 2.27). Erosional unconformities are commonly referred to as disconformities. During periods of large-scale degradation, older sediments and soils preserved in a stratigraphic sequence are completely or partially removed and reworked. Periods of erosion are triggered by changes in climate, a rise or fall in the ocean level, tectonic activity, poor land use, or internal changes in the depositional system. For example, an increase in rainfall may cause a river to cut a deep channel into its floodplain, waves may erode the coastline as the sea level rises and inundates the land, or a short drought may cause the vegetation stabilizing a sand dune to die, thus allowing the wind to erode and rework a previously stable dune.

Erosional unconformities are recognized by (1) the abrupt truncation of

FIGURE 2.27. A late Holocene alluvial section in Delaware Canyon in Oklahoma. Two buried paleosols—the Caddo (CS) and Delaware Creek (DCS) soils—are indicated. The modern soil (MS) has been buried by recent overbank flood sediments. The Caddo soil is a cumulic overthickened A horizon that formed between 2000 and 1000 B.P. Sometime between 900 and 600 B.P. a channel (the area filled with white sand left of the man) incised the Caddo soil and the underlying alluvium, and eroded the upper portion of the Caddo soil. The eroded channel was subsequently filled and the paleosol buried. The surface between the eroded paleosol and channel base and the overlying sediments is an erosional unconformity. Late Archaic archaeological horizons are present below the Caddo soil. Plains Woodland material is buried in the parent material of the Caddo soil, and Plains Village debris is buried in the parent material of the Delaware Creek soil. (Photograph by C. Reid Ferring)

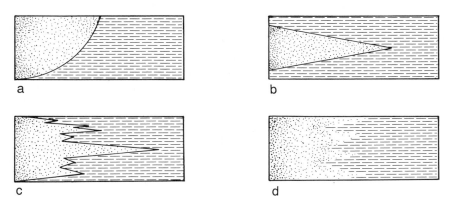

FIGURE 2.28. Lateral relationships between lithostratigraphic units: (a) abrupt truncation, (b) pinchout, (c) intertonguing or interfingering, and (d) gradational. (Modified from Boggs 1987)

either a lithostratigraphic or pedostratigraphic unit (Figs. 2.23, 2.25, and 2.27); (2) an abrupt discordance between underlying and overlying lithostratigraphic units or the removal of surficial horizons of a paleosol (Fig. 2.27); (3) the undulatory relief of the unconformable surface, especially the presence of channels (Figs. 2.23, 2.25, and 2.27); (4) a discordance in the numerical ages from lithostratigraphic units underlying and overlying the unconformable surface (Fig. 2.23); or (5) an abrupt change in the archaeological or biological assemblages above and below the unconformity. Sometimes, however, unconformities are difficult to recognize. The unconformable surface may appear to be a conformable bedding plane, with parallel beds above and below the surface of erosion. These are best discerned by recognizing unconformable contacts where they are obvious (e.g., where two lithostratigraphic units are truncated by a channel) and then tracing the unconformable surface away from this location (Fig. 2.23).

Contacts Between Laterally Adjacent Lithostratigraphic Units. Lithostratigraphic units do not extend indefinitely in a lateral direction; all eventually terminate. The lateral termination against another lithostratigraphic unit may be (1) abrupt, (2) characterized by a gradual pinchout, (3) interfingered, or (4) gradational (see Fig. 2.28). Abrupt terminations are usually the result of erosion, with lithostratigraphic units truncated by channels or other erosional surfaces. A pinchout refers to a lithostratigraphic unit that thins progressively to extinction. Pinchouts commonly thin away from the main loci of deposition. For example, sediments extending out of a channel thin to extinction toward the edge of the floodplain, and marine sediments thin to extinction as elevations increase in the direction of the shoreline. Interfingered contacts occur where the lithostratigraphic unit splits into a number of thin units that intertongue with an adjacent unit. Each of the smaller units reaches its own independent pinchout termination. Lateral gradational contacts are similar to vertical gradational contacts but differ in that there is a gradual and indistinct horizontal change from one unit to the other. Interfingering and gradational lateral contacts reflect facies relationships between depositional subenvironments and environments (see Fig. 2.14).

Pedostratigraphy

During periods of landscape stability, the landscape undergoes minimal aggradation and degradation. During this time, pedogenic processes alter the upper portions of exposed lithostratigraphic units, composed of previously deposited sediments, into soil profiles. The duration of landscape stability and other factors determine the degree of soil formation and the diagnostic surface and subsurface horizons that will form. These horizons develop on any exposed sediments and thus may cross-cut, or develop on more than one lithostratigraphic unit. If the environment again becomes an area of active sedimentation, the soil is buried and soil formation ceases. This buried soil, or paleosol, becomes part of the stratigraphy, recording a period of stability during which no erosion and no deposition occurred on the landscape. Thus, the contact between the top of the paleosol and the base of the overlying sediment (making up the overlying lithostratigraphic unit) is an unconformity representing the time elapsed during environmental stability before the next period of deposition (Figs. 2.22 and 2.29; Kraus and Bown 1986). This contact may be either time parallel or time transgressive depending on the rate and areal extent of later burial. If deposition was rapid and occurred over the entire soil surface, the contact is time parallel. If, however, burial incrementally covered the previously stabilized landscape, the surface is time transgressive. One cannot assume that the amount of time represented by the contact between the underlying paleosol and the overlying lithostratigraphic unit at all places is always the same. Consequently, artifacts on the paleosol may be contemporaneous or may represent sequential occupations.

Long periods of landscape stability are easily recognized in the stratigraphy by the imprint of a soil profile on a lithostratigraphic unit. Identifying paleosols in a stratigraphic sequence is crucial to interpreting the stratigraphic sequence and landscape change. Realizing their importance, the *North American Stratigraphic Code* (NACOSN 1983) has defined a category of units called pedostratigraphic units to designate buried soil profiles in a stratigraphic sequence.

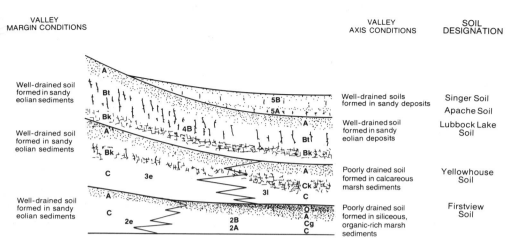

FIGURE 2.29. The upper portion of the lithostratigraphy and pedostratigraphy at
the Lubbock Lake site in Texas. Lithostratigraphic units include units 2A, 2B, and
3l (marsh facies found along the valley axis) and 2e, 3e, 4B, 5A, and 5B (eolian
facies found along the valley margin). Paleosols include the Firstview, Yellowhouse,
Lubbock Lake, Apache, and Singer profiles. The top of each paleosol is an unconformity, documenting five periods of landscape stability. Artifacts of mixed age
occur on these surfaces. Also, note that the calcic horizon (Bk) of the Lubbock Lake
soil, primarily developed on unit 4B, also extends in places into the underlying and
older unit 3e. The excavation of this calcic horizon as a stratigraphic unit led to
the mixing of temporally discrete artifacts, as discussed in the text. Also, note that
the Firstview soil developed on two different lithostratigraphic units (2B and 2e).
Likewise, the Yellowhouse soil developed on lithostratigraphic units 3l and 3e. This
led to the development of different soil profile characteristics within the same soil.
Also note that the Lubbock Lake soil is buried along the valley axis but exposed
along the valley margin. (Modified from Holliday 1990)

A pedostratigraphic unit is a unit composed of one or more soil horizons
developed on one or more lithostratigraphic units and overlain or buried by
another lithostratigraphic unit. All buried soils, or paleosols, are designated
as geosols by the *North American Stratigraphic Code* (Morrison 1967, 1978;
NACOSN 1983). However, the term *geosol* is not widely used by Quaternary
geologists and geoarchaeologists. Two other terms, *buried soil* and *paleosol*,
are more commonly used to designate buried pedogenic profiles. I use these
terms interchangeably here. The problems surrounding the term *geosol* are
discussed in Catt 1986 and Holliday 1990.

Buried soils are important to recognize because they represent periods
of landscape stability and substantial breaks in deposition between litho-

stratigraphic units. Whenever a paleosol is identified at a site, the stratigraphic relationship of the soil to lithostratigraphic units and landforms must be fully described. The areal extent of paleosols should be mapped to define the spatial extent of landscape stability and the nature of the paleotopography. Buried soils are either sequentially numbered within the stratigraphic succession from oldest to youngest or are given names.

It is important to understand the difference between pedostratigraphic and lithostratigraphic units—what they are composed of and what they represent. Sediments are accumulations of inorganic and organic materials that represent former periods of deposition. These accumulated sediments are used to define lithostratigraphic units. Soils are weathering profiles developed on sediments exposed at the surface during periods of landscape stability. These soil profiles, if buried, are used to define pedostratigraphic units. A paleosol, because it is superimposed onto a lithostratigraphic unit, is always younger than the unit on which it is developed. Because pedologic activity alters the original particle size distribution of the parent material and creates new structures, it often obscures important contacts between lithostratigraphic units, making stratigraphic interpretations difficult. Horizons should not be confused with geologic layering, because soil horizons have no relationship to geologic deposition (Fig. 2.15; Tamplin 1969). It cannot be overstressed that the color, textural, and structural characteristics of soil horizons bear little relationship to the original layering of sediments on which they developed. If two lithostratigraphic units of different ages are both exposed at the surface, pedogenesis will alter both units during a period of landscape stability and will create a laterally continuous soil profile. Consequently, artifacts of different ages buried in two different lithostratigraphic units may occur in the same soil horizon and lead to the erroneous conclusion that they are from the same time period (Holliday 1990).

At the Lubbock Lake site in northwest Texas, for example, artifacts of Archaic age occur in two different lithostratigraphic units but are found in the same calcic horizon of the Lubbock Lake soil (Fig. 2.29; Holliday 1990; Johnson and Holliday 1986). The calcic horizon of the Lubbock Lake soil is primarily confined to the lower portion of unit 4B, but in places it extends to depths where it has developed on the upper portion of unit 3e and thus is also superimposed over the upper portion of the Yellowhouse soil. Excavators in the 1930s did not distinguish between soil horizons and sedimentological units and excavated the calcic horizon as a stratigraphic unit. Consequently, the artifacts recovered from the calcic horizon could either be from unit 3e (and thus be as much as 6000 years old) or from unit 4B (and thus be less than 5000 years old). Failure to recognize the difference between sediment layering and soil horizonation led to the mixture of temporally discrete artifact assemblages.

Chronostratigraphy

In contrast to lithostratigraphy and pedostratigraphy, which are concerned with material units and their spatial relationships, chronostratigraphy is concerned with the temporal dimension of the stratigraphic sequence. Time is an irreversible continuum during which the landscape alternates between periods of deposition, erosion, and stability. Consequently, the passage of all time at an archaeological site is recorded by any one or a combination of (1) lithostratigraphic units (deposition of sediment); (2) pedostratigraphic units (landscape stability and soil profile development); and (3) erosional unconformities (degradation of the landscape). Chronostratigraphic investigations at an archaeological site are specifically concerned with determining (1) whether there were multiple episodes of deposition, erosion, and stability; (2) the relative order in which these intervals occurred; (3) when these episodes occurred in absolute time; (4) the absolute duration of each period of sediment accumulation, erosion, and pedogenesis; and (5) the placement of the site stratigraphy into established geologic time nomenclature.

The number of episodes of deposition, erosion, and stability and the order in which they occurred are determined by recording the superposition of lithostratigraphic units, pedostratigraphic units, and the contacts between them at an archaeological site. The timing and duration of deposition, landscape stability, and landscape degradation are determined by applying chronometric dating methods such as radiocarbon dating, archaeomagnetism, thermoluminescence, and other techniques.

Dean (1978) makes a distinction between the "sample age" generated by chronometric techniques and the event that is being dated, which he calls the "event age." The sample age is the geochronological age obtained on a sample that is a material inclusion in a matrix. This sample and the method used to date it are subject to a number of inherent limitations and avenues of contamination that affect the accuracy and precision of the finite age. Coleman and others (1987) stress this point by suggesting that the term *date* be replaced by *age*. Understanding the application, limitations, and reliability of absolute ages generated by geochronological methods is crucial to interpreting the temporal dimension of the site stratigraphy. Inappropriate techniques, the improper application of a dating method, and poor sample quality can generate unreliable ages that lead to false stratigraphic interpretations. The theory and application of different chronometric dating techniques are discussed in detail elsewhere (e.g., Mahaney 1984; Michels 1973;

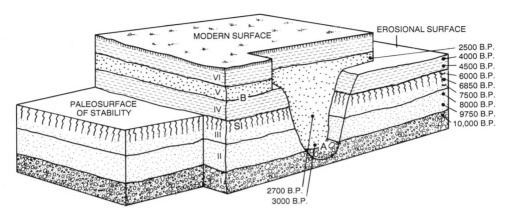

FIGURE 2.30. A cross section of a hypothetical alluvial exposure showing lithostratigraphic units (I–VI), a paleosol (S1), an erosional unconformity (the surface covered by unit V), and radiocarbon ages. Ideally, the duration of a lithostratigraphic unit is determined by dating the top, middle, and bottom of the unit. For example, unit III was deposited between 7500 and 6000 B.P. Additional ages from the top, middle, and base of the unit are needed to confirm these ages. The duration of landscape stability, represented by the formation of the soil (S1), is determined first by dating the uppermost portion of unit III. This dates the cessation of deposition and the beginning of landscape stability and soil formation. Next, the beginning date of renewed deposition is obtained by dating samples from the oldest portion of the lithostratigraphic unit (unit IV) that overlies the paleosol. This date determines the end of landscape stability and the first burial of the soil. The results of this methodology indicate that landscape stability and S1 soil formation occurred between 6000 and 4500 B.P. The surface buried by unit V is an erosional unconformity. This surface is dominated by an erosional channel, which cuts into preexisting deposits. The temporal value of the lacuna (degradational vacuity and hiatus; discussed below in the text) varies from a maximum at point A (7000 years, the difference between the ages of units I and V) to a minimum at point B (1500 years, the difference between the ages of units IV and V). At point A the degradational vacuity is much larger than at point B because of the greater removal of preexisting deposits at the former location. The hiatus is determined by comparing the ages from deposits that represent the very last period of deposition prior to erosion (the top of unit IV) and the very earliest deposition over the erosional surface (the base of unit V). A comparison of these ages indicates that the period of erosion occurred sometime between 4000 and 3000 B.P. (i.e., the maximum duration of the erosional event is 1000 years). Thus the degradational vacuity at point A is 6000 years, and that at point B is 500 years.

Mook and Waterbolk 1983; Rutter 1985; Taylor 1987) and are not covered here. This is not to diminish the importance of understanding the application and limitations of each dating technique, because the techniques used and the material dated determine the accuracy of chronostratigraphic interpretations. A classification of Quaternary dating methods according to accuracy is presented in Table 2.6. The emphasis of this discussion is on sample provenience and the determination of the event age (i.e., when periods of deposition, erosion, and stability occurred and how long they lasted).

Ideally, the duration of a depositional episode is determined by dating material from the base and the top of the sediments comprising a lithostratigraphic unit (Fig. 2.30). In this way the first and last episodes of deposition are determined. The archaeological and paleontological contents of the unit also provide useful data on the duration of sedimentation. Samples used to determine the initiation and cessation of deposition should be carefully collected and evaluated to prevent dating intrusive or secondary samples in the lithostratigraphic unit. If not recognized, the dating of samples that are not temporally associated with an event results in erroneous interpretations. For example, Blong and Gillespie (1978) showed that dispersed charcoal in alluvial units may sometimes yield radiocarbon ages that do not accurately reflect when deposition occurred. Taylor et al. (1986) illustrated how bioturbation of radiocarbon samples in the two-meter-thick midden at Encino Village in California led to date reversals in the stratigraphic sequence. To overcome problems of mixing and the statistical probabilities associated with dating techniques, multiple samples should be dated from the top and bottom of any unit. In addition, it is important to date additional samples in the unit to test the reliability of the ages derived from the top and bottom.

Even though the duration of the formation of a lithostratigraphic unit can be determined, deposition of that unit may not have occurred at a constant rate through time. The rate at which sediments accumulate varies from place to place and at any specific place through time. For example, on the floodplain of the Haw River in North Carolina, rates of sedimentation have varied from 0.8 to 7.4 cm per century (Larsen and Schuldenrein 1990). Determining the rate of sedimentation requires that numerous chronometric ages be obtained from the entire lithostratigraphic unit. The rate of sedimentation cannot be calculated simply by dividing the thickness of the sediment comprising the lithostratigraphic unit by the known duration of deposition.

The amount of time represented by landscape stability and soil formation may be roughly estimated from the degree of soil formation if the rate of pedogenesis is known (Birkeland 1984; Vreeken 1984). The absolute duration of landscape stability is determined by dating material from the paleosol (Vreeken 1984) and the overlying lithostratigraphic unit. Dates from the

Table 2.6 A Classification of Quaternary Dating Methods

TYPE OF RESULT[a]

======== Numerical Age ============

====== Calibrated Age ======

====== Relative Age ========

= Correlated Age =

TYPE OF METHOD[b]

Sidereal	Isotopic	Radiogenic	Chemical and Biological	Geomorphic	Correlation
Historical records	^{14}C	Fission-track	Amino acid racemization	Soil-profile development	Lithostratigraphy
Dendrochronology	K-Ar and ^{39}Ar-^{40}Ar	[c]	[c]	Rock and mineral weathering	Tephrochronology
Varve chronology	Uranium-series	Thermoluminescence	Obsidian and tephra hydration	Progressive landscape modification	Paleomagnetism
	Uranium-trend	Electron-spin resonance	Lichenometry	Rate of deposition	Archaeomagnetism
	Cosmogenic isotopes (^{210}Pb, ^{10}Be, ^{36}Cl, etc.)		Soil chemistry	Rate of deformation	Fossils and artifacts
			Rock varnish chemistry	Geomorphic position	Stable isotopes
					Orbital variations
					Tectites and microtectites

SOURCE: Coleman, Pierce, and Birkeland 1987.

[a] Classification of Quaternary dating methods based on the type of result (the level of information and degree of confidence):

Numerical Age: methods that produce quantitative age estimates;

Calibrated Age: methods that produce an age by measuring systematic changes resulting from individual unrelated groups of processes; the rates of these processes depend on environmental variables, such as lithology and climate, so that the process rates must be calibrated by independent chronological control;

Relative Age: methods that provide an age sequence; most also provide a measure of age differences between members of a sequence;

Correlated Age: methods that produce ages only by demonstrating equivalence to independently dated deposits or events.

Considerable overlap exists in these classes. Double dashed lines indicate the type of result most commonly produced by the methods below them. Single solid lines indicate the type of result less commonly produced by the methods below them.

[b] Classification of Quaternary dating methods. Methods grouped that share similar assumptions, mechanisms, or applications:

Sidereal (calendar or annual): methods that determine calendar dates or count annual events;

Isotopic: methods that measure changes in isotopic composition due to radioactive decay;

Radiogenic: methods that measure cumulative nonisotopic effects of radioactive decay, such as crystal damage and electron energy traps;

Chemical and Biological: methods that measure the results of time-dependent chemical or biological processes;

Geomorphic: methods that measure the results of complex, interrelated, time-dependent geomorphic processes, commonly including chemical and biological processes;

Correlation: methods that establish age equivalence using time-independent properties.

[c] Methods above this line routinely produce numerical ages. Methods below the line are more experimental and involve nonradioactive processes or processes whose effects on age estimates are not well established.

paleosol determine the beginning of landscape stability if the material dated was originally deposited in the uppermost portion of the sediments that comprised the parent material that was later altered into a soil profile. Ages from the base of the lithostratigraphic unit directly overlying the paleosol (pedostratigraphic unit) date the renewal of sediment deposition and thus the end of landscape stability and the cessation of soil formation (Fig. 2.30). Ages derived directly from the organic material in soil horizons provide approximate ages for soil formation because of the constant turnover of organic carbon in the soil (Birkeland 1984; Valentine and Dalrymple 1976; Vreeken 1984; Yaalon 1971). These are sometimes referred to as mean-residence ages, referring to the length of time it takes organic carbon to be cycled into and out of the soil.

Degradational episodes are represented by erosional surfaces. The total amount of time represented by an erosional unconformity is made up of two components, the hiatus and degradational vacuity, which are collectively called the lacuna (Fig. 2.30; Krumbein and Sloss 1963; Wheeler 1958). The hiatus refers to the duration of the erosional event. The degradational vacuity is the additional time represented by the unconformable surface that was created by the erosion of older preexisting material units (lithostratigraphic and pedostratigraphic units) during the episode of degradation (Fig. 2.30). The time value of the degradational vacuity often varies from place to place, depending on the severity of erosion. For example, if a channel downcuts into its floodplain, the degradational vacuity is greater at the base of a channel than near its margin because a greater volume of preexisting sediments is removed at the locus of entrenchment. The hiatus, however, is less time transgressive. Consequently, the total time represented by an erosional unconformity (i.e., the lacuna) may vary from one location to another. Ideally, the duration of landscape degradation—the hiatus—can be determined by dating samples from the youngest stratigraphic unit truncated by the unconformable surface and samples from the lowermost portion of the oldest unit overlying the unconformity.

The nature and structure of a stratigraphic sequence in any environment is determined by the number, timing, areal extent, magnitude, and duration of individual periods of deposition, degradation, and stability (Brookes et al. 1982; Kraus and Bown 1986; Sadler 1981). Over a given interval of time, individual episodes of deposition, stability, and erosion may be of long duration, with changes occurring infrequently, or they may be of short duration and alternate frequently. Furthermore, these episodes may affect a large region or only a small area. Consequently, different stratigraphic sequences of lithostratigraphic units, pedostratigraphic units, and erosional contacts are created.

The total duration of deposition, degradation, and stability determines how much of the time continuum of a stratigraphic sequence is recorded by material depositional units (lithostratigraphic units) versus the combined time represented by nondepositional intervals represented by surfaces of erosion (erosional unconformities) and surfaces of stability (pedostratigraphic units). Episodes of landscape degradation and stability create gaps in any depositional sequence and thus leave an incomplete geologic record of lithostratigraphic units. The ratio of the total amount of time recorded by the deposition of physical strata to the amount of time represented by nondepositional and erosional contacts between lithostratigraphic units produces a measure of the completeness of the stratigraphic sequence (Fig. 2.31; Sadler 1981). Generally this ratio is low because the contacts between and within lithostratigraphic units represent the passage of more time than the physical sediments themselves (Ager 1981; Kraus and Bown 1986; Sadler 1981).

Some individual stratigraphic sequences are more complete than others. In other words, some stratigraphic sequences have proportionally more time represented by periods of deposition of physical strata than by the surfaces and contacts created by erosion and stability. Generally, however, no single stratigraphic exposure has a complete range of late Pleistocene and Holocene sediments. To overcome part of the problem of incomplete stratigraphic sequences at individual exposures, more complete composite sequences may be constructed through regional stratigraphic studies. Spatially separated, incomplete stratigraphic sequences are correlated over a region in order to construct a composite stratigraphic record of material units (Fig. 2.31). In Whitewater Draw, an arroyo in southeastern Arizona, no single exposure preserved a complete sequence of stratigraphic units spanning the last 15,000 years. Instead, different portions of the late Quaternary record were preserved in individual exposures along the 25 km arroyo. By correlating one stratigraphic section with the next, a composite stratigraphic sequence representing most of the late Quaternary was constructed (Fig. 2.25; Waters 1986b). This procedure has been used widely. For example, composite stratigraphic sequences have been established for the lower Snake River in Washington (Hammatt 1977), the San Pedro River in Arizona (Haynes 1981, 1982a), and the Duck River in Tennessee (Brakenridge 1984).

In some cases, however, regional episodes of erosion or stability create widespread gaps in the stratigraphic sequence in which no deposits of a given time interval are present anywhere in a region (Fig. 2.31; Ager 1981; Brookes et al. 1982; Kraus and Bown 1986; Sadler 1981). This is well illustrated by the regional stratigraphic sequence of the Santa Cruz River near Tucson, Arizona, where sediments older than 5500 B.P. were eroded from the valley during a regional period of erosion (Haynes and Huckell 1986; Waters

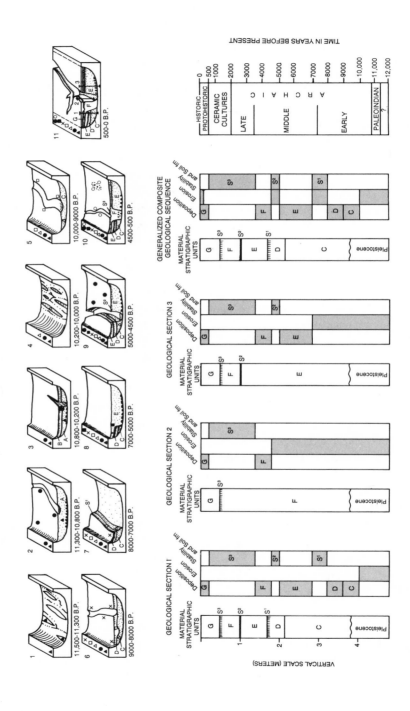

TIME IN YEARS BEFORE PRESENT

VERTICAL SCALE (METERS)

1988a, 1988b, 1988c). Sometime before 5500 B.P., the channel of the Santa Cruz River downcut into its floodplain, widened, and scoured its valley. Deposition resumed in the valley after 5500 B.P. This erosional episode was responsible for the destruction of most lithostratigraphic and pedostratigraphic units older than 5500 B.P. Similarly, a regional erosional event in western Iowa scoured deposits dating between 8000 and 3500 B.P. from many tributary valleys (Bettis and Thompson 1981, 1982, 1985; Thompson and Bettis 1980, 1982).

Finally, it is necessary to place the stratigraphic sequence defined at a site into established geologic time nomenclature. Geologists subdivide the 4.5 billion years of earth history into a number of intervals of fixed duration called geochronologic units. Geochronologic units are time units with

FIGURE 2.31. The sequence of landscape changes in a hypothetical valley, showing how an alluvial sequence is created and interpreted in terms of time (i.e., periods of deposition, erosion, and stability). Also shown is how the archaeological record is created within an alluvial environment. The series of block diagrams in the upper portion of the figure illustrate landscape changes from 11,500 B.P. to the present. Sites located on the landscape during these intervals are shown by various symbols. Some of these sites become buried and eroded within the dynamic floodplain environment. Evidence of all periods of occupation will be found on the surface of the stable Pleistocene terrace overlooking the floodplain. The lower portion of the figure illustrates the material stratigraphic record preserved at the three localities designated in diagram 11. Next to these stratigraphic sections are diagrams that interpret the stratigraphic section in terms of time—that is, each section records 11,500 years of time as a combination of depositional, erosional, and stable intervals. The preserved material units and the combination of time represented vary from section to section. The fourth diagram is a composite section of the alluvial stratigraphy. A comparison of the valley alluvial stratigraphy with the archaeological sequence shows that (1) the Paleoindian and the earliest Archaic remains have been eroded from the valley; (2) transitional material between the early and middle Archaic and some later middle Archaic remains were either eroded or may be found on the surfaces of paleosols S^1 and S^2; (3) transitional middle-to-late Archaic, late Archaic, and Ceramic period sites will be found compressed onto the surface of the S^3 paleosol and buried by a thin layer of historic alluvium; and (4) the deposits themselves will contain only early and middle Archaic, protohistoric, and historic remains. This figure also illustrates that the time represented by an unconformity also varies from place to place. The hiatus of each period of erosion is shown on the composite sequence, but the temporal value of the unconformities is greater in the various sections described. The difference between the hiatus and the temporal value of any of the unconformities in the specific geological sections is the degradational vacuity (i.e., the amount of time lost due to the erosion of preexisting sediments).

specific isochronus boundaries (i.e., the boundaries are everywhere the same age) and thus include the total assemblage of lithostratigraphic and pedo-stratigraphic units that formed during a specific interval of time (NACOSN 1983). Consequently, these units may or may not coincide with lithostrati-graphic or pedostratigraphic boundaries. Formal names are assigned to these intervals of earth history. Therefore, once the age of a sequence of lithostrati-graphic and pedostratigraphic units is determined by its fossil content or through chronometric dating techniques, it can be placed into one or more of the geochronologic units that define earth history.

In North America, all stratigraphic sequences that contain archaeologi-cal remains are assigned to the Quaternary period (1.8 my to the present). The Quaternary period is further subdivided into the Pleistocene epoch (1.8 my to 10,000 yr B.P.) and the Holocene epoch (10,000 yr B.P. to the present). The Pleistocene and Holocene are informally subdivided into early, middle, and late stages. For a discussion of the origin and meaning of this terminol-ogy, see Farrand 1990. All archaeological sites in North America can be placed into the late Pleistocene and Holocene epochs. These are broad chro-nostratigraphic units encompassing thousands of years and are used to group sediments into large blocks of time.

In summary, when defining the temporal relationships at a site, it is necessary to place the stratigraphic sequence in the Pleistocene and Holocene epochs. Furthermore, it is necessary to define the relative sequence of litho-stratigraphic units, pedostratigraphic units, and erosional unconformities, and then place these units and unconformities in absolute time to define the sequence and timing of deposition, stability, and erosion.

Correlation

Correlation is the demonstration of lithologic or temporal equivalency (Boggs 1987; Krumbein and Sloss 1963). Physical correlations demonstrate that lithostratigraphic units, pedostratigraphic units, and erosional contacts are the same from one exposure to the next. Temporal correlations determine the time equivalency between lithostratigraphic units, pedostratigraphic units, and erosional contacts, thereby illuminating facies relationships.

Stratigraphic units and contacts defined at an archaeological site are correlated across the site, and where possible the site microstratigraphy should be correlated with the regional geological stratigraphy. The best way to demonstrate the equivalency of geographically separated lithostrati-graphic units, pedostratigraphic units, and erosional unconformities is by direct correlation. If the units or contacts are continuous and well exposed, they can be physically traced from one point to another. In this way an unequivocal correlation is made. In many cases, however, stratigraphic units and contacts are discontinuously exposed because of erosion, slumping, and burial. As a result, indirect correlations are necessary to establish equivalency. Indirect correlations between units exposed in two geographically separated locations are demonstrated if (1) the lithologic or pedologic characteristics (e.g., texture, structure, or color) of the two units are similar; (2) the stratigraphic position of the units and contacts in the two sequences are similar; (3) the artifact, floral, and faunal assemblages in the units are similar; (4) the radiocarbon ages, archaeomagnetic ages, or ages generated by other chronometric dating techniques from both deposits are similar; and (5) the units show a similar stratigraphic relationship to a distinctive marker, such as a volcanic ash, that was deposited over a wide region during a brief interval.

Stratigraphic sequences at a site may be temporally correlated with stratigraphic sequences defined in other regions to elucidate regional patterns of landscape stability, erosion, and deposition. For example, correlations are commonly made between geographically separated river valleys to determine if changes in the landscape occurred at similar or different times. These correlations may show that spatially separated regions were undergoing similar and synchronous episodes of deposition, erosion, and stability. Synchroniety implies that geomorphic conditions (e.g., relief, position of the water table, sediment yield from the hillslopes, internal landscape thresholds, and vegetation cover) were similar from region to region and that external climatic changes triggered similar responses in each region. This creates stratigraphic sequences that are similar and that can be correlated over broad regions (Haynes 1968; Knox 1983), such as western Iowa (Thompson and Bettis 1980, 1982), the central Great Plains (Johnson and Martin 1987a, 1987b; Johnson and Logan 1990), the southern Great Plains (Hall 1990a), and the Llano Estacado (Stafford 1981).

Stratigraphic sequences may, however, vary from one region to another. In this case, there is no one-to-one correlation of depositional units, unconformities, and paleosols between the two spatially separated regions. This demonstrates that the two regions had different and nonsynchronous landscape histories. This occurs if climatic conditions during the late Quaternary varied from one region to another or if the landscape of each region adjusted in its own way to similar climatic conditions because each area possessed a unique set of geomorphic conditions. In addition, other factors, such as human land use or tectonism, may have triggered degradation, aggradation, or stability in one region and not another (Butzer 1980b; Patton and Schumm 1981; Schumm and Parker 1973; Waters 1985). For example, the late Quaternary stratigraphic sequences for four adjacent river valleys in southern Arizona (those of the Santa Cruz River, Cienega Creek, the San

Pedro River, and Whitewater Draw) show only minimal similarity (Fig. 2.32; Waters 1985, 1991). In some cases, these river systems responded roughly synchronously to broad climatic changes (e.g., arroyo cutting during the middle Holocene, though even this event is time transgressive), but for the most part the fluvial systems in each valley responded differently to long-term periods of climatic stability and short-term climatic iterations because each valley was characterized by different geomorphic conditions and internal landscape thresholds. Other factors, such as human land use (e.g., extensive farming or clearing of vegetation), appear to have triggered some local stream responses.

Lithostratigraphic units, pedostratigraphic units, and erosional unconformities that represent episodes of deposition, stability, and erosion may also be conceptually correlated with climatic events (e.g., the Altithermal or late Wisconsin glaciation), geologic events (e.g., earthquakes, volcanic eruptions, or sea level changes), or cultural events (e.g., abandonments or migrations). For example, soil formation, dune activity, and erosional events that occurred during the middle Holocene in the western United States are often correlated with a period of aridity known as the Altithermal (Haynes 1968; Holliday 1989b).

The Geoarchaeological Interpretation of Sediments, Soils, and Stratigraphy

Once the sediments and soils comprising the site matrix have been defined and the stratigraphy established, geoarchaeological investigations should focus on reconstructing the prehistoric landscape and evaluating natural site-formation processes.

Landscape Reconstruction

The geomorphic landscape is the physical platform on which all people, other animals, and plants live and interact. Portions of this landscape are relatively stable and remain unchanged over a given interval of time, while other areas are dynamic and are constantly changing over the same time period. This fact allows us to divide the landscape into two major components: the constant elements of the landscape and its dynamic elements (Fig. 2.33).

The question of whether components of the landscape should be considered constant or dynamic depends on the temporal scale of investigation. To geologists concerned with millions of years of earth history, the position of continents and the creation and denudation of mountain ranges are dynamic components of the landscape. However, the time frame of interest to North American archaeologists is generally the late Quaternary, the period when

TIME YR B.P.	ARCHAEOLOGICAL CULTURES	SANTA CRUZ RIVER (Waters 1988b)	CIENEGA CREEK (Eddy & Cooley 1983)	SAN PEDRO RIVER (Haynes 1981, 1982a)	WHITEWATER DRAW (Waters 1986b)
0	Historic / Protohistoric	Channel Cutting / Stable Floodplain / Channel Cut & Fill (VI) / Stable — V3a V3b V4 V1/V2 Stable	Channel Cutting / Channel Filling and Soil Formation (Units 1 & 2) / Arroyo Cutting	Channel Cutting	Channel Cutting
1000	Ceramic Cultures — Classic / Sedentary / Colonial / Pioneer (HOHOKAM)	Channel Cutting and Filling (Unit IV)		Channel Cutting and Filling (McCool Alluvium - Qmc)	Six Cycles
2000		Channel Cutting and Filling (Unit III)	Cienega, Colluvial and Shallow Stream Deposition (Units 3-7)		of
3000	Late	Filling of Large Channel with Unit II Alluvium		Channel Cutting and Filling (Hargis Alluvium - Qha)	Cienega Erosion and Deposition
4000		Localized Colluvial Slopewash (llsw) Along Edge of Channel | No Deposition in Main Channel			(Units J, K, L, M, N & O)
5000	Middle (ARCHAIC)			Channel Filling (Weik Alluvium - Qwk)	
6000		Channel Downcutting and Widening	Channel Downcutting and Widening		Arroyo Channel Cutting and Filling (Unit I)
7000				Channel Erosion and Widening	Four Cycles of Cienega Erosion and Deposition (Units E, F, G, & H)
8000		Remnants of Unit I Alluvium	(Major Erosional Unconformity)	Slopewash, Eolian Sediments (Donnet Silt - Qdo)	
9000	Early				Braided Stream
10,000		(Major Erosional Unconformity)		Cienega Deposition (Black Mat/ Clanton Clay - Qcl)	Deposition (Units Da & Db)
11,000					
12,000	PALEOINDIAN (Clovis)			Small Channel Cut and Filled (Graveyard Sand - Qgr)	

V1/V2 = Cienega Formation
V3a = Channel Cut & Fill
V3b = Gully-mouth Fan Formation
V4 = Sand Dune Formation

FIGURE 2.32. The correlation between the archaeological culture sequence for southern Arizona and the alluvial sequences for the Santa Cruz River, Cienega Creek (a tributary of the Santa Cruz River), the San Pedro River, and Whitewater Draw. Major periods of channel downcutting and widening that created major unconformities are indicated by the gray shading. This diagram graphically shows that there is little correspondence between the periods of channel downcutting and filling within these valleys. Furthermore, because of the staggered periods of erosion and deposition between these valleys, the alluvial record in each is different. Thus the archaeological record contained within the valley alluvium will vary from one valley to the next. For example, numerous buried Paleoindian sites are encountered in the San Pedro Valley, where sediments of this age are preserved, while Paleoindian sites are absent from the Santa Cruz Valley and Cienega Creek because the Clovis-age alluvium has been eroded.

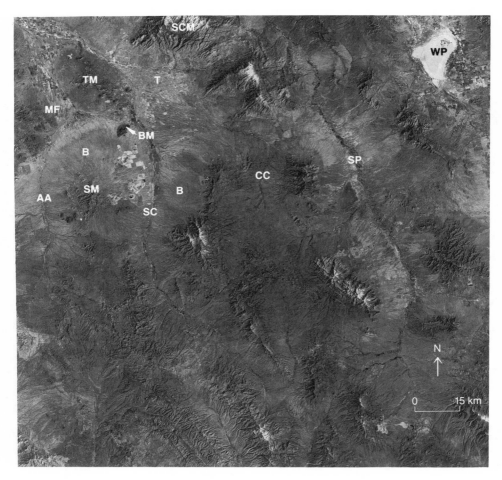

FIGURE 2.33. A Landsat photograph of southern Arizona and northern Sonora. The permanent features of the landscape include mountain ranges like the Sierrita Mountains (SM), the Santa Catalina Mountains (SCM), Black Mountain (BM), and the Tucson Mountains (TM). The stabilized depositional landforms include the extensive Pleistocene alluvial surfaces making up the upper portions of the bajadas (B) that emanate from the mountain fronts. The dynamic components of the landscape include the arroyo floodplains of the Santa Cruz River (SC), the San Pedro River (SP), Altar Arroyo (AA), and Cienega Creek (CC); the lower active portions of the bajadas; and the Willcox Playa (WP), the location of Paleolake Cochise. Also shown is an active arroyo-mouth fan (MF) at the terminus of the Altar Arroyo. The city of Tucson (T) is at upper left.

humans were present in the New World. Consequently, the constant portions of the landscape from an archaeological standpoint include (1) those geographic features that require millions of years to change, such as the location of valleys, mountain ranges, passes, and basins; and (2) the stabilized (inactive) depositional landforms that did not change significantly during the late Quaternary, such as early and middle Pleistocene age river terraces above the active floodplain, the 100,000-year-old surface of an alluvial fan, and the Pleistocene moraines of ancient glaciers. The dynamic components of the landscape are those depositional environments that were active and changed during the late Quaternary, such as a floodplain where a river changed its position and actively flooded adjacent lowlands, sand dunes that migrated downwind within a dune field, or a marine shoreline that was displaced with the rise and fall of the ocean. Through time, the dynamic portion of the landscape is characterized by alternating conditions of stability, deposition, and erosion. For example, previously stabilized areas may become active areas of deposition or erosion (e.g., a river may overtop its banks and deposit silt and clay over the previously stable floodplain). Similarly, areas that were once undergoing deposition could become stabilized (e.g., a river may stop inundating its floodplain, allowing a soil to form), and so on. Furthermore, different conditions may characterize different areas of the landscape at any given time. For example, the floodplain of a river is characterized by simultaneous erosion along the banks of its channel, deposition in the channel, and stability over the rest of the floodplain.

To elucidate human relationships with the land, it is essential to reconstruct both the dynamic and constant elements of the landscape (Butzer 1982; Davidson 1985; Gladfelter 1977, 1981; Hassan 1979, 1985a; Renfrew 1976). The keys to reconstructing the landscape are preserved in the sediments, soils, and erosional contacts making up the archaeological site matrix and the regional stratigraphy surrounding the site. Sediments provide information on depositional processes and the specific environments that were present; soils preserve evidence of landscape stability; and erosional unconformities record episodes of landscape degradation. Stratigraphic and geochronological investigations interpret the superpositioning of sediments, soils, and erosional contacts to define the spatial and temporal record of landscape aggradation, stability, and degradation. This evidence is used first to differentiate between the constant and the dynamic elements of the landscape and then to define the landscape history of the dynamic component in greater detail.

Reconstructions of the prehistoric landscape may be either synchronic or diachronic. Synchronic reconstructions define the geomorphic processes and configuration of the landscape that existed at and around a site at the time it was occupied, thus placing a site in its prehistoric landscape context. Site-specific synchronic reconstructions of the landscape are vital to the interpretation of site function and subsistence activity, while regional synchronic reconstructions provide an understanding of how coexisting landscape components affected the spatial patterning of settlements and activity loci (Butzer 1982; Davidson 1985; Gladfelter 1977, 1981; Hassan 1979, 1985a; Renfrew 1976). For example, the position of a prehistoric site, as well as the regional pattern of late prehistoric sites, may reflect the distribution of arable land and the hydrologic conditions of the region.

Diachronic landscape reconstructions at the site or regional level place prehistoric people in the context of an evolving landscape. The landscape is reconstructed at a number of different points in time, and then archaeological settlement data are compared to the corresponding diachronic landscape reconstructions. In this way, changes in the spatial distribution of geological processes (i.e., erosion, deposition, and stability) or changes in the depositional environments and subenvironments (e.g., a change from an inland to a coastal environment with a rise in sea level) are correlated with the changing loci of human activity through time (Butzer 1982; Davidson 1985; Hassan 1985a; Renfrew 1976).

Synchronic and diachronic reconstructions of the constant and dynamic elements of the landscape are crucial to archaeological interpretations of prehistory. In many cases the landscape has changed considerably since the site was last occupied. It must be recognized that prehistoric people occupied a landscape that may not have corresponded to the configuration of the existing one (Renfrew 1976). For this reason, the proper interpretation of human behavior requires us to place prehistoric sites in the context of both static and evolving prehistoric landscapes. These points are amplified with specific case studies in the chapters that follow.

The Preservation of Sites and the Formation of the Archaeological Record

The archaeological record has in large part been shaped by the same processes that have molded the landscape (Albanese 1978a; Thompson and Bettis 1982; Butzer 1982; Davidson 1985; Gladfelter 1985, Thorson 1990). Once people abandon a site, the geomorphic conditions characterizing the landscape determine whether it is initially preserved or destroyed. If the landscape is stable (i.e., if it is characterized by negligible erosion or deposition), an archaeological site may remain at the surface without becoming either buried or eroded away. However, if the site is situated in an area that is, or that becomes, subject to erosional conditions, all or part of the site will be destroyed. Similarly, if the site is situated in an area of active deposition, or if deposition begins sometime after abandonment, the site will be buried.

Buried archaeological remains are preserved in a number of different field situations: (1) they may be buried in the sediments of a lithostratigraphic unit, (2) they may be buried in a pedostratigraphic unit, or (3) they may be buried on the contact between a pedostratigraphic and a lithostratigraphic unit (Fig. 2.34).

Archaeological remains become incorporated into the sediments of a lithostratigraphic unit if the occupation correlates with a period of deposition (Fig. 2.34c). Such a situation occurs if the archaeological site is located in an area of active sedimentation, such as a floodplain during a short diastem, and is subsequently buried during the next episode of deposition. Multiple occupations may occur in a lithostratigraphic unit if the site is repeatedly inhabited through time and if the site is located in an area of active sedimentation. The vertical spatial separation between these episodes of occupation is determined by the rate at which sediments accumulate (Fig. 2.35; Ferring 1986a). If sedimentation is rapid, archaeological assemblages from different occupations will be clearly separated from one another. This situation makes it easy to distinguish temporally specific spatial patterns of archaeological remains at a site. However, if sedimentation rates are slow, archaeological assemblages from repeated occupations of a site may become mixed on a surface or may be separated only by thin strata. In this case, separating temporally discrete archaeological assemblages will be difficult or impossible. Sedimentation rates are not constant and vary from one environment to the next and from one time period to the next in the same environment. Consequently, increases and decreases in artifact densities in a stratigraphic unit may reflect corresponding increases and decreases in sedimentation rates over time rather than increases and decreases in the intensity of occupation. For example, if the rate of sedimentation at a site was slow, what was actually a number of discrete occupations at one locality by small bands of the same culture may appear to be a single large village occupation. Inversely, during periods of rapid sedimentation, intense occupation may be spread out over a greater vertical thickness of sediment and thus may not appear so intense. The influence that sedimentation rates can have on the archaeological record is shown by studies in Oklahoma at the Delaware Canyon site (Ferring 1986b), the Dyer site (Ferring and Peter 1987), and other sites on the Osage Plains (Hall 1988).

There are two ways in which archaeological remains can be preserved in a pedostratigraphic unit. In one case, the site is not buried by soil but by sediment after the site is abandoned. This sediment, and the buried site it contains, becomes stabilized and is close enough to the surface to be within the zone of active weathering. Soil forming processes alter the sediment into

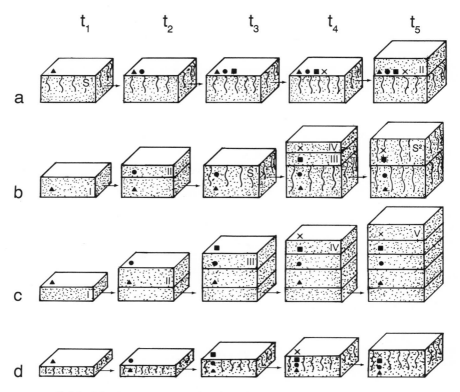

FIGURE 2.34. The incorporation of archaeological remains into soils and sediments. Time passes from t_1 to t_5, and symbols represent artifacts accumulated during each period. Wavy lines represent soil profile development. Series *a* shows the accumulation of artifacts on the surface of a soil (S^1) from t_1 to t_4 and its eventual burial by sand (unit II) at t_5. In this situation, artifacts of various ages are mixed on the surface of the paleosol and are overlain by a lithostratigraphic unit. Series *b* shows how artifacts become incorporated into a paleosol. At t_1 and t_2 artifacts become buried within sediments (units I and II). At t_3 the surface stabilizes and a soil (S^1) forms. Soil profile characteristics are imprinted onto the parent material (units I and II) that contains the archaeological debris. Thus, artifacts become incorporated into the soil horizons of soil S^1. At t_4 more sediment deposition occurs (units III and IV), and more artifacts are buried within these units. Also, the S^1 soil is buried. At t_5 stability returns and a new soil (S^2) is imprinted onto the sediments containing archaeological material accumulated during t_4. Series *c* shows how artifacts become incorporated into different lithostratigraphic units. During brief interruptions in deposition at t_1 through t_5, people occupied an aggrading surface (such as a floodplain). After each period of occupation, deposition occurred and buried the artifacts, incorporating them into a number of different sedimentary units

a soil profile, imprinting its horizons over the sediment and the buried archaeological remains, thus resulting in a site within a soil profile (Fig. 2.34b). For example, at the Lubbock Lake site in Texas, middle Archaic artifacts were buried in eolian sediments comprising stratigraphic unit 4B, deposited between 5500 and 4500 B.P. (Fig. 2.29). Deposition ceased and stability followed from around 4500 B.P. until 1000 B.P. A strongly developed soil profile, known as the Lubbock Lake soil, formed during this time in the upper portion of unit 4B. Thus Archaic artifacts are found in the pedogenic horizons of this soil (Holliday 1990).

In the second case, archaeological remains occur in cumulative soils, that is, soils formed in situations in which the accumulation of sediment is slow enough to permit simultaneous pedogenic alteration of the sediment (Fig. 2.34d). This process results in a very thick A horizon. In these situations, archaeological debris is buried in the overthickened A horizon as the profile accretes vertically. Thus, archaeological debris from multiple occupations will be spread out over the vertical soil profile. Because the rates of deposition and soil formation are so slow and because pedogenesis obscures bedding planes, great care must be taken to identify discrete occupation surfaces in the thick A horizon. For example, hearths and artifacts from multiple late Archaic occupations are stratified in the cumulative West Fork soil at site 41CO141 on the Elm Fork of the Trinity River in Texas. Here, debris from several late Archaic occupations dated between 1800 and 950 B.P. became incorporated into the soil when overbank deposition on the floodplain was slow and pedogenesis concurrently altered the floodplain silts and clays into an A horizon about 1.5 m thick (Ferring 1987, 1990a, 1990b; Prikryl and Yates 1987). Similarly, late prehistoric sites occur in the thick, cumulic A horizon of the Asa paleosol along the Brazos River in Texas (Fig. 2.21).

Evidence of human activity during prolonged periods of landscape stability will be found on the contact between pedostratigraphic and lithostrati-

---

(I–V). Series *d* shows how artifacts become incorporated into a cumulative soil profile. In this case, sedimentation is very slow and pedogenesis is concurrent (i.e., sedimentation and soil formation keep pace during a period of quasi stability). This commonly occurs on a floodplain where slow, incremental deposition alternates with periods of pedogenesis; a few centimeters of sediment are deposited during a flood, followed by pedogenic alteration of the sediment, followed by another increment of deposition a few years later, which in turn is pedogenically altered, and so on. When occupation occurs in this type of setting, artifacts become vertically superposed within a thick A horizon.

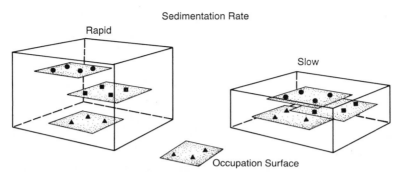

FIGURE 2.35. The spatial separation between three hypothetical occupation surfaces over the same interval of time in a setting with rapid and slow sedimentation
rates. Note the better spatial separation of the archaeological occupations in the setting characterized by rapid sedimentation. (Modified from Ferring 1986a)

graphic units (Fig. 2.34a). In this situation, occupation takes place on the
surface of the paleosol (pedostratigraphic unit). Archaeological debris will
accumulate on the surface until deposition resumes and covers it. Consequently, artifacts recovered from the surface of a paleosol could have been
left behind during any or all parts of the interval of stability. Thus, if discrete
multiple occupations occur at a site while the landscape is stable, the result
is a mixture of temporally discrete artifact assemblages and datable material
on the surface of the paleosol. Obviously, the longer a surface is exposed
prior to burial, the greater is the potential for mixed artifact assemblages to
be created. At the Lubbock Lake site, middle Archaic, late Archaic, and
ceramic period people camped on the surface of the Lubbock Lake soil from
4500 to 1000 B.P. Consequently, artifacts and datable organics spanning the
entire 3500-year interval of stability are compressed and mixed on the surface of the Lubbock Lake soil (Fig. 2.29; Holliday 1990).

Because cultural sequences and stratigraphic sequences are unrelated
phenomena that change independently through time, there is no consistent
relationship between archaeological cultures and stratigraphic units. Depending on the geomorphic conditions characterizing the landscape through
time and the duration of archaeological cultures and phases, remains of a
single phase or culture may occur (1) in a single lithostratigraphic unit, (2) in
more than one lithostratigraphic unit, (3) on the surface of a pedostratigraphic unit, or (4) in some combination of lithostratigraphic and pedostratigraphic units (see Fig. 2.23). Likewise, the remains of different cultures
and phases may occur in the same stratigraphic unit.

The nature and completeness of the buried archaeological record parallels the nature and completeness of the late Quaternary stratigraphic sequence. Recall that the structure of the stratigraphic sequence is determined by the number, magnitude, duration, areal extent, and timing of periods of deposition, erosion, and stability. These factors control how many sedimentary units, paleosols, and erosional surfaces are present, their spatial distribution and sequence, and the amount of time they represent. These same factors are important in the creation of the archaeological record because deposition, erosion, and stability work in concert to preserve, arrange, and fragment the evidence of human activity on the landscape (Fig. 2.31). Therefore, how well the preserved sites of a region approximate the original universe of archaeological sites that once existed must be evaluated before meaningful archaeological interpretations can be made (Butzer 1982; Schiffer 1987; Thompson and Bettis 1982).

The proportion of time represented by periods of sediment deposition versus periods of stability influences the archaeological record. The more periods of stability and the longer their duration, the greater the probability that assemblages of discrete occupations will become compressed and mixed on a common surface before burial. However, the greater the number and duration of depositional episodes, the greater the likelihood that assemblages of discrete occupations will become buried in sediments as spatially separated occupation surfaces (Ferring 1986a).

Even if sites are initially preserved, later degradation of the landscape affects their chance of surviving into the present. If the landscape enters a degradational mode, previously preserved sites may be destroyed. For example, if a river downcuts into its floodplain and widens its channel, previously preserved sites in the zone of entrenchment will be eroded (Fig. 2.31). Each subsequent degradational event diminishes the completeness of those portions of the geological and archaeological record that have survived into the present. The greater the number and duration of erosional events, the greater the destruction. For example, the Santa Cruz River has entrenched its floodplain five times since 5500 B.P. (Fig. 2.32; Haynes and Huckell 1986; Waters 1988a, 1988b, 1988c). Each time the river downcut into its floodplain and widened its channel, it eroded and reworked alluvial sediments and their archaeological contents. This repeated channel entrenchment fragmented the record of older alluvial sediments and archaeological sites. In general, the fewer the episodes of erosion and the shorter their duration, the more complete the stratigraphic sequence of material units and the contained archaeological record.

No single stratigraphic exposure in the field, however, has a complete record of late Pleistocene and Holocene sediments, let alone a representative sample of the archaeological record. Different portions of the geological and archaeological record are contained in a number of discrete stratigraphic sections over a region (Fig. 2.31). Compiling the isolated stratigraphic sequences permits us to construct a composite stratigraphic record of physical material units and archaeological sites. Recall that along Whitewater Draw, a 25 km arroyo in southeastern Arizona, no single exposure had a complete sequence of stratigraphic units spanning the last 15,000 years (Waters 1986b). It proved possible to construct a composite stratigraphic record, however, by correlating individual exposures that preserved different segments of the late Quaternary geological record. Archaeological remains of different age were preserved unevenly in these sections. When they were combined, a composite archaeological record emerged that documented the long continuum of Archaic occupation along Whitewater Draw (Figs. 2.25 and 2.32).

In some cases, regional erosional events completely remove older sediments and soils that may contain archaeological remains (Fig. 2.31; Brookes et al. 1982; Thompson and Bettis 1982; Turnbaugh 1978). In these cases, no deposits or soils of a certain time interval are present anywhere in a given region, which creates a break in the stratigraphic record and correspondingly in the archaeological record. This is well illustrated by the regional stratigraphic sequence of the Santa Cruz River near Tucson, Arizona, where sediments older than 5500 B.P. were eroded when the channel of the river downcut into its floodplain, widened, and scoured the valley. Deposition resumed after 5500 B.P. This erosional event was responsible for the destruction of most alluvial and soil units older than 5500 B.P., together with their potentially associated sites (Fig. 2.32; Haynes and Huckell 1986; Waters 1988a, 1988b, 1988c). As a result, there are no Paleoindian or early Archaic sites in the alluvial stratigraphic sequence of the Santa Cruz River. Clearly, gaps in occupation at a specific locality or in a region may just as likely be the result of erosion as they are of intentional abandonment.

The number, magnitude, duration, areal extent, and timing of erosional, depositional, and stable intervals may be either the same or different in adjacent regions. For example, spatially separated river valleys can have synchronous or nonsynchronous landscape histories. If the geomorphic variables of adjacent valleys are similar and if external changes in climate trigger similar responses in each valley, intervalley stratigraphic sequences will be similar (Haynes 1968; Knox 1983). In this case, similar temporal archaeological samples will be preserved in the two valleys.

However, if two valleys have different and nonsynchronous landscape histories—because climatic conditions varied from one valley to the next or because the geomorphic conditions of the two areas were different—the stratigraphic sequences of the two valleys will be different (Butzer 1980b; Patton and Schumm 1981; Waters 1985). In this case, different temporal archaeological samples are preserved in adjacent valleys. For example, the late Quaternary stratigraphic sequences preserved in four adjacent river valleys in southern Arizona (those of the Santa Cruz River, Cienega Creek, the San Pedro River, and Whitewater Draw) show only minimal similarity (Figs. 2.32 and 2.33). Correspondingly, the archaeological sample preserved in the alluvial sequence of each valley is unique (Waters 1991). Because of the middle Holocene period of erosion in the Santa Cruz Valley, only archaeological remains dating from 5500 B.P. to historic times are present (Waters 1988a). A similar period of erosion affected the archaeological sample along Cienega Creek (Eddy and Cooley 1983). In the San Pedro drainage, the alluvial sequence is well preserved, and as a result a nearly complete record of human occupation from 11,500 B.P. to historic times is preserved in the sediments (Haynes 1981, 1982a). The alluvial sediments in Whitewater Draw are likewise well preserved and contain an archaeological record dating from 10,000 B.P. through the historic period (Waters 1986b).

The differential structure of the archaeological record within and between regions has important implications for archaeological interpretation. Archaeologists must consider whether the observed patterns of occupation within and between areas accurately reflects the distribution of human activity or the biases of geological preservation. For example, consider the Paleoindian record of southern Arizona (Fig. 2.32). In the San Pedro Valley a large number of Clovis culture sites are preserved because of the favorable geological conditions that existed there during the late Pleistocene (Haynes 1981, 1982a). First, Clovis sites were buried soon after abandonment beneath an organic-rich clay, the black mat, which was deposited in a low-energy cienega environment. Second, subsequent Holocene erosion did not remove the Clovis-age surface. On the other hand, no Clovis sites have been found in Whitewater Draw even though sediments of this age are exposed in the arroyo (units Da and Db). This is due largely to the fact that even though units Da and Db are time transgressive, ranging in age from 15,000 to 8000 B.P., most of these sediments date between 10,000 and 8000 B.P., and only a few of the sand and gravel deposits are older than 10,000 B.P. What is more, if Clovis remains were found in units Da and Db, they would lie in secondary contexts because these sands and gravels were deposited in a high-energy braided-stream environment, which is not conducive to the preservation of systemic contexts. In the alluvial valleys of both the Santa Cruz River and Cienega Creek, erosional episodes have removed any Clovis sites that may once have existed. Therefore the intensity of Clovis use of the Santa Cruz, Whitewater Draw, and Cienega Creek floodplains cannot be gauged.

As a result, it cannot be determined whether the Clovis record of the San Pedro Valley represents a unique, intensive occupation of this valley alone during the late Pleistocene or whether the record instead reflects the biases imposed by different intervalley geological processes. If the latter is true, perhaps a similar level of Clovis activity occurred in the other valleys of southern Arizona. This, however, we shall never know.

Changes in the landscape also impose limitations on the later discovery of preserved archaeological sites (Bettis and Benn 1984; Gladfelter 1985; Thompson and Bettis 1982). Many preserved sites are not visible or detectable at the surface because of deep burial, subsidence, or submergence. Along the San Xavier reach of the Santa Cruz River, late Archaic remains occur at a depth of 7 m, Hohokam remains occur at depths of 1.25 to 5.5 m, and protohistoric remains occur at a depth of 0.5 m below the surface (Fig. 2.23; Waters 1987a, 1988a, 1988b). In addition, a half-meter-thick layer of historic alluvium overlies the floodplain. As a result, prehistoric sites are not visible on the surface of the floodplain; archaeological sites are only observable in the channel bank exposures. However, even though sites are visible in the late Quaternary sediments exposed along the banks of the entrenched floodplain of the Santa Cruz River, this alluvium is only a small portion of the total volume of late Quaternary sediments stored in the floodplain. There are certainly many more archaeological sites in the large tracts of undissected late Quaternary alluvium. The Aubrey site near Denton, Texas, provides another good example of the problem of site visibility. Here, Ferring (1989, 1990b) discovered a Clovis campsite overlain by 8 m of Trinity River alluvium. This site had not been detected during previous surface survey and was only found because a spillway constructed downstream from the Ray Roberts Reservoir cut a deep exposure into the floodplain. Undoubtedly, other Clovis sites still lay deeply buried in the alluvium of the Trinity River but are beyond our range of visibility.

To deal with the problems of differential site preservation, visibility, and detection, researchers must modify traditional archaeological survey techniques to include geomorphic site prediction modeling and testing (Artz 1985; Bettis and Benn 1984; Gardner and Donahue 1985; Thompson and Bettis 1982). Because the late Quaternary stratigraphic framework dictates the spatial and temporal structuring of the archaeological record, it provides the framework needed to determine which parts of the archaeological continuum are absent, which have potentially been preserved, and how fragmentary are the preserved portions of the record. By mapping the spatial distribution of the stratigraphic units and associated landforms of known age, a model can be established to predict the most probable locations of potential surface and buried cultural resources. This stratigraphic framework can be

FIGURE 2.36. The black mat (Clanton clay, the dark layer situated above the hammer) at the Murray Springs Clovis site in Arizona. The black mat is a marker horizon that buries Clovis-age paleosurfaces in the San Pedro Valley.

used to distinguish sediments that are too old to contain archaeological remains from those sediments dating to the time of human habitation of North America. Furthermore, attention can be focused on low-energy depositional settings, where sites would most likely be preserved, and away from high-energy depositional settings, where artifacts would occur only in secondary contexts. Geoarchaeological modeling maximizes valuable field time by allowing archaeologists to prospect for archaeological sites most effectively, thus optimizing site recording during an archaeological survey. This methodology helps researchers to obtain a representative sample of buried sites.

Modeling can also delineate strata, surfaces, and paleosols likely to contain sites of a particular age. For example, Haynes (1981, 1982a) used his knowledge of the alluvial history and deposits of the San Pedro Valley in Arizona to locate Clovis culture sites. He identified a distinctive thin organic deposit that was easily recognized and traced around the San Pedro Valley. He designated this deposit the Clanton clay or black mat (Fig. 2.36). The black mat was deposited in a cienega (marshland) environment between

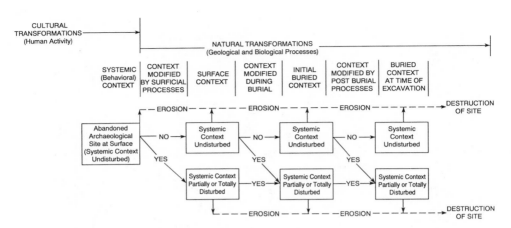

FIGURE 2.37. A model of the creation and physical modification of an archaeological site context by natural transformational processes.

10,800 and 9700 B.P., and it directly covers a Clovis age paleosurface. Haynes found the Murray Springs Clovis site by tracing this marker horizon north from the Lehner Clovis site, which is also buried under the black mat.

Geoarchaeological modeling can also be used to locate specific sites. Haynes (1989) used geoarchaeological methods to locate the ravine and identify the specific stratigraphic layer that probably contains the missing remains and artifacts of the 28 men of Company E of the Seventh Cavalry that were killed at the battle of the Little Big Horn in Montana on June 25, 1876. Geoarchaeological techniques were likewise used to locate the *Bertrand,* a steamboat buried under the alluvial floodplain of the Missouri River 40 km north of Omaha, Nebraska (Petsche 1974), and a Union gunboat, the USS *Eastport,* in the alluvium of the Red River floodplain in Louisiana (Albertson and Birchett 1990).

To summarize, the archaeological record does not accurately reflect the complete pattern of human sites that once existed in a given region through time but instead reflects the biases of geological preservation. Geomorphic processes associated with changing landscapes can significantly affect the temporal and spatial archaeological sample. Consequently, not all occupations that occurred in a given region over time are initially preserved. From the beginning, geomorphic processes operate on a site after its abandonment and determine whether it is initially preserved or destroyed. Subsequently, erosion may remove all or part of the evidence of preserved occupations at any time by completely removing the older sediments and soils that contain them. Further, the configuration of the modern landscape, whether dissected or undissected, reveals only a portion of this preserved record. Depth of burial, subsidence, submergence, and other factors obscure our knowledge of the archaeological record and limit our access to the exposed portions of it. In short, the completeness and nature of the stratigraphic record are critical limiting factors in the precision of archaeological interpretations because reconstructions of prehistoric human behavior and culture history can be no more complete than the stratigraphic sequence that contains the evidence. The degree to which geological processes have affected the archaeological sample varies from region to region and must be evaluated on a case-by-case basis. Meaningful interpretations of prehistory depend on our recognizing and understanding the limitations that geological processes have imposed on the archaeological record. Recognizing these factors in the formation of the archaeological record helps develop effective site survey and testing programs that utilize geoarchaeological studies to predict probable site locations.

The Context of Preserved Sites

So far we have considered whether sites as entities are preserved or destroyed, but we should also recognize that the systemic context of preserved archaeological sites—the three-dimensional spatial arrangement of artifacts, features, and ecofacts that reflect human behavior—is likewise unequally preserved in the stratigraphic record. This only increases the already fragmentary nature of the archaeological record due to geomorphic processes and further limits our interpretations of prehistory and human behavior.

The systemic context of an archaeological site is intact for a brief instant after site abandonment. Almost immediately, surficial geomorphic and biological processes begin to distort the original spatial relationships among the archaeological residues that reflect human behavior (Fig. 2.37; see also Butzer 1982; Gifford 1978; Kirkby and Kirkby 1976; Nash and Petraglia 1987; Schiffer 1987; Villa 1982). This spatial reorganization may be partial or complete, depending on (1) the length of exposure of the archaeological remains at the surface prior to burial, (2) the type and intensity of geomorphic and biological processes affecting the site surface, and (3) the processes responsible for the burial of the site.

Prior to burial, surficial geomorphic processes such as water sheeting over the ground (Isaac 1967; Petraglia and Nash 1987; Schick 1987), snowmelt (Savelle 1984, 1987), gravity processes (Rick 1976), freezing and thawing of the ground (Bowers et al. 1983), wind blowing over a surface (Lancaster 1986; Wandsnider 1984, 1987, 1988) and other factors can displace artifacts and destroy spatial patterns. In some cases, natural processes have restructured the archaeological debris into artificial patterns and features that are difficult to distinguish from those produced by human activity (Butzer 1982). These surficial processes of disturbance are fully discussed in the next four chapters.

Animals and plants may also alter the position of archaeological remains on a surface (Nash and Petraglia 1984). Humans and other animals may unintentionally kick artifacts as they wander over a site. Trampling may also damage artifacts and displace them into the substrate (Gifford-Gonzales et al. 1985; Villa and Countin 1983). Plants disperse archaeological debris when they fall over or when their branches sweep the surface as the wind blows.

Not only will the geomorphic and biological processes operating on the surface reorient artifacts and destroy associations prior to burial, but during exposure some artifact classes (especially those made of organic materials) will begin to break down as they weather. Weathering is usually a rapid process that leads to the differential destruction of organic materials.

The site will remain at the surface unless it is destroyed by erosion or covered by sediment. If burial occurs, the spatial associations between archaeological debris may also become altered or selectively eroded, depending on the geomorphic processes responsible for burial (Fig. 2.37; see also Butzer 1982; Schiffer 1987; Villa 1982). If the site is situated in a high-energy environment, such as on a sandbar in a river channel, chances are that the next high flow that inundates the bar will move the artifacts into a secondary context, thus destroying the original systemic context. However, if a site is situated away from the channel on the floodplain of the same river, the systemic context may be preserved with minimal alteration as floodwaters submerge and cover the site with sediment. These points are further discussed in the next five chapters.

Once buried, postdepositional physiogenic, biogenic, and chemical agents of modification begin to alter the archaeological debris and the spatial relationships between the remains. This results in the degradation of certain artifact classes and the total or partial mixing of debris within or between site layers (Fig. 2.37; see also Butzer 1982; Schiffer 1987; Wood and Johnson 1978). Biological processes of disturbance, often referred to as bioturbation, consist of (1) floralturbation, the disturbance of sediments and site context by plant growth; and (2) faunalturbation, the disturbance of sediments and site context by burrowing organisms. Physical processes capable of displacing archaeological debris include (1) cryoturbation, the freezing and thawing of the ground; (2) argilliturbation, the expansion and contraction of clays; and (3) crystalturbation, the precipitation and expansion of salt crystals. Soil forming processes also weather and displace material in the surficial parts of sediments affected by pedogenesis, and geochemical conditions can change at an archaeological site and affect the archaeological debris. Pedogenesis and geochemical processes can lead to the cementation of the site matrix, the deposition of secondary carbonate layers, the destruction of organic remains, and other changes in the chemical composition of the sediments and soils. In summary, the nature and intensity of biological, geological, pedological, and chemical processes operating after site burial determine the severity of the postburial alteration and modification of the systemic context.

Together, the preburial condition of the site, the length of time between abandonment and burial, the geomorphic process and energy level associated with burial, and postburial processes determine the extent of disturbance to the systemic context of a site. The degree of preservation of the systemic context ranges over a continuum from undisturbed (primary context) to completely disturbed (secondary context). Any given site can exhibit one level of preservation over its entire areal extent, or parts of the site may be differentially disturbed. If multiple occupations are present on a site, the systemic context of the various occupations may not be equally preserved as the debris of each occupation follows its own unique path to preservation or destruction.

Clearly, a number of natural transformational processes can alter the behavioral signature of the archaeological record before, during, and after burial. As stated by Butzer (1982), the proper interpretation of the archaeological context requires us to determine whether preburial, burial, and postburial processes have disturbed the context of a site. If they have, the types of processes and the extent to which the site has been altered must be identified. It cannot be assumed that because a site is buried it has not suffered some degree of disturbance. Regardless of how precise the recovery methods may be, the accuracy and precision of archaeological interpretations are always dependent on the degree of degradation of the archaeological record.

The Lubbock Lake Site: Interpreting Sediments, Soils, and Stratigraphy

The Lubbock Lake archaeological site is located in the Southern High Plains in Yellowhouse Draw, a dry valley in the city of Lubbock, Texas. The stratigraphic and archaeological sequence at the site fills an entrenched channel meander of Yellowhouse Draw. In the late Pleistocene, a channel 4.5 m deep was cut into the Pliocene Blanco Formation. During the next 12,000 years, clastic, chemical, and carbonaceous sediments filled the channel (Fig. 2.38). These sediments were deposited in different depositional environments (lakes, ponds, marshes, eolian settings, and a meandering stream) that occupied the channel bottom and its margin. Deposition was not continuous in

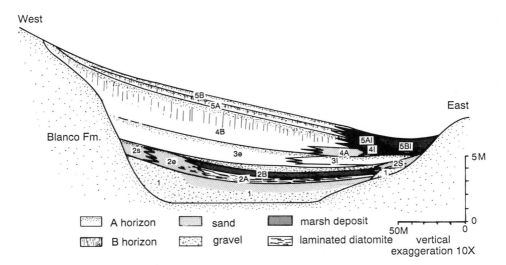

FIGURE 2.38. A generalized geologic cross section of the late Quaternary stratigraphic relationships at the Lubbock Lake site in Texas. (Modified from Holliday 1985a)

these environments; it was interrupted by five episodes of landscape stability, during which soils formed, and one period of minor erosion. Consequently, the stratigraphic sequence at the Lubbock Lake site reveals a complex late Quaternary history of deposition, degradation, and landscape stability. Humans repeatedly occupied this evolving landscape, and remains of their occupation have been incorporated into the sediments or buried on stable surfaces. The following discussion of the site illustrates how sediments, soils, and stratigraphy are created and later interpreted at an archaeological site.

The geology and archaeology of the Lubbock Lake site have been extensively studied (see Black 1974; Haas et al. 1986; Holliday 1985a, 1985b, 1985c, 1985d, 1986, 1989a, 1990; Holliday and Allen 1987; Holliday et al. 1983, 1985; C. Johnson 1974; E. Johnson 1987; E. Johnson and Holliday 1980, 1981, 1985, 1986, 1989; Stafford 1981). The following discussion of the late Quaternary sequence and archaeological record of the site is based on the most recent investigations by Holliday.

Holliday categorizes the sediments at the Lubbock Lake site into five major lithostratigraphic units, designated strata 1 through 5, from oldest to youngest. These lithostratigraphic units are separated into two facies: (1) clay, silt, diatomite, and sapropel deposited in the wetland environment along the channel axis; and (2) sand and silt deposited in the eolian and slopewash environments along the channel margin (Figs. 2.38 and 2.39). In some cases, the five major lithostratigraphic units are further subdivided. Five interbedded paleosols (pedostratigraphic units) occur in the stratigraphic sequence, and each is assigned an informal name (Figs. 2.29, 2.39, and 2.40). Chronostratigraphically, the sediments and soils date to the late Quaternary. Those dating before 10,000 B.P. belong to the Pleistocene epoch, while those postdating 10,000 B.P. belong to the Holocene epoch. Over 100 radiocarbon ages determine the timing and absolute duration of individual episodes of deposition, landscape stability, and erosion (Holliday et al. 1983, 1985).

The oldest late Quaternary sediments at the site, stratum 1, unconformably overlie the Blanco Formation. Stratum 1 is divided into three subunits: a basal gravel (substratum 1A) overlain by sand (substratum 1B) that fines upward into a clay (substratum 1C). These sediments were deposited in the stream that once flowed down the entrenched channel of Yellowhouse Draw. The beginning of stratum 1 deposition is unknown, but sediment accumulation ceased around 11,000 B.P.

A possible Clovis culture butchering and bone processing station, dated to approximately 11,100 B.P., was buried in stratum 1 sediments. Johnson and Holliday (1985) concluded that the bones of mammoth, camel, horse, bison, and other animals, were broken and scattered by humans on the surface of a gravelly point bar next to an active stream. However, taphonomic studies of the pattern of the megafaunal remains from stratum 1 by Kreutzer (1988) suggest that the bone distribution may instead be the result of natural stream flooding rather than human butchering. Shortly after creation of the bone bed, the point bar surface was covered with sand and clay during overbank flooding.

Stratum 1 is overlain by stratum 2, which is divided into four subunits that show complex facies relationships (Figs. 2.38 and 2.39). Substratum 2A, located along the axis of Yellowhouse Draw, is primarily composed of diatomite with interbedded lenses of sapropelic silt and clay. These sediments indicate an alternation between lacustrine and marsh environments. Radiocarbon ages from this unit show that deposition occurred between 11,000 and 10,000 B.P. Unit 2A is conformably overlain by unit 2B, a homogeneous sapropelic silt and clay that slowly accumulated between 10,000 and 8500 B.P. in a marsh environment. Along the margin of the valley, sandy slopewash (unit 2s) and eolian (unit 2e) sediments accumulated adjacent to the aggrading pond and marsh environments represented by units 2A and 2B. Where the valley margin (slopewash and eolian) and valley axis (lacustrine and marsh) deposits come into contact with one another, they interfinger. This facies relationship illustrates the contemporaneity of sediment accumu-

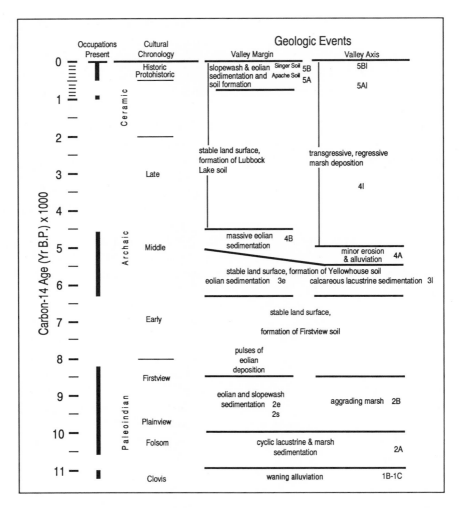

FIGURE 2.39. The geological and cultural history of the Lubbock Lake site. Note the different geologic histories of the valley margin and valley axis. The column labeled "Occupations Present" refers to the archaeological remains that were found at the site. (Modified from Holliday 1985a)

Pedostratigraphic   Lithostratigraphic
Units   Units

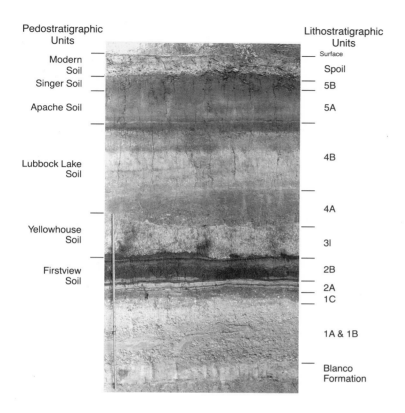

FIGURE 2.40. The major lithostratigraphic and pedostratigraphic units at the Lubbock Lake site. (Photograph by Thomas W. Stafford, Jr., courtesy of the Museum of Texas Tech University)

lation along the valley margin and wetland channel environments, and documents the relative position of each as the wetland and marginal environments expanded and contracted through time.

Stratum 2 contains an abundant Paleoindian record. Several Folsom culture bison kill and butchering locations, dating between 10,800 and 10,200 B.P., were excavated from the interbedded deposits of unit 2A. Plainview points and artifacts were associated with two small bison kill and butchering locations. One was buried in the base of substratum 2B just above the contact with unit 2A, while the other was buried in the slopewash sediments of unit 2s. Radiocarbon ages place these sites between 10,200 and 10,000 B.P. Firstview and other late Paleoindian period bison kill and butchering loci, dated between 10,000 and 8500 B.P., are buried in the upper parts of substrata 2B and 2s.

The positions of the Paleoindian loci in stratum 2 indicate that prehistoric hunting and butchering took place either along the floor of Yellowhouse Draw when it was occupied by a marsh with small isolated pools of water, or near the shore of a larger body of standing water. These loci of human activity were preserved because they occurred in a low-energy, aggradational environment and because they were buried by sediments soon after abandonment.

The deposition of unit 2 was followed by a period of landscape stability from 8500 to 6300 B.P., when the Firstview soil formed (Figs. 2.29, 2.38, 2.39, and 2.40). During the 2200 years of landscape stability, soil forming processes altered the upper portion of substrata 2B and 2e into a weak soil profile. Thin wedges of sand locally interfinger with the Firstview soil along the margin of Yellowhouse Draw. The sand was deposited episodically from 8500 to 6300 B.P. This relationship indicates that the valley margin alternated between long intervals of soil formation and short periods of sand deposition from 8500 to 6300 B.P., while the channel axis was stable during the same period.

No evidence of transitional or early Archaic period occupation has been found at the Lubbock Lake site (Fig. 2.39). Archaeological remains of this age should correspond to the geological period of landscape stability and Firstview soil formation. Consequently, transitional and early Archaic period artifacts could potentially be found only on the surface of the Firstview soil buried by overlying sediments, or buried in the 2e eolian sediments that were deposited periodically along the margin of the draw during the time of soil formation.

Following the period of landscape stability and the formation of the Firstview soil, stratum 3 was deposited. Stratum 3 is divided into two facies, subunits 3l and 3e (Figs. 2.29, 2.38, and 2.39). Substratum 3l is composed of fine-grained calcareous sediments that accumulated in a small pond or marsh along the axis of the valley, and substratum 3e is made up of clastic eolian sediments accumulated along the margin of the valley. Substrata 3e and 3l accumulated concurrently and interfinger where they come into contact with one another. Deposition of both substrata began around 6300 B.P., but the cessation date of deposition is unknown because radiocarbon samples were not found in the upper portion of these units. After deposition ceased, the landscape along both the axis and the margin of the valley again became stabilized, allowing pedogenic processes to alter the upper parts of both substrata 3e and 3l into a soil profile. This soil was named the Yellowhouse soil. The beginning of landscape stability and soil formation is not known. However, soil formation ceased along the channel axis around 5500

B.P. and on the channel margins by 5000 B.P., when deposition resumed in these areas. Thus the upper surface of the Yellowhouse soil is time transgressive across the valley. Considered together, the deposition of unit 3 and the formation of the Yellowhouse soil occurred between 6300 and 5500 B.P. along the valley axis and until 5000 B.P. along the valley margin, where the Yellowhouse soil was buried 500 years later. The deposition of unit 3 and the formation of the Yellowhouse soil is coincident with the end of the early Archaic and beginning of the middle Archaic cultural periods (Fig. 2.39). Sites of this age are primarily buried in substratum 3e, but a few bison kill and butchering loci were excavated from subunit 3l. Middle Archaic remains also occur scattered on the surface of the Yellowhouse soil.

A brief period of erosion occurred along the channel axis after the deposition of stratum 3 and the formation of the Yellowhouse soil. Following this, stratum 4, which is divided into a number of facies, was deposited. Substratum 4A, composed of sandy sediments interbedded with clayey deposits, unconformably overlies stratum 3 along the axis of the channel. This unit was deposited in a low-energy intermittent-stream environment between 5500 and 5000 B.P. Substratum 4B, made up of fine-grained clastic sediments, was deposited along the margin of the channel by eolian processes between 5500 and 4500 B.P. Substratum 4l is an organic-rich clay that interfingers with both substrata 4A and 4B. This unit was deposited in a marsh that existed along the axis of the channel from 5500 to 800 B.P.

Deposition along the valley margin ceased and the eolian deposits became stabilized around 4500 B.P. During the next 3500 to 4500 years, pedogenic processes altered the upper portion of the eolian sediments (unit 4B) into a strongly developed soil profile known as the Lubbock Lake soil (Figs. 2.29, 2.38, 2.39, and 2.40). Part of the Lubbock Lake soil became buried by renewed eolian deposition around 800 B.P., and soil formation ceased. However, near the margin of the valley, the Lubbock Lake soil was never buried, and soil formation continues today. Stability of the valley margin eolian sediments (substratum 4B) and formation of the Lubbock Lake soil occurred contemporaneously with the marsh deposition represented by unit 4l. Where the valley margin surface of stability came into contact with the marsh along the valley axis, organic-rich A horizons of the Lubbock Lake soil interfinger with the unit 4l marsh sediments. This complex facies relationship illustrates that portions of the landscape were stabilized and undergoing soil formation while other areas were more active loci of deposition. Furthermore, the penetration of individual fingers of marsh sediments into the Lubbock Lake soil represents repeated expansion and contraction of the marsh over the stable portion of the landscape from 4500 to 800 B.P.

The deposition of unit 4 and the formation of the Lubbock Lake soil correspond to the middle Archaic, late Archaic, and ceramic culture periods (Fig. 2.39). No loci of human activity are found in unit 4l, and only middle Archaic remains corresponding to the period of deposition are found buried in the eolian deposits of unit 4B. The late Archaic and early ceramic period record is compressed onto the surface of the Lubbock Lake soil rather than being found in discrete deposits. Temporally separate occupations may be spatially separated on this surface or mixed at a single locus. Consequently, nondiagnostic artifacts may be mixed and indistinguishable.

After 800 B.P. the Lubbock Lake site was characterized by episodic slopewash and eolian deposition along the margin of the channel and contemporaneous lacustrine deposition along its axis. Eolian deposition was interrupted by two periods of stability and soil formation. Along the margin of the valley, slopewash and eolian processes led to the accumulation of sand (unit 5A) from 800 to 600 B.P. This was followed by a brief interval of landscape stability from 600 to 450 B.P. during which pedogenic processes altered unit 5A into the Apache soil. Renewed eolian and slopewash deposition occurred along the margin of the valley from 450 to 100 B.P. and created unit 5B. Stability and soil formation followed over the next century to create the Singer soil. During this same 800-year interval, organic-rich clays (units 5Al and 5Bl) accumulated continuously in a marsh along the axis of the valley. These valley axis sediments are interbedded with the valley margin sediments and soils.

Late ceramic, protohistoric, and historic period campsites and hunting loci occur primarily in the valley margin facies (units 5A and 5B) and on the surface of the Apache and Singer soils (Figs. 2.29 and 2.39). However, some kill and butchering loci were identified in the marsh facies (units 5Al and 5Bl).

Holliday's interpretation of the sediments and soils, and their spatial and temporal relationships, permitted him to reconstruct the dynamic landscape context of human activity at the Lubbock Lake site. Reconstructions show that the prehistoric physical environment and topography at the site did not remain stable through time, but instead changed over time and that the prehistoric landscape did not resemble the modern landscape.

The archaeological record of the Lubbock Lake site was shaped by the changes in the landscape. The stratigraphic sequence reveals that the site area was dominated by deposition and stability, with only one minor episode of erosion. Consequently, because there was no major erosion at the site, the record of human occupation has the potential of being complete. However, the duration and timing of the episodes of landscape stability and deposition determine how this archaeological record is structured (Fig. 2.41).

Along the margin of the valley, where most human activity would have occurred, the total duration of depositional intervals accounts for only about

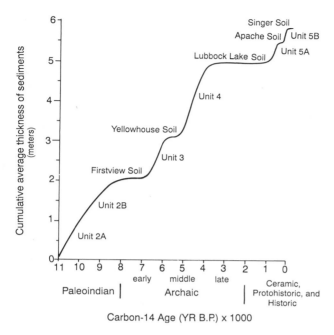

FIGURE 2.41. Sedimentation rates at the Lubbock Lake site over the last 11,000 years. Sloping segments of the curve indicate periods of deposition (the steeper the slope, the more rapid the sedimentation). Flat segments of the curve indicate landscape stability and episodes of soil formation. Note that depositional episodes are of shorter duration than the relatively long intervals of landscape stability and soil formation. Stratigraphic units and paleosols are noted. Archaeological periods are indicated along the horizontal axis of the graph. (Modified from Holliday 1985a)

40% of the last 11,500 years, while the time represented by the five intervals of soil formation when the landscape was stable accounts for almost 60% of the elapsed time. The longest periods of stability occurred from 8500 to 6300 B.P., during the creation of the Firstview soil, and from 4500 to 1000 B.P., spanning the formation of the Lubbock Lake soil. Consequently, late Paleoindian and early Archaic remains are encountered on the surface of the Firstview soil, while the middle Archaic, late Archaic, and much of the ceramic period records are mixed on the surface of the Lubbock Lake soil. Most of the Paleoindian and only a portion of the middle Archaic occupation of the site occurred when deposition prevailed. These remains are preserved as discrete loci buried in sediments of strata 1 through 5. Along the axis of the channel, where aggradation was more continuous during the last 11,500 years, deposition occurred for 75% of the time, soil formation occurred for 23%, and erosion for 2%. Here, more of the last 11,500 years is recorded by physical material units, and many activity loci are buried. Consequently, because deposition was occurring along the channel axis while stability and eolian deposition occurred on the channel margin, contemporaneous activity areas can be present in different stratigraphic positions. At the Lubbock Lake site, campsites are preserved on stable soil surfaces or in eolian sediments along the margin of the channel, and contemporaneous hunting and butchering localities are buried in the channel bottom sediments. Clearly, the timing of deposition and stability structured the archaeological record at the Lubbock Lake site.

Conclusion

Sediments and soils, and the contacts separating them, contain the information needed to reconstruct the landscape—the environments that were present at any given time and the changes that occurred to them through time. Geoarchaeological investigations provide not only detailed descriptions of sediments and soils and their stratigraphic relationships (which are important to fully documenting a site), but more important provide interpretations of these geological data that describe the dynamic relationship between the landscape and human behavior, and between landscape processes and the archaeological record.

3

Alluvial Environments

Flowing water is a dynamic geomorphic agent responsible for the erosion, downslope transport, and deposition of sediment. Landscapes dominated by running water are known as alluvial environments. They encompass a wide spectrum of settings, including braided streams, meandering streams, anastomosing streams, arroyos, and alluvial fans. These environments occur in a variety of climatic and geographic settings ranging from arid deserts to subpolar regions. It should be noted that the term *fluvial* is sometimes used as a synonym for *alluvial;* however, *fluvial* is more correctly used to describe only the processes and deposits of riverine environments.

Because alluvial environments have been intensively used through time for hunting, gathering, and in many places farming, archaeological remains are frequently incorporated into alluvial deposits. In this chapter the processes, landforms, and deposits of each major alluvial environment are reviewed. The geological references used to construct this summary include Blatt et al. 1972, Boggs 1987, Brakenridge 1988, Bull 1972, Butzer 1976, Cant 1982, Chorley et al. 1985, Collinson 1986a, Cooke and Reeves 1976, Cooke and Warren 1973, R. A. Davis 1983, Friedman and Sanders 1978, Galloway and Hobday 1983, Graf 1988, Knighton 1984, Leeder 1982, Leopold et al. 1964, Morisawa 1985, Nilson 1982, Reineck and Singh 1980, Richards 1982, Ritter 1986, Ruhe 1975, Rust 1978, Rust and Koster 1984, Schumm 1977, Smith 1983, and Walker and Cant 1984. General geoarchaeological discussions of alluvial environments include Butzer 1971, 1982; Cornwall 1958; Evans 1978; Gladfelter 1985; Hassan 1985b; and Pyddoke 1961. Following each geological review is a discussion of natural site-formation processes in each alluvial setting. The final section of this chapter discusses how alluvial processes shaped the archaeological record and how synchronic and diachronic reconstructions of alluvial environments amplify the interpretation of prehistoric land use.

Streamflow

Geomorphologists use the term *stream* to describe any body of flowing water that is confined in a channel, regardless of its size. Thus the term can delineate a small creek or a large river. In this discussion the terms *stream* and *river* are used interchangeably.

All the water flowing through a stream originates from a drainage basin, or watershed. This is the total catchment area drained by the stream and its tributaries that lie immediately upslope. The drainage basin consists of an integrated system of hillslopes and smaller interconnected channels that collect and funnel water downslope into ever larger channels. Drainage basins are separated from one another by topographic divides or ridges.

Because smaller streams successively drain into larger streams, any stream can be classified according to its relative position or rank in the drainage network. This concept is known as stream ordering (Fig. 3.1). Streams in North America are ranked from first-order to approximately tenth-order, based on the number of tributaries they have. First-order streams are small streams with no tributaries. They are typically found at the headwaters of drainage basins, which collect water running off slopes after rainfall. Second-order streams are formed by the joining of two first-order streams, and so on. Thus the drainage basin is made up of many low-order streams that funnel water into the single highest-order stream at the basin outlet.

Stream order strongly correlates with the size and regional significance of a stream. In general, as the stream order increases, the area drained by the stream and its tributaries also increases. For example, a small mountain creek may be a second-order stream, while the Mississippi River is generally considered to be a tenth-order stream.

The size of a stream at any point in the drainage network can also be defined in terms of its discharge. Discharge is the volume of water flowing through the channel in a given period of time, which is usually measured in cubic meters per second (cms) or cubic feet per second (cfs). Discharge varies from less than 1 cms in small creeks to thousands of cms in major rivers.

Stream discharge is maintained and affected by rainfall and snowmelt in the drainage basin. When rain strikes the ground or when snow begins to melt, water first infiltrates the hillslope sediments and soils (Fig. 3.2). Eventually, surficial soils become saturated to the point that water can no longer effectively soak into the ground, and a thin sheet of water begins to flow over the surface; this process is known as overland flow. Water flowing over the ground is quickly concentrated into small first-order channels, which then join together to form second-order tributaries that transport the water

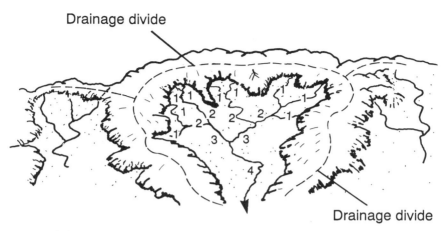

FIGURE 3.1. A typical drainage basin, showing the drainage divide that separates it from other basins. This basin is drained by a fourth-order stream. The numbers indicate stream ordering. (Modified from Marsh 1987)

to the main trunk channel. Surface runoff usually takes place within a few hours after rainfall, and if snow is present in the drainage basin, runoff will be sustained as it melts.

The water that infiltrates into the ground also flows downslope and contributes to stream discharge. Much of the water percolating through the soil finds its way to the groundwater zone. This is the subsurface zone where water fully saturates the voids between soil and sediment particles. The upper boundary of the zone occupied by groundwater is referred to as the water table. The position of the water table is not fixed but moves up and down as water is added to or drained from the saturated zone. Groundwater moves laterally downslope and seeps into streams where the water table and channel intersect. Groundwater continues to drain slowly into a channel as long as the water table intercepts the bed of the stream.

Some subsurface water also flows downhill above the water table in the upper meter or two of the underlying soil by a process known as interflow. Interflow occurs when the water percolating downward encounters a zone of low permeability, which impedes its passage. Then the water backs up into more permeable overlying zones and begins to flow downslope parallel to the barrier. Commonly, this barrier is an argillic or calcic horizon of a soil or an impermeable geologic stratum such as clay, while the more permeable zone through which the water passes could be an overlying A horizon or a layer of sand. Water traveling through the ground in this fashion eventually intersects the channel and gradually seeps into the stream. Typically, it takes several hours for interflow to begin, but once started, it may last for several days after rainfall has ended.

Based on the source and rate at which water is delivered to the stream channel, streamflow is divided into two categories: baseflow and stormflow. Baseflow is that part of the total discharge of the stream that is derived from groundwater seepage into the channel. Groundwater flow is usually very steady over long periods because the supply of groundwater is very large and is released very slowly. Baseflow is important because it can maintain the flow of water in a channel throughout the year, if the water table does not drop below the level of the streambed. Stormflow is the very rapid surface runoff generated by overland flow during or soon after a storm. Stormflow adds to the discharge already created by baseflow, thus resulting in brief above-normal flows and occasional floods. Interflow contributes to both stormflow and baseflow. The relationship between baseflow and stormflow is shown graphically in a hydrograph, which traces changes in stream discharge after a rainstorm (Fig. 3.3).

Discharge in a stream may be year-round or may temporarily cease for short or long periods, depending on the relationship of the channel to

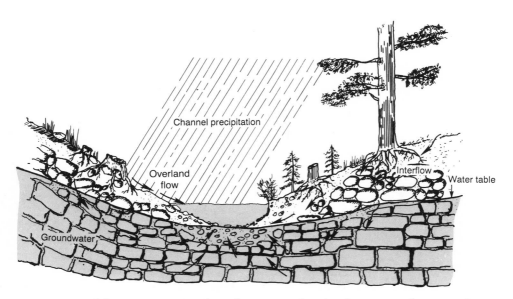

FIGURE 3.2. A cross section through a stream, showing the sources of water to the channel. (Modified from Marsh 1987)

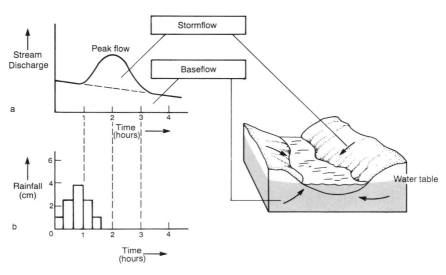

FIGURE 3.3. The relationship between stormflow, baseflow, and stream discharge: (a) a typical hydrograph showing baseflow (sloping solid and dashed line) and stormflow peak (bulge) caused shortly after a rainstorm (b). The hydrograph shows that soon after precipitation ends in the drainage basin, discharge increases, reflecting the rapid input in surface runoff (i.e., stormflow adds a surcharge to the baseflow). If the surcharge of water exceeds channel capacity, overbank flooding occurs. Stream discharge peaks and declines as overland flow diminishes and interflow continues. Eventually, stream discharge returns to baseflow conditions. (Modified from Marsh 1987)

baseflow and baseflow fluctuations. Variations in discharge are used to classify streams as perennial, intermittent, or ephemeral. Perennial streams are those that continually flow from year to year and that are supported by groundwater that ensures continuous baseflow even during periods of little or no precipitation. Discharge in a perennial stream may fluctuate above and below a mean value that reflects changes in baseflow (low discharge during dry periods, when less baseflow occurs because the water table is depressed; high discharge during wet periods, when more baseflow occurs because the water table rises). Perennial streams, maintained by base flow, are also known as effluent streams. Some perennial streams are also classified as exotic or influent streams. These are streams that originate in moist regions but flow across arid regions without drying up, such as the Colorado River of the American Southwest. The channel of an influent stream lies above the water table and receives no baseflow. Instead, water from the river percolates down to the water table beneath the streambed and ultimately recharges the aquifer.

Intermittent streams flow only during the moist season, when the water table rises and comes into contact with the streambed and when interflow is common. Intermittent streams become dry as the water table falls below the bed of the channel during the dry season, thus removing the stream from baseflow.

Ephemeral streams are dry most of the year and flow only after rainfall or snowmelt in the drainage basin. These streams receive their discharge almost exclusively from stormflow.

Sediment Erosion, Transport, and Deposition

When water flows over unconsolidated sediments, particles either remain stationary or begin to move. Entrainment, the initiation of grain movement, occurs only when the combined lift and drag forces produced by the flowing water exceed the gravitational and cohesive forces acting on the grain to keep it stationary. Consequently, water flow velocity and grain size are the primary variables critical for particle entrainment. Other factors, such as the shape and specific gravity of particles, the compaction and cohesiveness of sediments, the viscosity of the water, and flow turbulence, also affect the entrainment velocity of sediment particles.

A graph of water velocity against grain size, known as the Hjulstrom diagram (Fig. 3.4) shows the critical erosional velocity needed to dislodge and move particles of various sizes. This erosional velocity is lowest for sand-size particles, with a diameter of 0.5 mm. Greater velocities are required to move particles of larger or smaller size. Higher flow speeds are required to move particles larger than 0.5 mm because of their weight. High velocities are also needed to uproot clay and silt particles from the substrate because they are very cohesive.

Once particles of any size are set in motion, they will continue to move downstream if the current velocity remains high or even drops below the critical velocity needed to initiate grain movement. However, for a particle to remain in motion, the current-flow velocity must remain above the settling velocity of the grain. The Hjulstrom diagram shows that as particles increase in size, flow velocity must also increase to ensure transport of that sediment. High flow velocities are needed both to erode and to transport sand and gravel. Silt and clay particles are difficult to erode, but once entrained they will continue to be transported at very low velocities. Most streams do not maintain high flow velocities for very long, so most of the sediments transported during normal flow conditions consist of sand and finer particles.

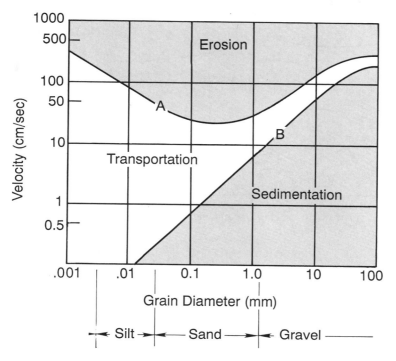

FIGURE 3.4. The Hjulstrom diagram showing the streamflow velocity needed to entrain, transport, and deposit clastic sediments. The upper line (A) is the minimum velocity needed for entrainment. The middle zone shows the velocities at which different-size particles are moved. The lower curve (B) is the velocity below which deposition occurs.

Gravels usually move only during flood episodes, when high flow velocities are maintained.

Once particles are set in motion, they are transported in several different ways, depending on their size and the speed and turbulence of the water (Fig. 3.5). Fine-grained sediments (clay and silt) are transported in suspension. These particles move great distances without coming into contact with the bottom or sides of the channel and are kept from settling by turbulent eddies. Sand-size particles, too heavy for suspended transport, are moved by a process known as saltation, in which sand-size grains bounce or hop along the bed of the channel. The energy needed for a sediment particle to leave the substrate is supplied by hydraulic lift or by already-saltating sand grains striking stationary grains. Saltating grains are confined to the bottom of the

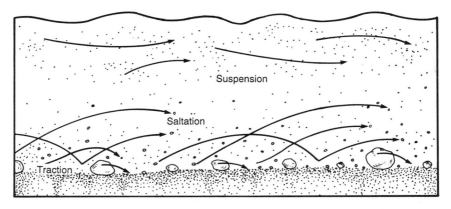

FIGURE 3.5. The transport of clastic sediments downstream within a channel by traction, saltation, and suspension.

stream and generally rise only 30 to 120 cm above the channel bed. The process of saltation is unable to move heavier particles of very coarse sand and gravel, which slide or roll downstream on the bed of the channel by a process known as traction. Together, the coarse clastic sediments transported by saltation and traction make up the total bedload of the stream.

Chemical constituents released during weathering (e.g., salts, ions, and oxides) are transported in solution. The soluble chemical constituents in the water are referred to as the dissolved load of the stream.

Grain movement eventually ceases and deposition occurs when the water velocity is no longer capable of initiating and sustaining particle motion. This occurs when the velocity of the flowing water is reduced below a grain's settling velocity (Fig. 3.4). As velocity decreases, the coarsest particles are deposited first, followed by progressively finer sediments. All stream-deposited sediments are referred to as alluvium.

Alluvium is temporarily or permanently stored in the streambed or along its margins. Sediments in the stream channel and near its banks are commonly stored for short periods before they are moved again. Sediments in areas away from the channel, such as those comprising the floodplain or inactive terraces, are more permanently stored and may remain stable for long periods. However, streams may erode these stored sediments at any time if the stream migrates or downcuts into its floodplain. Much of the sediment that is transported and repeatedly reentrained by rivers eventually finds its way to the terminus of the river, where it is deposited on alluvial fans or deltas.

Alluvial Environments: Rivers, Arroyos, Terraces, and Fans

No single set of properties and attributes can characterize the morphology, deposits, and landforms of all rivers. Differences in processes and floodplain morphology exist among rivers and even along different segments of the same river. However, even with this variability, rivers can be classified into four broad categories—straight, braided, meandering, and anastomosing—on the basis of shared characteristics and processes, especially channel morphology (e.g., number of channels, channel sinuosity, and channel landforms; see Fig. 3.6). These channel configurations reflect adjustments to (1) the amount and size of the sediment load being transported by the river, (2) the volume of, and variations in, discharge, and (3) the slope or gradient of the river. Of the four types, straight rivers are the rarest, while braided, meandering, and anastomosing are the most common. These latter three river types are ideal members of a nearly continuous spectrum of river morphologies. Although a single river may be classified as braided, meandering, or anastomosing, variations in river morphology commonly occur along its length. A single river may grade downslope from a braided pattern at its upper headwaters—where slopes are steep, abundant amounts of sediment are available for transport, and discharge is high—to a meandering pattern farther down-

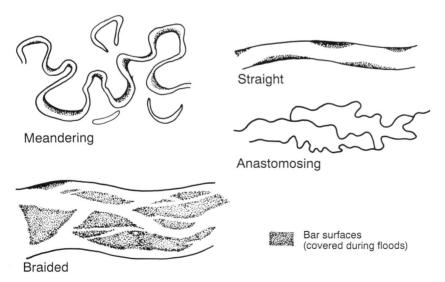

Meandering

Straight

Anastomosing

Braided

Bar surfaces
(covered during floods)

FIGURE 3.6. Map views of meandering, braided, straight, and anastomosing rivers. (Modified from Miall 1977)

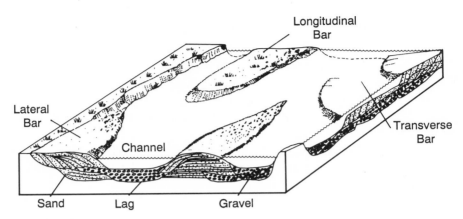

FIGURE 3.7. A generalized cross section through a braided streambed, showing the morphology and deposits of the channels and bars. Typical sequences through a longitudinal bar, a lateral bar, a transverse bar, and the channel are shown. Flow is toward the reader. (Modified from Galloway and Hobday 1983)

stream where the river traverses a valley in which the gradient is shallow and discharge is steady, and where it primarily transports a suspended load. Furthermore, the morphology of a river can change through time if the variables controlling slope, discharge, and sediment yield are changed.

Environments at the terminus of rivers include deltas and alluvial fans. These are the areas where most of the sediments transported by rivers ultimately accumulate.

The three most common types of rivers—braided, meandering, and anastomosing—are discussed below. Gullies and arroyos, ephemeral streams common to arid and semiarid regions, are discussed under a separate heading. In the final section of this chapter, alluvial fans are reviewed. Deltas are discussed in Chapter 6.

Braided Rivers

Braided rivers have a wide streambed characterized by a network of channels that diverge and rejoin around intervening bars and alluvial islands (Figs. 3.6 and 3.7). Bars consist of accumulations of gravel or sand, or a combination of both, that form topographic highs in the streambed. Braided streams, which range from straight to moderately sinuous, develop in areas with steep slopes, where an overabundance of coarse sediment (gravel and sand) is available for transport and where the stream banks are noncohesive and easily eroded. A braided river is unable to transport the total sediment load (especially the coarse component of the load) supplied to it. As a result, the channel becomes choked with its own alluvium.

Another characteristic of braided rivers is highly variable streamflow, with short periods of flooding followed by relatively long periods of low or moderate discharge or even complete desiccation. When low to moderate flow conditions prevail, the water is confined to the channels and directed around channel bars. Little erosion or sediment movement occurs during these periods. However, during the short periods of high discharge, the entire streambed is submerged and all sizes of particles are moved. During these conditions, channels shift position and bars are created and destroyed.

Although braided rivers share many common features, their sedimentological characteristics vary with the type of sediment load they transport. Braided streams are subdivided according to whether they transport primarily a gravel or sand bedload. Those transporting more than 10% gravel are known as gravelly braided streams, while those transporting mostly sand (less than 10% gravel) are referred to as sandy braided streams.

Braided rivers occur in all climatic zones and may flow year-round or intermittently. They are best developed in the distal parts of alluvial fans, on glacial outwash plains, and in the mountainous reaches of river systems.

Deposits and Landforms

The coarse clastic sediments transported in a braided stream accumulate in the channels and intervening bars and islands that make up the streambed. Three types of channel bars—longitudinal, transverse, and lateral—are defined on the basis of their morphology, size, and relationship to the channel banks (Fig. 3.7).

Longitudinal bars are elongate accumulations of the coarsest bedload particles, largely gravel or mixtures of gravel and sand, that occur in the middle of the streambed. The long axis of a longitudinal bar is always oriented roughly parallel with the flow direction. These bars are eroded at their upstream end and enlarge in length and height by the addition of sediment to their downstream and lateral edges. The particles making up longitudinal bars decrease in size both upward through the bar and downstream along its length. The internal structure of longitudinal bars may be massive, show crude horizontal bedding, or exhibit poorly developed planar crossbedding. The internal gravel fabric of the bar may develop an imbricate structure. Longitudinal bars are most prominent in gravelly braided streams.

Transverse bars are wedge-shaped bodies of sand oriented transverse to the main current flow. These bars have a broad upstream surface and a straight, lobate, or sinuous downstream margin, or slipface. When the bar is submerged, sand is transported across the bar surface and deposited on the downstream face of the bar, producing prominent cross-beds that dip downstream. Transverse bars are most common in sandy braided streams. Larger sand flats, 1 to 10 km in length, may be created by the coalescence of a number of transverse bars.

Lateral bars are large accumulations of sand attached to the channel banks. These generally develop on the inside of channel bends, where water velocity decreases.

Once a bar has formed, it may become stabilized by vegetation. If the bar is exposed, plants will begin to colonize the bar surface, and over time a dense growth of vegetation may develop, protecting it from further erosion. This process creates the vegetated alluvial islands common to many braided streams.

Channel deposits, occupying interbar areas, are highly variable in width and thickness. If gravels are present, they form massive horizontal beds that may exhibit a grain-supported fabric with internal imbrication. Channel sand deposits are usually massive or cross-bedded.

Fine-grained sediments—silt and clay—are minor constituents of the depositional record of a braided stream because periodic high flows tend to keep silt and clay in suspension and transport it through the system without allowing it to accumulate. Fine-grained deposition may occur locally as thin, discontinuous layers on the tops of bars or islands and in abandoned channel depressions, where silt and clay in ponded water can settle from suspension. These sediments generally rest directly on coarser-grained channel or bar sediments.

Site Formation Processes

The dynamic processes associated with braided rivers, especially the periodic high-energy flows, create a setting that is not conducive to the preservation of archaeological sites (Butzer 1982). During episodes of flooding, the systemic context of most sites situated on the bars and banks of a braided river is destroyed. Artifacts, hearthstones, charcoal, and other remains are swept from the surface of these sites and transposed into a secondary context. Artifacts and other archaeological debris influenced by streamflow are abraded and behave like natural sediment particles as they become incorporated into the active bar and channel sediments (Butzer 1982; Cornwall 1958; Gladfelter 1985; Isaac 1967; Limbrey 1983; Petraglia and Nash 1987; Schick 1986, 1987; Shackley 1974, 1978; Wymer 1976). Gladfelter (1985) refers to these reworked artifacts as "articlasts."

Artifacts incorporated into the streambed alluvium are the same age as the channel deposits if site occupation, stream erosion, and deposition were roughly contemporaneous. However, artifacts in a secondary alluvial context may have been eroded from sites buried in older sediments exposed in the channel banks, or they may be from older surface sites on terraces adjacent to the streambed. Remains in secondary alluvial contexts may also be from a combination of these sources. Consequently, streambed alluvium may contain a temporally related assemblage of artifacts or a mixture of temporally unrelated artifacts. If the latter situation goes unrecognized, it can lead to erroneous interpretations.

Near the town of Double Adobe in southeastern Arizona, a site was exposed in the channel banks of Whitewater Draw, a deeply entrenched arroyo. Milling stones and handstones of the Sulphur Spring stage of the Cochise culture, dated at other sites between 10,000 and 8000 B.P., are physically associated with late Pleistocene mammoth, horse, camel, and bison bones (Sayles 1983; Sayles and Antevs 1941) in sand and gravel deposits (Fig. 2.25). The association of groundstone artifacts of the Sulphur Spring stage with extinct fauna is at odds with the regional archaeology and the timing of late Pleistocene megafaunal extinctions in North America. This situation caused much controversy in North American archaeology. Some researchers suggested that it was a spurious association created by fluvial processes (Irwin-Williams 1979; Whalen 1971; Willey and Phillips 1958). Others (Haury 1953, 1983; Martin and Plog 1973) argued that the Sulphur Spring sites were late Pleistocene in age and represented plant gathering and processing stations of the Clovis culture. Clovis is the only culture in this area clearly associated with Pleistocene vertebrate fauna, such as at the Lehner, Murray Springs, and Naco mammoth kill sites, roughly 20 to 30 km west of Double Adobe. A geoarchaeological examination of the deposits at the Double Adobe site (Waters 1986a, 1986b) confirmed that the groundstone artifacts and extinct megafaunal remains physically occurred together in two lithostratigraphic units composed of gravel and sand (Fig. 2.25, units Da and Db). These deposits accumulated in the channels and bars comprising the streambed of a braided river that flowed through the Sulphur Springs Valley during the early Holocene. No features, artifact clusters, or articulated megafaunal remains were found in these alluvial units at the Double Adobe site. Instead, all artifacts, charcoal, hearthstones, and megafaunal remains were found isolated and dispersed in the gravel and sand. Examination of the pre-Holocene stratigraphy at the site revealed that megafaunal remains occurred in primary context in older Pleistocene age marls (Fig. 2.25, unit C) and alluvial terrace deposits (unit B). These older lithostratigraphic units formed the banks of the early Holocene braided stream channel. Based on several lines of evidence, it seems clear that the vertebrate megafaunal remains were eroded from the older sediments that made up the banks of the braided stream and that they were mixed into the younger gravel and sand deposits of the active early Holocene streambed. At the same time, artifacts from Sulphur Spring stage campsites situated on the banks and bars of the braided stream were eroded from these surfaces during floods. The temporally unrelated assemblages of bones and artifacts were reworked into the same gravel and sand deposits. Consequently, late Pleistocene megafaunal remains and early Holocene Sulphur Spring stage artifacts are physically associated with one another in the same alluvial units but are not temporally associated with one another (i.e., they are not the same age, the vertebrate remains being older than the Sulphur Spring artifacts).

Even archaeological remains that occur in secondary alluvial contexts provide valuable data. The artifacts dispersed in the sand and gravel at the Double Adobe site provide the only documentation of an early Archaic presence in Whitewater Draw. Without this information, the early Archaic occupation of southern Arizona would remain essentially unknown. In some cases, though less commonly, undisturbed archaeological sites may be preserved in the sediments accumulated in the streambed of a braided river. This occurs if an archaeological site located on a bar or channel bank is situated in an area protected from high discharge flows and is buried by alluvium soon after abandonment.

At the C. W. Harris site, a stratified archaeological site on the San Dieguito River in San Diego County, California, alluvial units IIIA, IIIB, and IIIC, 2 m below the surface, yielded San Dieguito culture artifacts dating to approximately 9000 B.P. (Fig. 3.8). These artifacts were buried in gravel and sand deposits accumulated in a gravelly braided streambed that was cut into the Tertiary age Torrey Sandstone (Rogers 1966; Warren 1966, 1967; Warren and True 1961). The flaked-stone artifacts and debitage recovered throughout the gravel and sand showed no indication of abrasion. In fact, several artifact concentrations were found, most notably in sand unit IIIB, where a hearth with charcoal, as well as numerous artifacts and camp debris, were discovered. Reconstructions based on the sedimentology and stratigraphy indicate that the San Dieguito occupation occurred on the surface of a lateral bar that was attached to the bank of the stream. The campsite was preserved because sand was deposited over the site shortly after abandonment. Other activity areas appear to have been located on longitudinal bars in the streambed. The C. W. Harris site illustrates that, though it is unusual, primary archaeological contexts may be preserved in a braided stream environment.

Meandering Rivers

In contrast to a braided river, streamflow in a meandering river is confined to a single, highly sinuous channel (Fig. 3.6). Meandering rivers also differ from braided rivers in that they (1) form in areas characterized by relatively

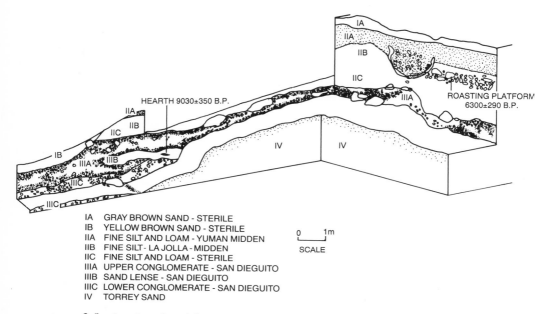

IA   GRAY BROWN SAND - STERILE
IB   YELLOW BROWN SAND - STERILE
IIA FINE SILT AND LOAM - YUMAN MIDDEN
IIB FINE SILT - LA JOLLA - MIDDEN
IIC FINE SILT AND LOAM - STERILE
IIIA UPPER CONGLOMERATE - SAN DIEGUITO
IIIB SAND LENSE - SAN DIEGUITO
IIIC LOWER CONGLOMERATE - SAN DIEGUITO
IV   TORREY SAND

0   1m
SCALE

FIGURE 3.8. Stratigraphy of the C. W. Harris site in California. San Dieguito artifacts were found in the braided stream alluvium (sand and gravel; units IIIA, IIIB,
and IIIC). (After Warren 1967)

low gradients; (2) have banks composed of cohesive sediments that are
difficult to erode; (3) typically transport a fine-grained suspended sediment
load; and (4) have a relatively steady discharge, with overbank flooding
typically occurring less than once a year. These conditions are most commonly encountered in the middle segments of rivers downslope from the
source area.

Stream Processes

Discharge in a meandering stream is characterized by two basic flow regimes: normal streamflow and overbank flooding. Normal streamflow refers
to the downslope movement of water in the confines of the channel. This
flow regime characterizes meandering rivers at most times. Periodically, however, overbank flooding occurs after periods of unusually high runoff generated by rainfall or snowmelt in the headwaters. Excess water enters the
stream system, fills the channel beyond its maximum capacity, and causes
the excess water to overtop the channel banks and spread laterally over the
adjacent lowlands.

Normal streamflow is responsible for erosion along the channel banks, deposition in the channel, and the lateral and downstream migration of the river. In the active channel, the zone of maximum water velocity is directed toward the concave bank of each meander (Fig. 3.9). The maximum-velocity current swings back and forth across the channel from one concave bank to the next. The lateral shift of the maximum velocity current in the channel causes the water to circulate in a strong, subaqueous spiral pattern known as helical flow. Helical flow circulates the water at the surface toward the outer concave bank of the channel and then deflects it downward toward the stream bottom, where it is redirected toward the inner convex bank of the channel and upward to the surface. As a result of helical flow, the concave

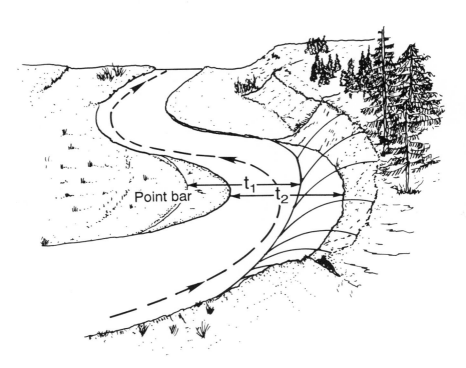

FIGURE 3.9. Erosion and deposition on a meandering river. The illustration shows the former position of the river channel at t_1, and its present position at t_2 as a result of lateral accretion (i.e., deposition on the point bar and erosion of the concave bank). The hatched area shows the amount of erosion along the cutbank between t_1 and t_2. Note the corresponding lateral accretion of the point bar. Curving arrows indicate the path of the maximum-velocity current during normal streamflow. (Modified from Marsh 1987)

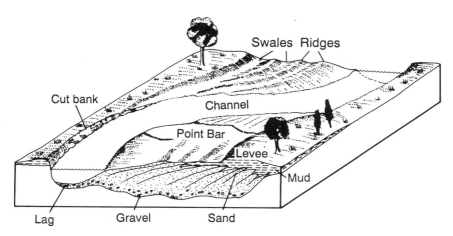

FIGURE 3.10. A generalized cross section through a segment of a meandering river, showing a typical channel, point bar, and levee, and typical sequences through them. Note the fining-upward sequences. Flow is toward the reader. (Modified from Galloway and Hobday 1983)

bank of the meander becomes the site of erosion, and the convex bank forms the locus of deposition on a gently sloping accretionary landform known as a point bar (Fig. 3.9).

Sediment is eroded from the concave side of the meander by sloughing and slumping. Sloughing is the gradual and continual erosion of noncohesive sediments from the channel banks. Slumping is the erosion of large blocks of cohesive sediment from the concave bank. Slumps are triggered when continual erosion undercuts the concave bank and a large mass of sediment falls as a cohesive unit into the channel. Eroded sediment is transported by helical flow up the sloping face of the point bar, where it is deposited under lower-velocity conditions. This creates the characteristic asymmetrical channel cross-section of meandering rivers, which have a steep concave bank and a gently sloping convex bank (Figs. 2.13 and 3.10).

Helical flow is not perpendicular to the channel but rather flows at an angle across the channel. Consequently, sediment eroded from the concave bank is not deposited on the point bar immediately opposite to it. Instead, the sediment from the cut bank is transported downstream and deposited on the point bar of the next meander or on another point bar farther downstream. Constant erosion on the concave banks and deposition on the convex banks of all meanders along the river cause the channel and its point bars gradually to migrate laterally and downstream. This results in lateral accretion. The continual horizontal erosion of the cut banks and deposition of sand and gravel in the channel and its point bars by normal streamflow processes creates a tabular body of channel gravel overlain by point bar sands (Figs. 2.24 and 3.10). During lateral accretion, the floodplain remains at a fixed elevation and does not build upward (i.e., the floodplain does not become thicker). Lateral accretion deposits are also known as bottom stratum deposits.

Overbank flow is responsible for the deposition of sediment on the low-lying areas adjacent to the river channel. This relatively flat land extending away from the channel to the edge of the valley is called the floodplain (Fig. 2.24). The floodplain of a typical meandering river is inundated at least once every two years. After each flood, sediments suspended in the floodwaters accumulate on it. The process of sequential upward growth of the floodplain as a result of repeated cycles of deposition associated with repeated episodes of overbank flooding is known as vertical accretion (Fig. 2.24). Vertical accretion deposits, also known as top stratum deposits, include the fine-grained sediments (fine sand, silt, and clay) that accumulate on the upper portions of point bars, natural levees, crevasse splays, oxbow lakes, and the floodbasin (Figs. 2.13 and 2.24).

In summary, a meandering river environment is a composite of basal lateral accretion deposits overlain by upper vertical accretion sediments accumulated in a number of different subenvironments (Fig. 2.24). The meandering river environment is dynamic, with different areas of the floodplain characterized by erosion, deposition, and stability. Furthermore, as the river migrates laterally and downstream it is constantly creating a new floodplain by reworking the older floodplain sediments.

Lateral Accretion Deposits and Landforms

Deposition in the meandering river channel during normal flow conditions occurs on the channel floor and in its associated point bars (Fig. 3.10). Point bars may be further modified during floods to create another sequence of channel and bar deposits called chutes and chute bars.

The channel floor of a meandering stream is characterized by high water velocity and turbulence. Consequently, this is where the coarsest material is transported and deposited by the river (Figs. 2.13 and 3.10). This coarse debris, the channel lag, consists of bedload gravel and sand, blocks of cohesive sediment eroded from the channel banks, and waterlogged plant debris. This lag is mobilized only during periods of high flood discharge. Fine-grained sediments are generally absent.

Point bars—which are attached to the inside, or convex, banks of meander loops—are the main loci of deposition in the meandering channel. Much

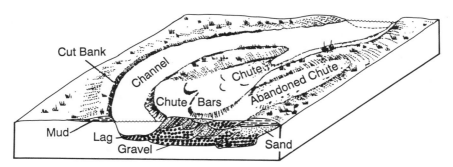

FIGURE 3.11. A generalized cross section through a segment of a coarse-grained meandering river characterized by chutes and chute bars. Typical sequences through a chute channel, chute bar, and the eroded portion of a point bar are shown. Flow is toward the reader. (Modified from Galloway and Hobday 1983)

of the sediment eroded from the concave channel banks accumulates on point bars as sediment is moved up the gently sloping bar surface by helical flow into areas of relatively low water velocity and turbulence. This gradual decrease in flow velocity upwards across the bar surface results in the deposition of coarser particles at the base and finer particles at the top of the point bar. The decrease in grain size upward is referred to as a fining-upward sequence (Fig. 2.13). Sediments making up the point bar sequence vary with the load transported by the river. Thus a bar may grade vertically from fine sand at the base to clay at the top, or from gravel to silt. Correspondingly, sedimentary structures also change upward through the point bar. A typical vertical sequence through a point bar may begin with a gravel channel lag at the base, which is overlain by large- to medium-scale cross-bedded coarse sand, which then grades upward into small-scale cross-laminated fine sand (Fig. 2.13). This sequence of lateral accretion sediments is capped by vertical accretion deposits, usually thin, horizontally laminated silts and clays washed over the bar surface during overbank floods. The surface of a point bar may be smooth or it may exhibit a surface topography consisting of a series of roughly concentric ridges and swales (Fig. 3.10).

Point bars may be modified during floods, when the zone of maximum current velocity straightens and cuts across the top of the inundated bar surface. When this occurs, a small channel or chute is excavated into the point bar surface, and large amounts of coarse bedload are funneled out of the main channel and through the chute (Figs. 2.13 and 3.11). A chute bar is created by the deposition of sediment at the downstream end of the chute adjacent to the point bar where the smaller chute channel rejoins the main channel (Figs. 2.13 and 3.11). These features are most commonly generated in meandering rivers of low sinuosity that transport an abundant coarse-grained load (mostly coarse sand and pebble- to cobble-size gravel) and that have a highly variable discharge.

Chutes slowly become filled with sediment during each successive flood. The chute channel deposits can be identified by their high concentration of imbricated gravels, cross-stratified sand, and lenses of fine-grained sediments (Fig. 3.11). Chute bars are characterized by relatively coarse-grained, cross-stratified sediments that prograde into the main channel. The internal structure of chute-modified point bars exhibits coarse-grained bedload sediments overlying and cross-cutting the typical point bar sequence (Fig. 3.11).

Vertical Accretion Deposits and Landforms

During periods of overbank flooding, coarse-grained bedload and considerable amounts of fine-grained suspended-load sediments are carried out of the channel and deposited on the floodplain. Water velocity rapidly decreases away from the channel; consequently, most of the coarse-grained sediment is deposited immediately adjacent to the channel margin, creating natural levees and crevasse splays. Fine-grained sediments, suspended in the water, are transported beyond the channel margin into the floodbasin. Deposition of these overbank sediments results in the upward aggradation or vertical accretion of the floodplain (Fig. 2.24).

Natural levees are one of the most prominent features on the floodplain (Figs. 2.13 and 3.10). They are wedge-shaped ridges of clastic sediment that form immediately adjacent to the channel on both the concave and convex banks of meander loops. Both the thickness and sediment grain size of levees decrease away from the channel. Levees are composite landforms that are constructed incrementally. During each episode of flooding, a layer of ripple-laminated and horizontally stratified sand, silt, and clay, usually a few decimeters thick, accumulates. Through time, deposition associated with recurrent overbank flooding accretes a thick natural levee. Because levees are exposed most of the time, they are commonly heavily vegetated, and plant debris often becomes incorporated into their sediments. Paleosols are also commonly interbedded in a levee sequence.

Natural levees are sometimes breached during a flood. Water from the main channel is funneled through the breach (a crevasse channel), and large amounts of bedload and suspended sediment are deposited on the floodplain as a fan or tongue-shaped mass. These deposits are known as crevasse splays (Fig. 2.13). The scale of crevasse splay deposits varies from square meters to square kilometers in area and ranges from centimeters to meters in thickness. Their abundance is determined by the flood frequency of the river.

Crevasse splay and crevasse channel sediments are coarser-grained than the associated levee deposits into which they are inset. Away from the river channel, sediments of a crevasse splay taper and become interbedded with the fine-grained sediments of the floodbasin. Crevasse splays are composed of a heterogeneous sequence of small-scale, horizontally and cross-stratified sands capped by ripple-laminated and horizontally laminated muds. Plant debris is commonly incorporated into the splay sediments. Crevasse splay deposits have extended periods of subaerial exposure; consequently, paleo-sols and root-disturbed zones are common in splay sequences.

The floodbasin occupies the area between the natural levees and the edge of the floodplain (Fig. 2.13). While the floodbasin is primarily a low-relief plain, the lowest-lying areas in the floodbasin are commonly occupied by swamps and shallow lakes. The floodbasin is dry most of the year and is inter-mittently inundated with water during brief periods of overbank flooding. Consequently, deposition on the floodbasin is sporadic. Fine-grained sedi-ments accumulate on the floodbasin as the sediments suspended in the flood-waters settle during the waning stages of the flood, forming massive to hori-zontally laminated deposits of silt and clay that are typically 1 to 2 cm thick. If vegetation is present on the floodbasin, the sediments may become organic-rich, and peats may develop locally in backswamp and lacustrine environ-ments. Because floodbasin sediments are exposed for long periods between floods, they are usually modified by burrowing animals, plant growth, and pedogenic processes. Eolian processes may cause local erosion, and dunes may cover part of the floodbasin. Along the margin of the floodbasin, alluvial fans may form where streams enter the lowlands from the adjacent highlands.

Channel Abandonment Processes and Deposits

Channel meander loops on the floodplain are periodically abandoned and form oxbow lakes. This abandonment may occur suddenly, by a process called neck cut-off, or gradually, by a process known as chute cut-off.

Neck cut-offs are created when the concave banks of adjacent meanders erode toward one another and the river breaches the narrow neck separating them (Fig. 3.12). This results in the sudden abandonment of an entire mean-der loop. Both ends of the abandoned loop become rapidly plugged with bedload sediment (gravel and sand), and an oxbow lake is created. After this, only suspended-load sediments (silt and clay) introduced during over-bank floods fill the abandoned channel. These processes generate a deposi-tional sequence composed of bedload channel sediments overlain by a thick sequence of flood-deposited silt and clay.

Rivers may also abandon meander loops by gradually reoccupying an old swale or eroding a chute into a point bar surface. During this process,

known as chute cut-off (Fig. 3.12), flow is gradually decreased in the main
channel as more discharge is funneled into the new channel. As the new
channel on the point bar surface becomes dominant (i.e., captures the main
flow of the river), the older channel slowly fills with coarse channel sediments. After the original channel is completely abandoned, an oxbow lake
is created. Sedimentation in the oxbow lake is then restricted to periods of
overbank flooding, when sediment-laden waters fill the abandoned channel
segment and silt and clay settle from suspension. This process results in a
thick sequence of coarse-grained channel sediments at the base overlain by
a thinner sequence of flood-deposited silt and clay.

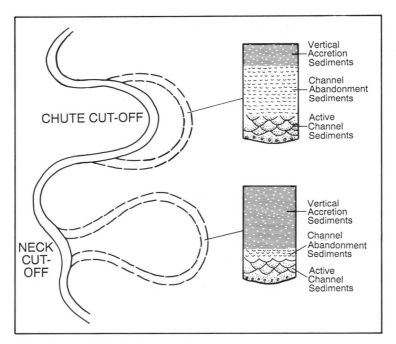

FIGURE 3.12. Meander loops, showing chute and neck cut-offs. The solid lines
show the position of the present channel, and the dashed lines indicate the abandoned channel segments. Corresponding vertical sequences of sediments created in
oxbow lakes as a result of chute cut-off and neck cut-off are also shown. Channel
sediments include cross-bedded sands and gravels deposited within the channel
while it was active. Abandonment sediments are cross-laminated sands that were
deposited during abandonment of the cut-off. Vertical accretion sediments are silts
and clays accumulated in the oxbow lake environment as a result of overbank flooding. (Modified from Walker and Cant 1984)

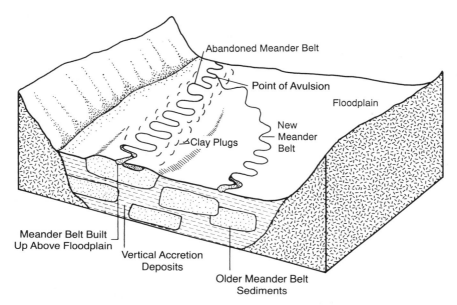

FIGURE 3.13. The avulsion of a very sinuous meandering river. Note that the river is confined to a narrow meander belt by the numerous clay plugs that formed within former oxbow lakes. Deposition within the meander belt has created a slight bulge on the floodplain. Avulsion occurred and created a new channel on the lowest portion of the floodplain. Also note that repeated avulsion has created a stratigraphic sequence of meander belt facies within floodplain facies. (Modified from Walker and Cant 1984)

The margins of oxbow lakes, whether created by neck cut-off or chute cut-off, are commonly densely vegetated. Consequently, sediments may be organic-rich, and beds of peat may be part of the oxbow lake sequence.

In another process, called avulsion, a long segment of a meandering river channel is rapidly abandoned (Fig. 3.13). Avulsion occurs in situations in which a highly sinuous meandering river channel does not freely migrate from one side of the valley to the other. The river's contorted pattern results in a high incidence of channel cut-offs and the subsequent formation of oxbow lakes. These oxbow lakes fill with fine-grained sediment and eventually form resistant clay plugs that gradually restrict the lateral movement of the channel to a narrow meander belt. The active channel can freely migrate in the predominantly sandy meander belt it establishes but cannot widen the belt. As deposition continues in the channel, point bars, and levees, an alluvial ridge is built above the level of the floodplain. This is an unstable situation that persists until a natural levee is breached during a flood and water is funneled to the lowest portion of the floodplain. The old meander belt is abandoned and a new channel is established. Avulsion is not a gradual process but occurs suddenly during an episode of flooding. Repeated episodes of avulsion will create a stratigraphic sequence of ancient meander belt sediments contained in the floodplain fill.

Site Formation Processes

Archaeological sites may be incorporated in the lateral accretion sediments of the meandering channel or in the vertical accretion deposits of the floodplain. In these settings, the systemic context of sites ranges from completely undisturbed to modified, depending on the energy level associated with deposition.

Artifacts incorporated into lateral accretion deposits—channel lags, lower and middle point bar sequences, and chute and chute bar sediments—generally occur in secondary contexts. Artifacts in these sediments are commonly eroded from previously buried sites in older sediments exposed along the concave meander banks of the channel or are derived from surface sites situated on the point bars or channel banks. Sediments in the channel environment are transported downstream by relatively high energy processes. In this situation, artifacts in the channel subenvironment behave like sediment particles and are integrated into the active channel sediments (Butzer 1982; Cornwall 1958; Gladfelter 1985; Isaac 1967; Limbrey 1983; Petraglia and Nash 1987; Schick 1986, 1987; Shackley 1974, 1978; Wymer 1976). For example, many of the proposed early bone artifacts from the Old Crow Flats in Canada are found in secondary contexts, reworked into channel lag and point bar sediments of the modern Porcupine River from two disconformities in the alluvial sequence exposed in the cut banks of the river (Morlan 1978, 1979, 1986).

Relatively undisturbed archaeological sites are more likely to occur in the vertical accretion sediments of the floodplain (upper point bars, natural levees, crevasse splays, oxbow lakes, and the floodbasin) (Butzer 1971, 1982). For archaeological material to become incorporated into floodplain sediments, occupation must take place on the lowlands adjacent to an active river channel during a period of stability. After abandonment, the site is inundated during a flood and buried as fine-grained sediments settle from suspension during the waning stages of flow. Repeated periods of stability and reoccupation of an aggrading floodplain creates a vertical sequence of horizontally stratified fine-grained sediment layers, sometimes with interbedded paleosols, or a cumulic soil profile (if sedimentation is slow) that contains archaeological debris. Floodplain aggradation ceases if the river

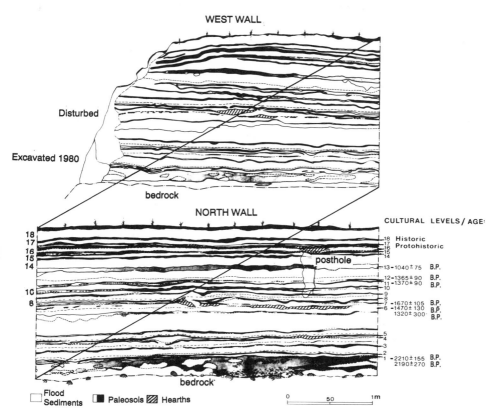

FIGURE 3.14. Vertical accretion floodplain sediments, paleosols, and archaeological surfaces at the Peace Point site in northern Alberta, Canada. The dark layers are
paleosols characterized by organic-rich A horizons, and the wider light beds are the
overbank silts deposited over the paleosols. Numbers show the position of the eighteen cultural levels buried in the floodplain stratigraphy. Associated radiocarbon
ages are indicated. (Modified from Stevenson 1985, 1986)

downcuts or if the hydraulic regime of the river is altered so that the lowlands adjacent to the channel are no longer flooded.

The Peace Point site in northern Alberta is an excellent example of site
formation in a floodplain setting (Fig. 3.14; Stevenson 1985, 1986). This site,
situated in the active floodplain of the Peace Point River, was repeatedly
occupied as it aggraded over the last 2500 years. At the site is a two-meter-
thick vertical sequence of horizontally stratified, fine-grained overbank sediments and interbedded paleosols. This sequence documents approximately
24 cycles of brief overbank flooding followed by longer intervals of stability

and soil formation. Eighteen discrete occupation surfaces were found at the site, each resting directly on the surface of a paleosol. At the Peace Point site, occupations repeatedly took place on the floodplain during the periods of stability, and the debris left by each occupation was subsequently buried during overbank flooding when silt and clay were deposited at the site. The systemic context of each occupation surface was virtually undisturbed by overbank flooding and burial. Because sedimentation was fairly regular and rapid, the assemblages represent temporally discrete encampments.

Archaeological debris may also be stratified in the cumulative soil profile created on a slowly aggrading floodplain (Fig. 2.34d). Here the archaeological remains are not separated by individual strata but instead occur in a massive, overthickened A horizon created by concurrent slow floodplain deposition and soil formation. A cumulic profile 1.5 m thick at site 41C0141, developed on the floodplain of the Elm Fork of the Trinity River in Texas, contained stratified late Archaic remains (Ferring 1987, 1990a, 1990b; Prikryl and Yates 1987).

Vertical accretion also occurs along the channel margin on point bar surfaces, natural levees, and crevasse splays. Here again, occupation occurred during periods of stability, and sites were subsequently buried during overbank flooding. At the Pen Point site in South Carolina, archaeological remains are buried in the top stratum deposits of a point bar on the Savannah River (Fig. 3.15; Brooks and Sassaman 1990). After initial construction of the subaqueous point bar platform by horizontal accretion and its subaerial emergence, the point bar surface remained relatively stable, with vertical accretion occurring four times during the last 10,000 years. Occupation took place during each period of stability, when the point bar surface was undergoing no deposition or erosion. Following each period of stability and occupation, floodwaters inundated the point bar surface and covered the stable surface and its associated cultural remains. As a result of repeated cycles of bar stability and overbank deposition, four discrete occupation surfaces were buried within the top stratum deposit, which was 100 cm thick. Because the intervals of stability were long and were punctuated by infrequent short episodes of deposition, multiple encampments by different groups are superimposed on one another. As a result, diagnostic artifacts of various phases and periods are mixed on each stable surface. Site formation in the upper portions of point bars are also well illustrated in the American Bottoms in Illinois, where Archaic, Woodland, and Mississippian sites once situated on the point bar ridges are buried to shallow depths beneath the floodplain alluvium (White and Emerson 1983; White et al. 1984). Similarly, Archaic and Woodland sites occur in the upper point bar top stratum deposits along the Missisquoi River in Vermont (Brakenridge et al. 1988).

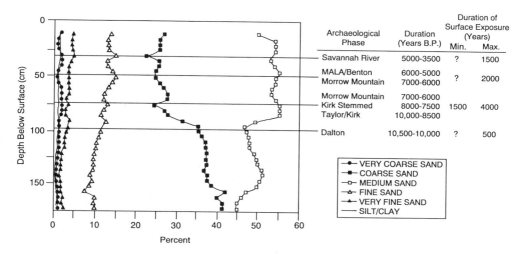

FIGURE 3.15. Textural data from the point bar sequence at the Pen Point site in South Carolina. Note the fining-upward sequence. The dramatic shift in grain size from coarse to fine at a depth of 100 cm is the break between lateral accretion (sub-aqueous bar platform) and vertical accretion (top stratum) deposits. Furthermore, each vertical depositional event is characterized by its own fining-upward sequence. Archaeological remains are found on the stable surfaces between depositional units. Because of the long duration of stability, numerous archaeological phases are compressed onto these surfaces. Furthermore, these breaks were not obvious in a visible examination of the stratigraphy but instead were discerned during sedimentological and archaeological investigations. (Modified from Brooks and Sassaman 1990)

Similar to the upper portions of point bars, natural levees and crevasse splays are incrementally built by vertical accretion during floods and may contain archaeological sites. Many late prehistoric sites in southern Louisiana occur on the surface or are buried in natural levees (Fig. 3.16; Coastal Environments 1977; Gagliano 1984; Gagliano et al. 1979, 1982). The Harper's Ferry site (Anderson and Schuldenrein 1985), the Gregg Shoals site (Tippitt and Marquardt 1984; Upchurch 1984), and the Rucker's Bottom site (Anderson and Joseph 1988; Anderson and Schuldenrein 1983a, 1983b, 1985), along the Savannah River separating Georgia and South Carolina provide excellent examples of natural site formation processes in natural levee environments.

Archaeological sites may also become incorporated within the channel fill sequences of oxbow lakes. While campsites are commonly situated on the floodplain next to oxbow lakes, they may also be located in the aban-

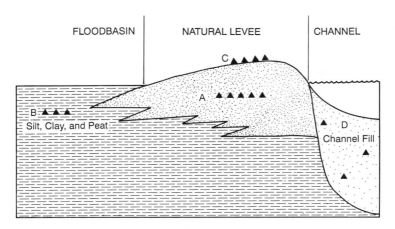

FIGURE 3.16. Archaeological sites within a natural levee and adjacent deposits:
(A) a site interbedded within the natural levee sediments; (B) a site interbedded
within floodbasin sediments; (C) a site on the surface of the natural levee;
(D) archaeological material within the channel fill. (Modified from Gagliano 1984).

doned meander on surfaces extending from the old channel banks onto the
abandoned channel floor during periods when the water table is low. Such
occupations are usually associated with very small ponds in the channel.
Evidence of this occupation becomes buried when overbank floodwaters fill
the abandoned meander and create an oxbow lake. The suspended silt and
clay settle out of suspension and cover the site. Because of the low energy
levels associated with the settling of suspended sediments in the oxbow lake,
the buried archaeological contexts are generally well preserved.

This situation is found at the Coffey site, which is adjacent to the Big
Blue River in northeastern Kansas (Schmits 1978, 1980). The stratigraphy at
this site revealed two separate oxbow lake sequences preserving a number of
discrete occupation zones. At the Coffey site, the first meander was abandoned by neck cut-off, creating an oxbow lake shortly after 6000 B.P. During
the next 1000 years, the abandoned meander was periodically filled with
deposits of laminated silt and clay following episodes of overbank flooding.
Between floods and when the water level of the lake was low, presumably
due to drought, Archaic period hunters and gatherers camped in the abandoned meander on the mudflats or shoreline next to a shallow pond in late
summer or fall to use the lacustrine and surrounding floodplain resources.
Evidence of their campsites, including artifacts, features, activity areas, and
faunal and floral remains, was buried intact and was not disturbed by sub-

sequent deposition. Twelve discrete occupation levels separated by alluvium and paleosols were discovered in these oxbow lake sediments. At the site, a second meander of the Big Blue River was abandoned around 2500 B.P., creating another oxbow lake. This lake was used by late Archaic people in a similar fashion to the first oxbow. A sequence of five discrete cultural levels was discovered in the fine-grained sediments that filled this later oxbow lake.

So far, the positive preservational aspects of site formation on the floodplain have been presented. However, the context of sites on a floodplain may also be partially or completely destroyed by water scouring the floodplain during overbank flooding (Butzer 1982; Turnbaugh 1978; Wilson 1983a, 1983b, 1990). Depending on the position of the site and the magnitude of the flood, sites situated on the surface or buried to shallow depths in floodplain sediments may be eroded and destroyed. Turnbaugh (1978) documented the effects of an exceptionally large flood on the floodplain of the west branch of the Susquehanna River in Pennsylvania. After the flood, he found that some sites were swept clean, with hundreds of artifacts and other debris left in windrows at the downriver ends of sites. Differential erosion carved pedestals at some sites, leaving features elevated above the scoured floodplain, and eroded deep potholes at others. This one flood substantially damaged the cultural resources on the floodplain, and this was just one of many floods that have occurred and will occur on the Susquehanna River. Wilson (1983a, 1983b, 1990) recorded the effect of overbank flows on an archaeological site in Calgary, Alberta. Here, cobble tools and fire-broken cobbles were reworked into lines, and lighter bone material was swept from the site. However, small flakes remained in activity clusters because they were protected by the grass in the litter mat of the prairie sod.

Anastomosing Rivers

Anastomosing rivers are characterized by a network of channels that divide and rejoin around alluvial islands (Fig. 3.17). While the morphology of an anastomosing river appears similar to that of a braided river, a number of characteristics differentiate the two river types. Anastomosing rivers have (1) channels that are relatively deep and narrow, with individual channel segments ranging from straight to sinuous; (2) alluvial islands that are extremely stable and commonly vegetated; (3) a well-developed floodplain, with backswamps that extend away from the river; and (4) perennial discharge that primarily carries a suspended load. Anastomosing rivers most commonly develop on alluvial plains that have extremely low gradients and that are rapidly subsiding. These conditions are often found in coastal and deltaic settings.

The channel sediments of an anastomosing river consist of a mixture of gravels and cross-bedded sands. Occasionally, narrow point bars composed of clastic sediments may develop on the inside of a channel bend, but alluvial islands and the floodplain are the dominant subenvironments of an anastomosing river system. The islands and floodplain are composed of fine-grained clastic sediments (silt and clay) and peats deposited in backswamps, natural levees, and crevasse splays.

The positions of the channels, islands, and floodplain are very stable because of the cohesive properties of the fine-grained sediments and the high degree of root binding by the vegetation. As a result, the river cannot migrate laterally, and sediments accumulate vertically during periods of overbank flooding on the islands and floodplain. Vertical accretion and rapid subsidence result in the accumulation of thick vertical piles of sediments characteristic of each subenvironment. The vertical stacking of channel sediments forms thick, narrow, elongate bands of sand and gravel that diverge and reunite around thick accumulations of fine-grained sediments.

Site Formation Processes

Except for the absence of oxbow lakes, the subenvironments of an anastomosing river are similar to those of a meandering river. Specifically, anastomosing rivers have channels, point bars (although less common and less well developed), natural levees, crevasse splays, and floodbasin subenvironments. As a result, archaeological sites may be encountered in situations similar to those described for a meandering river.

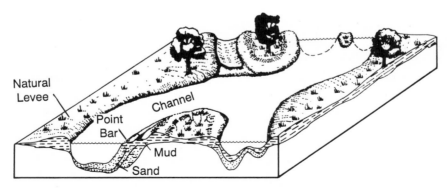

FIGURE 3.17. A generalized cross section of a segment of an anastomosing river. Typical sequences through the channel and a laterally accreting point bar are shown. Flow is toward the reader. (Modified from Galloway and Hobday 1983)

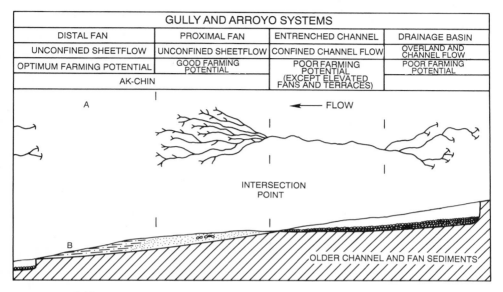

GULLY AND ARROYO SYSTEMS			
DISTAL FAN	PROXIMAL FAN	ENTRENCHED CHANNEL	DRAINAGE BASIN
UNCONFINED SHEETFLOW	UNCONFINED SHEETFLOW	CONFINED CHANNEL FLOW	OVERLAND AND CHANNEL FLOW
OPTIMUM FARMING POTENTIAL	GOOD FARMING POTENTIAL	POOR FARMING POTENTIAL (EXCEPT ELEVATED FANS AND TERRACES)	POOR FARMING POTENTIAL
AK-CHIN			

FIGURE 3.18. A generalized plan view (A) and a cross section (B), showing the components, flow characteristics, and deposits of a discontinuous gully and arroyo environment. The location of Ak-Chin fields and the farming potential of each segment are indicated. (From Waters 1987b)

Gullies and Arroyos

Many of the major rivers and streams in arid and semiarid regions, especially in the American Southwest, can be classified as ephemeral discontinuous gullies and arroyos (Fig. 3.18). Gullies and arroyos are entrenched channels that are dry most of the year and that flow for only a few hours or days after heavy rainfall occurs in their associated drainage basins. As a result, fluvial activity is sporadic, with erosion and deposition occurring rapidly during catastrophic flash flood events. Gullies and arroyos are characterized by similar processes and deposits, differing only in scale: gullies are smaller than arroyos.

Gullies begin upslope at a headcut or series of headcuts that merge downstream into a single entrenched channel. The walls of the entrenched channel gradually decrease in height downslope from the headcut because the slope of the channel bed is less than the slope of the previous valley floor into which the channel is entrenched. Eventually the walls and bottom of the channel merge downslope at a location known as the intersection point. Downslope from the intersection point, sediment eroded from the channel accumulates to form an alluvial fan. This gully-mouth fan is the terrestrial equivalent of a river delta (i.e., it forms on the land surface instead of underwater).

Discharge through a gully system is initiated after rainfall occurs in its watershed. Upslope of the intersection point, flow is generally confined to the channel, with floodwaters rarely overflowing the channel banks. During times of flow, gravel and sand are transported and accumulated in the channel bed. Downslope from the intersection point, shallow braided channels radiate across the proximal fan surface. Because the channels are shallow, unconfined sheetflow is generated. Sheetflows transport a combination of sand and gravel bedload and a suspended load of silt and clay. Vegetation on the fan slows the movement of the water, and deposition occurs. Coarse sediment accumulates in the braided channels, and finer sediments on the adjacent surfaces. These shallow channels frequently shift position on the fan surface as they become choked with sediment. The resultant fan deposits are laterally extensive layers of sand and silt interbedded with shallow sand- and gravel-filled channels. The sand and silt layers are commonly mixed into a massive deposit of silty sand as a result of bioturbation. Sediment-laden water traveling over the proximal fan surface continues to spread downslope over the distal fan. Because vegetation on the proximal fan filters out the coarser sediments, only the very fine sand, silt, and clay that remain in suspension reach the distal fan, where they accumulate into massive and laminated deposits.

Gullies may occur along the axis of a valley but are most common on the alluvial aprons or piedmonts, called bajadas, which extend from the base of the mountains (Fig. 2.33). Bajadas have a stratigraphy of superimposed channel and fan sediments because gullies are continually shifting position as one gully pirates the flow from another.

Arroyos are large gullies created by the deepening and expansion of a single gully or by the merger of a series of contiguous gullies into one uninterrupted channel. This occurs when the headcut of a gully erodes upslope and connects with a gully lying upstream. Once the gullies are connected, the newly formed arroyo deepens and widens its channel. Arroyos are common in the valleys of the American Southwest.

Arroyos are characterized by steep channel banks, usually several meters high, in unconsolidated sediments (Fig. 3.19). Most flows are confined to the channel, but during unusually heavy floods, water overflows the arroyo banks and spreads laterally over the valley floor. Because of the heavy sediment loads and ephemeral high-energy discharge in the arroyo channel, the streambed has a braided pattern, with small channels diverging and rejoining around channel bars. Therefore, arroyo channel sediments and structures are similar to those of gravelly and sandy braided rivers, with layers of imbri-

FIGURE 3.19. The Santa Cruz River, an arroyo, traversing the Tucson Basin in Arizona. Note the steep vertical banks and dry streambed, which exhibits a braided pattern. After heavy rainfall, floodwater may completely fill the channel.

cated gravels, cross-bedded to ripple-laminated sands, and occasional clay and silt layers. Typically, arroyo channel sequences become upwardly finer, with coarse gravel and sand at the base, then silty sand, and finally clay at the top. As with gullies, arroyo-mouth fans develop at the downslope terminus of arroyo channels. Arroyo-mouth fans are much larger than those of gullies, forming broad valley fills (Fig. 2.33). Like gullies, arroyos are unstable and have undergone numerous episodes of channel cutting and filling during the late Quaternary, creating complex alluvial stratigraphic sequences (see, e.g., Haynes 1981, 1982a; Waters 1986b, 1988b).

The channel bed of an arroyo is vulnerable to wind erosion during the long periods when it is dry. Wind-blown sand often accumulates in the form of dunes on the alluvial floodplain. If not destroyed by later flooding, these eolian sediments become incorporated into the alluvial sequence.

Marshlands—called cienegas in the American Southwest (Hendrickson and Minckley 1984; Melton 1965)—develop locally in an arroyo if the streambed intersects the water table. At these locations, water seeps to the surface and flows sluggishly through a shallow channel, which becomes heavily vegetated. Laminated, organic-rich, fine-grained sediments are commonly deposited in the shallow channel, and massive deposits of silt and clay accumulate on the adjacent wet meadows. Cienega sediments are frequently interbedded in arroyo channel fills.

Site Formation Processes

Archaeological sites in gully environments are commonly buried in gully-mouth fan alluvium. In these situations, sites are usually buried during sheet flooding, often with little disturbance of the original site context. Near Marana, Arizona, numerous Hohokam settlements (Rice 1987) are buried in proximal and distal gully-mouth fan sediments on the bajada emanating from the Tortolita Mountains (Waters 1987b; Waters and Field 1986). At this site, house floor assemblages and activity areas were not disturbed by burial. In some cases, however, archaeological remains may be reworked on the surface prior to burial. This occurred at several sites near Picacho, Arizona (Bayham et al. 1986), where Archaic lithic scatters were dispersed over the surface by sheetflooding prior to and during burial at the toe of a fan (Waters 1986c).

Artifacts buried in gully channel sediments are usually in a secondary context. This occurs when gullies entrench older sediments, erode artifacts from the channel banks, and rebury them in the channel alluvium.

Archaeological sites in a larger arroyo depositional system occur in situations similar to those described for gullies. Generally, archaeological remains in the sand and gravel deposits in the deeper portions of entrenched arroyo channel fills are in secondary contexts. In some situations, undisturbed evidence of riverine use may be preserved in bars and protected floodplain areas. At the San Xavier Bridge site near Tucson, Arizona (Fig. 2.23; Ravesloot 1987), undisturbed hearths, roasting pits, lithic scatters, and human burials of the Hohokam culture were encountered in the deeper portions of channel fill sequences (Waters 1987a, 1988a, 1988b).

Archaeological sites situated on the arroyo floodplain are commonly buried by fine-grained flood deposits. A protohistoric component at the San Xavier Bridge site was buried by silt during overbank flooding from the channel (Fig. 2.23). At the time of occupation, the site was situated on the floodplain adjacent to a large arroyo channel that was largely filled with alluvium.

Archaeological sites are commonly buried in the fine-grained sediments deposited in a cienega. Cienega deposits buried several Hohokam occupation surfaces at the San Xavier Bridge site (Fig. 2.23; Waters 1988a, 1988b), numerous Archaic period sites in Whitewater Draw (Fig. 2.25; Waters 1986b), and the Clovis occupation surfaces at the Lehner and Murray Springs sites in the San Pedro Valley (Fig. 2.36; Haynes 1981, 1982a).

Terraces

Terraces are landforms of alluvial origin that occur in many river valleys. These landforms have a relatively flat horizontal surface, called a tread, which is bounded at one end by a steep scarp, called a riser, and at the other end by the valley wall or the scarp of the next higher terrace (Fig. 3.20). Terrace treads are generally stable and are no longer inundated by overbank flooding. In some cases, however, terraces situated slightly above the active floodplain may become inundated and buried during unusually large floods. Terraces may also become veneered or buried by eolian, alluvial fan, and colluvial sediments.

Based on their mode of formation, alluvial terraces are classified as either depositional terraces or erosional terraces. Fill and cut terraces, as they are also known, can occur separately or in combination with one another in the same valley.

A depositional or fill terrace is one in which the tread of the terrace is created by deposition (Fig. 3.20a). In this case, the terrace tread represents an ancient floodplain. Consequently, the alluvial sediments beneath the terrace are genetically related to the tread surface. The creation of a depositional terrace is a two-step process. First, a thick valley fill accumulates as lateral and vertical accretion takes place on the floodplain. Second, the river cuts down into its valley fill and leaves the floodplain as an abandoned elevated surface. This abandoned floodplain becomes the terrace tread. Eventually the river stops downcutting and becomes stabilized at a lower elevation. As the river meanders back and forth, it erodes the older valley fill and creates a new floodplain (valley fill) below the elevation of the former floodplain. A steep erosional scarp separates the new floodplain and the abandoned surface. To create the next fill terrace, the river must aggrade and downcut again. This process of terrace formation may occur repeatedly through time to create a sequence of depositional terraces.

An erosional or cut terrace is one in which the tread of the terrace is created by the lateral erosion of preexisting older sediments (Fig. 3.20b). In this case, the terrace tread does not represent a former floodplain but is instead an erosional surface. Again, the creation of an erosional terrace is a two-step process. First, the tread is created when the river channel scours a flat surface while it migrates laterally from one side of the valley to the other. The migrating channel usually leaves only a veneer of coarse-grained alluvium over the cut surface. Second, the river downcuts, abandons the bev-

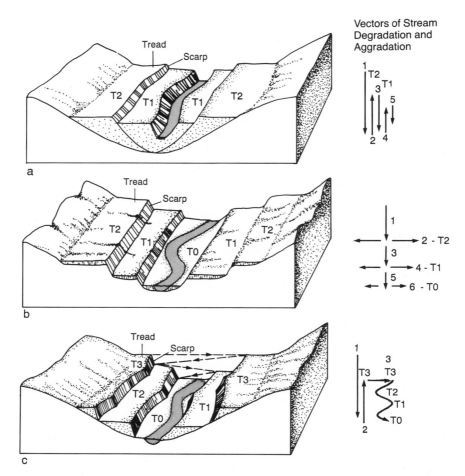

FIGURE 3.20. The formation of (a) depositional and (b) erosional stream terraces. Also shown are (a, b) paired and (c) unpaired terraces. The arrows to the right of each diagram show the changes in the river valley through time (1–6) and the corresponding terraces formed (T0–T3). Downward arrows indicate channel incision; upward arrows, floodplain aggradation; horizontal arrows, lateral channel planation; and sinuous arrows, concurrent channel downcutting and lateral planation. Note that terraces are numbered sequentially (T0, T1, T2, etc.) from the active floodplain (T0) to the highest terrace. (Modified from Muller and Oberlander 1984)

eled surface, which becomes the terrace tread, and in turn creates the terrace riser. Because this process does not involve the deposition of floodplain alluvium, as in the case of the fill terrace, sediments beneath the terrace (except for the channel lag) are not genetically related to the tread surface. Instead, the terrace tread is an erosional surface. If the tread of a cut terrace truncates bedrock, it is called a strath or rock-cut terrace.

The topographic relationship between terrace treads on either side of a valley is used to classify terraces as either paired or unpaired. Paired terraces are those with treads that occur at equivalent elevations on both sides of the valley (Fig. 3.20a and b). Matching terrace surfaces are usually presumed to be of equivalent age. Paired terraces are created when a broad floodplain or beveled surface is entrenched. Unpaired terraces are those that do not have a matching tread on the opposite side of the valley (Fig. 3.20c). Unpaired terraces that occur at staggered elevations on opposite sides of the valley are created by concurrent lateral erosion accompanying ongoing channel downcutting. In some situations, unpaired terraces may be confined to only one side of the valley (i.e., there are no terrace equivalents on the opposite side of the valley) as a result of differential erosion. In this case, terraces may have been created on both sides of the valley, but subsequent erosion scoured the terraces from one side. Paired and unpaired terraces can be either erosional or depositional in origin.

Commonly, a number of terraces occur in a valley, creating a sequence of stair-stepped surfaces extending from the active floodplain to the valley margin. Because terraces, whether depositional or erosional, are created by progressive lowering of the floodplain, the highest terrace is always the oldest, and the lowest terrace the youngest. Thus, terraces extending from the valley sidewall to the floodplain are chronologically ordered from oldest to youngest.

Site Formation Processes

Archaeological sites occur both on terrace treads and in terrace fills. Whether sites occur on the surface or are buried in a terrace depends on the age of the terrace and the period of occupation.

At any particular time, people occupying a river valley can camp on the active floodplain or on any of the higher terraces that lie above it. For example, Paleoindian sites could occur on the surface of terraces that were present at the time of occupation as well as in the alluvium of the then-active floodplain. However, Paleoindian sites would never occur on lower terraces, because these surfaces were formed after Paleoindian occupation. Only younger sites (e.g., Archaic and ceramic) will occur on the surface of any lower terraces.

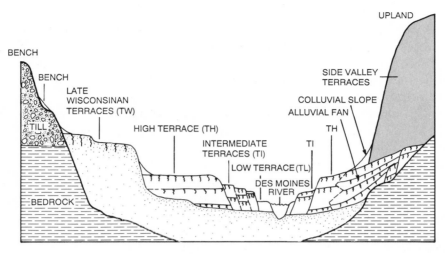

FIGURE 3.21. A generalized cross section showing the sequence of river terraces along the central Des Moines River Valley in Iowa. (Courtesy E. Arthur Bettis III)

In general, because terraces are a chronological set of landforms that progressively get younger toward the floodplain, higher terraces have been available for human occupation for a longer period than lower terraces. Consequently, the assemblages of surface artifacts on higher terraces could contain a greater mixture of older and younger artifacts than younger terraces. The mixture of temporally discrete assemblages becomes less severe on each terrace surface as the floodplain is approached. In other words, surface assemblages become less time transgressive as terraces become progressively younger, because they have been exposed for progressively shorter periods of time; thus, the potential for long-term occupation becomes less.

Several Pleistocene cut terraces, two late Pleistocene fill terraces, and three Holocene fill terraces occur along the Des Moines River Valley in central Iowa (Fig. 3.21; Benn and Bettis 1981; Bettis and Benn 1984; Bettis and Hoyer 1986). The highest cut terraces were stabilized before humans entered the valley, and the upper Pleistocene terraces (TW) became stabilized by 11,000 B.P. The highest Holocene terrace (TH) was stabilized around 4000 B.P., a series of intermediate terraces (TI) were abandoned around 750 B.P., and the lowest terrace (TL) is the active floodplain of the Des Moines River. Because of its long exposure, evidence of the very earliest occupation of the valley through the historic period potentially lies on the surface of the upper Pleistocene benches, while only post–11,000 B.P. remains could potentially be found on or near the surface of the late Pleistocene fill terraces. Likewise, only post–4000 B.P. remains could be found on the surface of the TH surface, only post–750 B.P. sites on the surface of the intermediate terraces (TI), and only historic occupation on the surface of the floodplain (TL).

Terrace sites remain exposed unless they become buried by slope colluvium, wind-blown sediments, or alluvial sediments during periods of exceptional overbank flooding. Portions of the intermediate terrace surface along the Des Moines River (TI) are mantled with recent overbank deposits. Several terraces, with sites situated on them, are buried by alluvium along the Duck River in southeastern Tennessee (Brakenridge 1984; Turner and Klippel 1989). Finally, along the Bow River in southern Alberta, alluvial fans emanating from the bluffs adjacent to the river have buried two Holocene terraces and their associated surface and buried archaeological remains (Wilson 1986).

Sites may also occur in terrace deposits. Whether or not sites are buried in a terrace depends on the age of the sediments underlying the terrace tread. If the age of the terrace fill is older than the antiquity of humans in North America (e.g., the sediments date to the early or middle Pleistocene), then archaeological remains will only occur on the tread surface and will not be buried in the fill. However, if the deposits underlying the terrace are late Pleistocene or Holocene in age, the alluvial fill could contain archaeological sites. Because the alluvium beneath each terrace was deposited during a discrete interval of time and because terraces develop sequentially through time, each terrace fill could potentially contain a different temporal assemblage of sites. For example, the deposits of the late Pleistocene fill terraces (TW) along the Des Moines River (Fig. 3.21 and Table 3.1) were created sometime between 12,600 and 11,000 B.P., the fill of the highest Holocene terrace (TH) accumulated between 10,500 and 4000 B.P., deposition of the intermediate Holocene terraces (TI) occurred between 4000 and 750 B.P., and the lowest terrace (TL) began forming after 750 B.P. Consequently, buried Paleoindian remains will only occur in the late Pleistocene fills; buried late Paleoindian and early and middle Archaic sites will occur only in the sediments of the fill of the TH terrace; buried late Archaic, Woodland, and late prehistoric sites will occur only in the deposits of the intermediate terraces (TI); and buried protohistoric and historic sites will occur only in the sediments of the the floodplain (TL).

Other studies that describe terrace sequences and their effect on site formation include those of Gardner and Donahue (1985) along the Little Platte River in Missouri; Holliday (1987b) along the South Platte River in Colorado; Hammatt (1977) along the Lower Snake River in Washington; and Albanese (1977, 1978a; Albanese and Wilson 1974) in various drainages in central Wyoming.

Table 3.1 Preservation Potentials for Buried Archaeological Sites in the
Central Des Moines River Valley in Iowa

Culture Period	Alluvial Fans	High Terrace	Intermediate Terraces	Low Terrace
Paleoindian	+ +	+ (late)	−	−
Early to Middle Archaic	+ +	+ +	−	−
Late Archaic	+ +	+	+ +	−
Woodland	+ −	−	+ +	−
Oneota and Great Oasis	+ −	−	+ +	+ −
Historic	−	−	+ −	+ +

SOURCE: Bettis and Benn 1984.

NOTE: Preservation potential is indicated by the following symbols:
− not possible
+ − low potential
+ moderate potential
+ + high potential

Alluvial Fans

Alluvial fans are fan-shaped wedges of sediment that extend from a mountain front or steep escarpment onto an adjacent lowland (Figs. 2.14 and 2.33). Fans form at the point where streams emerge from the mountains and dump their sediment loads. Slowly, as the sediments accumulate, a cone of debris is created.

Fans are commonly a kilometer or more in radius and grade downslope at angles between 3° and 6°. The size and shape of individual alluvial fans are strongly controlled by climate, drainage basin area, and drainage basin lithology. Alluvial fans may occur as individual landforms or may coalesce with adjacent fans to form a broad, sloping plain known as an alluvial piedmont or bajada (Fig. 2.33). Although fans are best developed in arid and semiarid regions where stream action is ephemeral, they also form in regions with humid climates.

Two processes—gravity-induced mass wasting and streamflow in gullies—are responsible for the erosion, transport, and deposition of sediments on alluvial fan surfaces. Mass wasting deposits are created by catastrophic flow events in which water-saturated debris moves rapidly downslope at rates of up to many meters per second, and transport and deposition of debris occurs in a matter of minutes. Debris flows and mudflows are the most common mass wasting processes on alluvial fans.

Debris flows are gravity-induced movements of water-saturated coarse-grained debris in a matrix of fine-grained sediments. When debris at the surface becomes saturated to the point that it overcomes the gravitational and cohesive forces resisting movement, a debris flow is triggered. Flows can occur on gentle or steep slopes and are capable of transporting boulders weighing several tons. Once movement has started, the debris is commonly funneled into a stream channel. Eventually the debris flow emerges from the channel and spreads outward to form a sheet or lobe-shaped deposit. Large particles tend to concentrate at the top and outer margins of the flow, where levees develop, producing an internal structure consisting of a poorly sorted mass of gravels in a fine-grained matrix, with little or no internal organization. Commonly, the matrix is winnowed by later wind and water erosion, accentuating the bouldery appearance of the deposit.

Mudflows are similar to debris flows except that they are composed almost entirely of fine-grained sediments (sand, silt, and clay). The morphology of a mudflow deposit ranges from a thin sheet to a thick lobate body, depending on the viscosity of the slurry. Mudflow deposits occur in both channeled and nonchanneled areas of the fan.

Gullies dominate the stream process on alluvial fans. Gully channels are commonly entrenched into the upper and middle segments of a fan and are the loci of coarse sand and gravel deposition. Gully-mouth sheetflow sediments most commonly accumulate in the lower portions of alluvial fans.

Deposition on a fan surface is neither uniform nor constant. The locus of deposition is constantly shifting, depositing sediments on one segment of the fan at a time. As a result, large areas of a fan may remain stable for thousands of years and develop lag pavements (a concentration of stones at the surface due to deflation caused by wind erosion) or well-developed soils. If the locus of deposition shifts, these stable areas may become buried by gully, debris flow, or mudflow deposits.

Fans in humid regions are generally dominated by stream processes, whereas those in arid and semiarid regions are dominated by mass wasting. Consequently, the internal structure of an alluvial fan in an arid region is composed of a combination of poorly sorted beds of gravel and sand deposited by debris flows and mudflows, better-sorted stream deposits of sand and gravel, and paleosols. Fans in humid regions are generally composed of better-sorted stream deposits, colluvium, and fewer mudflow deposits. In both regions, the coarsest sediments accumulate at the fan head, where most debris flows and mudflows occur, and grain size decreases toward the base of the fan. Alluvial fan sediments are commonly interbedded with fluvial, eolian, or lacustrine sediments near the toe of the fan, where they come into contact with these environments (Fig. 2.14). This can be seen along the Des Moines River in Iowa, where alluvial fans emanating from the bluffs adjacent to the floodplain interfinger with the alluvium of the highest terrace (Fig. 3.21).

Smaller fan-shaped bodies of sediments should not be confused with alluvial fans. Narrow, steeply sloping bodies of sediment deposited by small streams are called alluvial cones rather than fans, and the accumulation of coarse, bouldery debris at the base of a cliff as a result of rock fall rather than stream transport, is considered scree or a talus cone. Small fans deposited at the terminus of arroyos and gullies have already been discussed and are considered part of the gully or arroyo fluvial system.

Site Formation Processes

The preservation of archaeological sites on alluvial fans is determined by the position of the site relative to the processes operating on the fan. In regions where catastrophic debris flow and mudflow processes occur, sites in the upper and middle segments of a fan are generally preserved at the surface on the stable portions of the fan or are destroyed if they are in the path of a catastrophic flow. In the latter situation, artifacts are entrained in the flow and reworked into a secondary context farther downslope. This occurred at the Borax Lake site in northern California (Harrington 1948). Here, late Pleistocene and early Holocene fluted and stemmed projectile points are dispersed in two poorly sorted mudflow deposits (Meighan and Haynes 1970). These artifacts apparently were eroded from two temporally discrete surface contexts and mixed into a secondary context by two mass wasting events. At the Calico Hills site in California (Haynes 1973; Shlemon and Budinger 1990; Simpson 1978; Simpson et al. 1986), purported pre-Clovis artifacts were excavated from a secondary context in debris flow deposits. A similar situation also occurs at the Pinto Wash site in California, where crudely flaked artifacts are reported from gravelly alluvial fan deposits (Childers and Minshall 1980).

If sites are buried to sufficient depth before catastrophic flows pass over them, however, they may escape destruction. For example, undisturbed cultural horizons are buried in thin eolian silt layers situated between massive debris flow deposits at the Vermilion Lakes, Christensen, and Second Lakes sites in Canada (Fedje 1986). These sites are preserved because they were buried by eolian sediments prior to debris flow deposition. The most likely position for the preservation of systemic archaeological contexts on a debris-flow-dominated fan is near the toe, the lower segment of the fan. Here, debris flows and mudflows are less common, and sites may become buried by sheetwash alluvium associated with gully-mouth fans.

In humid regions, fan sedimentation is dominated by low-energy sheetwash processes and the deposition of colluvium by gravity processes. Mudflows are generally a minor component of humid fan sequences. In some cases, episodes of deposition can be episodic and then followed by relatively longer intervals of stability, during which soils form. Prehistoric occupations commonly occurred on these stable surfaces between depositional episodes. As a result, sites are often situated on the surfaces of buried paleosols that are overlain by alluvium or colluvium. At the Cherokee Sewer site in Iowa, three of the four cultural occupation surfaces were found on the surfaces of paleosols (Fig. 3.22; Hoyer 1980). Subsequent postdepositional processes have displaced some of the artifacts into the A horizons of these buried soils. In many areas in which sedimentation is more constant, with few periods of long stability during which a well-developed soil profile formed, occupation surfaces occur in lithostratigraphic units and cumulative soil profiles. For instance, the 23 stratigraphically discrete occupation surfaces at the Koster site in Illinois were buried in colluvium and sheetwash alluvium, on the contacts between these sediments, or in the overthickened A horizons of cumulic soils (Brown and Vierra 1983; Butzer 1977, 1978b; Hajic 1981, 1990; Wiant et al. 1983). Because humid fans are dominated by low-energy depositional processes, sites may be buried and the systemic context preserved regardless of location on the fan. Archaeological debris at the Koster site (Brown and Vierra 1983; Butzer 1977, 1978b; Hajic 1981, 1990; Wiant et al. 1983) occurs near the head of an alluvial fan that emanates from the bluffs adjacent to the Illinois River. The occupations at the Cherokee Sewer site occurred at the toe of the fan. Additional examples of site formation in humid fans occur in Illinois at the Napoleon Hollow site (Styles 1985; Wiant et al. 1983) and the Campbell Hollow site (Hajic 1985a).

Alluvial Landscape Evolution and the Archaeological Record

In the following discussion, the focus shifts from the processes, landforms, and deposits of different alluvial environments and their accompanying natural site formation processes to an examination of the preservation of archaeological remains in alluvial settings at a regional level. Instead of focusing on whether an individual site is preserved or destroyed based on its position in the alluvial environment and its relationship to alluvial processes, attention here is centered on the impact of landscape evolution on the total archaeological record of the alluvial environment.

By now it should be clear that alluvial environments are dynamic ero-

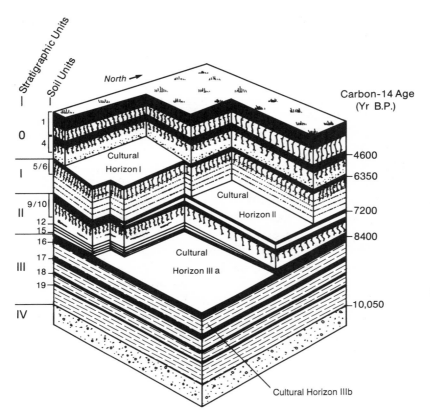

FIGURE 3.22. The stratigraphy of sediments and paleosols at the Cherokee Sewer
site in Iowa. The major sedimentary units and paleosols are designated on the left,
and radiocarbon ages are given on the right. The four cultural horizons, three of
which occur on the surface of the paleosols, are indicated. The black areas are the A
horizons of soils, and the wavy lines that in some cases extend below them indicate
that B horizons are present. (Modified from Hoyer 1980)

sional and depositional systems that are constantly changing. The physical
appearance and hydrological conditions of a floodplain can change dramatically over a short period. A river can change from a braided to a meandering
pattern, an arroyo can cut and fill several times, and a river can downcut into
its floodplain and create a terrace. These changes in a fluvial system are primarily triggered by changes in climate, tectonic activity, a rise or fall in the sea
level, internal geomorphic adjustments, and human land use (Chorley et al.

1985; Ritter 1986; Schumm 1977; Schumm and Brakenridge 1987). Changes in the fluvial landscape are recorded in the alluvial stratigraphic record, which is composed of sediments deposited during discrete intervals of time and separated by unconformities, diastems, and paleosols that represent periods of erosion, short episodes of nondeposition, and long periods of stability, respectively. As a result, the archaeological record contained in alluvium may not preserve the complete record of human use of a riverine environment.

Of all the archaeological surveys undertaken in river basins across North America, relatively few have been concerned with the effects of fluvial landscape evolution on the archaeological record. This is a crucial oversight because, as a number of geoarchaeological studies have shown, the archaeological record preserved in alluvial settings has been dramatically affected by fluvial processes through time (e.g., Bettis and Benn 1984; Gladfelter 1985; Thompson and Bettis 1982). The condition of the archaeological record must be addressed before archaeological interpretations are made from the site record contained in alluvial sequences. Absences or gaps in occupation at a specific locality or in a region may just as likely be the result of erosion as they are of cultural processes. Only when the alluvial history of deposition, erosion, and stability is reconstructed and their effects on both the spatial and temporal aspects of the archaeological record recognized are meaningful reconstructions of prehistoric human behavior in an alluvial setting possible. In short, the structure of the alluvial record that contains archaeological remains fundamentally limits archaeological interpretation in alluvial settings. The effects of fluvial landscape evolution on the archaeological record of a riverine environment and the usefulness of geoarchaeological site predictive modeling are illustrated in the following discussion on the archaeological record of western Iowa. A list of additional studies that illustrate these points is presented in Appendix A.

The Archaeological Record of Western Iowa

Gullies draining the Loess Hills of western Iowa have undergone a complex history of landscape change during the late Quaternary (Fig. 3.23). This record of landscape evolution is preserved in the alluvial stratigraphy that has been investigated by E. Arthur Bettis and his colleagues (Bettis et al. 1986; Bettis and Thompson 1981, 1982, 1985; Thompson and Bettis 1980, 1982). After studying the alluvial record of several gullies in western Iowa, Bettis defined the DeForest formation, which he divided into six members (Fig. 3.24). He also recognized a number of important erosional unconformities and paleosols in this formation. Bettis demonstrates in his study how a complex history of landscape degradation, stability, and aggradation has shaped the spatial and temporal archaeological record in western Iowa.

Between 12,000 and 10,500 B.P. the gullies in western Iowa cut deep channels that later filled with silty sediments derived from the erosion of Pleistocene loess that mantled the valley hillslopes (Fig. 3.23). This alluvium is known as the Soetmelk member of the DeForest formation. This period of deposition was followed by another episode of channel downcutting and widening. These newly created channels later filled with alluvium (designated the Watkins member) between 10,500 B.P. and 8000 B.P. Following a brief period of stability, gullies entrenched the Watkins floodplain. As their channels widened from 8000 to 3500 B.P., tremendous volumes of early Holocene and late Pleistocene alluvium were eroded. This major erosional unconformity, lasting approximately 4500 years, is called the DeForest Gap (Fig. 3.24). The sediments eroded from the small valleys during this interval

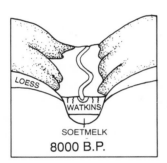
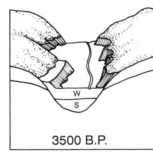
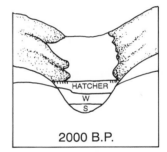
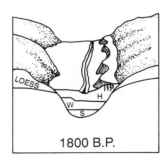
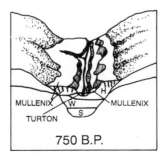
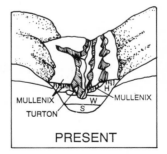

FIGURE 3.23. The evolution of small drainages in the Loess Hills of Iowa over the last 8000 years. The names of alluvial fills correspond to those mentioned in the text. (Modified from Thompson and Bettis 1982)

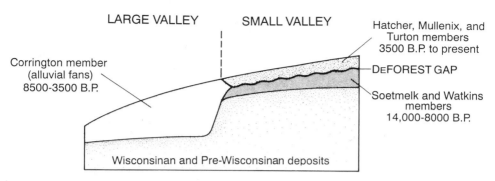

FIGURE 3.24. The temporal and spatial relationships of the DeForest formation. Note the DeForest Gap (unconformity), the position of alluvial units above and below this unconformity, and their relationship to the Corrington (alluvial fan) member. (Modified from Thompson and Bettis 1982)

accumulated downstream on alluvial fans where tributary streams joined larger rivers. The sediments comprising the alluvial fans are designated as the Corrington member. After 3500 B.P., deposition on the alluvial fans ceased. For the next 1500 years, the large gullies created during the middle Holocene erosional episode were filled with sediments of the Hatcher member (Fig. 3.23). Sometime between 2000 and 1800 B.P., gullies entrenched the Hatcher alluvium, and by approximately 1000 B.P. they had filled with alluvial sediments, designated the Mullenix member. The Mullenix alluvium was subject to yet another channel-cutting episode around 750 B.P., and by 250 B.P. the resulting channels had been filled with the Turton member alluvium. Modern gullies, created during the late nineteenth century, have cut into the older alluvial units of the DeForest formation. Historic alluvium, associated with the modern gullies, is designated the Camp Creek member.

Archaeological investigations of the tributary stream valleys show that sites dating to the late Archaic, Woodland, and later periods are buried in the post–3500-year-old Hatcher, Mullenix, and Turton alluvium, while no Paleoindian or early to middle Archaic sites are present (Paleoindian sites could potentially occur in the Watkins alluvium). Buried Paleoindian and early to middle Archaic sites occur only in the alluvial fan sediments of the Corrington member at the mouth of the tributary valleys. Later Archaic and Woodland sites occur on the surface of the fan.

The absence of early and middle Holocene archaeological remains from the tributary valleys of western Iowa and their presence in the alluvial fan sediments is the result of the erosion represented by the DeForest Gap (Fig. 3.24). Early archaeological remains, if originally present in the small tributary valleys, were eroded during the period of channel erosion and widening documented before 3500 B.P. The sediments eroded from the tributary valleys were transported to the channel terminus and deposited on the alluvial fans. Because the alluvial fans became the loci of deposition during the middle Holocene, sites dating between 8000 and 3500 B.P. became buried in the fan sediments and were subsequently preserved. Simultaneous erosion and deposition in different parts of the same fluvial system led to the differential preservation of middle Holocene sites. Likewise, because fan deposition ceased and the surface became stabilized after 3500 B.P., sites younger than 3500 B.P. are found on or near the surface of the alluvial fans, while sites of this age are buried in the Hatcher, Mullenix, and Turton alluvium in the small valleys.

Clearly, the archaeological record in western Iowa was shaped by the same processes that molded the landscape. As the alluvial environments changed through time, archaeological sites situated on the landscape were either destroyed by erosion or preserved through burial. Furthermore, because episodes of deposition, erosion, and stability from one end of the fluvial system to the other were not synchronous, there is differential preservation of Paleoindian and early to middle Archaic sites in the alluvial fan sediments and late Archaic and Woodland sites in the gully alluvium. This skews our understanding of how people used the landscape at different times.

Not only has the timing of cutting and filling episodes in the small tributary valleys dictated the preservation and destruction of remains from certain archaeological time periods, but repeated periods of gully formation during the late Holocene have also diminished the completeness of the archaeological record buried in the Hatcher and Mullenix alluvium. Each time the channel entrenched its floodplain and widened, it eroded and reworked alluvial sediments that had been deposited during previous periods of aggradation. Thus, an unknown number of late Archaic and Woodland sites in the Hatcher and Mullenix alluvium were partially or wholly removed by the erosion associated with later gully cutting. This has further fragmented the archaeological record.

Changes in the fluvial landscape also imposed limitations on the later discovery of preserved archaeological sites (Bettis and Benn 1984; Gladfelter 1985; Thompson and Bettis 1982). Many subsurface sites preserved through burial are not visible or detectable at the surface or in cut-bank exposures along the tributary channels. Archaeological remains in the Watkins member are deeply buried by up to 5 m of alluvium, and some late Archaic remains in the Holocene alluvium occur at depths of 4 m. Further, a thin layer of historic alluvium overlies the floodplains of the tributary streams and conceals late prehistoric archaeological sites. Thus, prehistoric sites are not visible on the surface of the floodplains but only in the channel bank exposures.

Even though some sites are visible in the cut banks, the majority of the valley fill of each stream is not entrenched and must surely contain archaeological sites. Therefore, an indeterminate number of undetected archaeological resources must lie beneath the vast portion of each undissected valley fill. Additionally, the depth of channel entrenchment is not uniform, and older sediments may not be exposed everywhere along the length of the channel or may be covered in places where there has been recent alluvial deposition or where banks have slumped.

Clearly, the archaeological record preserved in the alluvium of the small valleys of western Iowa does not accurately reflect the total universe of archaeological sites that once existed in these valleys through time. Instead the archaeological record reflects the biases of geologic preservation. These combined factors limit our knowledge and interpretation of the human prehistory of the region. By recognizing how fluvial processes have structured the archaeological sample, improved reconstructions of past human behavior are possible. Only when the alluvial history of deposition, erosion, and stability is reconstructed and their effects on the archaeological record are recognized will meaningful and comprehensive reconstructions of prehistoric human interaction with the alluvial environment be possible. Finally, this study provides the geologic framework for a site prediction model for the Loess Hills of western Iowa by defining the temporal and spatial distribution of cultural resources.

Alluvial Landscape Reconstruction

It is important to realize that the landscape setting of an archaeological site during excavation is not necessarily the setting of that site when it was occupied by prehistoric people. In many cases, alluvial processes and landscapes have changed significantly through time, as illustrated by the discussion of the alluvial valleys of western Iowa. Reconstructing the landscape setting of a site at the time of occupation and understanding how it has changed through time are necessary to interpreting site function and subsistence activities. Likewise, reconstructing the regional landscape setting of a group of sites at the time of occupation and understanding how the regional landscape changed through time are important to our understanding of site patterning.

Site-Specific Synchronic and Diachronic Alluvial Landscape Reconstruction

Site-specific synchronic landscape reconstructions place a site in its prehistoric landscape context by defining the fluvial processes and configuration of the environment at and adjacent to the site at the time of occupation. This type of reconstruction also helps to elucidate how and why a specific locality was used at a particular time.

Site-specific diachronic landscape reconstructions determine how the alluvial landscape at a specific locality changed through time and how these changes affected the use of that locality. In some cases, a site is occupied only when a specific environment or combination of environments is present, and the site may be used less frequently or abandoned when the landscape is disrupted. The objective of diachronic landscape reconstruction is to track the evolution of the fluvial landscape and concurrent changes in human behavior.

The value of site-specific synchronic and diachronic landscape reconstructions is illustrated by the geoarchaeological investigations at the Colby site in Wyoming and the Coffey site in Kansas. A list of additional site-specific synchronic and diachronic landscape reconstructions is given in Appendix B.

The Colby Site: A Site-Specific Synchronic Landscape Reconstruction

The paleoenvironmental reconstructions at the Colby site on the eastern side of the Bighorn Basin in Wyoming by John Albanese (1977, 1978a, 1978b, 1986) provide an excellent example of the need to place sites in their prehistoric landscape context in order to understand human behavior. At the Colby site the remains of seven mammoths were found in sediments containing Clovis projectile points and butchering tools (Frison and Todd 1986). Differential weathering of the mammoth bones indicated that the skeletal remains accumulated over an extended period rather than representing a single kill. From the distribution of bones, it also appeared that meat from some of these mammoths was stored in snowbanks during the winter. This evidence clearly indicated that mammoths were repeatedly attacked and butchered by Clovis hunters at the Colby site, but what do the sediments, soils, and stratigraphy at the Colby site reveal about the landscape at the time of the mammoth kills and the procedure Clovis hunters used to trap mammoths?

The Colby site is presently located on a tributary of Slick Creek. The bones and artifacts were recovered from alluvial sediments exposed in two erosional terraces along this tributary (Fig. 3.25). By examining the sediments and soils at the site, Albanese determined that the artifact-bearing

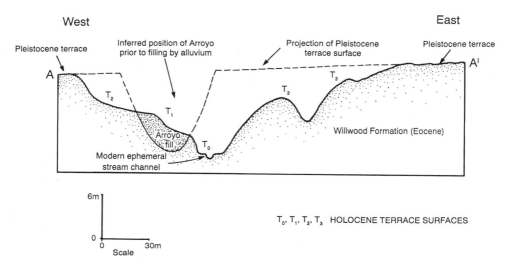

West   East

Pleistocene terrace   Inferred position of Arroyo   Projection of Pleistocene   Pleistocene terrace
                       prior to filling by alluvium   terrace surface

A   A'
         T_2 T_3
                           T_1 T_3

                    Arroyo   Willwood Formation (Eocene)
                     fill T_0
      Modern ephemeral
       stream channel

6m

                                        T_0, T_1, T_2, T_3 HOLOCENE TERRACE SURFACES
0
    0   30m
       Scale

FIGURE 3.25. The ancient and modern topography and stratigraphy at the Colby site in Wyoming. Note the presence of the 11,000-year-old arroyo fill that contained the mammoth and archaeological remains and its relationship to the modern channel and terraces. The position of the cross section is shown in Figure 3.26. (Modified from Albanese 1986)

alluvium had originally been deposited in the bottom of a paleoarroyo channel. Mapping these sediments showed that the paleoarroyo was approximately 0.8 km long and paralleled the course of the modern channel (Fig. 3.26). At the Colby site, this arroyo would have been about 12 m wide and 7.5 to 9 m deep. Downstream, the arroyo widened to about 60 m. Albanese concluded that at the time of the mammoth kills, 11,000 years ago, the site was situated at the head or upstream terminus of a deep arroyo three-quarters of a kilometer long. In a sense, the Colby site was a natural, steep-sided cul-de-sac.

Frison and Todd (1986) combined the landscape reconstruction with the archaeological and paleontological data into a holistic reconstruction of a Clovis hunting strategy. They suggest that Clovis hunters would ambush and wound a single mammoth and then drive it into the arroyo. The wounded animal fleeing the Clovis hunters would tire and become trapped at the head of the arroyo, where it could be easily killed. The presence of seven butchered mammoth carcasses suggests that this was a planned and patterned strategy that was repeatedly successful (Fig. 3.27).

Landscape reconstruction was crucial to proper interpretation of the

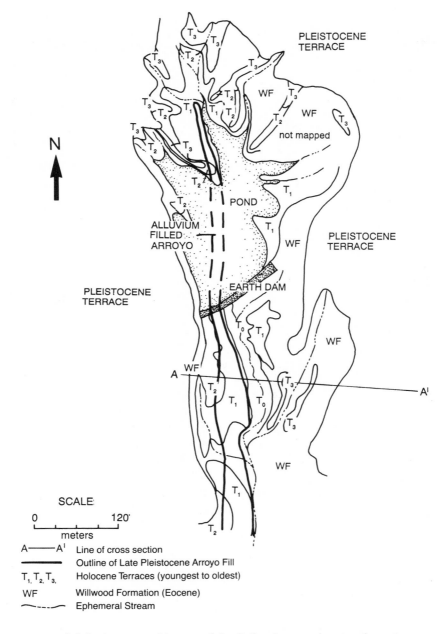

FIGURE 3.26. A geomorphic map of the Colby site area showing the major ter-
races and bedrock geology. Superimposed on the map is the position of the late
Pleistocene arroyo used to trap mammoths 11,000 years ago. (Modified from
Albanese 1986)

FIGURE 3.27. A pile of mammoth bones (bone pile no. 2) draping the steep east bank of the paleoarroyo at the Colby site. (Photograph by John P. Albanese)

Clovis hunting behavior at the Colby site. Reconstruction of the 11,000-year-old landscape illustrated that an arroyo existed and presented a natural trap that the Clovis hunters used many times. Without this important contribution, the understanding of the site would be far less precise.

The reconstruction of the prehistoric landscape at the Colby site also illustrates that there is no relationship between the modern channel topography and the position and appearance of the prehistoric arroyo (Figs. 3.25 and 3.26). The modern cut terraces did not exist during the time of the mammoth kills but developed later in the Holocene. Also, the modern channel is much broader than the paleoarroyo and has gently sloping banks rather than steep walls. The modern configuration of the landscape has evolved only within the last 1500 years and is considerably different from that occupied by the Clovis hunters.

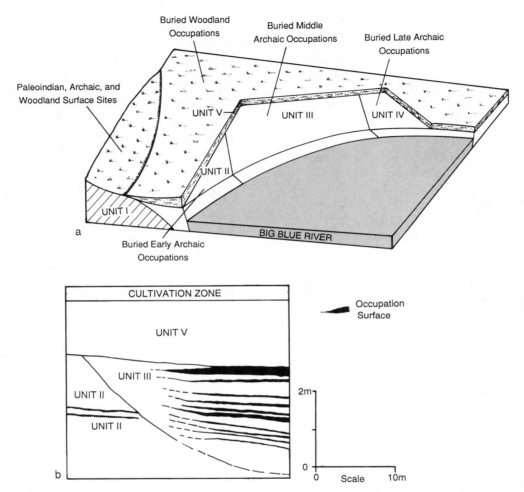

FIGURE 3.28. The Coffey site in Kansas: (a) the major stratigraphic units, and (b) detailed cross section through the older oxbow lake sediments (unit III) showing a number of the occupation surfaces within it. (Modified from Schmits 1978, 1980)

The Coffey Site: A Site-Specific Diachronic Landscape Reconstruction

A stratigraphic sequence of five major fluvial lithostratigraphic units is defined by Schmits (1978, 1980) at the Coffey site, which is situated adjacent to the meandering Big Blue River in northeastern Kansas. The stratigraphic sequence preserves evidence of environmental and topographic changes that occurred at the site through the Holocene, and the archaeological record shows how human activity correlates with these changes.

The alluvial sequence begins with the downcutting of the Big Blue River during the late Pleistocene, which resulted in the formation of a fill terrace (unit I in Fig. 3.28). During the Holocene, the terrace was repeatedly occupied, and Folsom, late Paleoindian, early through late Archaic, and Woodland artifacts have been found on the surface of its tread. The accumulation of artifacts on the terrace surface, covering 10,000 years of prehistory, indicates that it was a stable surface throughout the Holocene, undergoing neither deposition nor erosion. However, the floodplain below the terrace was dynamic and constantly changing.

Four alluvial lithostratigraphic units (labeled II through V in Fig. 3.28) were deposited on the newly created floodplain of the Big Blue River during the Holocene. The first Holocene deposition on the floodplain occurred around 6300 B.P. when laminated fine-grained sediments (unit II) were deposited during overbank flooding. These sediments became overlain by sands deposited in a natural levee and crevasse splay near the margin of a meandering paleochannel. Evidence of two Archaic period occupations are contained in these lower floodplain sediments. Shortly after 6000 B.P., the channel of the Big Blue River meandered into the site area and truncated unit II. An oxbow lake was created at the site when the meander loop was cut off from the main river channel and abandoned as the active channel migrated to the other side of the floodplain. Over the next 1000 years, the abandoned meander was periodically filled with sediment-laden water whenever the Big Blue River left the confines of its channel and inundated the floodplain. Sediments suspended in the floodwaters that filled the oxbow lake settled from suspension to create a laminated deposit of silt and clay (unit III). Between floods and when the water level of the lake was low, presumably due to drought, Archaic period hunters and gatherers established seasonal camps in the abandoned meander. These camps were situated adjacent to small ponds in the bottom of the channel on the mudflats that extended from the banks of the former paleochannel. Based on archaeobotanical and zooarchaeological investigations, this occupation occurred in the late summer or fall, when the lacustrine and surrounding floodplain resources were used. Twelve discrete occupation levels separated by alluvium with paleosols were discovered in the oxbow lake sediments. During this time, camps were also located on the stable terrace surface.

After filling of the oxbow lake by approximately 5000 B.P., the floodplain in the area of the site remained relatively stable until approximately 2500 B.P., when the river again meandered into the site area and truncated the older abandoned channel fill sediments (unit III). Again, a meander was abandoned by the main channel through neck cut-off to form a second oxbow lake. Late Archaic people used the newly created oxbow environment in a fashion similar to the way earlier Archaic people had used the older oxbow lake environment. A sequence of five discrete cultural levels was buried in the fine-grained sediments that filled the second oxbow (unit IV).

Decades or centuries after the channel meander became filled with unit IV, overbank flooding resulted in the accumulation of 2 m of fine-grained sediments (unit V) over the three older Holocene alluvial units. This floodplain was used by Woodland people, whose artifacts are found in and on the surface of the floodplain deposits. The modern Big Blue River has meandered onto the site again and has exposed the Holocene sediments, stratigraphy, and archaeology at the site in its cut bank.

Clearly, some portions of the landscape at the Coffey site remained stable while others changed. Throughout the Holocene a stable terrace was present, while the lower floodplain alternated between periods of stability and environmental change as the Big Blue River meandered across its valley. The various floodplain environments that were present at one time or another at the site included oxbow lakes, an aggrading floodplain, an open channel, and a natural levee and crevasse splay. In addition to the physical environment, landscape changes also affected the spatial location of floral and faunal communities on the floodplain and the human cultural systems adapted to these biotic communities. The greatest diversity of biotic resources occurred on the floodplain whenever the oxbow lakes existed. Correspondingly, this was the time of greatest human use of the Coffey site floodplain. After the oxbow lakes filled with sediments, the biotic resources declined and the floodplain at the Coffey site was no longer used as intensively. Archaic hunters and gatherers, who used the oxbow lake environments at the site as part of their subsistence base, probably shifted to other oxbows in the floodplain environment. When the oxbow lake environment and its associated biotic resources returned to the Coffey site, it was again intensively used.

Regional Synchronic and Diachronic Alluvial Landscape Reconstruction

Regional synchronic landscape reconstructions place a group of contemporaneous sites in their prehistoric landscape context. Comparing the regional settlement distribution for a particular period over the corresponding reconstruction of the regional landscape elucidates how a specific region was used at a particular time. These regional reconstructions help us to understand how the types and the distribution of fluvial processes and landforms affected the regional patterning of human settlements and activity loci.

Regional diachronic landscape reconstructions define how coexisting alluvial processes and landforms changed through time and how these changes influenced the use of that region. In practice, the landscape is reconstructed at a number of points in time that show the changing distribution of alluvial processes and landforms. Then diachronic archaeological settlement data are superimposed over the corresponding diachronic landscape reconstructions. Placing a sequence of settlements and activity loci in the context of an evolving regional landscape illuminates the dynamic relationship between the landscape and the people. These reconstructions provide the context necessary to evaluate the influence of the fluvial landscape on regional prehistoric settlement patterns and subsistence strategies through time.

The following examples from the Tucson Basin in Arizona and the Swan Lake Meander in Mississippi illustrate how regional synchronic and diachronic reconstructions of the fluvial landscape are used to enhance our understanding of human behavior. A list of additional regional synchronic and diachronic landscape reconstructions is given in Appendix C. Many of these studies are combined into wider human ecological syntheses.

Hohokam Settlements in the Tucson Basin: A Regional Synchronic and Diachronic Landscape Reconstruction

A group of agriculturalists known as the Hohokam occupied the semiarid Tucson Basin of southern Arizona from about A.D. 300 to 1500 (Haury 1976; Fish 1989; see Fig. 2.32). These prehistoric people used many different environments but depended heavily on the alluvial environments that dominate the Tucson Basin: the alluvial piedmonts (bajadas) that emanate from the surrounding mountains, and an arroyo, the Santa Cruz River, that traverses the axis of the Tucson Basin (Fig. 2.33). Both the locations of Hohokam settlements at any particular time and changes in settlement location through time were closely tied to the distribution of the fluvial systems, the evolution of these fluvial environments, and the farming potential of the ancient landscape (Waters 1991).

Hohokam farming settlements are commonly found on the bajadas fringing the Tucson Basin (Fig. 2.33). Regional archaeological surveys have shown that these sites are not randomly dispersed across the bajada but consistently occur in a particular zone (Fish 1989; Fish et al. 1985; Waters 1987b, 1987c; Waters and Field 1986). Before the prehistoric Hohokam settlement patterns can be deciphered, it is necessary to understand historic farming techniques used by the Native Americans in the Tucson Basin (historically called the Papago, they are now known as the Tohono O'odham).

In this semiarid basin, rainfall is sporadic and is unevenly distributed over a wide area. Historic Indian groups knew that the moisture provided to fields by direct rainfall was inadequate for crops to mature on a reliable basis and thus to sustain a sedentary population. Additional and more reli-

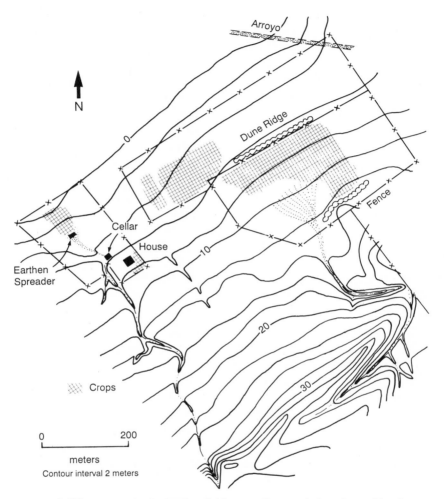

FIGURE 3.29. Two typical Ak-Chin fields on gully-mouth fans farmed by the Hopi in the Talahogan Valley in Arizona. Note that the house is located slightly above the intersection point of the gully. (Modified from Hack 1942)

able sources of moisture were required for successful farming. Consequently, historic peoples farmed areas on the bajadas that were naturally flooded on a regular basis. The areas most often farmed by the Tohono O'odham were the fan environments at the terminus of ephemeral gullies on the bajadas (Figs. 3.18 and 3.29; see also Bryan 1929b; Castetter and Bell 1942; Hack 1942; Nabhan 1979, 1986a, 1986b). These gully-mouth fan surfaces were especially desirable for farming because the runoff generated by rainfall in any part of the watershed, even kilometers away from the fan, would be funneled into the main gully channel and would eventually make its way to fields on the fan surface. The fans are called Ak-Chin, a Tohono O'odham term for an arroyo mouth (Bryan 1929b; Hack 1942; Nabhan 1986a). They required little or no modification to direct the streamflow, except perhaps brush or rock structures to slow and spread the water over a broader area.

By reconstructing the paleolandscape of several bajadas, delineating stable Pleistocene alluvial fan surfaces and late Holocene gully and gully-mouth fan environments, and comparing this to the distribution of Hoho-kam settlements, researchers discovered that Hohokam settlements were consistently situated in areas dominated by gully-mouth fans (the prehistoric environment that was optimal for floodwater farming), not in areas domi-nated by gully channels (Fig. 3.30; Waters 1987b, 1987c; Waters and Field 1986). This site distribution is analogous to the position of historic sites where Ak-Chin farming was pursued. The correspondence between the posi-tion of Hohokam agricultural settlements and gully-mouth fans becomes clearer when the bajada environment is understood in the context of other landscape elements.

Near Marana, Arizona, large habitation sites are concentrated in areas dominated by gully-mouth fan environments on the lower bajada (Fish 1989; Waters 1987b; Waters and Field 1986). Habitation sites are not pres-ent on the stable Pleistocene surfaces. Instead, these areas were used for gathering wild plant resources and growing agave (a plant with minimal moisture and soil requirements; Fish 1989; Fish et al. 1985). A regional archaeological survey of 1650 km^2 in the vicinity of Marana and com-plementary geomorphic mapping shows that the lower bajada alluvial sur-faces conducive to floodwater farming make up only 23.5% of the total alluvial landscape (all Pleistocene and Holocene surfaces) but are the loci of 56.3% of the Hohokam sites (Field and Lombard 1987). This is more than would be expected by chance. Thus, if we note the analogy with the historic Ak-Chin floodwater farming technique, the strong correspondence between Hohokam settlements and the distribution of late Holocene gully-mouth fans, and the avoidance of areas dominated by channelized flow, it is clear that the prehistoric Hohokam farmers preferred to locate their settlements on the bajada in those areas well suited to floodwater Ak-Chin farming. At the time of occupation, Hohokam sites were probably located slightly above the intersection point (the junction of the gully channel and the fan head), and farming was pursued on both the distal and proximal gully-mouth fan surfaces (Figs. 3.18 and 3.29).

Not all bajadas were used equally, nor were settlements evenly distrib-

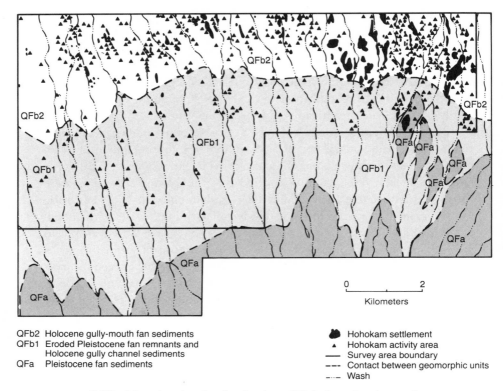

QFb2 Holocene gully-mouth fan sediments
QFb1 Eroded Pleistocene fan remnants and
      Holocene gully channel sediments
QFa   Pleistocene fan sediments

🐾 Hohokam settlement
▲ Hohokam activity area
— Survey area boundary
--- Contact between geomorphic units
-·-· Wash

FIGURE 3.30. Map showing the distribution of Hohokam farming settlements superimposed on the geomorphology of the bajada emanating from the north side of the Sierrita Mountains in Arizona (see Fig. 2.33). Note that most sites are situated in the lower portion of the bajada, which is dominated by gully-mouth fan environments where Ak-Chin farming could be easily pursued. Only limited-activity areas occur above these areas in the environments dominated by entrenched gullies. (Modified from Waters 1987c)

uted over a single bajada. Other factors, especially the nature and thickness of the sediments comprising the gully-mouth fan, the fan slope (Dart 1987), the substrate underlying it, and drainage basin characteristics (e.g., size, the distance from the drainage basin to the fan field, and the hillslope composition) made some areas better suited for farming than others and thus affected the location of agricultural settlements. In general, the optimal areas, characterized by soils with strong water-holding and water-availability characteristics and desirable drainage basin features (e.g., basins of small size with impermeable slopes that are located a short distance from fields) were used heavily, while less-desirable areas on the bajada were used only marginally.

Ak-Chin fields do not occupy fixed locations on the bajada and would have been abandoned frequently because of the migration of headcuts through the fan surfaces. The entrenchment of a fan destroyed the usefulness of a field by channelizing the former sheetflow. When this occurred, old fields were abandoned and new ones were selected for planting. This shifting occurred on a small scale, displacing fields and settlements on the order of tens or hundreds of meters across the bajada surface. As a consequence, Hohokam settlements appear concentrated around the same position on the bajada through time and became buried as the gullies shifted position.

Ak-Chin farming appears to have been widely used by the Tucson Basin Hohokam, as evidenced by the numerous bajada-Hohokam associations. Furthermore, this agricultural strategy appears to have been long-lived, as it was practiced from the Pioneer through the Classic periods (ca. A.D. 300–1500).

The Santa Cruz River floodplain was also heavily used by the Hohokam. Changes in the landscape and hydrologic conditions on the floodplain influenced the position of Hohokam settlements and agricultural strategies. This is well illustrated along the 15 km segment of the Santa Cruz arroyo traversing the San Xavier Indian Reservation south of Tucson. Here, the location of settlements is well documented for six separate Hohokam phases dating between A.D. 800 and 1500 (Doelle et al. 1985). The geomorphic history of the landscape is also well established (Haynes and Huckell 1986; Waters 1987a, 1988a, 1988b). When the settlement patterns are superimposed over the corresponding landscape reconstructions, it becomes clear that the changing configuration of the floodplain influenced prehistoric Hohokam use of the riverine environment (Fig. 3.31).

Prior to the Rillito phase, the channel of the Santa Cruz River was entrenched around 50 B.C. Over the next 1000 years the channel filled with alluvium, and by A.D. 950 the floodplain had stabilized. The last 150 years of aggradation, from A.D. 800 to 950, coincided with the Rillito phase, when settlement was characterized by occupation at five primary villages and a number of hamlets on the western side of the floodplain. Floodplain stability continued into the early Rincon subphase (A.D. 950–1000), and the settlement pattern closely resembles that during the Rillito phase, but the number of hamlets and the intensity of occupation at primary villages increased. The floodplain during both the Rillito and early Rincon was characterized by a broad, sandy surface that was probably traversed by a shallow channel or draw. Discharge across most of the floodplain would have been ephemeral; however, small isolated seeps may have been present. This environment was well suited to floodwater farming. Crops could have

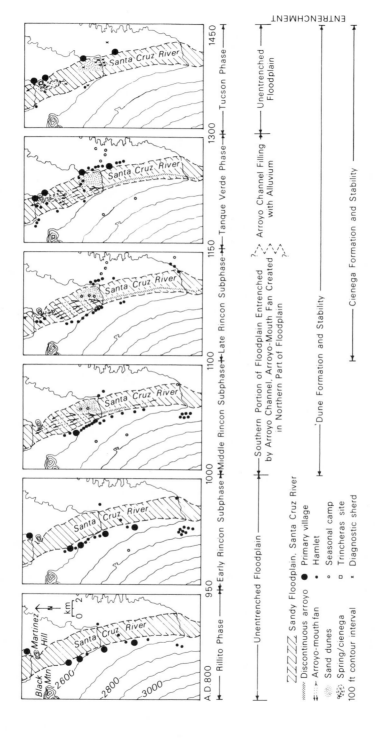

FIGURE 3.31. Landscape changes along the San Xavier reach of the Santa Cruz River in Arizona from A.D. 800 to 1450 and their effect on Hohokam settlement patterns. (Modified from Waters 1988b)

been planted on the floodplain, where they would have been watered during overbank flows, and along the margin of the floodplain, where gullies draining the bajada emptied out onto the floodplain. Villages were located immediately adjacent to the floodplain next to major washes entering it but above areas of active flooding. Additional floodwater Ak-Chin farming could have been pursued on the gully-mouth fans on the bajada to the west.

At the beginning of the middle Rincon subphase (A.D. 1000–1100), arroyo cutting occurred in the central portion of the floodplain and extended southward. Channel entrenchment led concurrently to the formation of an arroyo-mouth fan and sand dunes to the north. Thus the arroyo destroyed arable land in the south but in the process created arable land to the north. Ak-Chin farming was possible on the gully-mouth fan, and dry farming on the sand dunes. These landscape changes appear to have triggered settlement reorganization. During the middle Rincon, the number of primary villages decreased from five to one, and settlements generally shifted northward. A second entrenchment episode during the late Rincon subphase (A.D. 1100 to 1150) resulting in the formation of a cienega (spring-fed marsh) in the northern part of the floodplain. Also, the arroyo in the southern portion of the floodplain continued to destroy arable land to the south. Correspondingly, Hohokam settlements shifted to the northern and eastern edges of the floodplain.

During the subsequent Tanque Verde phase (A.D. 1150–1300), the landscape remained much like that of the previous 150 years. The cienega expanded and stabilized, and the arroyo channel in the southern portion of the floodplain began to backfill. During this time the number of settlements continued to decline on the western side and increase on the eastern side of the floodplain. New primary villages were established around Martinez Hill and the dune complex, and the number of hamlets also increased.

The settlement shift to the northern and eastern sides of the floodplain, completed by the Tanque Verde phase, appears to have been a response to the destruction of arable land in the southern and western parts of the floodplain and the creation of environments suitable for farming to the north. Major villages were established next to the cienega and the sand dunes, and smaller sites occurred around and within these two environments, which represented the optimal areas for farming in the newly created landscape. Water could have been drawn from the cienega to fields situated on its margin, and dry farming could have been pursued on the sand dunes. Floodwater farming could have been conducted on the gully-mouth fan and along the undissected portions of the floodplain-bajada interface on the eastern side of the floodplain. Clearly, the unentrenched northern and eastern portions of the floodplain offered favorable agricultural conditions.

By the beginning of the Tucson phase (A.D. 1300–1450), the arroyo had filled with alluvium, and the floodplain was no longer entrenched, while the cienega and sand dune environments remained. The population appears to have concentrated into the primary villages established during the Tanque Verde phase. A few small sites are present, and diagnostic sherds of the Tucson phase are found on activity loci on the floodplain.

Major entrenchment of the Santa Cruz floodplain followed the Tucson phase around A.D. 1450. This widespread environmental degradation would have again rendered the floodplain unfarmable, and following the entrenchment, the large primary villages were abandoned. Occupation is not documented along the San Xavier reach of the Santa Cruz River until sometime after A.D. 1650 (Ravesloot 1987), by which time the arroyo channel was largely filled.

From this we can see that the landscape of the San Xavier reach of the Santa Cruz River changed dramatically during the period of Hohokam occupation and clearly influenced Hohokam settlement patterns. In addition to landscape changes, social factors may account for some of the observed patterns (Doelle et al. 1985; Ellis and Waters 1991). However, the adverse effect of the channel entrenchment on floodplain farming and the emergence of the cienega, arroyo fan, and sand dune environments as alternative locations for agriculture were probably the most important factors responsible for the disruption of settlement stability.

Some of the changes on the Santa Cruz River floodplain may have been triggered by human activity. An examination of the alluvial record for the last 7000 years reveals a striking increase in the frequency of floodplain entrenchment during Hohokam use of the San Xavier reach. Over the 500-year period between A.D. 950 and 1450, the floodplain was entrenched twice. In contrast, during the preceding 7000 years the floodplain had been entrenched only three times (Haynes and Huckell 1986; Waters 1988a).

The entrenchment of the Santa Cruz River floodplain prior to agricultural activity is attributed to the creation of repeated unstable internal geomorphic threshold conditions and flooding (Waters 1988b). Sediment deposition on the floodplain oversteepened particular reaches of the floodplain and made them very susceptible to entrenchment. These unstable segments of the floodplain became gullied during flooding. The introduction of historic and prehistoric agriculture to the floodplain appears to have been a major factor leading to the increased frequency of arroyo cutting.

The historic Santa Cruz River channel, which is approximately 80 km long and 6 to 8 m deep in places (Fig. 3.19), was created by a combination of the development of unstable geomorphic threshold conditions, flooding, and human modification of the floodplain (Cooke and Reeves 1976). In the late 1800s, two farmers dug small ditches in oversteepened areas of the floodplain. Following intense flooding a few years later, these ditches enlarged, connected, and subsequently became the channel of the Santa Cruz River. Similarly, the Hohokam agriculturalists, much like their historic counterparts, modified the landscape. They probably cleared natural vegetation from fields on the floodplain, concentrated the runoff from drainages on the bajada to the edge of the floodplain, collected undergrowth and deadfall from mesquite thickets for firewood, created well-worn compacted paths across the floodplain, and perhaps constructed small diversion structures, short canals, and ditches on the floodplain. All of these modifications would have unintentionally made the ground more susceptible to erosion. The disturbed areas and ditches may have served as loci for erosion and entrenchment. Based on the historic analogy, prehistoric ditches may have expanded during floods to become the paleoarroyos visible in the alluvial record. Although there is no direct evidence to support the hypothesis that human actions on the floodplain resulted in entrenchment, the temporal correlation between the occupation of the Santa Cruz River by the Hohokam agriculturalists and the increased frequency of floodplain entrenchment is striking. It appears that the Hohokam agriculturalists may have made the same mistakes that historic farmers made in the late nineteenth century.

The Swan Lake Meander: A Regional Diachronic Landscape Reconstruction

A scenario for settlement pattern changes along the Swan Lake meander, an abandoned channel segment in the active meander belt of the Mississippi River in west central Mississippi, has been proposed on the basis of geological and archaeological studies (Weinstein 1981; Weinstein, Glander et al. 1979). During the last 2500 years, the Swan Lake meander evolved from an active segment of the Mississippi River to an oxbow lake that eventually filled with sediment. During its evolution, both the aquatic biotic resources (reptiles, mollusks, fish, plants, and birds) and the terrestrial biotic resources (plants and mammals) also changed, which influenced the position of human settlements along the meander. Figure 3.32 illustrates the sequential geomorphic changes along the Swan Lake meander, the documented settlement patterns, and the inferred habitats for six archaeological periods.

Prior to A.D. 1 the Swan Lake meander was part of the active Mississippi River. The cut bank of this open channel meandered northward, while the upstream and downstream reaches of the channel on either side of the point bar eroded the interfluve separating them. No prehistoric occupation

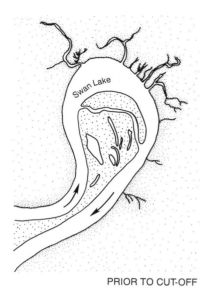

PRIOR TO CUT-OFF

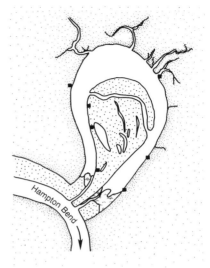

MARKSVILLE

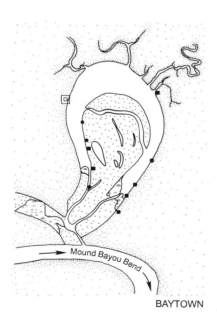

BAYTOWN

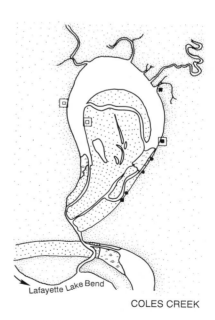

COLES CREEK

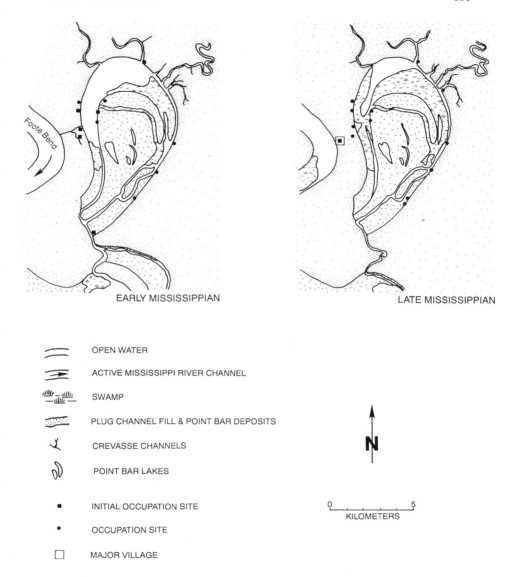

EARLY MISSISSIPPIAN

LATE MISSISSIPPIAN

OPEN WATER

ACTIVE MISSISSIPPI RIVER CHANNEL

SWAMP

PLUG CHANNEL FILL & POINT BAR DEPOSITS

CREVASSE CHANNELS

POINT BAR LAKES

INITIAL OCCUPATION SITE

OCCUPATION SITE

MAJOR VILLAGE

N

0   5
KILOMETERS

FIGURE 3.32. The evolution of the Swan Lake meander of the Mississippi River in west central Mississippi during the last 2000 years, and corresponding changes in settlement location. (Modified from Weinstein 1981)

was associated with this stage of meander development because active riverine processes and low habitat diversity probably made the banks of the river less desirable for occupation than other areas in the floodplain.

By about A.D. 1 the interfluve that separated the active channel on either side of the point bar had been breached by neck cut-off and the Swan Lake meander had been abandoned. Sand and gravel plugged the ends of the channel, creating an oxbow lake. This setting was characterized by a number of different habitats (lacustrine, swamp, and riparian environments around the oxbow and the open channel of the adjacent Mississippi River) that offered diverse resources to prehistoric people. As a result, seven hamlets were established around the edge of the oxbow lake and on the abandoned point bar of the old channel during the Marksville period, between A.D. 1 and 400. These sites were situated near the arms of the old meander, where environments were most diverse and where there was easy access to the active river channel (Hampton Bend).

During the subsequent Baytown period, between A.D. 400 and 700, the Swan Lake oxbow became a desirable site for habitation. Five new hamlets were established, and occupation continued at all but one of the original Marksville period sites. One of these sites expanded into a major village. During this period the Mississippi River abandoned the Hampton Bend and began to flow through the Mound Bayou Bend. The Swan Lake oxbow continued to receive fresh water from the Mississippi River during episodes of overbank flooding, which replenished oxygen in the lake and allowed aquatic life to flourish. Sediment deposited during these floods continued to plug the southern portion of the lake and created more land and swamp, thereby decreasing the size of the oxbow lake. These changes produced even more diverse habitats. The expansion of settlements in the region was probably due to the greater productivity of the entire system, a result of increased natural productivity of the area coupled with the probable pursuit of limited maize agriculture on the old point bar and natural levees.

Environmental conditions were probably similar during the succeeding Coles Creek period, from A.D. 700 to 1000. During this interval the southern portion of the Swan Lake oxbow continued to fill, Mound Bayou Bend was abandoned, and Lafayette Lake Bend became the new course of the Mississippi River. The resource-rich natural environment, coupled with agriculture on the natural levees and the point bar, supported a more intensive occupation than during the preceding period. Intensive Cole Creek period occupation is documented by the presence of three major villages and five hamlets.

During the following Mississippian period, from A.D. 1000 to 1700, the intensity and nature of the occupation around the Swan Lake meander changed as the oxbow environment evolved. These settlement changes coincided with the deterioration of the environments on the eastern side of the meander as the oxbow lake filled with sediment and became isolated from the active river, which was flowing to the west through the Foote Bend. Also, a crevasse splay developed from the active channel of the Mississippi River (Foote Bend) and extended to the western side of the oxbow. Overbank flooding associated with the crevasse splay environment provided fresh water to the constricted oxbow lake. As a result of these landscape changes, the western side of the Swan Lake meander became the preferred locus of habitation during the early Mississippian period. Some new hamlets were established, and the remaining villages shrank to hamlets. Some of the new sites established during this period were located directly on the banks of the crevasse channel and on the surface of the splay, which offered a dry land connection between the oxbow lake and the freshwater resources of the active channel. Weinstein postulates that had the crevasse splay not developed, the site area might have been abandoned. By late Mississippian times, no new settlements were being established around the Swan Lake meander, and the intensity of occupation at the remaining sites had declined. During this period the Mississippi River migrated away from the site area, the Foote Bend became an abandoned-channel oxbow lake, and the Swan Lake oxbow was almost completely filled with sediment or covered with swamp. The sites around the Swan Lake oxbow at this time were probably small camps visited to procure biotic resources in the swamp. The people who had once occupied the Swan Lake meander probably moved to more recently created oxbow lakes, where more desirable conditions existed. In fact, a new village site was established adjacent to the abandoned Foote Bend meander. In short, the settlement patterns and subsistence activities around the Swan Lake meander over the last 2000 years appear to have been controlled in large part by changes in the riverine landscape and the biotic environment.

Conclusion

Alluvial environments are dynamic and constantly changing. Because of this, the archaeological record contained within them is severely fragmented. This concept is important to consider for the proper interpretation of a site or regional settlement system. Reconstructing alluvial landscapes is also important because there is a direct relationship between alluvial landscapes and human activity. The choice of settlement location and changes in activity and settlement loci are strongly influenced by changes in the landscape. Finally, not only does the landscape affect people, but people also affect the landscape. The introduction of agriculture to a floodplain may cause erosion or trigger some other change. In short, understanding the archaeological record and properly reconstructing prehistoric human behavior associated with alluvial environments require geoarchaeological investigations of the alluvial landscape.

4

Eolian Environments

Eolian deposits and landforms are created by the erosion, transport, and deposition of sediment by the wind. Eolian processes and deposits may bury archaeological remains or erode them from preexisting contexts. Further, the configuration of eolian landscapes influenced prehistoric use of these environments. The summary of the major eolian processes, deposits, and landforms in the first part of this chapter is based on Ahlbrandt and Fryberger 1982, Bagnold 1954, Blatt et al. 1972, Boggs 1987, Brookfield 1984, Butzer 1976, Chorley et al. 1985, Collinson 1986b, Cooke and Warren 1973, R. A. Davis 1983, Friedman and Sanders 1978, Galloway and Hobday 1983, Greeley and Iversen 1985, Leeder 1982, McKee 1979, Péwé 1981, Pye 1987, Reineck and Singh 1980, Ritter 1986, and Ruhe 1975.

Sediment Erosion, Transport, and Deposition

In any region, regardless of its climate, wind may erode, transport, and deposit sediment where (1) there is a source of unconsolidated sediment that is available for transport, (2) the wind is strong enough to mobilize and transport sediment particles, and (3) there is no vegetation or other obstacles to protect the ground surface and inhibit wind erosion. Eolian processes and landforms most commonly occur in arid and semiarid deserts, where these three conditions often coincide. Eolian activity may take place in humid regions, but there it is generally confined to beach and riverine settings, where large amounts of erodible sediment are present and winds are locally strong.

Wind is the driving force behind the entrainment and transport of sediment particles. The most important wind attributes are velocity, direction, and turbulence. Wind velocity determines which particles move and which remain stationary. Direction is responsible for the formation and preservation of bedforms, while the degree of turbulence, especially the presence of spiraling currents (eddies), affects the erosion of grains and the shape of eolian landforms.

Much like the fluvial environment, particle movement in an eolian setting begins when the critical fluid threshold velocity is reached. This varies according to the size of the particle (Fig. 4.1). Particles with a diameter between 0.1 and 0.84 mm are the most easily entrained. High fluid threshold velocities are needed to entrain particles with a diameter of less than 0.1 mm because they are very cohesive, and individual grains or aggregates of smaller grains larger than 0.84 mm are difficult to move because of their weight and generally represent the upper limit of unaided entrainment. Entrainment is impeded in the natural environment by such variables as the amount and type of vegetation on the surface, sediment moisture content, the degree of cementation binding the grains, and sediment compaction.

Once particle motion is initiated, sediment entrainment can occur at lower velocities. This reduced velocity is called the impact threshold, which is reached when falling airborne particles strike stationary grains on the surface and set them into motion. This process permits particles larger than 0.84 mm to become entrained even though the velocity of the wind is not by itself strong enough to initiate grain movement.

Once particles are set in motion, they are transported by the wind in suspension, by saltation, or by surface creep, depending on the size of the clastic sediment particles (Fig. 4.2). Saltation is the process by which fine- to medium-size sand grains move downwind by hopping or skipping along the ground. At some point after a grain becomes airborne, the free-fall velocity of the grain exceeds the velocity of the wind, and the grain falls and collides with the ground. Upon impact, the grain rebounds or sets other particles into motion. Usually the bulk of the saltating load is concentrated in a one-meter zone above the ground. Saltation is the dominant mechanism by which the wind transports sediment.

Up to 25% of the load never becomes airborne but moves by surface creep. Creep occurs when saltating grains strike the surface and roll or shove heavier particles without displacing them vertically. This is the dominant mechanism responsible for the movement of coarse sand and granules.

Silt and clay particles are transported in suspension. These fine-grained sediments are launched into the air by the impact of saltating grains and are then buoyed to great heights by wind turbulence. Because of their small free-fall velocities, suspended sediments are transported great distances before settling.

Sediments transported by the wind are eventually deposited in a variety of forms downwind from the source area. Silt and clay accumulate to form

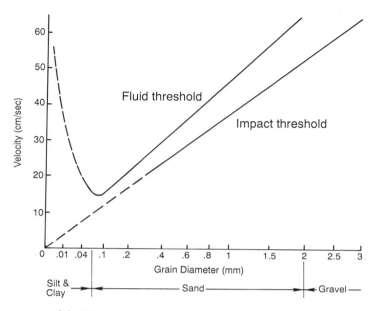

FIGURE 4.1. The relationship between particle size and wind velocity. The fluid threshold velocity is the minimum wind speed necessary to initiate grain movement by the force of the wind alone. The impact threshold velocity is the minimum wind speed needed to initiate particle movement as a result of grain impact. Deposition occurs when wind velocity drops below the impact threshold velocity.

blanketlike deposits known as loess or dust that mantle the preexisting topography. Sand is generally concentrated into dune fields, and gravel, which cannot be transported by the wind, remains at the source area, forming a lag pavement. Thus wind is an effective sorting agent that can winnow a preexisting mixed-grain-size deposit and separate it into well-sorted accumulations of gravel, sand, and silt and clay.

Sand Dunes

Sand dunes are the most common eolian landforms. A dune is an accumulation of wind-blown sand that develops an equilibrium profile characterized by a gently sloping (10°–15°) windward surface called the backslope, a crest, and a steeply dipping (30°–35°) slipface on the leeward side of the dune (Fig. 4.3).

Dunes usually originate around a topographic irregularity or obstruction, such as a bush or a channel bank, where wind velocity decreases and sand begins to accumulate. Slowly the patch of sand grows into a mound and develops a slipface. Once formed, dunes generally migrate downwind unless they are stabilized by vegetation. The movement of sand dunes creates two distinctive types of deposits: avalanche deposits and accretion deposits.

Avalanche deposits develop on the steeply inclined slipface as sand grains move up the backslope of the dune by saltation and surface creep and accumulate on the crest of the dune. Eventually the upper portion of the slipface becomes oversteepened (i.e., the angle of repose exceeds 35°) and a mass of sand avalanches down the slipface, creating a tongue-shaped deposit. The entire length of the slipface is not uniformly avalanched at a single time. Instead, only a part of the slipface avalanches at any time. Repeated avalanching creates a superimposed sequence of inclined avalanche tongues, which are reworked into steeply dipping cross-beds by oblique and longitudinal winds along the slipface. Individual cross-beds dip downwind at angles between 30° and 34° and are usually 1 to 5 cm thick.

Cross-stratified avalanche deposits with a similar orientation are combined into larger units called sets, which are typically 1 to 2 m thick. Sets of cross-strata are separated by erosional contacts or bounding surfaces. Bounding surfaces are created when older dune deposits are eroded and a beveled surface is created and subsequently buried. This occurs as a result of local fluctuations in wind direction and strength, as well as by changes in dune configuration. Steep bounding surfaces, dipping 15° to 25° in a downwind direction, occur near the slipface. In the upper part of the dune body, bounding surfaces are roughly horizontal or dip upwind at low angles.

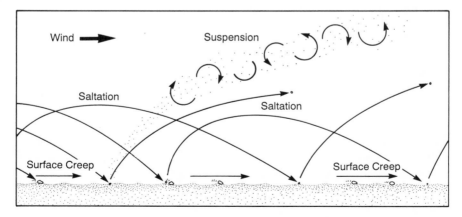

FIGURE 4.2. The wind-borne transport of sediment particles by suspension, saltation, and surface creep.

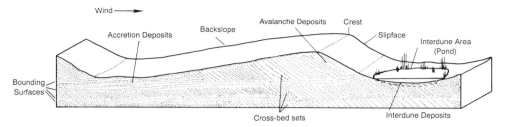

FIGURE 4.3. A cross section showing the typical morphology and internal structure of a sand dune. (Modified from Ahlbrandt et al. 1978)

Accretion deposits form on the gentle windward dune slope. These sediments are characterized by thin (1–4 mm) laminae of sand that are horizontal or that dip 1° to 3° upwind. These deposits are created whenever more grains come to rest on the windward slope than are entrained by saltation.

Small ripples, generally a few centimeters in height, are commonly superimposed on sand dunes. The most common are impact ripples, which are created when the sandy surface of a dune is bombarded by saltating grains. As a result of the bombardment, elongate hollows are eroded and sand particles are displaced downwind into ridges. Both the hollows and the ridges lie transverse to the dominant wind direction. Consequently, small-scale ripple cross-stratification may be present in a dune sequence. Ripple laminations are created as ripples migrate over the dune surface and accrete over one another.

Small-scale deformation structures—such as contorted bedding, folds, and small-scale faults—are common in eolian sand deposits. Disturbance by plants and animals is also common, and in many cases it obliterates stratification and creates a homogeneous mass of mixed sediments.

Classification of Sand Dunes

Dunes develop varied morphologies depending on the direction and strength of the prevailing wind, the size and supply of sand, and the characteristics of the surface over which the sand is deposited (especially the presence or absence of vegetation and relief). Many classifications of dunes have been proposed, but McKee's (1979) morphological classification is the most widely used. McKee defines several dune types based on the morphology of the dune and the number and position of the slipfaces (Fig. 4.4). McKee's dune types represent ideal members within a broad continuum of morphologies.

Sand dunes may occur as solitary landforms isolated from one another, or they may occur together in colonies. Also, when two or more dunes of the

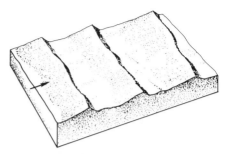

Transverse dunes

Dome dunes

FIGURE 4.4. Basic eolian dune
forms as defined by McKee. Arrows
indicate the direction of wind move-
ment. (Modified from McKee 1979)   Blowout dunes

same type but of different size become superimposed (e.g., a small barchan
on a large barchan), compound dunes are created. When two or more dune
types overlap, they are known as complex dunes (e.g., a star dune on top of
a transverse dune).

Barchan Dunes

A barchan dune is a crescent-shaped ridge of sand with its extremities or
"horns," pointed downwind (Fig. 4.4). Barchans form in areas where there
is a strong unidirectional wind, where the supply of sand available for trans-

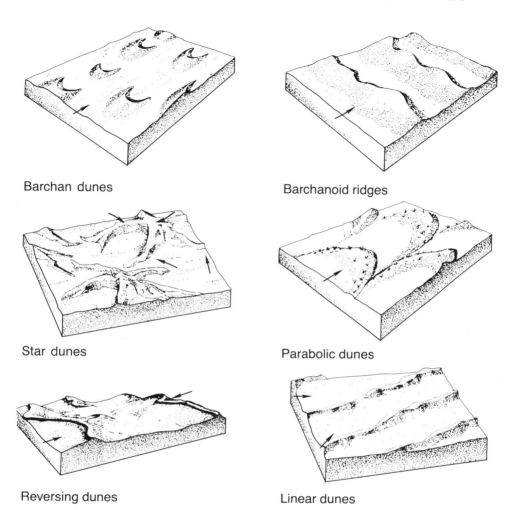

Barchan dunes

Barchanoid ridges

Star dunes

Parabolic dunes

Reversing dunes

Linear dunes

port from the source area is limited, and where the landscape is sparsely vegetated. Because of the strong unidirectional wind, barchans develop a single slipface in the central portion of the dune. Sediments that accumulate on the slipface produce an internal structure characterized by planar cross-beds that are inclined downwind at angles greater than 30°. The sand making up the horns of the dune generally dips less than 30° at right angles to the dominant wind direction. Barchan dunes migrate downwind and maintain their characteristic crescent shape because the horns in front of the main body of the dune migrate downwind more rapidly than the central body of the dune. Barchans may occur as single isolated dunes, linked together in chains, or they may coalesce into a large dune field. If individual dunes merge and form parallel wavy ridges, they are known as barchanoid dunes.

Transverse Dunes

Transverse dunes are straight, elongate ridges of sand oriented perpendicular to a strong unidirectional wind. Transverse dunes have a single slipface and form in areas where vegetation is absent and where there is an abundant supply of sand. These sand ridges are usually regularly spaced and separated by broad interdune areas. Internally, transverse dunes are characterized by high-angle cross-beds that dip downwind.

Star Dunes

Star dunes are isolated hills of sand characterized by three or more ridges of unconsolidated sand that radiate from a high central peak. Star dunes develop in areas where the wind blows from several different directions. As a result, multiple slipfaces are created, and the dune tends to accumulate vertically rather than migrating laterally. The internal structure of star dunes is complex and is characterized by sets of high-angle cross-beds that dip in multiple directions.

Parabolic Dunes

Parabolic dunes are crescent-shaped ridges of sand with their extremities, or "horns," oriented upwind. These dunes develop in a unidirectional wind regime through the modification of preexisting dunes. The characteristic parabolic shape is produced where the ends of a transverse or barchan dune are anchored by vegetation and the middle part of the dune advances downwind with respect to the arms. The central migrating part of the dune develops a single downwind slipface. This generates intermediate-angle cross-bedding, often with organic matter accumulated along the bedding planes.

Dome Dunes

Dome dunes are isolated circular or elliptical mounds of sand with no downwind slipface. Dome dunes originate where strong winds bevel the top of a preexisting barchan dune and inhibit its upward growth. In coastal regions, moisture and vegetation are important in the stabilization and development of dome dunes. The internal structure of the dune is characterized by a barchan core with steeply inclined slipface deposits oriented in a single direction. The eroded barchan core is overlain by flat-lying sediments that grade into low-angle foreset beds that dip downwind in all directions.

Reversing Dunes

Reversing dunes are formed in areas characterized by seasonal changes in the dominant wind direction. Responding to these changes, reversing dunes migrate short distances in one direction and then advance in the opposite direction. Because one wind direction usually dominates over the other, it molds the general morphology of the dune. Reversing dunes look roughly like barchan or transverse dunes, but in response to the seasonally shifting winds, reversing dunes differ from them in developing a seasonal slipface in the direction opposite to that of the primary slipface. The deposition of sand on two opposite slipfaces results in a complex internal structure dominated by high-angle foreset laminations oriented in opposite directions.

Linear Dunes

Linear dunes (also known as longitudinal or sief dunes) are straight to sinuous elongated ridges of sand oriented parallel to the prevailing wind direction. These dunes usually occur together in a series of long parallel rows, with broad interdune areas separating individual dune ridges. Longitudinal dunes are formed and maintained by a strong uniform wind direction and spiral wind cells or eddies that flow parallel to the axis of the dune on either side of the dune crest. Deposition occurs on slipfaces that develop on both sides of the dune crest. Consequently, two sets of high-angle cross-beds develop that dip at right angles to the dune axis.

Blowouts

A blowout is a circular, craterlike depression in sand that is stabilized by plants, moisture, or both. Typically, blowouts are created where the vegetation cover in a stabilized dune field is disturbed and a vegetation-free surface is exposed to wind erosion. Sand is scoured from the surface, and a depression is excavated by the wind. The sand eroded from the depression accumulates downwind on the margin of the crater. The blowout continues to enlarge until it becomes stabilized by renewed plant growth, which inhibits further erosion and expansion of the depression. Consequently, blowouts vary widely in size and shape.

Topographic Dunes

A variety of dune types, collectively categorized as topographic dunes, form where wind laden with sediment encounters an obstacle (e.g., a bush, a cliff, or a channel bank). Properties such as the height, width, shape, and orientation of the obstacle are important to the morphology of a topographic dune.

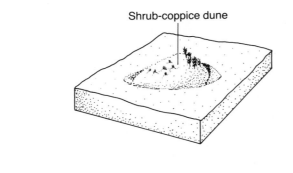

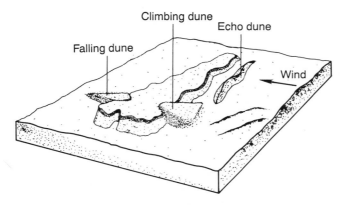

FIGURE 4.5. Topographic dune types. (Modified from Cooke and Warren 1973)

Lee dunes, or shadow dunes, are accumulations of sand that form down-wind behind small hills or patches of vegetation. As the wind diverges around these obstacles, it loses velocity and deposits its saltating load. Dunes formed behind and around a plant core are commonly referred to as shrub-coppice dunes (Fig. 4.5). Once sediment begins to accumulate at the base of a plant, more sediment is trapped, and it eventually engulfs the entire plant to form a low mound. The dune grows larger as more vegetation takes root on the mound and traps even more sediment.

Dunes also form on the windward side of long ridges and large hills (Fig. 4.5). If sediment-laden winds encounter a bedrock ridge or mountain with steep slopes, echo dunes form. These are ridges of sand that accumulate on the lowlands below the steep scarp and that run parallel to it. If the ridge or mountain is characterized by a gently sloping scarp, a climbing dune may accumulate on the windward slope. Sand passing over the top of the hill accumulates as a wedge on the opposite side. This is called a falling dune.

In humid coastal regions, retention ridges (also known as precipitation dunes) develop against a forest barrier as sand blown from the shoreline advances inland and is stopped by trees and other plants in its path. Vegetation takes root and stabilizes the dune into a long, narrow body oriented parallel to the shoreline.

Interdune Areas and Sand Sheets

Interdune areas are the flat, exposed regions between sand dunes. The extent of interdune areas depends on the size and spacing of the dunes, but they commonly occupy more total area than the dunes (Fig. 4.3). Interdune environments are either deflationary or depositional.

Deflationary interdune areas are dominated by erosional processes. Here very coarse sand, granules, and gravel accumulate as the fine-grained matrix of a preexisting deposit is winnowed away by the wind. Ventifacts may also be present on the deflated surface. The processes and effects of deflation are discussed later.

Depositional interdune areas, on the other hand, are dominated by aggradational processes in a number of different environments. Clastic sediments may accumulate in the interdune area as a result of intermittent alluvial sheetflooding or eolian processes. Water may also become impounded in these interdune areas and create small, ephemeral ponds, or in some cases more permanent ponds if the water table is close to the surface (Fig. 4.3). Laminated to massive deposits of silt and clay, commonly rich in salts and sometimes organic matter, form in such environments.

Sand sheets are flat to slightly undulatory blanketlike deposits of sand that surround dune fields and that mark the transition between eolian and non-eolian environments. Generally, sand sheets do not have definable dune forms. Deposits in this marginal area are characterized by horizontal to moderately dipping (0°–20°) cross-stratified layers of pebbles and coarse sand. Eolian sediments are commonly interbedded with sediments of adjacent terrestrial environments, such as ephemeral stream deposits.

Site Formation Processes

Archaeological remains are commonly buried either in or beneath sand dunes (Butzer 1971; Evans 1978). Artifacts and features may also occur on the surface of dunes or in deflated interdune areas. However, in many cases the original systemic context of these sites has been modified or destroyed by eolian processes.

The spatial relationships between archaeological debris on the surface of sand dunes can be substantially modified prior to burial by surficial eolian processes (Beckett 1980; Butzer 1982; E. L. Davis 1978; Lancaster 1986;

Schiffer 1987; Wandsnider 1984, 1987, 1988). Artifacts can move laterally in the direction of the prevailing wind and even opposite to the prevailing wind when they fall into small depressions scoured on their upwind side. Artifact movement varies depending on (1) the size, shape, and weight of the artifact; (2) the nature of the substrate; and (3) yearly meteorological conditions. Small-scale slumping on dune slopes also displaces artifacts. Consequently, the original systemic context of a site on the surface of a sand dune can be modified to the extent that behavioral patterning no longer exists.

Preservation of the systemic context of a site occurs only if an occupation surface is rapidly buried by shifting sands after site abandonment and the dune is stabilized (Albanese 1977, 1978a, 1978b). Rapid burial minimizes surficial alteration of the systemic context by eolian processes, and stabilization of the dune (commonly by vegetation) protects the archaeological site from erosion. If stabilization does not occur, the buried site contexts are susceptible to later destruction by wind deflation (Butzer 1982; Schiffer 1987). However, even stabilized sand dunes become reactivated when the vegetation cover is reduced during short droughts or longer periods of aridity. When this occurs, sand comprising the older dunes is eroded and reworked into new dunes. Artifacts and features in the dune are excavated by the wind and deflated to a common surface as the sand matrix surrounding the debris is winnowed away. For this reason, it is very common to find artifacts and scattered hearthstones lying on the hard substrate in interdune areas and in depressions associated with blowouts or parabolic dunes. If more than one archaeological horizon was present in the dune prior to deflation, the artifacts from each horizon become mixed on the deflated surface. Clearly, the same eolian processes that bury the site and preserve it for a period of time may also later destroy the site (Curry 1980). Deflated remains may later become buried by drifting sands, thus creating a potentially confusing situation for archaeologists.

Between the time a site is abandoned and the time it is later discovered, it may have been disturbed by surface processes, buried, modified while buried (see Chapter 7), reexposed to the surface due to deflation, and later reburied. The confusion and frustrations of site formation in sand dune environments is well illustrated by the Ake site on the San Augustin Plains of western New Mexico (Beckett 1980; Weber 1980).

The Ake site (Fig. 4.6) is situated in and around a small dune at the edge of a playa (an ephemeral desert lake). Artifacts spanning 11,000 years of human occupation (including the Folsom; early, middle, and late Archaic; ceramic period Mogollon; Spanish; and later historic periods) were found together in a single eolian stratum (unit D) and on the adjacent deflated interdune surfaces. In one deflated area, a hearth was preserved under playa

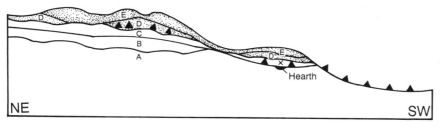

FIGURE 4.6. A generalized cross section through the Ake site in New Mexico. Units A, B, and Ĉ are older playa lake deposits. Unit D, a bed of eolian sand, contained all the buried archaeological remains, ranging in age from Paleoindian through historic. Unit E is modern eolian sand. Unit X is the playa deposit that overlies the surface on which a late Archaic hearth and Folsom projectile points were found. Triangles represent the position of artifacts. (Modified from Weber 1980)

lake clays (unit X). Material associated with the hearth included Folsom projectile points (diagnostic artifacts that are 11,000 to 10,000 years old), lithic debris, and bison tooth enamel. However, charcoal from the hearth yielded two radiocarbon ages averaging 3400 B.P. The mixed cultural assemblages and the anomalous association between diagnostic Folsom artifacts and a late Holocene radiocarbon-dated feature indicate that eolian processes have been at work at the site, continually deflating and reburying archaeological remains over time.

The systemic context of a site within a sand dune has the best chance for preservation if it is buried soon after abandonment and stabilized, and if in addition a resistant seal that inhibits further wind erosion develops over or within the dune sediments containing the site (Albanese 1977, 1978a, 1978b). Wind cannot effectively scour or entrain particles from deposits that are well cemented or cohesive. The two most common "seals" that protect eolian sediments from later erosion are paleosols, especially argillic and calcic horizons, and interdune pond sediments, such as clays or marls.

At the Claypool site in Colorado (Dick and Mountain 1960; Malde 1960), Cody complex activity areas (ca. 8000 B.P.) became buried by dune sand soon after abandonment, which was then stabilized by vegetation. While stabilized, a soil with a clay-rich argillic horizon developed in the dune sediment containing the Cody remains. This clay-rich soil horizon sealed and protected the site from subsequent wind erosion for 8000 years. The protective seal created by the paleosol was breached by severe erosion during the Dust Bowl era of the 1930s (Albanese 1977). Destruction of the clay horizon by wind scour resulted in the excavation and destruction of much of the systemic context at this site. Cody artifacts are now found at the surface in the deflation hollow of the blowout that developed.

A similar situation occurs at the Buried Dune site in the Picacho Basin in Arizona (Bayham et al. 1986; Waters 1986c), where an Archaic Pinto phase occupation surface was preserved in dune sediments beneath the calcic horizon of an eroded paleosol. Here, the systemic artifact patterning and intact features were preserved, including hearths with charcoal dating to 4300 B.P. This site, which was situated on the top of a coppice dune at the time of occupation, must have been covered with eolian sediment soon after abandonment and the sand stabilized by vegetation. Subsequent soil development sealed and protected the site from destruction. Wind later eroded the upper portion of the paleosol but could not breach the calcic horizon. Younger dune sediments accumulated over the eroded paleosol and are now stabilized by vegetation. The dune sediments overlying the paleosol have been extensively disturbed by plant growth and burrowing animals (bioturbation); consequently, archaeological contexts in the younger dune sediments are thoroughly mixed. The older dune sediments containing the Pinto phase occupation under the paleosol were not disturbed by these processes because roots and burrowing animals generally could not penetrate the calcic horizon. However, burrowing mammals did breach the paleosol at a few spots, and the archaeological contents of the lower and upper dunes are completely mixed. In some places, the buried paleosol was so extensively disturbed that pieces of the calcic horizon were suspended in bioturbated eolian sand. The dramatic effect that the calcic horizon had on preservation at the Buried Dune site is illustrated by the widespread disturbance of eolian sediments and archaeological contexts at other sites in the same dune field. During the testing of 25 other archaeological sites and the excavation of over 1.5 km of backhoe trenches in the Picacho Dune Field, the paleosol was not encountered. This suggests that wind erosion following the period of soil formation was effective in destroying the paleosol in most areas. The deposits and systemic contexts of the other 25 archaeological sites in the dune field were severely modified by eolian processes and bioturbation. In short, the Buried Dune site is a unique locality in the Picacho Dune Field in which a sequence of fortuitous geological circumstances occurred to preserve the site.

Calcareous interdune pond sediments have sealed and protected the archaeological horizons at the Casper and Finley sites in Wyoming. At the Casper site (Fig. 4.7; Albanese 1974a, 1974b, 1977, 1978a, 1978b), an intact Hell Gap period bison kill was preserved in the deflation hollow of a parabolic dune. Fortuitously, a pond formed in the depression shortly after the kill, and calcareous silty sand (unit C) was deposited over much of the site. Those portions of the site under the protective seal of the cemented pond

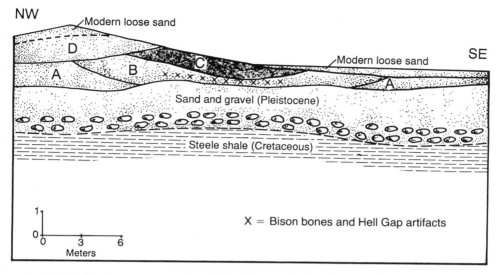

FIGURE 4.7. A cross section through the Casper site in Wyoming, showing the major stratigraphic units. Unit A is older eolian sand. Unit B is eolian sand filling the depression of the parabolic dune that contained the Paleoindian artifacts and bison bones. Unit C is the overlying pond sediment, which sealed and protected the site. Unit D is modern eolian sand. (Modified from Albanese 1974a)

sediments were preserved, whereas those sections of the site that were covered only by unconsolidated dune sand were destroyed by wind erosion. A similar situation preserved the Cody age bison kill at the Finley site (Ahlbrandt 1974; Albanese 1977; Hack 1943; Howard 1943; Moss 1951), where artifacts and bison bones were protected in muddy interdune pond sediments.

Deposition is also an important factor in the distortion of the regional archaeological record of a dune field. Extensive blankets of sand often bury sites, making them undetectable by surface survey. The Casper site in Wyoming, which was buried by 6.5 m of eolian sand, was not detected by an archaeological survey of the region but was exposed during land leveling associated with a construction project (Albanese 1974a). Also, because sand in a dune field is constantly shifting from year to year or season to season, new sites are exposed and old sites covered. Consequently, sites may be annually or seasonally buried and exposed. Therefore their discovery can depend on the year or season in which a survey is conducted (Wandsnider 1987, 1988).

The poor preservation potential of archaeological contexts in sand dune settings and the problem of site detection bias our knowledge of how humans used sand dune landscapes. Archaeologists working in eolian environments must address these limitations, adjust the level of their investigations to the level of preservation, and develop methodologies to explore for buried sites, especially those in unique preservational settings. If sand dunes and their archaeological contents are disturbed, it may be possible to obtain information only on the chronology of occupation, activities that occurred on the dunes, and the intensity and duration of human use of the dunes. However, where sites are well preserved by fortuitous geological circumstances, much information about human behavior can be obtained. Additional examples of dune stratigraphy and site preservation include geoarchaeological investigations of the Skull Creek Dunes in Oregon (Mehringer and Wigand 1986), the Corn Creek Dunes in Nevada (Williams and Orlins 1963), the Ash Meadows Dunes in Nevada (Mehringer and Warren 1976), and the sand sheet near the Jarilla Mountains at White Sands, New Mexico (Blair et al. 1990).

Landscape Reconstruction at the Casper Site

Because the geological and archaeological record is usually poorly preserved in sand dunes, few landscape reconstructions that illustrate the relationship between human activity and the eolian landscape have been possible. However, where landscape reconstructions have been possible, they have provided valuable insights into human behavior. This is well illustrated by the reconstruction of the landscape context of the Casper site in east central Wyoming (Albanese 1974a, 1974b, 1977, 1978a, 1978b; Frison 1974).

The Casper site is situated in a large dune field on a Pleistocene terrace about 90 m above the North Platte River. Buried by 6.5 m of unconsolidated eolian sediment and later exposed during land leveling were the skeletal remains of 74 *Bison antiquus* associated with Hell Gap culture artifacts. The presence of projectile points, butchering tools, and disarticulated bison remains indicated that this was a 10,000-year-old bison kill and butchering site. However, it was unclear how this kill took place in a dune field. Consequently, reconstructing the site landscape was crucial to understanding how the bison were procured by the Hell Gap hunters. The stratigraphy of the Casper site consisted of four lithostratigraphic units of Holocene age (Fig. 4.7; units A, B, and D were unconsolidated eolian dune sand, and unit C was cemented silty sand that had accumulated in a pond). These Holocene units rested directly on a unit of Pleistocene river gravel and sand 1.5 m thick, which in turn rested on Cretaceous bedrock. The eolian sands of unit B contained the bison and archaeological remains. Based on the sedimentology and stratigraphy at the site and analogies with the modern dune landscape,

FIGURE 4.8. A typical parabolic dune near the Casper site in Wyoming. This area is analogous to the prehistoric landscape in which bison were herded and trapped 10,000 years ago. (Photograph by John P. Albanese)

Albanese reconstructed the site landscape before, during, and after the Hell Gap bison kill.

Before 10,000 B.P., unit A was deposited on a Pleistocene terrace as the wind blew in a northeast direction. Later the wind scoured an elongate, troughlike depression through unit A and into the underlying Pleistocene sand and gravel deposits. The preserved depression was 93 m long, 23 m wide, and 1.8 m deep. Albanese concluded that this depression was a remnant of a much larger deflation hollow associated with a parabolic dune. Modern parabolic dunes in the region range from 365 to 550 m long, 120 to 150 m wide, and 10 to 15 m deep (Fig. 4.8). While the original dimensions of the prehistoric dune are unknown, Albanese believes it was probably similar in size to the modern dunes. A thin veneer of eolian sand (Fig. 4.7, unit B) accumulated in the depression before the bison kill. Around 10,000 B.P., at least 74 bison were herded into the parabolic dune by the Hell Gap hunters. The crescent-shaped parabolic dune would have been a natural trap. The high, steep sides and loose sand of the surrounding dune, perhaps even covered by snow, would have prevented the escape of the animals. When the bison were killed, bones and artifacts became distributed for 60 m along the axis of the parabolic dune depression. After the bison were butchered and the site was abandoned, the depression continued to fill with drifting sand (unit B). Shortly after the deposition of unit B, a pond formed in the depression, and unit C, a massive brown silty calcareous sand and sandy silt, was deposited. This unit sealed and protected the site from destruction by wind deflation for 10,000 years. Additional eolian sediments (unit D) eventually buried the site to a depth of 6.5 m.

Reconstructing the method used by the Hell Gap hunters to trap bison at the Casper site required the reconstruction of the landscape setting at 10,000 B.P. However, other aspects of human behavior associated with the kill site are impossible to reconstruct. Because the paleotopography has long since been either destroyed or altered by wind erosion, it was not possible to reconstruct how the ancient dune topography was used to channelize the bison into the trap. Likewise, any associated sites, such as a campsite that may have been situated close to the kill area, have been destroyed because they were not sheltered by a protective seal.

Loess and Dust

Fine-grained sediments are eroded by the wind from areas poorly protected by vegetation and are transported great distances in suspension before being deposited. These fine-grained sediments settle to the ground when the wind velocity is reduced or when the sediment particles are washed from the atmosphere. Once settled, the grains are kept in place by the protective grip of grasses and other vegetation. This results in a blanketlike or sheetlike deposit called loess.

Loess is primarily composed of silt-size particles and minor amounts of clay and very fine sand. These deposits can cover thousands of square kilometers and any surface, regardless of topographic position. Consequently, loess tends to mantle and smooth the preexisting relief. It is generally massive and devoid of stratification, and it ranges from a few millimeters to more than 50 m in thickness. Loess is thickest near its source, and both particle size and bed thickness decrease downwind.

Widespread loess deposits are present in the Midwestern United States and Alaska. Much of the silt comprising the loess was derived from the streambeds of braided outwash rivers downslope from glaciers during the Pleistocene. Loess is still accumulating in Alaska where outwash plains are active. Silt and clay can also be derived from actively deflating arid and semiarid desert basins, especially dry streambeds, bajadas, and dune fields. Accumulations of fine-grained sediments derived from nonglacial sources in semiarid and arid regions are commonly called dust instead of loess.

Not all loess or dust will remain at the original site of deposition. Much of the fine-grained sediment deposited on unstable hillslopes is eroded downslope and reworked into secondary colluvial and alluvial deposits.

Site Formation Processes

Archaeological remains are found under, within, and on the surface of loess (Thorson 1990). Unlike sand dunes, once loess is deposited it cannot easily be reentrained by the wind, because of its cohesiveness. As a result, the systemic context of archaeological remains at a site are more likely to remain undisturbed once they are buried in the loess. Also important to site preservation is the topographic position of the loess. If a site is situated in loess that rests on a stable surface where it is protected from colluvial and alluvial processes (e.g., a terrace tread), the chances of preservation are better than if the site was situated in loess that had been deposited in an unstable topographic position where it could be reworked by colluvial and fluvial processes (e.g., a hillslope or river floodplain).

The Dry Creek site in central Alaska provides an excellent example of the preservation typical of sites in loess (Fig. 4.9; Thorson and Hamilton 1977). The Dry Creek site is situated on a glacial outwash terrace 25 m above the active streambed of Dry Creek. The stratigraphy at the site consists of a two-meter-thick sequence of seven lithostratigraphic units of loess and four units of eolian sand. The particles making up the eleven eolian units were eroded from the streambeds of Dry Creek and the adjacent Nenana River, transported downwind, and deposited on the terrace. The deposition of eolian sediments was interrupted by five periods of stability and soil formation. These are recorded in the stratigraphic sequence by five paleosols. Preserved in the loess are four discrete occupation surfaces. The three lower occupations occurred between 11,000 and 8500 B.P., and the upper occupation occurred between 4700 and 3400 B.P. Additional sites along the Nenana River and its tributaries, such as Moose Creek and Walker Road, also contain early archaeological remains in correlative loess deposits (Powers and Hoffecker 1989).

The sites in the Nenana Valley were preserved because the loess that contained them was deposited on stable surfaces and the highly cohesive nature of the loess prevented the wind from eroding it and destroying the artifact contents. However, unusually strong winds may locally erode older loess deposits. Thorson and Bender (1985) suggest that strong katabatic winds have removed all loess older than 12,000 B.P. in the Nenana River Valley. Consequently, this would be a poor place to look for pre–12,000 B.P. sites. More recently, Hoffecker (1988) studied the regional Quaternary history of drainages on the north side of the Alaska Range in central Alaska

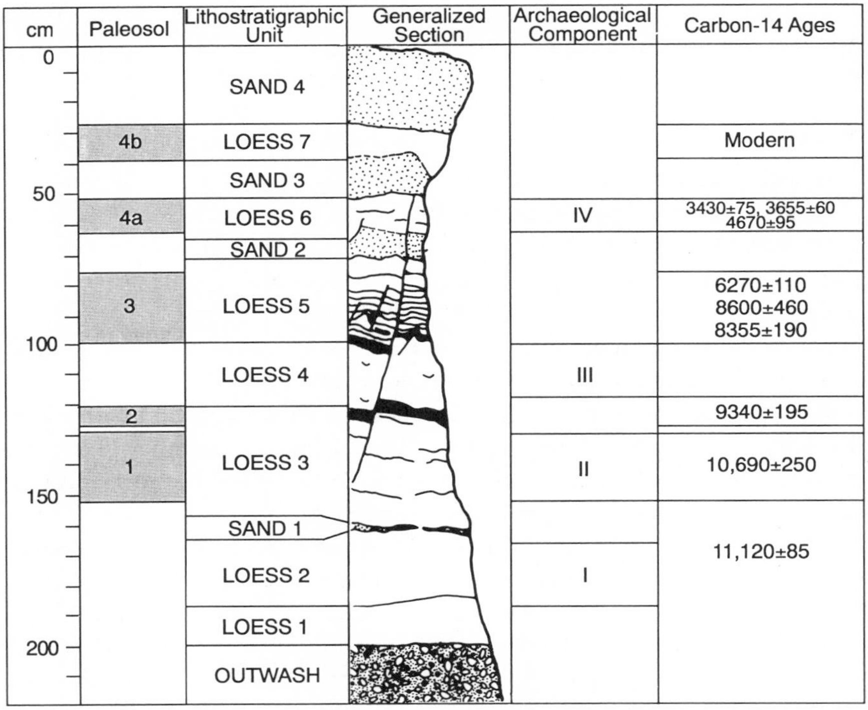

cm	Paleosol	Lithostratigraphic Unit	Generalized Section	Archaeological Component	Carbon-14 Ages
0		SAND 4			
	4b	LOESS 7			Modern
50		SAND 3			
	4a	LOESS 6		IV	3430±75, 3655±60 4670±95
		SAND 2			
	3	LOESS 5			6270±110 8600±460 8355±190
100		LOESS 4		III	
	2				9340±195
	1	LOESS 3		II	10,690±250
150		SAND 1			11,120±85
		LOESS 2		I	
		LOESS 1			
200		OUTWASH			

FIGURE 4.9. A generalized stratigraphic section of the Dry Creek site in Alaska showing the loess and eolian sand lithostratigraphic units, major paleosols, radiocarbon ages in years B.P., and occupation surfaces. (Modified from Thorson and Hamilton 1977)

(which includes the Nenana River and its tributaries) and developed a geoarchaeological model identifying pre–12,000 B.P. landforms and deposits where sites of this age may occur.

Stone Pavements

A stone pavement is a one-pebble-thick concentration of gravel that mantles a stable surface (Fig. 4.10). Stone pavements vary from a tightly packed mosaic of stones that completely armor a surface to a loosely packed layer of gravel and coarse sand that incompletely veneers a surface. Stone pavements form anywhere that gravelly deposits are present but are especially common on alluvial fans, fluvial terraces, pediments, and ancient beaches. They are most common in arid regions, where they are known as desert pavements. Because these surfaces are stable, soil development is common under desert pavements.

The traditional explanation for the formation of a stone pavement is to view the surface as a lag gravel produced by deflation. Deflation is the process by which the fine-grained sediment fraction of a preexisting gravelly deposit is removed by wind and water erosion, and the heavier particles that cannot be moved become concentrated on a common surface (Fig. 4.11). Alternatively, Springer (1958) suggested a mechanical process for the formation of pavements, whereby pebbles and cobbles migrate to the surface due to repeated wetting and drying of the gravelly sediment matrix. When a gravelly deposit contains expandable clays, such as montmorillonite, it expands when wet and contracts when dry. When expansion occurs, a stone is slightly lifted from its original position, creating a void under the stone. As the soil dries, the matrix around the stone shrinks, distorting the void. Because the shape of the stone no longer matches the shape of the void, it cannot fall back into its original position, and fine-grained particles fill the void. The net effect is the upward displacement of stones to the surface,

FIGURE 4.10. Typical desert pavement coated with desert varnish on a terrace overlooking the Colorado River near Cibola, Arizona. Note the two "sleeping circles" (circular cleared areas). The exposed area in the sleeping circles is the silt underlying the desert pavement. The notebook in the closest circle indicates the scale.

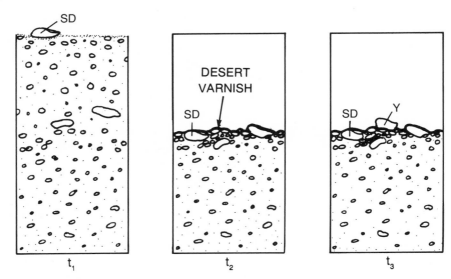

FIGURE 4.11. The formation of a desert pavement by deflation. At time 1 (t_1), a San Dieguito I artifact (SD) is left on an undeflated surface. As wind deflation occurs (t_2), the artifact and the gravels that were present in the matrix are lowered to a common surface, forming a desert pavement. At this point the San Dieguito artifact is embedded into the pavement. After the pavement is stabilized, all the exposed stones become coated with desert varnish. Sometime after pavement formation and varnishing (t_3), Yumans (ceramic period people) left an artifact (Y) on the pavement surface. This artifact is unvarnished. (Modified from Rogers 1966)

where they can concentrate to form a desert pavement. This mechanism for the formation of pavements is supported by laboratory experiments and field observation of a stone-free layer directly beneath many pavements. Recently McFadden, Wells, and Jercinovich (1987) have shown that many desert pavements may also be "born" and maintained at the land surface in rocky terrains. They suggest that as eolian sediments accumulate in a rocky terrain, they become trapped in rock fractures. This accelerates the mechanical fragmentation of rocks and produces the source material for the pavement. The rubble produced by mechanical weathering eventually covers the eolian surface and creates a stable gravel lag or pavement. This process also accounts for the silty, gravel-free layer under many pavement surfaces. Regardless of the mechanism responsible for the origin of a desert pavement, once a surface is completely covered by gravel, it is stabilized.

The time required for pavement formation varies greatly from place to place. Shlemon (1978) reports that tank tracks scored onto the pavements in the Mojave Desert of California during military maneuvers in the early 1940s show no evidence of healing. However, Cooke (1970) and Péwé (1978) have observed incipient renewal of artificially removed pavement in experimental plots in as little as four years in western Arizona and southern California.

Desert varnish, a black-to-brown coating of iron, manganese, and clay, commonly forms on exposed rock and artifact surfaces that are embedded in desert pavements (Dorn and Oberlander 1982). Also, a light buff to orange-red coating of clay and iron develops on the undersides of the desert-varnished cobbles that rest in the pavement. This is sometimes called a ground patina. Desert varnish forms in arid regions as a result of organic microbial activity on the rock surface, which fixes the iron and manganese.

Site Formation Processes

Artifacts and archaeological features either occur on a pavement surface or are embedded to some degree within it (Fig. 4.11; Hayden 1965, 1967, 1976, 1982). Artifacts incorporated into a pavement were originally deposited on the pavement surface as it formed. Consequently, the worked edges of arti-facts display the same degree of patination and desert varnishing as the nonartifact stones comprising the pavement. Artifacts that lie on the pave-ment surface postdate pavement formation, and the worked edges of these younger artifacts do not exhibit the same degree of desert varnishing or ground patination as the stones comprising the pavement (Fig. 4.11). Older artifacts are sometimes uprooted from the pavement by humans, animals, or geologic processes. These displaced artifacts are easily recognized because the thickness, color, and chemical composition of the desert varnish on the artifacts is identical to the other stones in the pavement. If the gravel armor of a pavement is disturbed, younger artifacts on the surface occasionally become incorporated into the pavement as the disrupted surface regenerates its lag. Intrusive artifacts are easily recognized because they do not have the same degree of desert varnish or patination as the original pavement. Thus, artifacts can be chronologically separated at a site by their position on or in a desert pavement and by their relative degree of desert varnishing. These relationships are well documented by Hayden (1967, 1976) in the Sierra Pinacate in Sonora, Mexico, and by Rogers (1939, 1966) in the deserts of California. Kearns, Dorn, and Stanford (1990) have recently tried to quan-tify the chronological relationship between San Dieguito I and Clovis arti-facts in southeastern Utah using cation ratio values derived from the desert varnish that coats these artifacts.

If a number of desert pavement surfaces are present in a region, they can be chronologically ordered from oldest to youngest; thus, any archaeological sites in these pavements are also placed in sequential order. Desert pavement surfaces and their associated archaeological sites are chronologically ordered from youngest to oldest by (1) defining the sequential development of landforms in the region (e.g., lower terraces are younger than higher terraces); (2) establishing a soil chronosequence based on the relative degree of soil development beneath the pavements (e.g., a soil with an argillic horizon is older than one with a cambic horizon, so the overlying pavements are respectively older and younger); and (3) determining the presence or absence and degree of desert varnish development. Rogers (1939, 1966) and Hayden (1965, 1967, 1976, 1982) developed this methodology (sometimes called horizontal stratigraphy) to establish a relative sequence of cultural occupations in the arid portions of the American Southwest. The oldest Malpais artifacts, thought to be 20,000 years old, are darkly varnished and are found in old pavement surfaces with strong soil horizon development. San Dieguito I artifacts, thought to be between 15,000 and 10,000 years old, are lightly varnished and occur in younger pavements with moderately developed soils (or on the surface of the older Malpais pavements). Later Archaic and ceramic period artifacts have no desert varnish and occur in surfaces with weakly developed pavements and soils (as well as on the surface of the older Malpais and San Dieguito pavements).

Archaeological features—such as cleared circles, trails, and intaglios (ground figures)—are also commonly etched into the desert pavement surface (Fig. 4.10; Hayden 1967, 1976, 1982). These features indicate that the pavement was in existence at the time the feature was created.

Eolian Erosion

Wind laden with sediment is a powerful erosional force that can considerably abrade anything in its path. Abrasion occurs as airborne sand particles, moving by saltation or in suspension, strike obstacles (e.g., rock outcrops, artifacts, stones, and buildings) exposed on the surface. The effectiveness of wind abrasion—or sandblasting, as it is commonly called—depends primarily on (1) the wind velocity, (2) the hardness and concentration of the abrading particles, (3) the hardness of the abraded surface, (4) the density and distribution of vegetation, and (5) the nature of the topography.

Ventifacts, wind-faceted stones, are one of the most common products of wind abrasion. Facets are developed on surfaces facing the prevailing wind as airborne sand particles slowly abrade the exposed face of a gravel-size particle. Facets do not form on surfaces oriented parallel to or facing away from the prevailing wind. Ventifacts have multiple facets, with angular to rounded intersections. Multiple facets are created as the orientation of

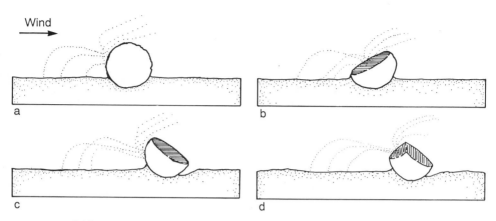

FIGURE 4.12. Stages in the formation of a ventifact: a stone is abraded by saltating grains (a), and the side facing into the wind eventually develops a facet (b). When the pebble is displaced into a hollow excavated by the wind into the surface on its downwind side (c), a new face of the stone is exposed to saltating grains. Slowly, a new facet develops (d). Later reorientation of the pebble will create more facets on the ventifact. (Modified from Hamblin 1989)

the ventifact shifts and a new surface of the cobble is exposed to wind scour (Fig. 4.12). Ventifacts are reoriented by frost action, animal disturbance, or when the stone falls into a pit scoured under the downwind side of the cobble by the wind. Thus, a number of facets are created on a single cobble in a unidirectional wind regime. Fine-grained suspended sediments often polish the surface of stones to a high luster and may also groove, pit, and frost the surface.

Sandblasting also shapes rock outcrops. Yardangs—elongate ridges 10 to 30 m high and aligned parallel to the prevailing wind—are common features of wind erosion. Grooving of bedrock surfaces is also common, resulting in parallel furrows ranging from tiny elongate flutes a few centimeters long to giant hollows more than a kilometer wide and up to 10 m deep.

Site Formation Processes

Archaeological remains in the path of sediment-laden winds are vulnerable to erosion. Architectural features can be scoured, petroglyphs obliterated, and stone and ceramic artifacts substantially eroded. In the Mojave Desert of California, Emma Lou Davis (1967, 1978) noted that sandblasting usually subdued or obliterated the flake scars on chipped-stone artifacts and beveled and dulled their edges. Soft ceramic artifacts are easily eroded. Grooves 0.5

cm deep have been observed in ceramics dating between A.D. 1000 and 1500 in the Salton Trough in California. Often the edges of these sherds are rounded and polished.

The degree of abrasion on the surface of an artifact depends on the hardness of the artifact material, the position of the artifact in relation to the path of sediment-laden winds, and especially the amount of time it has been subjected to abrasion. Artifact abrasion may not be constant through time, because the artifact may repeatedly be buried and exposed as eolian processes and landscapes change. Consequently, different sides of the same artifacts may be differentially eroded, artifacts of different ages may show the same degree of abrasion, and artifacts of the same age may show different degrees of abrasion. Both Clovis (ca. 11,500 to 11,000 B.P.) and middle Archaic (ca. 5500 to 3500 B.P.) projectile points from surface sites around China Lake in the Mojave Desert of California were in some cases abraded to a similar degree (E. L. Davis 1978). Also, the assemblage of Clovis projectile points from China Lake ranged from heavily eroded (flake scars and ridges obliterated or faintly visible) to lightly eroded (flake scars and ridges fresh in appearance).

Borden (1971) separated an assemblage of artifacts from a surface site in the Mojave Desert into four categories based on differential surface erosion and suggested that these categories represented temporally discrete assemblages. His report indicates that diagnostic Lake Mojave projectile points (typically no older than 10,000 B.P.) are more severely eroded in some cases than 11,000-year-old Clovis fluted projectile points. Because too many variables must be held constant over time at a site, the relative degree of artifact abrasion is not a reliable indicator of relative age.

Volcanic Ash (Tephra)

The origin and depositional processes associated with volcanic sediments, or tephra, and their characteristics are discussed in chapter 2. The importance of these sediments as stratigraphic markers and the effects of volcanic activity on human behavior are considered in this section.

Of all the various types of pyroclastic sediments, volcanic ash is the most important to archaeologists in North America. These fine-grained particles produced during volcanic eruptions are transported great distances downwind from their source and form distinctive, widespread layers that are compositionally unique (Kittleman 1979; Steen-McIntyre 1985).

Because volcanic eruptions occurred along the northern Pacific coast of North America during the late Pleistocene and Holocene, volcanic ash is commonly found in the stratigraphy of sites in the northwestern United

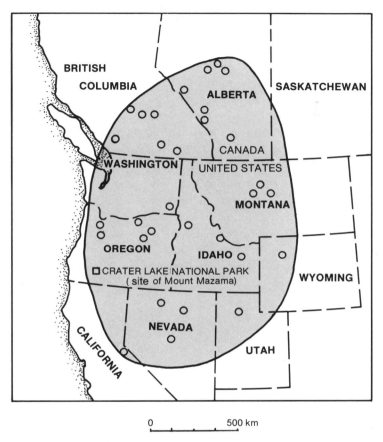

FIGURE 4.13. The known extent of the Mazama Ash across western North America. The circles mark some of the sites where the ash has been identified. The volcanic source of the ash is also indicated. (Modified from Sarna-Wojcicki et al. 1983)

States, western Canada, and Alaska (Butzer 1982; Schiffer 1987; Steen-McIntyre 1985; Thorson 1990; Wilson 1990). Many volcanic ashes have been identified, mapped, and dated in these regions and thus are important time horizons that can be correlated between archaeological sites (Sarna-Wojcicki et al. 1983; Steen-McIntyre 1985). The Mazama Ash, for example, is found over much of the northwestern United States and southwestern Canada (Figs. 2.11 and 4.13). This ash was derived from the eruption of Mount Mazama, now Crater Lake, in Oregon during a series of eruptions between 7000 and 6700 B.P. Ash from these eruptions blanketed 1.7 million square kilometers. Mazama Ash has been found in stratigraphic contexts at such sites as the Marmes Rockshelter in Washington (Sheppard et al. 1984), Fort Rock Cave in Oregon (Bedwell 1973), the Wasden site in Idaho (Miller and Dort 1978), Hidden Cave and Gatecliff Shelter in Nevada (J. O. Davis 1983, 1985), and the terraces of the Snake River in Washington (Hammatt 1977). Many other ashes, such as the Glacier Peak and Mount St. Helens tephra sets, are equally useful for dating in the Northwest (Sarna-Wojcicki et al. 1983). Dixon and Smith 1990 and Thorson 1990 discuss the application of tephrochronology to the establishment of cultural chronologies in Alaska.

The effects of volcanic eruptions on prehistoric people are not well documented. People living in the vicinity of the crater where volcanic activity was most severe and where biotic communities were greatly affected were surely displaced for short periods following volcanic eruptions. For example, maritime Aleutian populations in the Alaskan Peninsula were displaced short distances after a volcanic eruption but soon returned to their original sites (Dumond 1979; Workman 1979). Dumond and Workman believe that volcanic eruptions had no significant long-term impact on the development of Aleutian culture.

In areas away from the erupting volcano, where only ash fall occurred, there was probably no significant effect on the landscape, biotic communities, or people. Grayson (1979) points out that ash fall in the Fort Rock Basin in Oregon, which is over 100 km from Mount Mazama, had only a minimal effect on the fauna hunted by prehistoric peoples in eastern Oregon. In another example, the eruption of Sunset Crater in northern Arizona in A.D. 1064, once thought to have been the major factor in demographic and cultural change in the area, is now recognized as having played a minor and localized role in settlement and culture change (Hevly et al. 1979; Pilles 1979). Pilles points out that the magnitude of post-eruptive Sinagua culture change in northern Arizona was no greater than that occurring elsewhere in the American Southwest at this time. Furthermore, the eruption of 1064, rather than being an isolated episode of volcanic activity, was just one of many eruptions that occurred over a period of 200 years. In contrast, Workman (1979) suggests that late Holocene ash fall in the interior of northwestern Canada may have made a portion of that region uninhabitable for at least a few years and forced people to migrate into unaffected surrounding areas. Because of the limited carrying capacity of the interior region, Workman believes conflicts developed between the displaced groups and the people already living in the unaffected surrounding areas. He suggests that the rejected refugees were forced southward and that this migration may account for the linguistically documented movement of Athapaskan speakers twelve centuries ago. Also, volcanic activity did have disastrous effects on societies in Mesoamerica causing the abandonment of regions and social reorganization (Sheets 1979; Steen-McIntyre 1985). For the most part, however, it appears that volcanic disasters in North America did not trigger social change, because the stress placed on prehistoric cultures by volcanic eruptions did not exceed the support and adaptive capacities of the affected societies (Grayson and Sheets 1979; Sheets and Grayson 1979).

Conclusion

Eolian environments were used by prehistoric people from the very earliest times. Consequently, archaeological sites are found in sand dunes and loess, and on desert pavements. The natural site formation processes and examples of landscape reconstruction in these eolian landscapes have been presented in this chapter. Clearly, sites in loess deposits will most likely be preserved with their systemic contexts intact. However, interpreting archaeological sites in dune and pavement settings is especially challenging because of the problem of site context preservation. For the behavioral context of a site in a sand dune to be preserved, the site must be rapidly buried after abandonment, stabilized, and a cemented or cohesive layer formed over the site that will protect it from later wind erosion. However, even if these conditions are met, sites may still be disturbed by postburial processes (especially bioturbation) and during periods of extreme aridity, when eolian erosion may intensify. Thus, if a site is buried in a sand dune with its systemic context intact, it is truly unique. Also, because of the constant reworking of eolian dune sediments, the geological information needed to reconstruct the landscape is poorly preserved as well. These factors severely limit our understanding of how people utilized some eolian landscapes.

5

Springs, Lakes, Rockshelters, and Other Terrestrial Environments

Springs, lakes, slopes, glaciers, and rockshelters are important archaeological settings, and the evolution of these environments has affected human behavior and the archaeological record. This chapter reviews the geological processes, landforms, and deposits of each of these terrestrial environments. Each geological review is followed by a discussion of natural site formation processes and landscape reconstruction.

Springs

Springs are localized environments where groundwater emerges at the surface through natural openings in lithified rock or unconsolidated sediment (Brune 1981; Haynes 1985; Meinzer 1923, 1927, 1939). This water is derived from an underground water reservoir known as an aquifer. Depending on the position of the water table associated with this aquifer, discharge from the spring may be perennial or ephemeral. Perennial spring discharge may fluctuate diurnally or seasonally. The amount of dissolved solids and the temperature of the emerging water also varies between springs.

Springs are classified as either gravity or artesian springs. Gravity springs, also called seeps, develop where the surface topography intersects or is cut below the level of the water table (e.g., at the base of a hillslope, as in Fig. 5.1). At this intersection, water slowly drains from the underground source to the surface through fissures or small openings in the porous bedrock or unconsolidated alluvium by the force of gravity. The water discharging from a seep is under no confining pressure. Seeps are also encountered in streambeds where subsurface water moving through porous channel sand and gravel is deflected to the surface by an impermeable stratum.

In contrast, artesian springs are those from which groundwater emerges at the surface under pressure (Fig. 5.2). Artesian springs develop where an underground water-saturated stratum becomes confined. As a result of the pressure, the water erodes a conduit to the surface through the overlying unconsolidated sediment or bedrock. Conduits usually form along a zone of weakness, such as a fault or fracture, in the host sediment or rock. The conduit enlarges and erodes a depression, which then becomes a pond. Both the size and the configuration of the conduit and pond are adjusted to the spring's discharge. An artesian spring may also build a circular to elliptical mound above the level of the adjacent land surface if its water carries a high concentration of calcium carbonate.

A spring boil develops at the orifice of the conduit where the artesian water emerges. This boil is characterized by a roiling fountain of water and sand. Because of the constant water motion, silt and clay are suspended in the water and pushed to the edge of the pond. Gravel, if present in the host sediment, is too heavy to be buoyed by the artesian pressure and accumulates as a lag in the lowest part of the conduit. As the water motion in a conduit subsides, it becomes filled with well-rounded and well-sorted sand grains that are frosted and polished.

Deposition of the silt and clay occurs away from the conduits in the more quiescent waters of the pond (Figs. 5.2 and 5.3). These sediments accumulate over the conduit only after it becomes inactive. Typically, these fine-grained sediments are horizontally laminated and may be locally deformed around the conduits. If the water is alkaline, fine-grained deposits of calcium carbonate called marls may precipitate in the spring. Peats and organic sediments also accumulate in spring environments as vegetation around the pond dies, becomes waterlogged, and sinks. As spring discharge declines, waterlogged vegetation may encroach over the inactive conduits and produce a continuous layer of peat, which covers the spring (Fig. 5.2). Thin lenses of sand may become interbedded in the peat, fine clastic sediments, and marl if artesian pressure returns and erodes a new conduit. In general, springs are characterized by a complex microstratigraphy of interbedded clastic, carbonate, and carbonaceous sediments overlying conduits filled with well-sorted sand and gravel (Haynes 1985; Laury 1980).

Tufa and travertine form around springs and seeps if the water is alkaline. They precipitate on bedrock and clastic particles, and on the leaves and stems of plants. Thin coatings of silica, called sinter, form around hot springs.

Site Formation Processes and Landscape Reconstruction

Human groups commonly used spring environments because springs provided plant resources, fresh water, and attracted animals. As a result, artifacts and features are commonly found around springs and in spring sediments.

Artifacts in a spring conduit occur in a secondary context because they

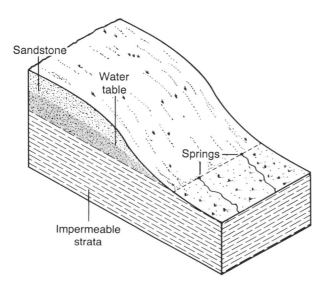

FIGURE 5.1. A typical gravity spring created where the water table intersects the surface topography. Water seeps to the surface and creates a marsh in the lowlands. (Modified from Strahler and Strahler 1989)

have been constantly moved by the agitated waters at the mouth of the conduit. In addition, these artifacts have commonly been abraded and polished by the sand particles in the roiling water. At the Blackwater Draw site in New Mexico, highly polished Clovis, Folsom, Midland, Agate Basin, and Archaic projectile points were recovered from well-sorted spring conduit sands (Boldurian and Agogino 1982; Haynes and Agogino 1966; Hester 1972). Apparently these artifacts were intentionally thrown into the spring by prehistoric hunters.

Likewise, in the most active parts of the spring the constant movement of the water disarticulates and disperses the remains of animals that have fallen into the spring. Bones often become lodged in conduits and highly polished. At the Tule Springs site in Nevada, polished bones of Pleistocene megafauna occur in sand-filled artesian spring conduits (Brooks et al. 1967; Haynes 1967). Disarticulated bones may also be pushed to the edge of the spring, where they are concentrated into windrows, as seen in a number of ancient artesian spring ponds along the Pomme de Terre River in Missouri (Fig. 5.2; Chomko 1978; Haynes 1985; King 1988; Saunders 1988).

Archaeological sites in primary context are commonly found on the surfaces adjacent to springs or are buried in the sediments accumulated in

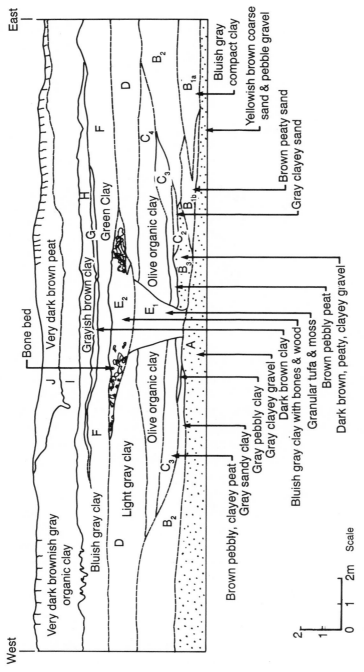

FIGURE 5.2. Late Pleistocene stratigraphy of Boney Springs, which is on a terrace of the Pomme de Terre River in Missouri. Unit A is the aquifer through which water flowed underground, unit E_1 is the spring conduit or feeder, and unit E_2 is the spring pond. The remains of 31 mastodons were found concentrated in a bone bed along the edge of the pond. Organic remains and spruce logs within the bone bed date to approximately 16,000 B.P. This is a typical example of the complex stratigraphy associated with artesian springs. (Modified from Haynes 1985)

the quieter water environment of the pond and channel sediments that lead away from the spring. At Blackwater Draw in New Mexico, four butchered mammoth carcasses associated with Clovis culture artifacts were found in the laminated pond sediments, away from the spring conduits (Haynes and Agogino 1966; Hester 1972). At the Lehner site in Arizona, the remains of 12 mammoths and associated Clovis artifacts were recovered from sediments that filled a channel leading downslope from a seep (Antevs 1959; Haury et al. 1959; Haynes 1982a).

Spring-fed ponds are also created in bedrock sinkholes. Here, a pond develops where groundwater seeps into the sinkhole and rises to the level of the water table. The Warm Mineral Springs and Little Salt Spring sites in Florida (Clausen, Brooks, and Wesolowsky 1975; Clausen et al. 1979; Cockrell and Murphy 1978), are excellent examples of spring-fed sinkholes. During the late Pleistocene, humans occupied the ledges adjacent to these ponds when the water table and sea level were lower. These sites became submerged when the water table and sea level rose at the end of the Pleistocene.

Springs are not static environments. Through time they may be active during one period, become dormant, and later reactivate. Also, the discharge and the size of the pond of any active spring can fluctuate over time. Changes in spring activity are usually triggered either by climatic fluctuations that cause the water table to rise and fall or tectonic activity, which may alter the flow of the underground aquifers supplying water to the spring. During the middle Holocene Altithermal in the American Southwest (a period of aridity and drought) the water table fell and many springs that had been active during the late Pleistocene became dry. During this time, Archaic people in search of water excavated wells into the dry spring beds and associated pond sediments. At Mustang Springs in Texas, more than 60 wells were excavated into older spring-pond sediments (Meltzer 1991b; Meltzer and Collins 1987). Similar wells were excavated during the Altithermal into the spring sediments at Blackwater Draw in New Mexico (Haynes and Agogino 1966; Hester 1972). Changes in spring discharge over time are also well documented at a number of other archaeological and paleontological sites, such as the Hiscock site in New York (Laub et al. 1988; Muller and Calkin 1988), at several springs along the Pomme de Terre River in Missouri (Haynes 1985), at the Hot Springs site in South Dakota (Agenbroad 1984; Laury 1980, 1990), and at Tule Springs in Nevada (Haynes 1967).

Lakes

Natural lakes are bodies of fresh or saline water that occupy topographically closed basins or that are impounded behind natural dams (e.g., glacial ice,

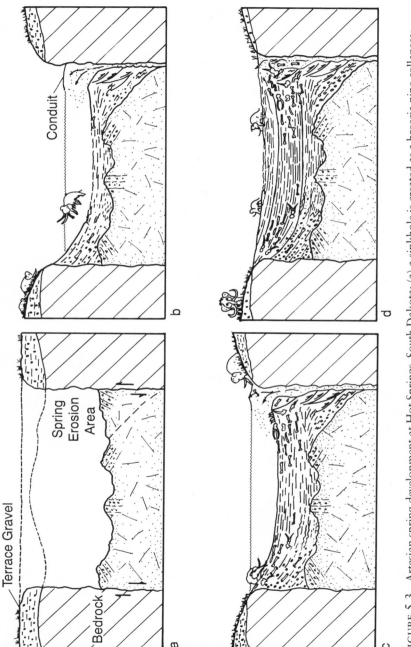

FIGURE 5.3. Artesian spring development at Hot Springs, South Dakota: (a) a sinkhole is created as a breccia pipe collapses; (b) groundwater erodes a conduit and emerges at the surface within the sinkhole, fine-grained sediments accumulate in the pond environment away from the spring orifice, and mammoth bones begin to accumulate in the spring; (c) pond sediments and mammoth bones continue to accumulate; (d) the water table drops, the spring becomes inactive, well-sorted sand fills the conduit, and colluvium fills the remaining depression. (Modified from Laury 1980)

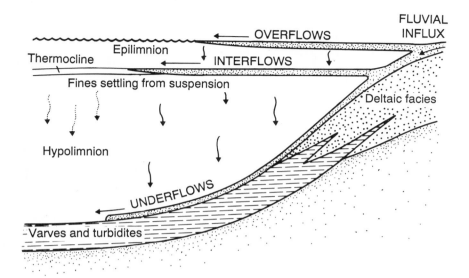

FIGURE 5.4. A cross section through a lake showing temperature stratification of the water. A river enters the lake at the right, and coarse sediments accumulate to form a delta, while fine-grained sediments are dispersed into the lake by overflow and interflow. (Modified from Galloway and Hobday 1983)

landslides, or lava flows). They occur in all environmental settings from mountains to desert lowlands and in different environmental associations, such as on riverine floodplains, between sand dunes, and on deltaic plains. Lakes vary in size, configuration, depth, water chemistry, temperature, and numerous other characteristics. The following geological review is based on Allen and Collinson 1986, Fouch and Dean 1982, Galloway and Hobday 1983, Leeder 1982, Picard and High 1972, and Reineck and Singh 1980.

Processes

Water circulation and sedimentation in lakes are controlled by the temperature and salinity differences in the water and wind-generated waves and currents.

Water temperature varies between lakes and within a lake. If a lake is shallow, there is little difference in temperature between the surface and bottom of the lake. However, if a lake is deep, a layer of less-dense warm water called the epilimnion overlies a body of denser cold water known as the hypolimnion (Fig. 5.4). These two layers of water are separated by a zone called the thermocline. The epilimnion is generally well oxygenated because of continual circulation from the surface, while the lower hypolimnion is generally stagnant and anoxic. Temperature stratification may also be enhanced by salinity layering. In this case, more-dense saline water sinks to the bottom of the lake and is overlain by less-dense, less-saline water. A halocline separates lower-salinity surface waters from more-saline bottom waters.

Wind blowing over the surface of a lake is responsible for generating the waves and currents that circulate surface and subsurface water. If the lake is not density stratified, the entire body of water is mixed. However, circulation in a density-stratified water body is confined to the epilimnion, with little or no circulation in the hypolimnion. Some density-stratified lakes undergo complete mixing on a seasonal basis, once or twice a year, by a process known as lake overturn. This occurs if the temperature of the epilimnion becomes equivalent to the temperature of the hypolimnion. Also, cold water may upwell from the hypolimnion, and warmer water of the epilimnion may sink due to wind forcing.

Wind-generated waves and currents resemble those developed along marine coastlines (see Chapter 6), but lacustrine waves have a shallower wave base and lower energy levels. Swash and backwash occur on the beachface, and longshore currents flow parallel to shorelines in a manner analogous to their marine counterparts. Shoreline zones are also strongly affected by storms. A major difference between marine and lacustrine shoreline processes is the absence of tides in lakes.

Landforms and Deposits

Clastic, chemical, and carbonaceous sediments accumulate in lakes. Most of these sediments are ultimately derived from the rivers that drain the surrounding uplands. Lesser amounts of sediment also come from the erosion of the lake basin and from inputs of volcanic ash and eolian dust and sand that may blow directly into the lake.

The coarsest sediments transported by the river are deposited at the point where it enters the lake. These bedload sediments usually form a delta (Fig. 5.4) unless they are mobilized by waves and currents and reworked into depositional shoreline features (e.g., beaches). The remaining suspended load of silt and clay is dispersed over a much broader area of the lake by overflow and interflow. Overflow is the dispersal of sediment into the central portion of the lake in the epilimnion. This occurs if the river water entering the lake is less dense than the waters of the epilimnion. Interflow is the dispersal of suspended sediments across the lake along the top of the thermocline. This occurs if the river water is denser than the water of the epilimnion but less dense than the water of the hypolimnion. In either case, the silt-size particles dispersed across the lake eventually settle to the lake bottom, while the finer clay-size particles remain held in suspension in the thermocline. The latter particles are seasonally released during overturning and settle to the lake floor. In this way, rhythmically laminated sediments (varves) are created.

Underflows, also known as turbidity flows, occur if dense, cold stream waters mixed with sediment enter a body of less-dense lake water (Fig. 5.4). The denser stream water travels along the bed of the lake basin and transports sediment into the deeper parts of the lake. Deposits generated by underflows are a mixture of coarse to fine clastic particles that show graded bedding. These deposits are called turbidites.

Lacustrine shoreline features are created by nearshore waves and currents that erode and deposit sediment along the lake margin. Lacustrine shoreline landforms and sediments are similar to those produced along marine coastlines and include both erosional and depositional features that differ little from their marine counterparts (e.g., beaches, bars, spits, estuaries, mudflats, and wave-cut cliffs and platforms).

In addition to the clastic sediments, rivers that enter a lake basin also carry a dissolved chemical load. In many lakes, the concentration of the dissolved load may be small, especially if an outlet allows water to leave the lake. However, in some basins with restricted circulation, where overflow does not occur or is minimal, the concentration of the dissolved load increases and chemical sediments precipitate.

Evaporites form in closed-basin lakes in arid and semiarid regions, where salts dissolved in the water entering the lake become concentrated into saline brines due to intense evaporation. Minerals precipitate in the brine and accumulate to form an evaporite deposit (e.g., layers of halite and gypsum). The composition of the brine determines the type of minerals precipitated.

Marls are commonly created near the shoreline in freshwater and brackish lakes. They develop where carbonate clasts and shells accumulate or where organic or inorganic precipitation of calcium carbonate takes place. Calcium carbonate may also be deposited as tufa on the rock surfaces exposed along the shoreline of the lake (Fig. 2.10).

Organic matter is commonly incorporated into lacustrine sediment. Peats and sapropels are created as waterlogged plant debris accumulates in anoxic lake waters, where bacterial activity is minimal.

Playas

Playas are broad, shallow depressions with no external drainage. Typically, a playa occupies the topographically lowest portion of a basin (Fig. 5.5), but one may also form in an interdune area or in the depression of a parabolic dune or blowout. Direct rainfall and runoff from the adjacent highlands

FIGURE 5.5. Looking south across the Drinkwater Playa in the central Mojave Desert in California.

occasionally fill a playa with water to create a shallow lake. Because water is not constantly supplied to the playa, the water eventually evaporates. Consequently, playa lakes are ephemeral and are usually dry most of the year. Playas are generally found in the arid and semiarid regions of the western United States.

Playa lake sediments are characterized by both fine-grained clastic sediments and chemically precipitated mineral layers. Clastic sediments are transported to the playa from the adjacent highlands by both fluvial and eolian processes. As the water in the playa evaporates, the sediment suspended in it settles to the playa floor, and salts dissolved in the water concentrate and precipitate. Repeated filling and desiccation of a playa results in the creation of thin interbedded layers of sand, silt, clay, and evaporites. These sediments are very susceptible to destruction by later wind erosion. Desiccation features, such as polygonal mud cracks, are common at the surface of a playa. Many playas in the western United States occupy the lakebeds of Pleistocene pluvial lakes. These were perennial bodies of water that filled the same basins but were much greater in size and depth than the modern playas.

Along the margin of a playa, waves and currents are not strong enough to transport sediment and construct shoreline features. Instead, the shoreline of a playa lake is usually defined by a concentration of coarse sand and gravel. This lag is created as waves winnow the fine-grained sediments from deposits fringing the playa and leave behind the particles that are too heavy to be entrained and transported by the water.

Site Formation Processes and Landscape Reconstruction

Because lacustrine processes, landforms, and deposits are similar to those of the coastal marine environment, the same general concepts of site formation, preservation, and destruction due to transgression and regression are applicable to lake environments (see Chapter 6). Consequently, this discussion does not deal with the mechanics of site formation and preservation but instead focuses on lacustrine landscape evolution and its influence on the spatial and temporal distribution of the sites of lacustrine-adapted people.

Lakes, like most environments, are constantly changing over time. Analogous to the rise and fall of sea level, the level of a lake also fluctuates, with periods of transgression onto the land and regression from it. The level of a lake is a balance between the loss of water due to evaporation and groundwater recharge and inputs of water from direct precipitation, runoff from the watershed, and interbasin groundwater transfers. If inputs of water exceed losses, the level of a lake rises unless a spillway draining excess water from the basin limits the maximum level it can attain. Conversely, when water losses from a basin are greater than inputs, the lake level falls. If the latter conditions prevail long enough, the lake disappears.

The most dramatic fluctuations in lake levels occurred during the late Pleistocene in western North America, where large pluvial lakes formed within internally drained and closed basins (Fig. 5.6; Benson and Thompson 1987; Flint 1971; Smith and Street-Perrott 1983). The most prominent pluvial lakes included Lake Bonneville, which covered much of northwestern Utah; Lake Lahontan, which inundated and connected many basins in northwestern Nevada; and the Searles Lake system, which stretched through the Mojave Desert of California. These lakes formed because temperatures decreased (reducing evaporation rates) and precipitation increased during the late Pleistocene. Pluvial lakes later desiccated during the Holocene when temperatures rose and precipitation declined. The basins occupied by these paleolakes are now either dry (e.g., Searles Lake is now a playa) or are occupied by much smaller lakes (e.g., the Great Salt Lake in Utah now occupies a portion of the Lake Bonneville Basin).

As lake levels rose and fell, lacustrine resources (plants, fish, shellfish, and waterfowl) were displaced. Prehistoric people who depended on these resources followed the movements of the shoreline. Consequently, fluctuations in the lake level determined the spatio-temporal distribution of lacus-

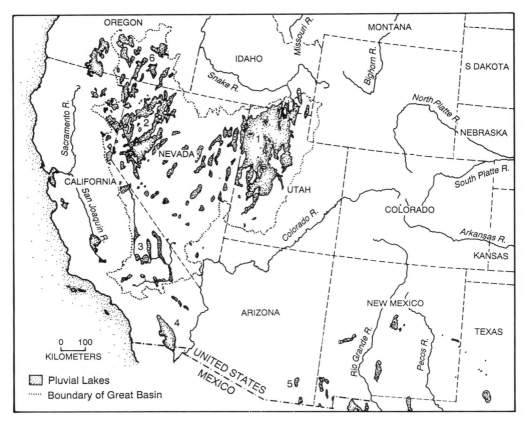

FIGURE 5.6. The distribution of pluvial lakes in the western United States during the late Pleistocene: (1) Lake Bonneville, (2) Lake Lahontan, (3) the Searles Lake system, (4) Lake Cahuilla, (5) Lake Cochise, and (6) the Alkali Lake Basin. (Modified from Smith and Street-Perrott 1983)

trine-focused sites. In the Great Lakes region, for example, Larsen (1985) showed that lake levels in the Lake Michigan and Lake Huron basins have fluctuated repeatedly during the past 14,000 years. As a result, Paleoindian, earliest Archaic, latest Archaic, and Woodland period sites can be found on or near the surface of shorelines that developed at different elevations. Also, because the lakes in the Michigan and Huron basins sometimes rose to the same level at different times in the past, different cultures and periods of occupation are in some cases superimposed on the surface or buried to shallow depths on the same shoreline. Many early and middle Archaic sites associated with periods when the lake levels were below their present position are either submerged or have been eroded during subsequent transgressions. However, Larson showed that early and middle Archaic sites, once thought to be completely absent from the region because they were submerged below the modern levels of Lake Michigan or Lake Huron, can be found in deeply buried contexts under younger shorelines. This is because there were intermittent high lake stands during the early and middle Archaic periods. These surfaces and associated sites became buried beneath younger shoreline sediments by a later rise in the lake level around 4500 B.P. Similar oscillations in the level of Lake Minong (an earlier and deeper stage of Lake Superior) eroded and buried much of the late Paleoindian and early Archaic archaeological record around Thunder Bay, Ontario (Julig et al. 1990; Phillips 1988).

Surface and buried sites are also found on and below the prominent late Holocene shoreline of Lake Cahuilla in the Salton Basin of California (Fig. 5.6; Wilke 1978). Here the lake rose and fell at least four times between A.D. 700 and 1580 (Waters 1983). Because the lake rose to the same level each time, evidence of human use of the littoral zone during high stands of the lake is compressed onto the surface of a single shoreline. Buried sites are encountered below the shoreline where people camped on the dry lakebed whenever the lake level fell or the lake dried up. In many cases these sites became buried by alluvium shedding off the hillslopes and later by laminated lake basin sediments during a subsequent rise in lake level (Fig. 5.7). These sites were protected and preserved from the shoreface erosion associated with a later transgression of the lake because the overlying alluvium was thick and the lake rose rapidly.

The configuration and hydrologic condition of a lake also affected the location of settlements along its shoreline. Willig (1984, 1988) suggests that the presence of the Dietz Clovis site on the margin of a small lake in the Alkali Basin in southern Oregon (Fig. 5.6) and the absence of Clovis sites along the shoreline of two larger lakes in the basin is due to a relationship between drainage basin size and lake surface area. The Dietz site is situated next to a lake basin with a small surface area that is fed by a large drainage basin. This small lake would have provided a reliable source of water and would have been characterized by a marsh, which would have attracted mammals and waterfowl. The larger lake basins nearby drained smaller watersheds and thus could not sustain a reliable water supply for any length of time. Furthermore, artifacts of the Clovis and Western Stemmed point traditions (Lake Mojave) are temporally and spatially segregated around the lake basin. Clovis artifacts occur along the shoreline of an extremely small (2.4 km^2) and shallow (40–50 cm deep) playa marsh in the center of the Dietz Basin, while stemmed points and artifacts are found fringing the

FIGURE 5.7. A hearth containing charcoal (directly above the shovel) interbedded between late Holocene lacustrine deposits exposed below the 12 m shoreline of Paleolake Cahuilla. This feature was excavated by people who camped on the ancient lakebed during a low stand of the lake. The hearth was subsequently buried by alluvium and later overlain by lacustrine sediments during a rise of the lake.

shoreline of a lake that was 2 m deep and had a surface area of 14 km². Along the shoreline of Glacial Lake Algonquin in Ontario, Paleoindians located sites in areas that maximized visibility (i.e., provided unobstructed views along the shoreline) and where the shoreline was indented (Mason 1981; Storck 1982, 1984). Indented shorelines provided situations in which a larger area of shoreline and more diverse environments were available within a short distance of a site. Buchner and Pettipas (1990) suggest a close relationship between the distribution of Paleoindian sites dated between 11,500 and 7700 B.P. and the fluctuations of Lake Agassiz in Manitoba.

   The most extreme changes in a lacustrine landscape occur where a basin is cycled between contrasting periods of rich lacustrine resources and terrestrial conditions. These changes affected adaptations and the prehistoric use of many basins. For example, Lake Cahuilla (Fig. 5.6) was intermittently formed during the late Holocene whenever the Colorado River, which typically flows into the Gulf of California, was diverted into the arid Salton Basin of California (Waters 1983; Wilke 1978). The level of the lake was stabilized at an elevation of 12 m, and excess water flowed to the south through an outlet channel. At this elevation, Lake Cahuilla had a surface area of over 5,700 km² and a maximum depth of 95 m. When the Colorado River was rediverted to the Gulf of California, inflow into the lake ceased, the lake desiccated, and arid conditions returned to the basin. Reconstruction of the lacustrine history of the lake shows that there were at least four periods of filling and desiccation between A.D. 700 and 1580 (Waters 1983). Filling the lake required only 12 to 20 years, and desiccation occurred within 60 years. Thus regional changes in the Salton Basin occurred over a span of one to three generations.

   The question of how people adapted to the changes in the Salton Basin has not been resolved. Wilke (1978) believes that there was dense sedentary occupation along the shoreline and that the people depended on the lacustrine resources. He believes that the final desiccation of the lake caused demographic changes in southern California and even facilitated the adoption of agriculture in the basin. However, Weide (1976) believes that because the lake frequently fluctuated, it was too unreliable to allow a sedentary lifeway. She believes that instead the shoreline was occupied for brief intervals by small hunter-gatherer groups that readily adapted to the presence or absence of lacustrine conditions. When the lake was absent from the basin, these groups would focus on the terrestrial desert resources, and when the lake reappeared, they would use the lacustrine resources. Recent investigations along the shoreline of Lake Cahuilla (Gallegos 1986; Schaefer 1986) tend to support Weide's reconstruction.

A similar opportunistic adaptation by Archaic hunter-gatherers seems to have characterized the semiarid Willcox Basin in Arizona. Three times during the Holocene, water filled the basin and created Lake Cochise (Fig. 5.6; Waters 1989). Lake Cochise had a maximum surface area of 190 km^2 and was 11 m deep. The high stands of Lake Cochise, however, were maintained only for brief intervals. During most of the Holocene, Lake Cochise did not exist, and the Willcox Basin was characterized by ephemeral playa lakes and desert conditions. An archaeological survey of the basin indicates that only small camps occur on the shoreline, and there were no periods of intense occupation around the shoreline at any time. Larger residential camps are located on the upland bajadas. Waters and Woosley (1990) suggest that the lacustrine resources of Lake Cochise were incorporated into a wider pattern of seasonal exploitation whenever the opportunity afforded itself (i.e., when the lake was present), but its absence did not substantially affect Archaic subsistence in the basin.

Slopes

Mass movement (also called mass wasting) is the downslope movement of rock, sediment, and soil under the influence of gravity without the aid of other agents of erosion such as flowing water, wind, or ice (Chorley et al. 1985; Ritter 1986; Young 1972). Mass movements range from rapid, catastrophic landslides in which large masses of debris are transported off a slope within a matter of seconds or minutes to the imperceptible slow creep of individual particles down a gradual slope. These types of movements may be triggered by the vibrations from earthquakes or the mechanical pushing or heaving of particles downslope, or they may occur spontaneously if the gravitational forces exceed the forces holding the material to the slope. Five basic types of mass movements are defined, based on the type of movement involved: falls, slides, slumps, flows, and creep (Fig. 5.8).

Falls are created by the free fall of rocks or coherent masses of sediment from steep cliffs. The coarse debris that breaks loose from the cliff tumbles over the slope and accumulates to form talus or scree deposits at the base of the slope. Slides are slope failures in which a large mass of rock and debris slips downslope along a zone of weakness, usually a bedding plane or structural surface (e.g., a fault or joint). The debris removed from the slope may come to rest anywhere from a meter to a kilometer downslope. A scar is left on the slope delineating the area in which the debris originated. Slumps are generated when a block of sediment breaks loose from its bed and slides downward and outward as a coherent unit along a curved failure plane. As the failed block rotates from its original position, it produces a scarp or

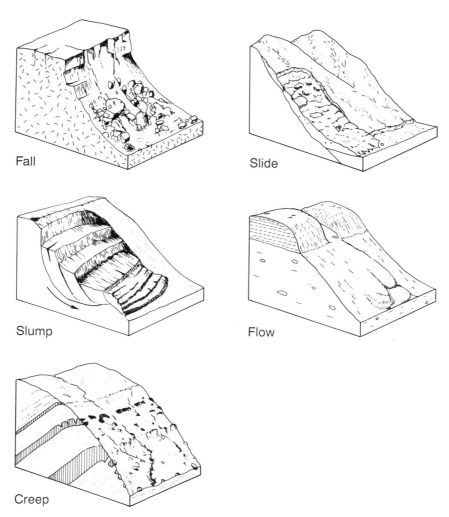

FIGURE 5.8. Five basic types of mass movements on slopes.

concave scar on the slope. Sliding and slumping may occur suddenly in one great mass movement or in a series of small displacements that take place over months or years. Flows are created by the downslope movement of water-saturated debris. The material being transported may remain semi-coherent or may become jumbled and mixed. These soggy masses may move rapidly downslope in a few minutes (e.g., mudflows and debris flows on alluvial fans; see Chapter 3) or at a rate of only a few centimeters or meters per hour or day for a short period (e.g., solifluction and gelifluction; see Chapter 7). Creep is the extremely slow, almost undetectable downslope movement of soil particles in the upper meter of the soil caused by a variety of mechanisms. Particles may simply roll down the hillside, burrowing animals may push sediment down the slope, or particles may slowly move downslope due to heaving and slumping associated with wetting and drying or freezing and thawing (see Chapter 7).

The term colluvium is used to describe sediments that are eroded, transported, and deposited on and at the base of slopes by gravity. Colluvial deposits range from accumulations of coarse rock fragments to clay-size particles but are commonly a poorly sorted mixture of both coarse and fine-grained particles.

Site Formation Processes and Landscape Reconstruction

Archaeological sites are commonly disturbed by slope processes and buried in mass movement deposits. The disturbance of sites by slope processes, especially creep and flow, is discussed in Chapter 7. The following discussion focuses on the burial of sites in mass movement deposits (i.e., viewing mass movement as a process of burial and preservation) and the effects of slope processes on people.

Archaeological debris is commonly buried in mass movement deposits at the base of slopes. Archaeological remains situated on the failed slope or in the path of the mass movement are incorporated into the moving debris. When later discovered, these archaeological remains are clearly not in their original behavioral context. For example, archaeological remains in mudflows and debris flows are usually jumbled in the flow deposits (e.g., the Borax Lake site in California; see Chapter 3) or may form reworked colluvial deposits at the base of the slope (e.g., the Rincon Point site in California; see Chapter 7). However, in some cases the systemic context of a site may be well preserved under a mass movement deposit. At the Ozette site in Washington, a mudslide engulfed a whale-hunting settlement around A.D. 1750, preserving much of the spatial integrity of the site (Kirk and Daugherty 1974, 1978). Likewise, at the base of cliffs once used as animal jumps, bone beds are often buried in multiple layers of colluvium (see, for example, Davis and Wilson 1978; Frison 1978; Kehoe 1973).

Mass movement deposits and the scars they created on slopes provided landscape settings that were used by humans. A small slump on the Battle River in central Alberta was the setting for a bison jump (Quigg 1977; Wilson 1990). Similarly, moist local microhabitats that attracted humans were created at the heads of rotational slump blocks on the slopes above Forty Mile Coulee in southern Alberta (Brumley and Dau 1988; Wilson 1983c, 1990).

Mass movements have also affected the location of human settlements and regional settlement and subsistence patterns. For example, prior to A.D. 1820 the Wet'suet'en people fished for salmon at Moricetown, British Columbia, along the Bulkley River (Cassidy 1987; Morice 1906). A rockfall into the Bulkley River in 1820 downstream from Moricetown created a cascade that was too high for salmon to ascend. This change in ecological conditions caused by the rockfall forced the Wet'suet'en people, whose subsistence depended on salmon fishing, to establish a new village (called Hagwilget) 40 km downstream from Moricetown near the newly created cascade. Eventually the rockfall debris was eroded by the river, which allowed the salmon to pass upstream again. This, in turn, allowed some of the inhabitants of Hagwilget to return to Moricetown.

On a larger scale, Hayden and Ryder (1991) suggest that landsliding in the Lillooet region of British Columbia was responsible for the abandonment of a large area. From 3000 to 1100 B.P. a number of large and socially complex hunter-gatherer villages emerged along the Fraser River. Subsistence in these settlements was based largely on salmon procurement from the river. Around 1100 B.P. all the large villages in the region were abandoned, and they were never reoccupied to any significant degree. While numerous explanations for this settlement change have been proposed, the failure of the salmon runs is the most likely explanation for the abandonment. Hayden and Ryder (1991) suggest that the abandonment of the region coincided with a catastrophic landslide that temporarily dammed the Fraser River. This landslide prevented the salmon from traveling to spawning grounds upstream from the landslide, which undermined the economic foundations for subsistence and trade. Because other resources in the area were limited and there was no alternative subsistence strategy to be followed, the ecological catastrophe triggered by the landslide forced the migration of people out of all the communities along the Fraser River upstream from the landslide.

Along the Columbia River the opposite appears to have happened. Sanger (1967) notes that for several thousand years prior to A.D. 1200–1300, there is very little evidence for salmon fishing upstream from Celilo Falls, an area characterized by waterfalls and rapids. After A.D. 1200–1300 there was a shift in subsistence to intensified salmon fishing accompanied by more extensive use of the river floodplain. This shift coincided with the Cascade landslide, which occurred around A.D. 1265. This landslide dammed the river for a short period, but more important, it reduced the stream gradient around Celilo Falls and created natural fish ladders, which permitted the upriver passage of salmon to new spawning grounds. Sanger (1967) believes the sudden improvement in the resource potential of the Columbia River above Celilo Falls accounts for the settlement and cultural changes at this time.

Glaciers

Glaciers are large, slow-moving masses of ice that can erode valleys, scour vast surfaces, and transport and deposit large masses of sediment (Easterbrook 1982; Edwards 1986; Eyles and Miall 1984; Flint 1971; Leeder 1982; Reineck and Singh 1980; Ritter 1986). During the Quaternary there were at least twenty major glacial-interglacial cycles, when glaciers formed, expanded, retreated, and disappeared from the landscape (Bradley 1985; Catt 1986, 1988; Nilsson 1983; Sibrava et al. 1986). At the height of the latest Wisconsin glaciation, 20,000 to 18,000 years ago, ice covered nearly one-third of the earth's surface. In North America, two large ice sheets, the Laurentide and Cordilleran, covered most of Canada and the northern border of the conterminous United States, and glaciers extended down many mountain valleys (Fig. 5.9).

On the basis of their morphology and physiographic position, glaciers are classified as (1) valley glaciers, ice that is confined within mountain valleys; (2) piedmont glaciers, ice that emerges from the confines of a valley and spreads over the adjacent lowland beyond the mountain front; or (3) ice sheets, extensive masses of ice that form and spread over large continental areas. Although each of these types of glaciers is characterized by its own mode of movement and erosional and depositional landforms, the following generalizations can be made about glaciers.

Glaciers are created in areas where the amount of accumulated snow exceeds the amount of melted snow over a number of years. As more snow accumulates, it becomes compacted and recrystallizes into glacial ice. As more ice is formed, a glacier slowly moves outward from its source due to the stresses created by its own weight through processes known as internal creep and basal slip. Once formed, a glacier will advance or retreat, depending on the balance between the amount of new ice created at the source of the glacier and the amount of old ice lost due to melting and evaporation. Thus glaciers are in a constant state of motion, always adjusting to yearly climatic conditions.

Glaciers transport tons of clastic debris in their ice. Sediment becomes incorporated into glacial ice as the ice advances over frost-shattered bedrock or when debris falls onto the surface of the ice. These clastic sediments become embedded in the ice and then erode and polish the underlying bedrock over which the ice passes, scouring deep valleys and large, flat plains. Even the stones within the ice become faceted, striated, polished, and pulverized.

Much of the debris transported in the ice is eventually deposited along the base, sides, and terminus of the glacier (Fig. 5.10). Glacially deposited sediment is known as drift. Drift is divided into two types: till, or unstratified

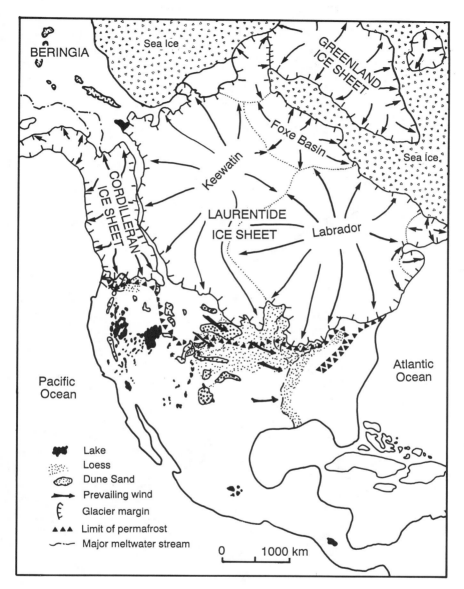

FIGURE 5.9. A paleogeographic map of North America showing the extent of continental glaciation, the configuration of the continent as a result of lowered sea levels, and other environmental conditions during the last glacial maximum 20,000 to 18,000 years ago. (Modified from Porter 1988)

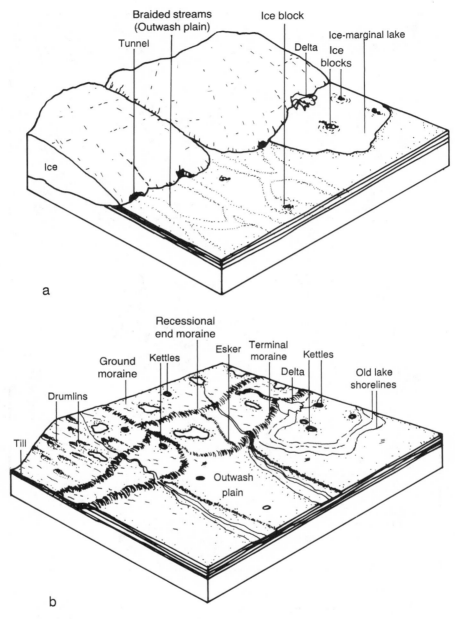

FIGURE 5.10. Landforms and deposits left by continental glaciers: (a) the environment at the time of glaciation; (b) landforms and deposits created as a result of glaciation. (Modified from Strahler and Strahler 1989)

FIGURE 5.11. Late Pleistocene glacial till deposited at the mouth of a glaciated valley on the western flank of the Flint Creek Range in Montana. Note the poor sorting and the matrix-supported nature of the deposit. Here ablation till (AT, the bouldery layer) abruptly overlies lodgement till (LT). The bank is approximately 3 m high.

drift, which is sediment deposited directly by ice transport; and stratified drift, which is composed of deposits created by running water in contact with the ice.

Till is a poorly sorted, unstratified deposit of boulders, cobbles, pebbles, sand, silt, and clay that is deposited directly from the ice. Two common forms of till are lodgement till and ablation till (Fig. 5.11). Lodgement till is a layer of till plastered onto the ground surface beneath the glacier. Ablation till is a layer of drift that is created where glacial ice stagnates and the clastic debris in the ice is concentrated at the surface by melting of the ice matrix. Ablation till forms at the terminus of the glacier and commonly overlies lodgement till. If the glacier remains stationary for a time, till is often accumulated into ridges known as moraines along its sides and terminus (Fig. 5.10). The outermost moraine is called the terminal moraine and marks the maximum expansion of the glacier. Recessional moraines are often nested behind the terminal moraine and represent short periods of stability during

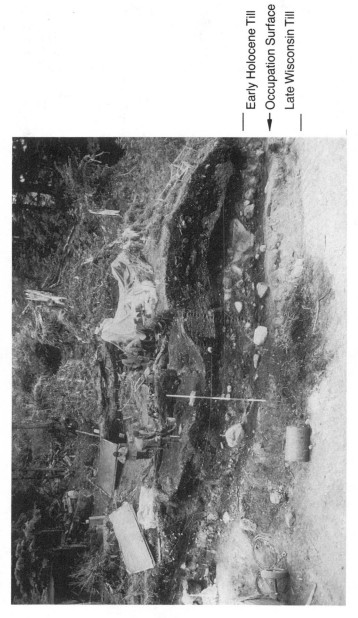

— Early Holocene Till

→ Occupation Surface

— Late Wisconsin Till

FIGURE 5.12. A 9500-year-old occupation surface preserved between late Wisconsin till and early Holocene till at the Hidden Falls site in Alaska. Younger units and archaeological components overlie the Holocene till. (Photograph by Stanley D. Davis)

the retreat of the glacial ice. Kettles are depressions created by the melting of blocks of ice in till and are common on till surfaces.

Meltwater flows through streams that occur on, within, and under the ice. The clastic deposits created by these streams, usually well-sorted deposits of sand and gravel, are called stratified drift. Two of the most common landforms composed of stratified drift are eskers and kames. Eskers are linear ridges of sand and gravel deposited by streams confined by the glacial ice, usually in tunnels at or near the base of the glacier. Kames are mounds of stratified drift created by the accumulation of sand and gravel in cavities in the glacial ice.

Beyond the terminus of the glacier are outwash plains, which are characterized by a network of braided channels that diverge and rejoin around gravel bars. Here sediment transported by meltwater from the glacier accumulates into deposits like those described for gravelly braided streams in chapter 3.

Three other depositional environments—glaciolacustrine, glaciomarine, and eolian—are associated with glaciers. Lakes commonly form either directly against the glacial ice at the terminus of a glacier or farther downstream in former glaciated terrain where meltwater collects. Delta, shoreline, and fine-grained basin sediments may accumulate in this glaciolacustrine environment (Fig. 5.10). Glaciomarine sediments are those that accumulate on the ocean floor in areas where glacial ice extends into marine waters. Eolian environments form when silt and sand winnowed from the outwash plains accumulate in adjacent regions as loess and sand dunes.

Site Formation Processes and Landscape Reconstruction

In North America, glacial deposits do not commonly contain archaeological remains, but in a few cases glaciers have advanced over sites and artifacts have become incorporated into drift and buried beneath it. This rare situation is well illustrated by the Hidden Falls site on the Pacific coast of Baranof Island in southeastern Alaska (Fig. 5.12; S. D. Davis 1989; Swanston 1989). At this site, the oldest of four cultural layers, dating to approximately 9500 B.P., is overlain by glacial till. More than 600 artifacts were recovered from the basal lodgement till, the overlying ablation till, and a stratified glaciofluvial deposit. The stratigraphy at the site indicates that at around 9500 B.P. maritime-adapted people camped on the surface of late Wisconsin till. After the site was abandoned, artifacts and features were incorporated into an organic-rich unit, which later became weathered into a soil. Sometime around 8000 B.P., a glacier advanced over this buried site. As glacial ice covered the site, the systemic patterning of the archaeological debris was altered as the artifacts and stones making up features were reworked into the lodgement till or incorporated into the ice and later deposited as part of the ablation till when the ice over the site stagnated as the glacier retreated. Some artifacts were picked up by water running over the stagnating ice and were deposited in ice-contact stratified drift. One hearth feature, composed of a concentration of fire-fractured stones, charcoal, and artifacts, occurred primarily in the underlying paleosol but was also partly reworked into the overlying lodgement till. Most of the artifacts had no noticeable edge damage and were probably not transported far from their original context. Had the artifacts been transported any distance, they would have become more scattered and the archaeological site probably would have been completely destroyed. At the Timlin site in New York, controversial early stone tools have been recovered from within and under glacial till (Timlin and Raemsch 1971).

During the late Pleistocene, glaciers covered large parts of North America. Consequently, they prevented the occupation of certain regions, created barriers to early population movement, and molded much of the landscape of North America on which later Holocene occupation took place (Fig. 5.9; Flint 1971; Fulton 1989; Nilsson 1983; Porter 1988; Ruddiman and Wright 1987; Wright and Porter 1983). The northern migration of people into Canada was limited by the rate at which the continental ice sheets retreated and exposed the land (Fulton 1989; Harris 1987). Also, the expansion and contraction of the Laurentide and Cordilleran ice sheets were responsible for closing and opening the ice-free corridor between Alaska and the conterminous United States, thereby dictating the times when humans could or could not travel through the corridor (Bobrowsky et al. 1990; Catto and Mandryk 1990; Rutter and Schweger 1980; Wilson 1990). Continental glaciation also influenced climate patterns in North America, the timing and magnitude of changes in the sea level, the distribution of vegetation in nonglaciated areas, and fluvial, eolian, and lacustrine processes (Bonnichsen et al. 1985; COHMAP 1988; Porter 1988; Ruddiman and Wright 1987; Wright and Porter 1983). Consequently, even though glacial drift rarely serves as an archaeological matrix, glaciation had a profound influence on landscape evolution in glaciated and nonglaciated areas that directly and indirectly affected human groups.

Rockshelters and Caves

Both rockshelters and caves are naturally formed recesses within bedrock, but rockshelters are shallow niches or ledges under overhanging bedrock, while caves extend beyond their opening into subterranean passageways and chambers. Caves and rockshelters can form in a variety of different litholo-

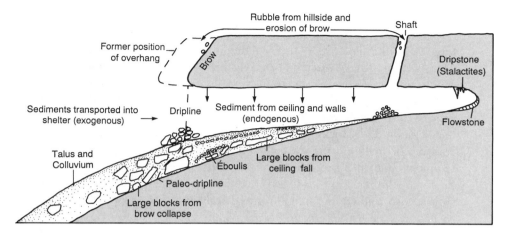

FIGURE 5.13. A generalized cross section through a rockshelter.

gies, but most develop in limestone or sandstone. Small tubes or blisters in basaltic lava also form bedrock shelters.

The environment at the mouth of a cave and in a rockshelter is generally within the reach of daylight and the influence of outside weather. These areas were the preferred sites of human habitation. The interior cave environment is beyond the reach of daylight and is characterized by its own local atmosphere, which is commonly wet. Such areas were not conducive to human habitation, and the interior chambers of caves were generally restricted to ritual and artistic activities. For this reason, this discussion emphasizes the environment of cave mouths and rockshelters. References for this discussion are Butzer 1971, 1982; Donahue and Adovasio 1990; Farrand 1985b; Laville 1976; Laville et al. 1980; Lowe and Walker 1984; Schmid 1969; and Straus 1990. The term *rockshelter*, as used in this chapter, includes cave mouth environments. Interior cave environments are discussed in Ford 1976.

The edge of the bedrock overhang of a rockshelter is called the brow (Fig. 5.13). Directly below the lip of the brow, on the lower ledge of the rockshelter, is the dripline. This is the area where water flowing or dripping off the brow strikes the ledge. A pile of debris typically accumulates on the ledge below the brow. Depending on the morphology of the debris pile, water is either directed into or out of the rockshelter. Commonly, an apron of talus and colluvium extends downslope from the entrance of the rockshelter.

Some of the sediments making up the fill of a rockshelter are created by physical and chemical weathering processes operating in the shelter. Weath-

ering of the bedrock comprising the ceiling and walls of a shelter can produce individual silt-to-sand-size grains, coarse angular rubble (*éboulis*), and
large slabs and blocks that accumulate on the shelter floor. For example, at
Meadowcroft Rockshelter in Pennsylvania a slow but continuous rain of
sand-size particles caused by grain-by-grain disintegration of the sandstone
bedrock making up the shelter walls and ceiling was a major depositional
process responsible for filling the shelter (Donahue and Adovasio 1990).
Large slabs and blocks in the Meadowcroft stratigraphy record several
episodes of spalling from the ceiling and brow of the rockshelter. Chemical
sediments may also precipitate in rockshelters and are referred to as spelothems. Spelothems are classified as either dripstones or flowstones. Dripstones, also known as stalagmites and stalactites, are deposits of calcium
carbonate (travertine) created as chemically charged water drips from the
ceiling of the rockshelter. Dripstones may be found near the back of a
rockshelter but are generally found in the inner chambers of caves. Flowstones are thin crusts or veneers of calcium carbonate, gypsum, or other
evaporite or carbonate minerals that precipitate on the walls or floor of the
rockshelter. These crusts are created as chemically charged water trickles
over exposed surfaces and precipitates salts from solution onto these surfaces. For example, a breccia (a deposit of coarse angular rubble) containing
Folsom artifacts is overlain and underlain by dripstones at Sandia Cave in
New Mexico (Haynes and Agogino 1986). Chemically charged water may
also percolate into older deposits and cement them. The lower levels of Ventana Cave in Arizona, which contain early San Dieguito I artifacts, were
cemented by calcium carbonate and silica (Bryan 1950; Haury 1950). The
clastic and chemical sediments produced in a cave are referred to collectively
as endogenous sediments.

The type of endogenous sediments created in a rockshelter are in large
part controlled by the lithology of the bedrock (Donahue and Adovasio
1990; Farrand 1985b). Sandstone shelters are dominated by clastic endogenous sedimentation, while shelters composed of limestone may have both
clastic and chemical endogenous sediments.

Rockshelters are also effective sediment traps. Sediments from outside
the rockshelter, known as exogenous sediments, commonly find their way
into the shelter through the entrance and any fissures in its roof or walls (Fig.
5.13). They enter the rockshelter by fluvial, eolian, gravity, glacial, lacustrine,
marine, and human processes. The type of exogenous sediments accumulated in a rockshelter depends on (1) the shape, size, and orientation of the
shelter entrance or other openings; (2) the depositional environments present outside the shelter; and (3) the height of the shelter entrance above active
depositional areas. For example, alluvial sediments may accumulate in a

shelter if floodwater rises to the level of the shelter's entrance or if the flood-plain next to the shelter is aggrading. At Thorne Cave in southeastern Utah (Fig. 5.14; Day 1964; Malde and Schick 1964), alluvium filled and buried the cave during an interval of valley aggradation and was later reexposed as the channel downcut into its floodplain. Similarly, the entrance to Gatecliff Shelter in Nevada was completely buried by alluvium as the valley filled, was later reexposed during valley downcutting, and was again partially filled with alluvium as the valley aggraded for a second time (Melhorn and Trexler 1983a, 1983b). Marine or lacustrine water may enter a shelter and deposit sediments if the site is situated along a fluctuating marine or lake shoreline. At Danger Cave in Utah, which is situated on the slopes below the Stansbury shoreline of Pluvial Lake Bonneville, lake water entered the shelter and filled the lowest portion of the cave with beach sands and gravel (Jennings 1957, 1978). Lacustrine beach sands, quiet-water clays, and tufa were deposited in the lowest portions of Hidden Cave in Nevada as Pluvial Lake Lahontan rose and covered the shelter during the late Pleistocene (J. O. Davis 1985; Thomas 1985). Eolian and ash deposits also accumulate in rockshelters. The Mazama Ash, for example, is present in the stratigraphy at both Gatecliff Shelter and Hidden Cave in Nevada (J. O. Davis 1983, 1985; J. O. Davis et al. 1983; Thomas 1983, 1985). Gravity debris flow, slopewash, and col-luvium also find their way into shelters. These deposits make up part of the stratigraphic sequence of both Hidden Cave and Gatecliff Shelter. Sediments may also enter through vertical openings in the shelter. At the Seminole Sink site in Texas, a talus cone and exogenous sediments accumulated directly below a vertical shaft entrance and contained Archaic burials and crema-tions (Byrd 1988; Turpin 1988).

Exogenous sediments also include the biological material left by animals and humans. This includes the nests built by packrats, guano deposited by birds and bats, and layers of coprolites left by sloths, mammoths, and other creatures, as encountered at such sites as Gypsum Cave in Nevada (Harring-ton 1933). Humans also transport biological material into shelters and create middens.

The stratigraphic sequence in any rockshelter is unique because of differ-ences in shelter lithology, weathering processes, hydrologic conditions, and the types of depositional environments present outside the shelter. Thus, rockshelter sequences are composed of many combinations of endogenous and exogenous sediments. These sediments may be continuous layers across the shelter or discontinuous layers that were deposited only in one part of the shelter. Also, the exogenous sediments can be derived from multiple sources at any one time, and the source of the intrusive sediments can change over time. The rate of sedimentation in a rockshelter also varies over time and can even be interrupted by periods with little or no deposition, creating hiatuses in the stratigraphic sequence. For example, over the last 21,000 years the sedimentation rate at the Meadowcroft Rockshelter in Pennsylvania has varied from 6.9 cm to 267 cm per 1000 years (Donahue and Adovasio 1990). Pedogenesis and other postdepositional alterations of previously deposited sediments may occur during hiatuses in deposition.

In general, once sediments are deposited in a shelter, they are generally not eroded away. In many cases, roof fall may seal and protect the underlying sediments. However, erosional unconformities can be present in the stratigraphy of a shelter, documenting periods when previously deposited sediments were scoured. For example, much of the early stratigraphic record in Ventana Cave in Arizona was eroded when water flowed across the floor of the shelter (Bryan 1950; Haury 1950).

Site Formation Processes and Landscape Reconstruction

Rockshelters and the entrances to caves were common sites of human occupation. The archaeological debris of these occupations becomes incorporated into or buried by the sediments that entered or formed within the shelter. Excellent examples of this phenomenon can be found at Gatecliff Shelter in Nevada (J. O. Davis 1983; J. O. Davis et al. 1983; Melhorn and Trexler 1983a, 1983b; Thomas 1983); Hidden Cave in Nevada (J. O. Davis 1985; Thomas 1985); Danger Cave in Utah (Jennings 1957, 1978); Thorne Cave in Utah (Day 1964; Malde and Schick 1964); Modoc Rockshelter in Illinois (Ahler 1976; Styles et al. 1983); Ventana Cave in Arizona (Bryan 1950; Haury 1950); Dirty Shame Rockshelter in Oregon (Kittleman 1977); Jaguar Cave in Idaho (Dort 1975); the Wasden site in Idaho (Miller and Dort 1978; Moody and Dort 1990); Meadowcroft Rockshelter in Pennsylvania (Donahue and Adovasio 1990); and Sandia Cave in New Mexico (Bryan 1941; Haynes and Agogino 1986).

The history of deposition, erosion, and stability in a rockshelter influences the vertical and spatial separation and completeness of the archaeological record. If buried occupation surfaces are present in the shelter, the rate of sedimentation determines their vertical separation. The greater the rate of sediment accumulation, the greater the separation of discrete occupations. During periods of stability, temporally distinct occupations may become superimposed upon one another. Apparent hiatuses in occupation may be created during periods of erosion, when previously deposited sediments and artifacts are removed. For instance, the erosional period in Ventana Cave in Arizona, noted above, significantly fragmented the archaeological record of the late Pleistocene and early Holocene occupation of the shelter (Bryan 1950; Haury 1950). Gaps in the occupation of a shelter may also be the result

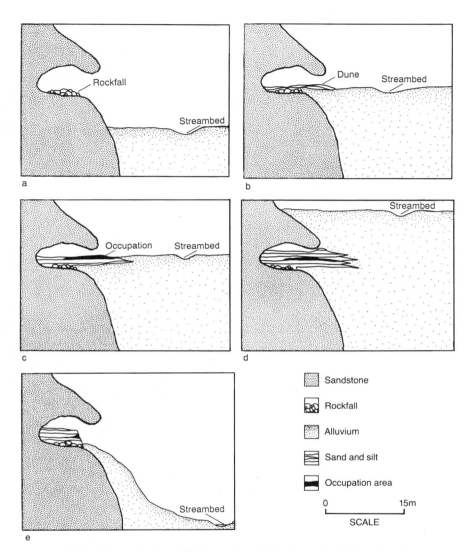

FIGURE 5.14. The evolution of Thorne Cave in Utah: (a) the shelter lies above
the streambed of Cliff Creek before 4000 B.P.; (b) the floodplain of Cliff Creek
continues to aggrade and enters the shelter (eolian sediments also accumulate);
(c) occupation occurs as the floodplain continues to aggrade and the shelter continues to fill with sand and silt; (d) alluvium completely covers the entrance to the
shelter and prevents occupation; (e) sometime around 3000 B.P., Cliff Creek downcuts into its valley and reexposes the shelter. (Modified from Day 1964)

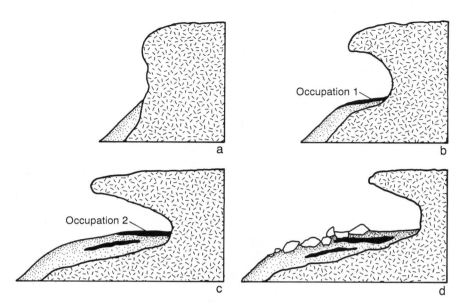

FIGURE 5.15. The evolution of a rockshelter. A cliff face (a) undergoes physical and chemical weathering to produce a shelter (b). The shelter continues to enlarge, and debris from the walls and ceiling begin to collect outside the shelter and on its floor. After the shelter has become sufficiently large, human occupation takes place and middens are created (b and c). Eventually the brow of the shelter collapses, and boulders accumulate on the floor (d). Note that the oldest occupation (no. 1) is buried beneath the rockfall in front of the shelter and would not be discovered if excavations were conducted at the back of the shelter. (Modified from Laville et al. 1980)

of periods when the rockshelter was not accessible to prehistoric people. This occurs if the shelter is submerged by rising lake or marine waters or if the entrance of the shelter becomes blocked by sediment. The floodplain of Cliff Creek, adjacent to Thorne Cave in Utah, aggraded and reached the level of the cave entrance by approximately 4000 B.P. (Fig. 5.14). Occupation occurred in the shelter until the alluvium covered the entrance and prevented any further habitation. Sometime after 3000 B.P., Cliff Creek downcut into its valley, reexposed the cave, and made it again accessible to people (Day 1964; Malde and Schick 1964). Thus the hiatus in occupation at Thorne Cave was created by the depositional history of the landscape.

Like other landscapes, rockshelters evolve through time (Collins 1991; Farrand 1985b; Laville et a. 1980). Shelters erode deeper into the host bedrock and overhangs collapse (Fig. 5.15). For example, Donahue and Adovasio (1990) mapped the progressive retreat of the brow of Meadowcroft Rockshelter over the last 21,000 years. Because of this retreat, hearths and activity areas excavated near the mouth of a shelter may represent activities that originally occurred toward the back wall of the shelter. Also, because of rockfall from the brow, the oldest archaeological remains in a shelter may lie beneath the collapsed brow debris immediately in front of extant overhangs and thus go undetected if excavations are conducted toward the back of the shelter (Fig. 5.15). Bryan (1977) and Collins (1991) point out that rockshelter degradation may account for the small sample of Paleoindian remains from rockshelter sites in North America and suggests that future excavations should sample the sediments beneath the collapsed brow debris for Paleoindian and Pre-Clovis remains. In some cases the rockshelter overhang may completely collapse, leaving no morphological indication that a shelter ever existed. In this situation, the cave fill would lie on the slope and would be covered by coarse angular debris. Other changes also occur in shelters. For example, the size of the habitation area in the shelter is reduced as sediment accumulates in it, or the shelter may at times be inaccessible to people because it is covered with sediment or submerged by lake or marine waters. In short, rockshelters have rarely remained unchanged between the period of prehistoric occupation and excavation (Farrand 1985b; Laville et al. 1980).

Conclusion

Springs, lakes, rockshelters, slopes, and glaciers are all dynamic depositional environments that can become archaeological matrices. This chapter has reviewed natural site formation processes associated with each of these environments. It has also shown how these environments have changed through time and have influenced human behavior and the archaeological record.

6

Coastal Environments

The coastal zone is the area along the margin of a continent where the sea and land meet and where there is an interplay between marine and terrestrial processes. This chapter reviews the processes, landforms, and deposits of coastlines. The geological review is based on Blatt et al. 1972; Boggs 1987; Butzer 1976; Chorley et al. 1985; Clifton 1982; Coleman 1988; Coleman and Prior 1982; R. A. Davis 1983, 1985; Elliott 1986a, 1986b; Friedman and Sanders 1978; Galloway and Hobday 1983; Leeder 1982; McCubbin 1982; Miall 1984; Morgan 1970; Reineck and Singh 1980; Reinson 1984; Ritter 1986; and Weimer et al. 1982. The chapter concludes with a discussion of archaeological site preservation and landscape reconstruction of coastal areas.

Coastal Processes

Waves, tides, and the currents they generate are the active agents that sculpt the coastal landscape. Waves, probably the most important, are created in the open ocean, where the wind distorts the surface of the water into swells. At the surface, swells have a distinctive "wave form" (Fig. 6.1) characterized by a crest (the maximum height of the water above the level of calm water) and a trough (the maximum depression of the water below the level of calm water). Other characteristics of these surface waves include the wavelength (the horizontal distance between two adjacent crests) and the wave height (the total vertical distance between the crest and the trough of a wave). In addition to the surface wave, the column of water directly under each swell moves in a circular motion. This orbital motion decreases rapidly below the surface and becomes negligible at a depth equal to approximately half the wavelength, a level known as the wave base. This orbiting water does not move forward; rather, only the surficial wave form advances toward the land.

As the surface waves enter shallow water, the water circulating beneath them comes into contact with the sea floor for the first time at a point known as the fair-weather wave base. When this occurs, the orbital motion beneath the wave becomes distorted, and the surface waves rise and tilt forward as they pass through the shoaling zone. As waves continue to approach the land, they become oversteepened and collapse, causing the water circulating beneath the waves to move forward, creating breakers. As the breakers approach the land, they are transformed into translation waves, or bores, in the surf zone. The surf runs up onto the land as a thin uprush of water, called a swash (Fig. 6.2). This is followed by an even thinner, seaward-directed return flow referred to as a backwash. Together, these constitute the swash zone.

The water circulating beneath the waves erodes sediment from the submerged substrate in the zone extending from the fair-weather wave base to the top of the swash zone (Fig. 6.1). These sediments, once entrained by the waves, are transported by beach drift, longshore currents, and rip currents.

Beach drift is the unidirectional lateral transport of sediment in the swash zone (Fig. 6.2). This occurs in areas where the upwash travels diagonally up the beachface and the return flow is roughly perpendicular to the shoreline. This causes sand to move in a roughly zig-zag pattern across the beach.

In the surf and breaker zones, wave processes generate longshore and rip currents (Fig. 6.3). Longshore currents are strong unidirectional currents that transport large volumes of sediment parallel to the shoreline. Sediments can also be transported by narrow rip currents that flow in a seaward direction through the breaker zone.

Coastlines can be substantially modified during storms or if there are

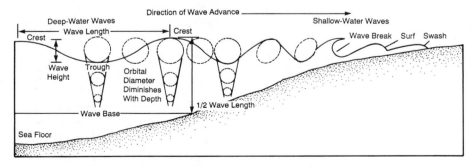

FIGURE 6.1. The terminology associated with near-shore waves. Circles show the orbital motion of water as the wave advances.

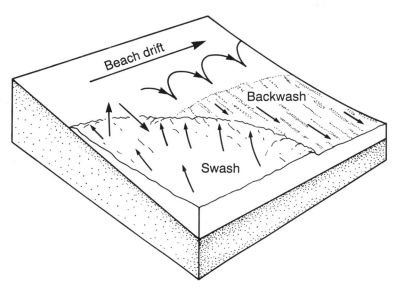

FIGURE 6.2. Beach drift in the swash zone. (Modified from Strahler and Strahler 1989)

seasonal changes in the intensity of wave processes. During these periods the fair-weather wave base is lowered and large volumes of sediment are scoured from the coastline and transported offshore. Much of this sediment is returned to the coast when the normal wave and current regime is reestablished.

Tides are also important shoreline processes. They are the rhythmic rise and fall of the ocean produced (twice every 24 hours) by the gravitational forces of the moon and sun. The difference between the high and low water levels is referred to as the tidal range. Tides affect the coastal zone in three ways: (1) the constant rise and fall of the water generates tidal currents that may erode the ocean bottom and transport sediment; (2) erosive wave processes are displaced landward and seaward with each rise and fall of the tide; and (3) if the tidal range is large enough, wave processes are neutralized.

Late Quaternary Sea Level Changes

Although the coastal zone has been relatively stable and fixed in its present position for several thousand years, during the Quaternary coastal environments were displaced several times in both a seaward and landward direction (Bloom 1983a; Flint 1971). These sea level changes were worldwide and

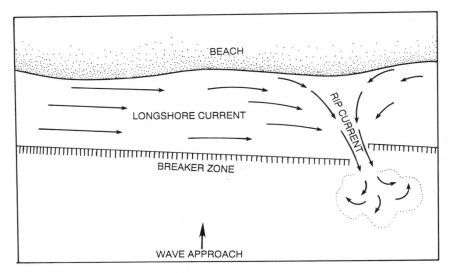

FIGURE 6.3. Longshore and rip currents along a coastline. Longshore currents run parallel to the shoreline and transport sediments laterally. Rip currents funnel water and sediment back to the ocean. (Modified from Elliott 1986a)

were synchronized with the creation and disappearance of continental ice sheets. During periods of glaciation, water evaporated from the ocean basins was used to create and nourish the massive ice sheets covering much of North America and Europe. Also, because temperatures were lower than today, runoff to the ocean basins from melting snow and ice was reduced. As a consequence, sea level fell, exposing extensive portions of the continental shelf, the low sloping platform that extends seaward from the modern coastlines. Conversely, during periods of deglaciation, meltwater from the retreating ice sheets was funneled into rivers and returned to the ocean basins. As a consequence, sea level rose to its present position.

The position of sea level over the last 40,000 years has been reconstructed by coring the continental shelf and dating in-place organic remains such as submerged peats, shells, and tree stumps (Flint 1971; Kellogg 1988). These ages and their corresponding elevations are used to construct curves showing the position of former coastlines.

A number of curves showing the position of sea level over time along different coastal segments of the United States have been constructed (Fig. 6.4; Berger 1983; Bloom 1983a, 1983b; Coastal Environments 1977; Flint 1971; Kraft 1985; Kraft et al. 1985; Nilsson 1983; Stright 1990). These curves are not the same; they vary from one another because of localized upwarping and downwarping at the continental margin, faulting, the compaction of sediment on the continental shelf, and the quality of the radiometric ages (Kellogg 1988). As a result of these variations, a universal worldwide curve documenting spatial and temporal sea level displacements does not exist. However, even though there is regional variation in these curves, they do show enough similarity to support certain generalizations.

Prior to the last period of continental glaciation, about 30,000 to 40,000 B.P., sea level stood at approximately its present position. As the large Laurentide and Cordilleran ice sheets of North America and the extensive Scandinavian Ice Sheet of northern Europe began to develop, sea level fell and the coastline was displaced seaward. Sea level reached its lowest position around 18,000 B.P., when continental ice sheets were at their maxi-

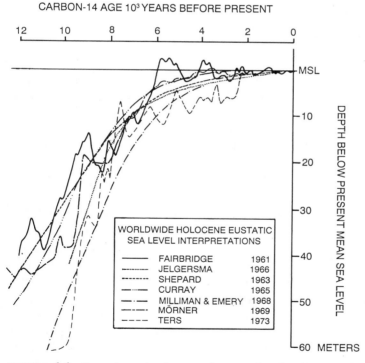

FIGURE 6.4. Eustatic sea-level curves documenting the rise in sea level over the last 12,000 years. Local geological factors, geochronological control, and interpretation of the evidence accounts for the differences among the curves. Note that all curves show a rapid rise in sea level until about 6000 B.P. (Modified from Kraft 1985)

mum. Sea level at that time was at least 90 m, possibly even 130 m, below its present position (Bloom 1983a).

Over the next 18,000 years as the ice sheets melted, sea level rose and the shoreline advanced over the continental shelf, reclaiming the land. In general, the consensus is that between 18,000 and 6000 B.P., sea level rose rapidly (Fig. 6.4). During this period there may have been oscillations in sea level and even brief intervals of stability. For the period after 6000 B.P., there is disagreement concerning when the oceans reached their present level and what has happened since that time. Fairbridge (1961) and others (e.g., Colquhoun and Brooks 1986; Colquhoun et al. 1981; DePratter and Howard 1981; Holmes and Trickey 1974) believe that sea level reached its present position at around 6000 B.P. and has since fluctuated above and below this level. However, other researchers (e.g., Berger 1983; Hoyt et al. 1990; Pinter and Gardner 1989) believe that sea level rose at a slow but constant rate after 6000 B.P., reached its present position by 4000 B.P., and has been relatively stable since that time.

Coastal Environments: Erosional, Submerged, and Depositional Coastlines

As a result of coastal processes and the displacement of the ocean level during the late Quaternary, many different coastal environments have been created, such as sea cliffs, beaches, estuaries, tidal flats, and barrier islands. Although there are many ways to classify these environments, they can be grouped for convenience into three broad categories: erosional coasts, submerged coasts, and depositional coasts.

Erosional Coasts

Erosional coasts are, of course, those dominated by erosion (Fig. 6.5). This usually occurs where bedrock directly fronts the open ocean and little sediment is available for beach formation. Continual wave pounding and supplementary biological and chemical weathering slowly disintegrate and wedge the rocks apart, carving a wave-cut cliff. At the base of the cliff, an indentation marks the zone of the most intense wave erosion. This is called the wave-cut notch. As the notch is enlarged, the overhanging bedrock collapses and the cliff retreats. The collapsed rubble is broken up and transported to sea. As the cliff retreats landward, waves bevel the underlying bedrock, creating a wave-cut platform, a smooth, gently sloping surface that extends from the cliff outward to the sea. Erosional coastlines are common along the Pacific and northeastern coasts of North America.

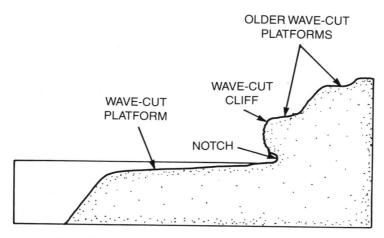

FIGURE 6.5. Wave-cut features associated with an erosional coastline. (Modified from Strahler and Strahler 1989)

Submerged Coasts

Submerged coasts have an irregular configuration, with embayments that extend inland from the coast and headlands that jut into the ocean. These embayments are known as estuaries and fjords.

Estuaries are coastal embayments that submerge the lower part of an unglaciated river valley. Modern estuaries, such as Chesapeake, Mobile, and Delaware bays, are located where terrestrial river valleys were inundated with seawater as the ocean advanced landward during the late Quaternary.

Estuaries are complex environments where both terrestrial and coastal processes interact to produce a brackish-water environment rich in marine fauna. Most of the sediments that accumulate in an estuary are derived from the river that flows into it. In most cases, waves and tidal currents rework these sediments into tidal flats and marshes around the margin of the estuary and into spits and baymouth bars that may build across its front.

Fjords are a special type of embayment in which seawater inundates a valley cut by glacial ice. These deep troughs are most common along the Pacific coast of British Columbia and Alaska, where valley glaciers extended onto the continental shelf during the Pleistocene. The glacial valleys were drowned at the end of the Pleistocene as glacial ice retreated into the headlands and as sea level rose.

Depositional Coasts

Depositional coasts are those in which sediments are accumulating to create landforms. These shorelines are dominated by either marine coastal processes, terrestrial fluvial processes, or a combination of both. Fluvial processes and landforms dominate the coastal landscape at points where rivers carrying large sediment loads empty into the ocean and sediment accumulates faster than coastal processes can rework it. In these areas, deltas are created. However, along most of the coastline of North America, coastal processes are able to rework all the clastic sediments transported to the mouth of a river. Depending on the interplay of waves and tides, features such as beaches, barrier islands, and tidal flats are created. Where both coastal and fluvial processes interact, cheniers are formed. The most common clastic depositional environments created by waves, tides, and fluvial processes are reviewed below.

Beaches

Beaches are narrow zones of unconsolidated clastic sediment attached to the land (Fig. 6.6). These are best developed in coastal regions characterized by a relatively flat, low-gradient coastal plain, an abundant sediment supply, intense wave activity, and low to moderate tidal ranges.

The profile of an active beach is divided into three distinct shore parallel zones. From offshore to onshore these zones are the shoreface, foreshore, and backshore. The backshore includes the nearly level berm that extends from the landward margin of the beach (marked by sand dunes, bluffs, or bedrock cliffs) to the normal high-tide level. The backshore is normally dry and is inundated with water only during unusually high tides or when storm waves overtop the berm crest. When this occurs, sediment suspended in the waves is deposited on the backshore. This creates horizontal to landward-dipping layers of sand and silt.

The foreshore, also known as the beachface, gently slopes seaward from the berm crest and occupies the intertidal zone. Swash and backwash processes on the beachface create distinctive cross-stratified deposits of sand, gravel, and shell fragments that dip seaward. Changes in sediment supply or wave regime result in low-angle discordances between cross-bedded units.

The shoreface is the wide zone that extends from the low-tide mark offshore to the fair-weather wave base (Fig. 6.6; approximate depth: 10 m). This includes the high-energy surf and breaker zones. In general, grain size decreases and biological activity increases across the shoreface in a seaward direction, corresponding to a decrease in wave activity offshore.

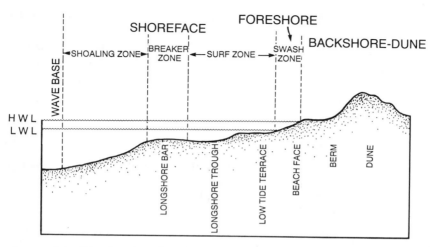

FIGURE 6.6. The shoreface, foreshore, and backshore areas of a beach. Also indicated are the wave zones and various morphologic features mentioned in the text. HWL is the high-water or high-tide level; LWL is the low-water or low-tide level. (Modified from Reinson 1984)

If the coastline is indented by an embayment, longshore currents may extend the mainland beach into the open water, forming a spit. In places, mainland beaches are characterized by multiple beach ridges separated by swales. These beaches are called strandplains.

Barrier Islands

Barrier islands are elongated bodies of sand oriented parallel to the shore that are separated from the mainland by a lagoon (Fig. 6.7). The seaward side of a barrier island is much like that of a mainland beach, with a backshore area often covered by sand dunes, and foreshore and shoreface zones farther seaward. The specific configuration of a barrier island and its associated environments depends primarily on tidal range and wave activity. Along wave-dominated coastlines with low tidal ranges (e.g., along the Texas coast), barrier islands are long and narrow, with only a few inlets. Lagoons in these settings are typically brackish or hypersaline, and tidal flats are poorly developed. Washover fans (lobate deposits of sand created where storm-generated waves overtop the barrier island and transport sand landward into the lagoon) are abundant and commonly coalesce to form an apron of sand on the back side of the barrier. Barrier islands along coastlines that are influenced equally by tidal and wave processes are separated by numerous inlets (e.g., along the Carolina and Georgia coasts). Individual island segments tend to be short and relatively wide. Lagoons in this setting usually have normal salinities because the tidal inlets permit ocean water to enter and exit the lagoon freely. In these areas, tidal flats and marshes commonly develop along the edges of the lagoon, while washover fans are essentially absent.

Tidal Flats and Marshes

Tidal flats and marshes are platforms of mud that extend from the mainland out into the open ocean along tide-dominated coasts where wave activity is minimal (Fig. 6.8). Tidal flats also develop in lagoons, estuaries, and embayments where they are protected from wave erosion (Fig. 6.7). The main parts of a tidal flat occupy the areas above and between the level of high and low tide.

The intertidal zone of a tidal flat is characterized by a relatively flat, seaward dipping plain traversed by a network of sinuous tidal channels. Twice a day the intertidal zone is inundated as ocean water enters and fills the tidal channels. As the tide continues to rise, the channels overtop their

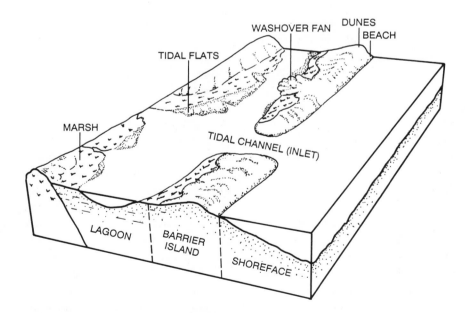

FIGURE 6.7. Cross section through a typical barrier island. (Modified from Reinson 1984)

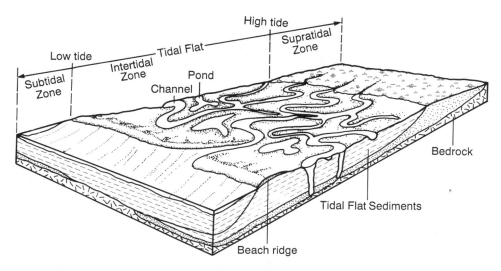

FIGURE 6.8. A typical tidal flat, with its supratidal, intertidal, and subtidal zones and various morphological features. (Modified from Boggs 1987)

banks and submerge the adjacent flats. When the tide falls, the water covering the tidal flat drains through the channels, and the flats are reexposed. The intertidal zone generally does not support vegetation.

Constant daily inundation and exposure of the tidal flat creates widespread deposits of laminated fine sand, silt, and clay. Tidal channel deposits are characterized by a lag of shell debris, coarse sand, and mud clasts. Tidal flat and channel deposits are usually extensively burrowed by marine organisms.

The supratidal zone of a tidal flat lies above the normal high-tide mark. This zone is also incised by tidal channels but is only inundated during storms and extreme high monthly tides. The supratidal zone is subaerially exposed most of the year. In warm temperate areas, salt marshes dominated by halophytic grasses develop on the supratidal portion of a tidal flat. Salt marshes are characterized by deposits of laminated clay, silt, and organic matter that are extensively homogenized by bioturbation. In warm, humid climates, mangrove swamps commonly form in this zone.

Cheniers

Cheniers are isolated, elongated, shore-parallel ridges of sand and shells separated by mudflats and marshes (Fig. 6.9). They are commonly a few meters high and 20 to 200 meters wide, and they may extend laterally for

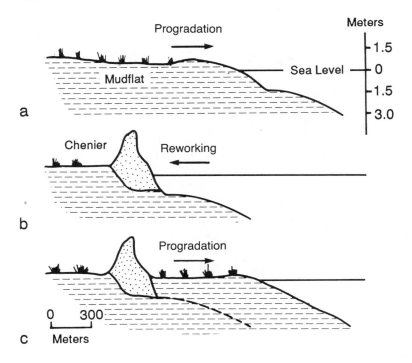

FIGURE 6.9. Formation of a chenier: first a mudflat progrades seaward (a), then there is a period of reworking and chenier formation (b), and finally there is renewed mudflat accretion into the ocean (c). Another period of reworking would create a second chenier. (Modified from Boggs 1987)

many kilometers. Cheniers form in coastal regions characterized by (1) low to moderate wave energy; (2) low tidal ranges; (3) strong longshore currents; and (4) most important, a fluctuating sediment supply. Cheniers are most commonly located adjacent to areas where rivers intersect the coast. They are constructed when the sediment supply to the coastal plain is reduced. This allows waves and longshore currents to winnow fine-grained sediments from the mudflats and concentrate shell debris and coarse sediments into a ridge. When the supply of fine-grained sediment from the river increases, waves and longshore currents cannot rework and transport all of this sediment. Consequently, mudflats and marshes begin to develop in front of the chenier ridge and continue to build seaward until the supply of sediment from the river decreases. As this process is repeated, a chenier plain is developed, consisting of a series of cheniers and intervening mudflats. A prominent chenier plain is located west of the Mississippi Delta in Louisiana.

Deltas

A delta is a lobate body of sediment deposited at the mouth of a river where clastic sediments accumulate faster than they can be reworked by marine processes (Fig. 6.10). Because of the interaction between marine and fluvial processes, a delta is a diverse and complex environment.

Deltas are divided into subaerial and subaqueous components. The subaerial portion of the delta, also known as the deltaic plain, is further subdivided into upper and lower segments. The upper deltaic plain lies above the high-tide level and is the oldest part of the delta. This area is dominated by the floodplain of the river, which nourishes the delta and is not affected by coastal processes. The lower deltaic plain occupies the intertidal zone, which is submerged by water during high tide and exposed during low tide. Consequently, this portion of the delta is affected by both fluvial and marine

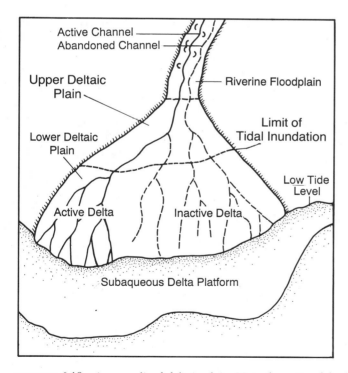

FIGURE 6.10. A generalized deltaic plain. Note the active delta lobe forming at the mouth of the active river channel and also the abandoned river course and inactive delta lobe. (Modified from Gagliano 1984)

processes. The lower deltaic plain is characterized by distributary channels that branch and fan out over the delta surface. The area between the channels—which is composed of natural levees, tidal channels, bays, crevasse splays, marshes, swamps, lagoons, and lakes—makes up the largest part of the lower deltaic plain. Overall, the subaerial delta plain has a wide variety of saline, brackish, and freshwater environments within a short distance.

The subaqueous portion of the delta lies below the low-tide mark and extends seaward from the lower deltaic plain. This zone receives fluvial sediments that are reworked by marine processes to form a base or platform onto which the subaerial delta progrades.

Deltas are environments that build outward, or prograde, into the open ocean. A delta does not prograde seaward along its entire length simultaneously but instead progrades in only one area at a time as sediment is accumulated into a delta lobe at the mouth of the active distributary stream system. The position of a delta lobe is not fixed. Periodically a delta lobe is abandoned and a new one is created as hydrologic conditions change upstream from the mouth of the river. This is commonly the result of avulsion, which occurs when the river establishes a new and shorter route to the ocean. When this happens, the margin of the abandoned delta lobe is reworked by coastal processes into beaches and barrier islands, while a new delta lobe builds seaward at the mouth of the newly established river course. Repeated shifts in the site of deposition over thousands of years create a number of delta lobes that coalesce to form the deltaic plain. Thus, deltas are composite landforms created by the overlapping and coalescence of numerous delta lobes of different ages. The Mississippi Delta is a composite of nine major delta lobes laid down at various times over the last 12,000 years (Coleman 1988; Gagliano 1984).

Coastal Landscape Evolution and the Archaeological Record

The spatial and temporal distribution of the archaeological record of coastally adapted cultures in North America must be understood in the context of the evolving coastal landscape and the configuration of the continental shelves. Reconstructions show that sea level fell by at least 90 m at 18,000 B.P. and subsequently returned to its present position sometime between 6000 and 4000 B.P. Since then, the modern coastal environments have developed.

Consequently, archaeological sites on the surface of extant coastal landforms and in the sediments of these landforms can be no more than 4000 to 6000 years old. The oldest sites with evidence of coastally adapted prehistoric cultures on the extant coastal features along the Gulf of Mexico date to 4500 B.P. (Aten 1983; Gagliano 1984). Similarly, the oldest sites with littoral adaptations on the barrier islands off the Georgia and Carolina coasts date to a maximum of 4500 B.P., with most sites dating later in time (Crusoe and DePratter 1976; DePratter and Howard 1981; Garrett 1983; Mitchell 1986).

Prehistoric sites older than 4500 B.P. that show evidence of coastal adaptations are typically buried in coastal sediments that are submerged offshore of the modern coastline (Bryan 1977; Edwards and Emery 1977; Emery and Edwards 1966). For example, Paleoindian and early Archaic shell middens are submerged in Tampa Bay in Florida (Goodyear and Warren 1972; Warren 1964). An 8000-year-old shell midden was discovered buried in estuary sediments 12 km from the Louisiana coast and under 18 m of water (Pearson et al. 1986). Other submerged sites are known to occur offshore along the Atlantic coast (Cockrell 1980; Cockrell and Murphy 1978; Salwen 1967), the Gulf coast (Cockrell 1980; Goodyear et al. 1980; Ruppé 1980, 1988), and the Pacific coast (Inman 1983; Masters 1983; Pierson et al. 1987). A complete list of submerged sites can be found in Stright 1990. These sites were occupied when sea levels stood at lower elevations.

The offshore location of sites associated with lower stands of the sea varies primarily with shelf width and slope, because these factors determine the horizontal displacement of the shoreline (Emery and Edwards 1966). Along the Pacific coast of California, the continental shelf is generally narrow and steeply inclined, while along most of the Atlantic and Gulf coasts it is a broad, gently sloping platform. Consequently, during the time of maximum sea level lowering, the shoreline was displaced only 0.5 to 10 km from the present Pacific coast (Fig. 6.11), while the same prehistoric shoreline would have been between 100 and 150 km from much of the present Atlantic and Gulf coasts (Fig. 6.12). As a result, submerged sites could potentially occur farther offshore along the Atlantic and Gulf coasts than along the Pacific coast.

In places where the continental shelf is narrow and steeply inclined, and thus where the horizontal displacement of the prehistoric shoreline from the modern coast was not great, some evidence of pre–4500 B.P. coastal adaptation is present along the extant coastline. These older sites are found on the stable portions of the landscape adjacent to the present coastal environment but not on the extant coastal landforms or in coastal deposits. Many sites with evidence of coastally adapted cultures dating to 9000 B.P. are found near the modern coastline of southern California (Warren and True 1961). These sites are situated on the highlands alongside estuaries or on the bluffs overlooking the present coast. At the time these sites were occupied, the

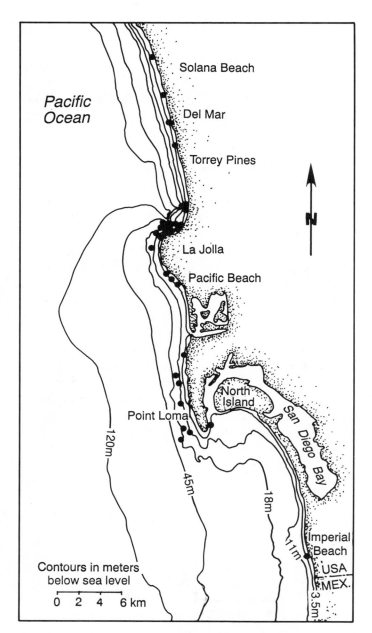

FIGURE 6.11. The coast and continental shelf of southern California and known submerged archaeological sites (large solid circles). Depths on the continental shelf are shown in meters below sea level. Most submerged sites are approximately 6000 to 9000 years old and belong to the La Jollan culture. Many of these sites are found 10 to 18 m below sea level, which in most cases is less than 1 km from the modern coastline. Other La Jollan shell middens of similar age are found on the bluffs overlooking the ocean. (Modified from Masters 1983)

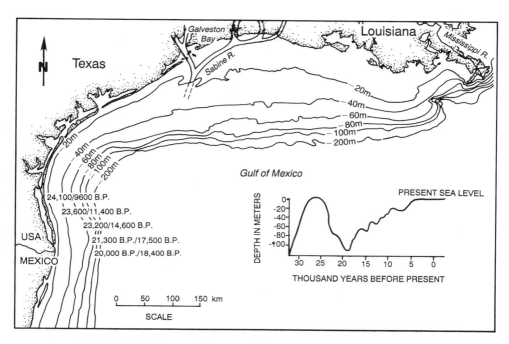

FIGURE 6.12. The Gulf Coast of the United States and the approximate position of shorelines at various times during the late Quaternary. The inset shows the sea level curve for the Gulf of Mexico. The former position of the Sabine River is shown. Note that the − 20 m shoreline is many tens of kilometers from the modern coastline in the Gulf, while the same shoreline on the southern California coast (Fig. 6.11) is generally less than 2 km from the modern coastline. (Modified from Stright 1986b)

prehistoric shoreline was not displaced very far from the modern coastline, and people could have easily transported shellfish the short distance to higher ground (Fig. 6.11).

Along most of the Atlantic and Gulf coasts, however, no older coastally adapted prehistoric sites are found along the modern coastline, even on stable terrestrial landforms. This is because former shorelines that could have been occupied by Paleoindian and Archaic peoples would have been located many kilometers from the modern coastline on the broad shelves extending from these coasts (Fig. 6.12; Emery and Edwards 1966). Any shell middens that would have been created by early coastally adapted peoples during periods of lower sea level were probably within a short distance of the former shoreline. These localities are now submerged on the continental shelf. Thus, along most of the Atlantic and Gulf coasts, evidence of coastal adaptations older than 4500 B.P. will occur only on the submerged continental shelf, not on coastal highlands. It is important to note, however, that even along the California coast, the early Holocene coastal sites on the highlands adjacent to the modern shoreline are only part of the total archaeological record of these coastally adapted people; many of their sites are submerged offshore (Fig. 6.11; Inman 1983; Masters 1983).

Sites with a terrestrial focus are also submerged offshore. During periods of lower sea level, large portions of the continental shelf surrounding North America were exposed behind the displaced shorelines and became covered by terrestrial depositional environments (e.g., rivers, springs, and lakes; Coastal Environments 1977; Edwards and Emery 1977; Edwards and Merrill 1977; Emery and Edwards 1966). Humans used these environments, and the sites they created became buried in terrestrial sediments (Bryan 1977). These sediments and any associated sites were submerged during the subsequent rise in sea level during the late Quaternary. For example, a 7000-year-old Archaic site formerly associated with a perennial upland stream is now submerged off the west coast of Florida (Goodyear et al. 1980).

The late Quaternary rise in sea level also environmentally displaced inland Paleoindian and Archaic period sites. Many older sites adjacent to the modern coast represent sites that were farther inland when occupied and contain evidence of inland adaptations. In short, the present coastal position of these sites is a consequence of rising sea levels and does not represent their original landscape position.

This situation is well illustrated by the Island Field site on the west coast of Delaware Bay, a major marine estuary (Fig. 6.13; Kraft 1977, 1985; Kraft et al. 1985; Kraft and John 1978). Today the Island Field site is situated on a low ridge extending into the tidal salt marsh next to the Murderkill River less than half a kilometer from the bay. However, during the late Paleoindian and early Archaic periods, the Island Field site was farther inland, many kilometers from the coast. Even during the late Archaic and Woodland periods, from 3000 to 1000 B.P., the Island Field site was farther inland than its present position suggests. This knowledge was important to the interpretation of subsistence activities at this site.

The effects of coastal landscape evolution on the archaeological record are summarized in Figure 6.14. This is a hypothetical time-geographic diagram showing the position and displacement of coastal and terrestrial sites relative to a changing sea level, the changing subsistence activities at these sites, and their modern position.

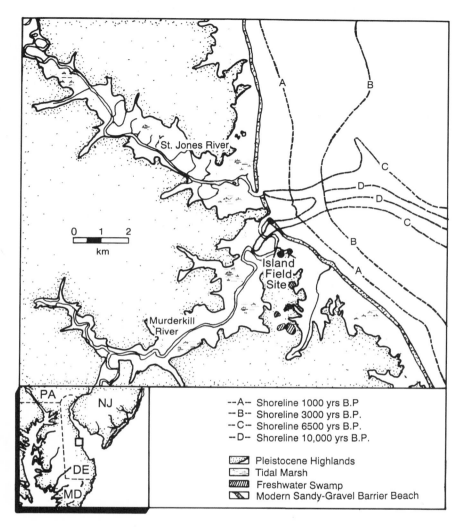

FIGURE 6.13. The Island Field site on the western side of Delaware Bay. The position of the shoreline from 10,000 B.P. to the present is indicated. Note that the Island Field site, which is now adjacent to the modern coastline, was farther inland during much of the Holocene. The square on the inset map shows the location of the site area. (Modified from Kraft 1985)

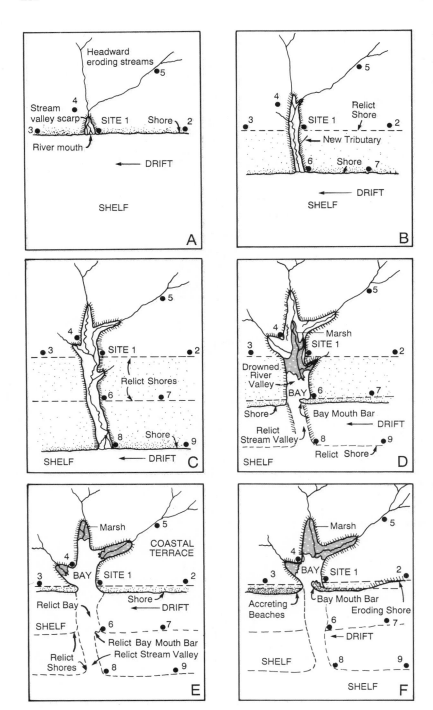

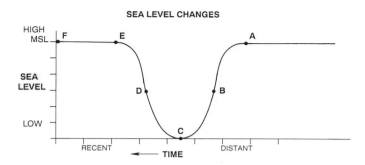

SEA LEVEL CHANGES

STAGE	SITES								
	1	2	3	4	5	6	7	8	9
A	MEU	MU	MU	U	RU	—	—	—	—
B	RU	U	U	U	RU	MEU	MU	—	—
C	RU	U	U	RU	RU	RU	U	MEU	MU
D	EU	U	U	RU	RU	MEU	MU	—	—
E	MU	U	U	EU	RU	—	—	—	—
F	MEU	MU	U	EU	RU	—	—	—	—

M - marine shore - beach - dune - bay mouth   E - estuarine - marsh
R - riverine   U - uplands

FIGURE 6.14. The diagrams on the opposite page show a hypothetical sequence of landscape changes along a coastline as a result of changes in sea level. Archaeological sites are indicated by the solid circles with numbers. Above, the upper curve shows changes in sea level from time A to time F (corresponding to A to F on the maps), and the lower diagram shows the changing environments around sites 1 through 9. This diagram illustrates how environments changed at a number of sites as a result of sea level changes. At stage A, site 1 was in a coastal setting, and marine, estuary, and upland resources could be used. As sea level dropped, the landscape around site 1 evolved into a more riverine and upland setting. As sea level rose, the original environmental conditions returned to the site. Thus, if excavations were undertaken at site 1, a long sequence of occupation would be encountered, and each occupation period would be characterized by a different assemblage of cultural remains and ecofacts, reflecting the changing environmental conditions around the site through time. Similar environmental changes occurred at the other sites. Also, note that sites 6, 7, 8, and 9 (which record marine adaptations at times B, C, and D) are now submerged on the continental shelf.

Site Formation on the Extant Coastline

Prehistoric people occupied those areas of the coastal zone that were elevated above tidal or wave inundation. Along wave-dominated depositional coastlines, sites are typically found on the surface or buried to a shallow depth on beach berms, backshore dunes, and cheniers behind the high-energy swash zone. Sites may also occur in low-energy environments such as the marshes of a delta or lagoon, or in tidal flats fronting the ocean (Coastal Environments 1977; Gagliano 1984; Gagliano et al. 1982). These sites often subside into the mud and become buried (Britsch and Smith 1989; Coastal Environments 1977; Gagliano 1984; Gagliano et al. 1982; McIntire 1971). For example, the Bayou Jasmine site, a Poverty Point midden dating between 3500 and 3000 B.P. near Lake Pontchartrain in Louisiana, has subsided 5.5 m below the surface of the modern swamp (Gagliano and Saucier 1963). Similarly, the shell middens and mounds located on natural levees at the Magnolia Mound site in Louisiana, dating from 1000 to 2000 B.P., have subsided 2.2 to 3 m below the modern marsh surface (Gagliano 1984; Gagliano et al. 1982). Only the tops of these mounds are now visible.

Because coastlines are generally high-energy environments characterized by waves and tidal processes, the preservation or destruction of sites on the extant coastline depends on the position of the site relative to shoreline processes (Coastal Environments 1977; Gagliano 1984; Kraft 1985; Kraft et al. 1985). Depending on the interplay between sediment supply, subsidence, coastal processes, and tectonic activity, present-day shorelines have (1) transgressed landward, (2) stabilized and maintained a neutral or unchanged configuration, (3) prograded seaward, or (4) tectonically emerged or risen above the modern sea level.

Transgression of the sea onto the land occurs where the sediment supply to the coast is diminished or the coastline is actively subsiding. If the shoreline is transgressing landward, the preservation of archaeological sites with undisturbed systemic contexts is unlikely. Erosion associated with the swash and backwash processes on the beachface, erosion accompanying wave processes and rip and longshore currents in the surf and breaker zones of the shoreface, and erosion caused by intensified waves and currents during storms will rework archaeological sites on and in preexisting coastal landforms and sediments (Fig. 6.15; Coastal Environments 1977; Gagliano 1984). When high-energy coastal processes come into contact with buried sites, the fine-grained fraction of the site matrix is winnowed and the artifacts and heavier archaeological debris are abraded and reworked into a lag along the beach. If a number of sites of different ages are eroded and reworked by shoreline processes, the beach lag will be composed of a mixture of tempor-

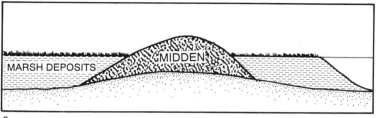

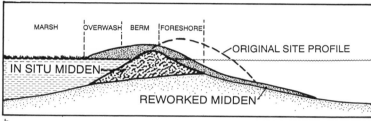

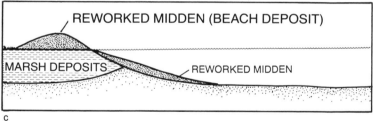

FIGURE 6.15. The destruction of a midden by wave processes associated with marine transgression. As sea level rises (a), erosion in the surf and swash zones destroys the marsh deposits and eventually reworks the midden (b). The sea level stabilizes (c), a new beach is created, and the midden contents are further reworked along the beach. (Modified from Gagliano 1984)

ally diagnostic artifacts. At the McFaddin Beach site in Texas, a mixed assemblage containing Clovis, Eden, and San Patrice projectile points, along with mammoth, camel, and horse bones, has been concentrated on the beachface by the erosion of late Quaternary terrestrial deposits in the shoreface zone (Aten 1983; Coastal Environments 1977; Long 1977). Similarly, sites are eroding from the bluffs along the California coast and are becoming reworked into the beaches below as the sea cliffs retreat landward. Even though the context of a site is destroyed by transgression, not all archaeological value is lost. Information on the presence, age, and function of the site may still be obtained from the reworked debris.

Stable coastal configurations have been achieved and maintained in areas where there is a balance between sediment supply, subsidence, and coastal processes. On a stable coastline, archaeological site preservation is more likely. However, sites along stable coasts can be destroyed by intense wave activity generated during storms (Hughes and Sullivan 1974; Milanich and Fairbanks 1980) or by minor transgressions associated with sea level oscillations, when waves can erode the higher portions of the landscape.

Progradation of the coastline occurs in areas of high sediment supply and low to moderate coastal subsidence. This most commonly occurs along the fronts of barrier islands, cheniers, strandplains, tidal flats, and deltas. Prograding coastlines provide the best preservation potential for archaeological sites. As shoreline landforms build in a seaward direction, former coastal sites are left behind in an inland position (Fig. 6.16; Coastal Environments 1977; Gagliano 1979, 1984; Gagliano et al. 1982) and are thus removed from destructive coastal processes.

A progradational sequence creates a chronologically ordered sequence of littoral landforms on which chronologically ordered archaeological sites

FIGURE 6.16. The distribution of archaeological sites on a prograding shoreline, in this case a chenier plain. Both map and cross section views are shown. The location of the cross section on the map is indicated by x–x′. Chenier B dates to 3000 B.P., chenier C to 2200 B.P., chenier D to 1750 B.P., and chenier E to 750 B.P. People occupied these landforms during the Poverty Point (oldest), Tchefuncte, Marksville, and Mississippian (youngest) periods. In this scenario, whenever a new chenier was constructed and stabilized, the older chenier was abandoned and a new site established on the new chenier, which would have been more biologically productive than the older cheniers behind it. Thus, a chronologically ordered set of landforms and initial occupation sites was created. It should be noted that prehistoric people could also reuse older cheniers at any time. This is why younger sites occur on older cheniers. The time depth of the archaeological sites on each landform is limited by its age. Thus, archaeological assemblages from chenier B could be from all the time periods (Poverty Point through Mississippian) because the chenier has been stable for 3000 years, while chenier E would have the least time-transgressive assemblage of sites because it has only been stable for 750 years. The cross section shows only initial occupation sites (i.e., the first and oldest occupations to occur on a landform once it was habitable). Of all the sites, site A could have the greatest time depth (going back to the Paleoindian period) because it was situated on a stable upland surface adjacent to the prograding shoreline. (Modified from Gagliano 1984)

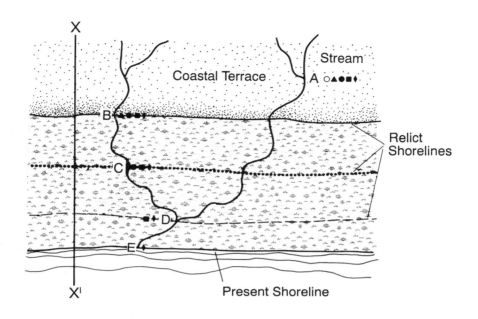

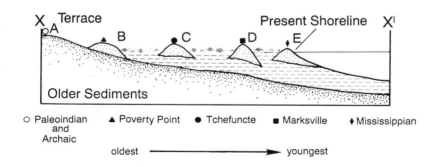

○ Paleoindian   ▲ Poverty Point   ● Tchefuncte   ■ Marksville   ♦ Mississippian
  and
  Archaic

             oldest ⎯⎯⎯⎯⎯⎯⎯⎯⎯⎯⟶ youngest

may be found (Fig. 6.16; Coastal Environments 1977; Gagliano 1984; McIntire 1971). The basic assumption behind the chronological ordering of archaeological sites on a prograding shoreline is that prehistoric people found it advantageous to locate their sites in close proximity to the ocean, where they had easy access to marine resources. Then, as the shoreline prograded seaward and new beach ridges developed, new sites were established on the newly created shoreline landforms, and the older beach ridges were abandoned. Consequently, the oldest sites are farther inland on the older landforms, with sites becoming progressively younger in a seaward direction where the youngest landforms are preserved. Chronologically ordered archaeological sequences have been documented along multiple beach ridges in western Alaska at Cape Krusenstern and at St. Lawrence Island (Collins 1937; Giddings 1966; Mason and Ludwig 1990). Similarly, DePratter and Howard (1977) documented the sequential prehistoric occupation of a prograding barrier island on the Georgia coast. Likewise, on the chenier plain of western Louisiana, the distribution of initial occupation sites corresponds to the sequential development of major chenier ridges (McIntire 1971). Older Tchefuncte period sites (ca. 500–100 B.C.) are found on the most inland cheniers, more than 10 km from the modern coastline. Plaquemine period sites (ca. A.D. 1000–1400) occur on the most seaward ridges. Troyville and Coles Creek period sites (ca. A.D. 300–1000) occur on a pair of intermediate cheniers. Sites on a prograding shoreline may be destroyed during large storms or if progradation is interrupted and the shoreline is subsequently subjected to wave erosion. Large storms have produced unconformities in the beach ridge sequences in western Alaska (Collins 1937; Giddings 1966; Mason and Ludwig 1990). During this time, artifacts and other debris are winnowed from their contexts and incorporated into beaches.

Emergent coasts are those that are rising above the level of the ocean due to faulting or isostatic readjustments of the earth's crust. These coasts are characterized by a series of elevated shoreline features that become progressively older with increasing elevation. Along the California and Alaska coasts (Schwartz and Grabert 1973), where faulting is actively occurring, a sequence of uplifted wave-cut cliffs and beaches are present in many places. In the Canadian Arctic, isostatic rebound of the crust is occurring in areas that were once under the Laurentide Ice Sheet (Edwards and Merrill 1977). In these areas the weight of the ice depressed the earth's crust by approximately one-third of the ice thickness. Since the ice has melted, the crust has been rebounding, and the coastline has been rising at rates of up to 3 m per century. Along the Canadian Arctic coast, there are many well-developed but abandoned post–glacial-age shorelines elevated to 180 m above modern sea level (Andrews et al. 1971; Fitzhugh 1977). Many of these elevated shorelines contain archaeological sites. Sites on emergent coasts are protected from coastal erosion processes and preserve a chronologically ordered record of coastal occupations.

Preservation of Submerged Sites

Paleoindian and Archaic period archaeological sites on the continental shelf have been affected by coastal processes during the last marine transgression. During periods of lower sea level, terrestrial and coastal environments advanced seaward and occupied the area formerly covered by the oceans (Emery and Edwards 1966). The type of environments and their spatial configuration would have been like those that exist today, only displaced seaward. Terrestrial environments such as river valleys, sand dunes, springs, and lakes, would have passed offshore into a coastal zone, perhaps characterized by a lagoon and barrier island, which in turn would have passed into deeper-water marine environments. As transgression occurred, these adjacent terrestrial, coastal, and marine environments retreated landward in a subparallel fashion. Ideally, deposits associated with these laterally adjacent coexisting environments should overlap one another and become vertically superimposed as the sea advanced landward through time. That is, as the shoreline rose, the area previously covered by terrestrial environments and sediments would have been covered by coastal sediments, while the area formerly occupied by the coastal environment would have been covered by marine sediments, and so on. This would create a vertical sequence on the continental shelf with terrestrial sediments at the base, coastal sediments in intermediate stratigraphic position, and shallow- and deep-water marine sediments at the top.

Transgression does not occur this way, however. Instead, it is primarily a destructive process that does not create ideal depositional sequences (Belknap and Kraft 1985; Kraft 1971, 1985; Kraft et al. 1983, 1987). Episodes of transgression are periods of erosion. Consequently, the process of shoreline retreat is important to site preservation. Transgression may occur in two ways: (1) by shoreface retreat, when the coastline slowly advances landward, or (2) by stepwise retreat, when in-place drowning of coastal features occurs.

Shoreface retreat is the term used to describe the erosion of previously deposited sediments by wave and current processes as the shoreline transgresses. As sea level rose during the late Quaternary, the beachface and shoreface erosional zones sequentially passed across those portions of the continental shelf that had previously been exposed (Fig. 6.17a). Thus, older sediments that had been deposited in coastal and terrestrial environments behind the shoreline were reworked, first by the swash and backwash processes of the beachface and then by the waves and currents associated with

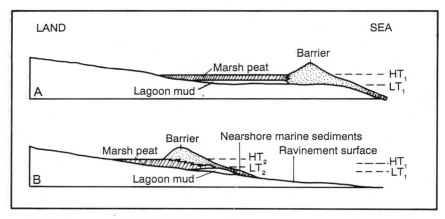

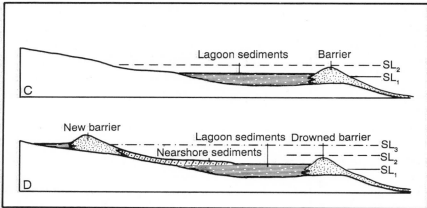

FIGURE 6.17. Marine transgression by shoreface retreat (A and B) and in-place drowning (C and D). In A and B, erosion associated with a rise in sea level removes the older barrier island deposits and creates an erosional surface known as the ravinement surface (the high-tide level [HT] and the low-tide level [LT] are shown at times 1 and 2). In C and D, the shoreline jumps landward as sea level (SL) rises rapidly from a lower position (SL₁) to a higher position (SL₃). As a result, the erosional surf and swash zones have little time to erode the older barrier island sequence, thus preserving it. A new barrier island is created farther inland. (Modified from Reinson 1984)

the upper shoreface breaker and surf zones. The erosion associated with the slow and continuous transgression of the sea reworked these deposits into a thin transgressive lag. Reworked terrestrial and coastal sediments are referred to as palimpsest sediments (Swift et al. 1971), and the erosional surface, marking the depth of maximum disturbance by transgression, is known as the ravinement surface (Fig. 6.17a; Belknap and Kraft 1985; Kraft 1971). Shoreface retreat is most common in areas where the sea level rose slowly and subsidence rates were low.

Alternately, transgression may occur by stepwise retreat, which is the sudden inundation or in-place drowning of coastal landforms and sediments (Fig. 6.17b; Rampino and Sanders 1980; Sanders and Kumar 1975a, 1975b). Stepwise retreat most commonly occurs in areas of rapidly rising sea level, where the coast is rapidly subsiding and the gradient of the transgressed surface is shallow. In this case, instead of the waves and currents of the shoreface and beachface sequentially reworking older sediments during transgression, the breaker and surf zones jump from the active shoreline to a point farther inland and submerge the older coastal landforms and sediments. The surf and breaker zones then stabilize and develop a new shoreline farther inland. In-place drowning has preserved barrier island and lagoonal sequences and other relict shoreline features on the Atlantic coast (Rampino and Sanders 1980; Sanders and Kumar 1975a, 1975b). This process is less common than shoreface retreat.

The preservation of archaeological remains on the continental shelf depends in large part on whether transgression occurred by in-place drowning or shoreface retreat. If coastal and shelf conditions are favorable for in-place drowning to occur, sites in the skipped sediments are more likely to be preserved, unless they are reworked by later marine processes. Preservation of sites is less likely in areas where shoreface retreat occurs.

Because shoreface retreat is the dominant transgressive process, the great majority of Paleoindian and Archaic period archaeological sites that were once on the continental shelf were probably destroyed during the late Quaternary as sea level rose to its present position. Waves and currents associated with the slow and continuous shoreface retreat during the last rise of sea level eroded and reworked most previously deposited sediments. However, some coastal and terrestrial landforms and sediments (e.g., glacial, eolian, fluvial, beach, and lagoon) escaped destruction and are preserved on the continental shelf, and undisturbed sites are known to exist within them. Therefore, there must be other factors and conditions that protect sites from the erosive processes of transgression or that minimize their impact.

A major factor determining the severity of erosion during shoreface retreat, and as a consequence the preservation potential of late Quaternary sediments and any contained sites, is the rate at which the sea level rises (Belknap and Kraft 1981). If the sea level rises rapidly over the continental shelf, erosion will be of short duration and the underlying sediments will have a greater potential for preservation. If the sea level rises slowly, the erosion associated with shoreface retreat is of longer duration over a single location and results in greater erosion of the underlying substrate.

More important than the rate of sea level rise and probably the most important factor controlling sediment and site preservation is the configuration of the topography on the continental shelf prior to transgression (Belknap and Kraft 1985; Kraft 1971). If a site is located and later buried in a topographic position that will not be eroded during transgression, it will be preserved under the ravinement surface. The topographic situations that offer optimum protection of relict sediments and sites are topographic low-points in the pretransgressive surface of the continental shelf (Belknap and Kraft 1985; Masters and Flemming 1983). In Pearson et al. 1986 and Kraft et al. 1983, the authors point out that river valleys incised into the continental shelf during periods of lower sea level provide the most likely places where relict sediments and sites may be preserved, because sites buried in submerged river valleys or other similar topographic situations are placed beneath the impact of shoreface erosion (Fig. 6.18). Other factors that influence site preservation on the continental shelf include (1) the energy level of coastal processes and the depth of the wave base (i.e., the depth of effective erosion); (2) the cohesiveness of sediments comprising the site matrix; (3) the amount of subsidence prior to transgression; (4) the gradient of the continental shelf; (5) the tidal range; and (6) sediment import and export processes. These and other factors are discussed in Aten 1983; Belknap and Kraft 1981, 1985; Flemming 1983; Hoyt et al. 1990; Kraft 1971, 1985; Kraft et al. 1983; Masters and Flemming 1983; Pearson et al. 1986; and Stright 1986a, 1986b, 1990.

Gagliano and his associates have developed and tested a model to locate archaeological sites on the continental shelf extending into the Gulf of Mexico (Fig. 6.12). This project was carried out in several stages over a number of years. During the first stage, all information of settlement patterning, submerged site locations, and the Quaternary geology of the Gulf Coast were compiled to develop a model of site-landform associations (Coastal Environments 1977). Before the model was tested, the sedimentological characteristics of Gulf Coast archaeological sites were studied to establish criteria for identifying prehistoric sites from core samples (Gagliano et al. 1982). In the final stage, the Sabine River Valley, submerged off the Louisiana coast, was selected for testing the model. Eighteen kilometers offshore, submerged relict landforms were identified by seismic profiles (Pearson et al.

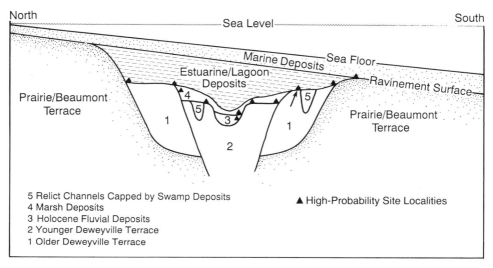

FIGURE 6.18. A generalized cross section showing that the most likely location for the preservation of late Quaternary deposits and sites on the continental shelf is under the ravinement surface within river channels that became entrenched on the shelf during low stands of the sea. Coastal and terrestrial deposits and sites above the ravinement surface have been eroded by shoreface retreat. This model is based on studies of the submerged portion of the Sabine River Valley off the coast of Louisiana, as discussed in the text. The arrow points to the location where the 8000 B.P. *Rangia* shell midden was encountered during coring. It rested on the Older Deweyville Terrace and was overlain by estuarine/lagoon sediments. (Modified from Pearson et al. 1986)

1986; Stright 1986a, 1986b). Based on the landform-site association model established in stage 1, the areas of greatest potential for site occurrence and preservation were then cored. The sediments brought to the surface were compared with the sedimentological characteristics of coastal sites established in stage 2 of the project, and two likely submerged sites were identified on a terrace in the incised valley of the Sabine River. These sites are now covered by marine sediments beneath the ravinement surface (Fig. 6.18).

In a similar project, Kraft, Belknap, and Kayan (1983) constructed a predictive model for the occurrence of archaeological sites along the Delaware coast based on field situations. This model has been elaborated in a more recent paper by Hoyt, Kraft, and Chrzastowski (1990). Inventories of known sites, Quaternary coastal environments, and predictive models have been established for: (1) the Atlantic Coast from the Bay of Fundy to Cape

Hatteras (Harvard University 1979); (2) the Pacific coast from Morro Bay to the Mexican border (Pierson et al. 1987); and (3) the coast of Alaska (Dixon et al. 1986). Most of these areas have not been tested. Stright (1990) provides a discussion of ways to predict the location of inundated sites on the continental shelf and methods to locate these sites. In general, the prerequisite for site preservation on the continental shelf is site burial in terrestrial or low-energy marine sediments prior to the transgression of the ocean. Then, if the site remains below the depth of shoreface erosion during the marine transgression, it will be preserved.

Coastal Landscape Reconstruction

Just like other environments, the coastal landscape has evolved through time. Sea level rose and fell during the Quaternary, displacing both terrestrial and coastal landscapes. Also, since the extant coastline was established, many shorelines have prograded seaward or transgressed landward. Consequently, it is important to place archaeological sites and the human behavior they represent into their prehistoric landscape context. The following examples illustrate site-specific and regional diachronic landscape reconstructions.

The Sabine River Valley: A Site-Specific Diachronic Landscape Reconstruction

An examination of the Sabine River Valley dramatically shows that the present landscape position of a site does not always reflect its prehistoric landscape context (Pearson et al. 1986). Pearson and his colleagues reconstructed the evolving landscape surrounding an 8000-year-old *Rangia* shell midden that now lies buried in estuary sediments submerged under 18 m of water 12 km south of the present Louisiana coast.

Prior to 10,000 B.P., when the sea level was approximately 30 m below its present level, the floodplain of the meandering Sabine River extended onto the exposed continental shelf (Fig. 6.19a). This floodplain, known as the older Deweyville surface, was characterized by an active meandering channel and numerous abandoned channels and backswamps. Older fluvial terraces (known as the Prairie and Beaumount terraces) flank the older Deweyville floodplain. This floodplain may have been occupied by Paleo-indians, but no sites were discovered in the testing phase of the project.

Between 10,000 and 8800 B.P., the Sabine River downcut and created a new floodplain at a lower level, known as the younger Deweyville surface, and the abandoned floodplain became the older Deweyville terrace (Fig. 6.19b). During this time the coastline was approximately 22 m below its present level. Shortly thereafter, between 8500 and 8000 B.P., the sea level rose and inundated the younger Deweyville floodplain, creating an estuary (Fig. 6.19c). The older Deweyville terrace was not flooded by seawater, and a fresh-to-brackish-water marshland developed on its surface. Early Archaic people camped next to the estuary sometime around 8000 B.P. on the older Deweyville terrace. They collected *Rangia* from the estuary and adjacent marshlands, and this debris accumulated into a shell midden that grew to 60 m in diameter (Figs. 6.18 and 6.19c).

After 8000 B.P., the sea level rose, salt water inundated the site, and estuarine muds buried the shell midden (Fig. 6.18). Because of the position of the site within the incised channel of the Sabine River and its subsequent burial, which placed it below the ravinement surface, the site was protected from shoreface erosion during the continued transgression of the sea to its present location.

Cape Henlopen: A Regional Diachronic Landscape Reconstruction

An example of how shoreline evolution affected the human use of the extant coastal landscape is provided by Kraft's geoarchaeological investigation of the evolution of Cape Henlopen on the Atlantic coast of Delaware (Kraft 1977; Kraft and John 1978; Kraft et al. 1978). At this site, a number of Woodland period shell middens occur on a spit that is prograding northward from the end of a barrier island. The presence of shell middens containing species that are not abundant in the present environment suggests that the modern configuration of the landscape did not characterize the landscape at the time of occupation. Based on coring of the sediments at and adjacent to the site, Kraft documented the following changing landscape scenario (Fig. 6.20).

Around 7500 B.P., Cape Henlopen was part of a quiet-water salt marsh fringing Delaware Bay (Fig. 6.20a). The active shoreline lay many kilometers to the east. As the sea level rose, the area around Cape Henlopen was gradually transformed into a wide barrier beach, which was separated from the mainland by a lagoon around 4000 B.P. (Fig. 6.20b). By 1500 B.P. (Fig. 6.20c), sea level had risen farther, and the broad barrier island had been reworked into an elongate barrier beach by northward-flowing longshore currents. Sediment derived from the beach drifted to the north and created a recurved spit at the end of the barrier beach which prograded into the bay. The spit continued to develop and eventually created a shallow lagoon behind it. This lagoon became rich in shellfish and other marine resources. Middle and late Woodland people used these resources intensively and left

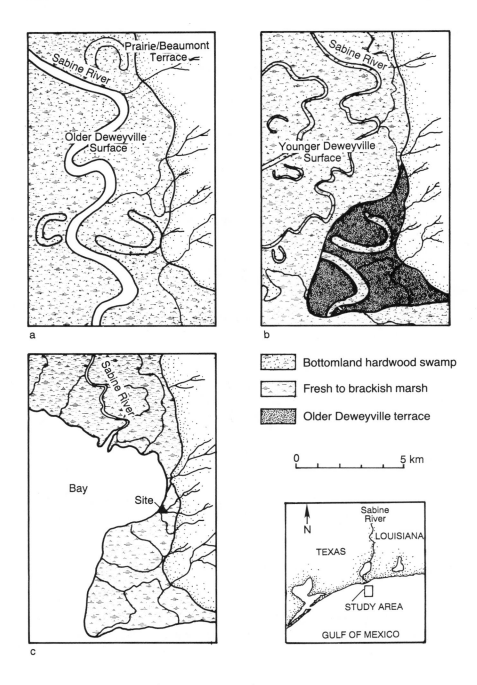

a

b

c

Bottomland hardwood swamp

Fresh to brackish marsh

Older Deweyville terrace

0   5 km

N

Sabine River

LOUISIANA

TEXAS

STUDY AREA

GULF OF MEXICO

behind a number of shell middens on the spit and the adjacent coastal plain surrounding the lagoon. The barrier grew and the lagoon became isolated from the ocean as sea level rose to its present level (Fig. 6.20d). The isolated lagoon no longer supported rich marine shellfish resources and filled with mud, and the region was abandoned. A salt marsh now occupies the position of the former lagoon. Thus the evolution of the landscape over 8000 years played a major role in shaping its biological resources, which in turn affected prehistoric human use of the region.

Similarly, changes in coastal processes and landscapes along other coast-lines in North America influenced the distribution of shellfish and thus the prehistoric people who used these resources. Along the California coast, many estuaries became filled with sediment as the sea level rose and stabil-ized during the Holocene. Along the Santa Barbara coast, middens indicate that early Holocene people survived primarily by consuming plants and shellfish (Erlandson 1988). Most of these early, Millingstone Horizon sites are situated around what were productive estuaries. However, as the estu-aries filled with silt during the middle and late Holocene, shellfish productiv-ity declined. Correspondingly, the dietary contribution of shellfish declined, and the middens indicate that there was an increased emphasis on hunting and fishing. At Batiquitos Lagoon, an estuary 30 km north of San Diego, prehistoric shell middens record a similar story (Gallegos 1985; Gallegos and Carrico 1985). Middens predating 7000 B.P. are dominated by *Agopec-ten,* a species that flourishes in deep, open lagoons. However, middens dating between 7000 and 3500 B.P. are dominated by *Chione,* a species that lives in shallow lagoons dominated by mudflats. This biological shift corresponds with the silting in of Batiquitos Lagoon as a consequence of a rising and stabilizing sea level. An absence of archaeological sites in the area dating

FIGURE 6.19. A sequence of paleogeologic maps of a submerged portion of the Sabine River off the Louisiana coast at different times. Map *a* is a reconstruction of the landscape prior to 10,000 B.P., when the older Deweyville surface was the active floodplain of the Sabine River. The active Sabine River channel and abandoned meanders are indicated. Map *b* is a reconstruction between 10,000 and 8800 B.P. The Sabine River downcut and created a new floodplain (the younger Deweyville surface) and left the older Deweyville surface as a terrace. Map *c* is a reconstruction around 8500 to 8000 B.P. The younger Deweyville surface was flooded by ocean water as sea level rose and the Older Deweyville surface became a marsh on the edge of an estuary. At this time, humans occupied the marsh and the *Rangia* shell midden was created. Continued sea level rise submerged the marsh and site. (Modi-fied from Pearson et al. 1986)

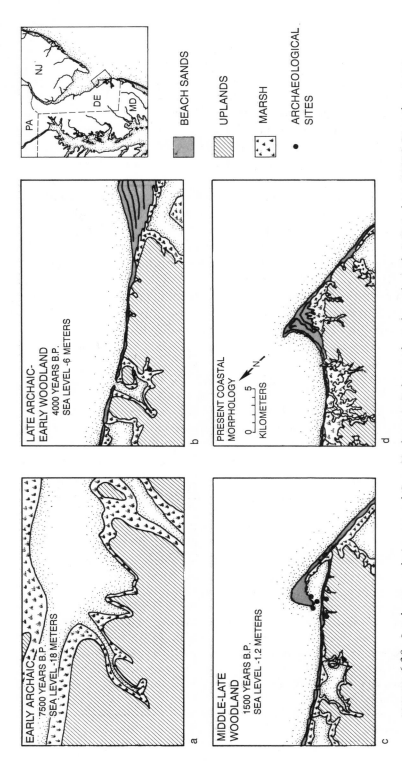

FIGURE 6.20. Landscape evolution around Cape Henlopen in Delaware from the early Archaic Period (ca. 7500 B.P.) to the present. Map *a* shows the configuration of Cape Henlopen at 7500 B.P. During the late Archaic and early Woodland periods (Map *b*) the spit had not yet formed, and occupation occurred only in the uplands to the west. The most intensive use of the area occurred during the middle-to-late Woodland period (Map *c*), when a spit and a small bay were present. Map *d* shows the modern configuration of Cape Henlopen, with the enclosed marsh. The rectangle on the inset map shows the location of the study area. (Modified from Kraft 1977)

BEACH SANDS

UPLANDS

MARSH

• ARCHAEOLOGICAL SITES

LATE ARCHAIC–
EARLY WOODLAND
4000 YEARS B.P.
SEA LEVEL -6 METERS

b

PRESENT COASTAL
MORPHOLOGY

N

0   5

KILOMETERS

d

EARLY ARCHAIC
7500 YEARS B.P.
SEA LEVEL -18 METERS

a

MIDDLE-LATE
WOODLAND
1500 YEARS B.P.
SEA LEVEL -1.2 METERS

c

between 3500 and 1500 B.P. is suggested to represent a period of closure of the lagoon, which resulted in a decline in *Chione* productivity and thus abandonment of the area. Shell middens dating to the last 1500 years indicate that only small *Chione,* in limited numbers, were collected. This indicates an open but not highly productive lagoon. Shell middens on Grape Island, in Hingham-Hull Bay (Boston Harbor) in Massachusetts, show that closure of the bay to the open ocean around 890 B.P. transformed a once highly productive shellfish harvesting ground that was heavily used by prehistoric people into an area of low shellfish productivity that was no longer used by humans (Jones and Fisher 1990). Similar shifts are also noted along the Louisiana coast by McIntire (1971) and Coastal Environments (1977). In short, changes in shellfish use as reflected by the concentration and type of shellfish in middens may reflect not only cultural factors (a change in cultural preference from one shellfish species to another or a shift due to overpredation of a species) but also changing environmental variables.

The Mississippi Delta: A Regional Diachronic Landscape Reconstruction

The pattern of prehistoric human use of a delta landscape follows the cyclic phases of delta lobe formation, florescence, and deterioration (Fig. 6.21; Coastal Environments 1977; Gagliano 1984; McIntire 1958, 1971). Paralleling the evolution of the delta landscape, the biological resources (mammals, amphibians, reptiles, fish, plants, and shellfish) on the delta lobes also changed. Occupation of a delta lobe usually begins shortly after the subaerial deltaic plain becomes established and intensifies as the lobe expands and biological productivity increases. During this time, sites are most often situated on the natural levees above the deltaic wetlands at the junction of distributary channels that fan across the delta lobe (Coastal Environments 1977; Gagliano 1984). Periodic avulsion of the river upstream from the delta lobe causes the river to change its course, abandon the delta lobe, and create a new one. Occupation of the abandoned delta lobe continues, even after the lobe is no longer active, until biological productivity begins to decline. At this point, the older delta lobe is slowly abandoned and the intensity of occupation increases on the active delta lobe.

The evolution of the Mississippi Delta is an excellent archaeological example of the interaction between people and an evolving delta landscape (Britsch and Smith 1989; Coastal Environments 1977; Gagliano 1979, 1984; Gagliano et al. 1975, 1979; Weinstein, Wiseman et al. 1979). The lower channel of the Mississippi River has avulsed at least nine times during the last 12,000 years, initiating nine periods of delta lobe formation in different locations. A study of the human interaction with the delta landscape shows

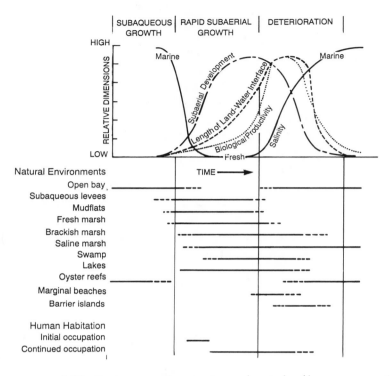

FIGURE 6.21. Environmental succession and periods of human occupation during an idealized cycle of delta lobe formation, growth, and degradation. (Modified from Gagliano 1984)

a strong correspondence between the sequence of delta lobe formation and the spatial pattern of occupation from the Paleoindian through the historic period.

Between 12,000 and 8500 B.P., when sea level stood 15 to 25 m below its present level, the Mississippi River branched downstream into three separate deltaic lobes, collectively known as the Lafayette deltaic complex, which prograded into the Gulf of Mexico (Fig. 6.22a). Landward of the delta complex was a large swamp, which was traversed by crevasse channels from the Mississippi River. Both environments were biologically rich. East of the Lafayette delta was an embayment and a chain of uplifted salt-dome islands. Paleoindian and early Archaic peoples occupied the Lafayette delta lobe, and their sites have been found on the floodplain of the Lafayette meander belt of the Mississippi River and on the edge of the embayment in association with one of the salt domes (e.g., the Avery Island site; Gagliano 1967, 1970).

Sites of this age have also been found in the inland swamp along crevasse channels and in the upland areas to the east.

Around 8500 B.P., sea level rose, but it remained approximately 12 m below its present position. At this time the Mississippi River abandoned the Lafayette deltaic lobe and began flowing into the embayment to the east, creating the Maringouin delta lobe. This lobe continued to grow until approximately 6000 B.P. Middle Archaic occupation coincided with Maringouin delta lobe formation. Sites of this age have been found on the margin of distributary channels associated with this delta lobe.

The sea level rose to its present elevation sometime between 6000 and 4000 B.P. and submerged and reworked much of the Lafayette and Maringouin delta lobes. A new delta lobe, the Sale-Cypremort, developed in almost the same location as the older lobes but was slightly displaced to the east. Archaeological sites from this period of lobe formation are poorly represented.

A major new meander belt and delta lobe, the Metairie lobe, began to develop by 4000 B.P. in the eastern portion of the delta plain, and Poverty Point people began to use this new, highly productive landscape. Most of the sites were small, special-activity, fishing-hunting-gathering camps situated on the natural levees of active distributary channels flowing over the delta lobe. During this time Poverty Point people also continued to use the deteriorating environments associated with the older abandoned delta lobes.

During the following Tchefuncte and Marksville periods, between approximately 2500 and 1700 B.P., the Mississippi River had two major courses and was building two delta lobes (Fig. 6.22b). The La Loutre lobe, to the east, was an extension of the older Metairie lobe. The Teche lobe, to the west, began building when the Mississippi River reoccupied the old meander belt that flowed downslope to the abandoned Sale-Cypremort lobe.

Deposition on the La Loutre lobe continued and expanded after 1700 B.P. into the Plaquemines lobe (Fig. 6.22c). At the same time, another delta lobe known as the Lafourche lobe developed over the older Teche lobe. During this time a number of major distributaries flowed across both these delta lobes and were intensively occupied during the Troyville, Coles Creek, Plaquemine, and Mississippian periods. These lobes deteriorated at the end of the Mississippian period, and historic delta formation began on the Balize lobe. Only historic sites occur on this delta lobe.

Another example of multiple delta lobe formation occurs at the mouth of the Trinity River in Texas. Over the last 2500 years, the Trinity River has produced a sequence of five delta lobes (Aten 1983). Each lobe underwent its own cycle of formation, florescence, and atrophy. Here too the sequence of occupation and abandonment of the delta lobes followed the changing landscape.

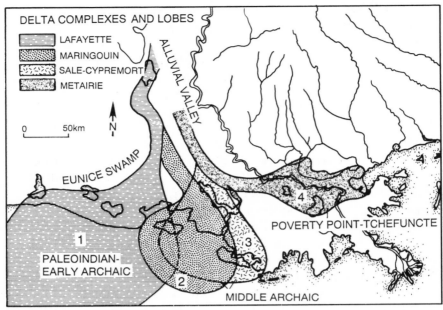

a

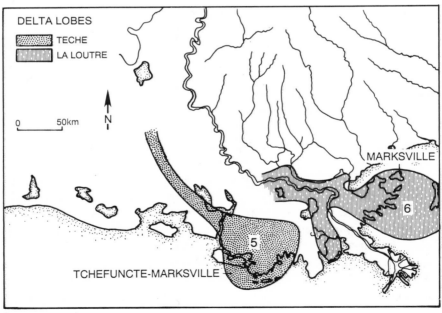

b

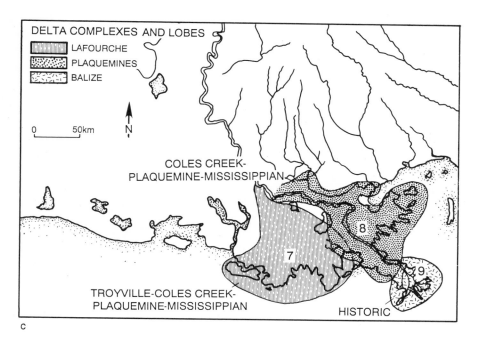

FIGURE 6.22. The evolution of the Mississippi Delta and the succession of occupation on the delta lobes: (a) from 12,000 to 2500 B.P.; (b) from 2500 to 1700 B.P.;
and (c) from 1700 to the present. The numbers indicate the chronological succession of the delta lobes. (Modified from Gagliano 1984)

Land Connections and Passageways

During periods of lower sea level, land connections were created between
continents that are presently separated by oceans. These land connections
were subsequently drowned whenever the sea level rose. The best-known
land connection was the Bering Land Bridge, which connected northeast
Asia and North America (Fig. 5.9). The Bering Land Bridge was created
during the Quaternary whenever the sea level fell and exposed the continental shelf under the Bering Sea. This land connection was more than 1000 km
wide and quickly became covered with terrestrial environments (Dixon et al.
1986; Hopkins 1967, 1979; Hopkins et al. 1982). The presence or absence of
Beringia most likely influenced the movement of people into North America.

Land connections were also created between the Channel Islands off the
coast of California during lower stands of the sea (Johnson 1978, 1983).
Lower sea levels also created a potential migration route for early humans
out of Beringia along the Pacific coast of North America when large portions

of the continental shelf were exposed (Fladmark 1978, 1979, 1983; Luternauer et al. 1989). Thus, landscape changes caused by sea level fluctuations
significantly influenced the arrival and dispersal of humans into North America at the end of the Pleistocene.

Conclusion

Changing sea levels during the late Quaternary have dramatically affected
the distribution and preservation of sites of early coastally adapted peoples.
Most of these sites are destroyed; the few that remain are situated offshore
from the modern coastline. Since the middle Holocene, modern shorelines
have developed and evolved. These landscapes preserve the evidence of later
coastally adapted cultures. Furthermore, the evolution of these landscapes
has affected the loci of human activity.

7

The Postburial Disturbance
of Archaeological Site Contexts

In the previous five chapters it was shown that an archaeological site is preserved because of a set of fortuitous natural circumstances and that the systemic context of a site (i.e., the three-dimensional patterning of occupation debris that reflects human behavior) is disturbed to some degree prior to and during burial. However, even when a site is buried, it is not static. The sediment and soil matrix surrounding archaeological remains is dynamic and is constantly in motion as animals and plant roots burrow through the soil, sediment slowly creeps downslope, and the matrix expands and contracts (Hole 1961). These and other postburial physiogenic and biogenic processes mechanically disturb the systemic context of a buried site by moving archaeological remains upward, downward, or laterally in the matrix and by differentially sorting and concentrating artifacts into artificial layers that may be difficult to distinguish from those produced by human activity (Butzer 1982). Depending on the type, intensity, and duration of postdepositional disturbance processes, the original three-dimensional patterning among artifacts, features, and ecofacts on a site may become partially or completely rearranged.

At a site in which mixing and churning is intense, the systemic context may be completely destroyed and the archaeological debris concentrated into a single layer or redistributed into multiple layers (Villa 1982). If these situations are not recognized, serious errors in archaeological interpretation may occur. For example, at site 21CA58, situated on a terrace of the Gull River in central Minnesota, five temporally discrete assemblages dating from 800 B.C. to the historic period were mixed and homogenized by postdepositional turbation processes into a zone 5 to 30 cm below the surface (Neumann 1978). This matrix had no perceptible cultural or natural stratigraphy. In another situation at the Cave Spring site in Tennessee, archaeological remains of the same age were found in three different stratigraphic units (early and late Holocene alluvium and a middle Holocene paleosol; see Fig. 7.1 and Hofman 1986). This material was translocated by postdepositional processes from a single occupation surface (presumably on or in the paleosol). Had lithic studies not demonstrated that artifacts from the three separate layers could be refitted—in many cases, to the same core—it might have been assumed that three stratigraphically superposed occupations were present.

In most cases, however, postdepositional disturbance processes have not completely disrupted the systemic context of a site. Most sites retain sufficient contextual and stratigraphic integrity to allow meaningful interpretations of human behavior. Postburial disturbance of archaeological remains must, however, be recognized before accurate behavioral interpretations can be made from the archaeological context. Evaluating postdepositional disturbance includes (1) identifying all disturbance processes that have operated on the site since its creation (the absence of disturbance processes at a site at the time of excavation does not necessarily preclude the possibility that displacement processes previously affected the site); (2) determining the timing, intensity, rate, and duration of these disturbances; (3) determining the spatial extent of the disturbance (i.e., determining whether postdepositional processes affected the entire site or only a portion of it); and (4) evaluating the specific effects of the disturbance processes on the archaeological remains.

Most archaeological site contexts have undergone some sort of postdepositional movement. Consequently, the present position of buried cultural remains may not reflect their original behavioral position. Therefore it can never be assumed that the buried archaeological debris at a site is in a systemic position (Butzer 1982; Nash and Petraglia 1987; Schiffer 1987). Postdepositional processes of site degradation must be recognized before a correspondence between artifact patterning and human behavior can be convincingly demonstrated. When postburial disturbances—as well as modifications of the site context prior to and during burial—are understood, then behavioral interpretations that depend on artifacts, being in their original position are possible.

This chapter highlights the major physical and biological processes that cause the mechanical movement of objects within an archaeological site. Summary discussions of these processes can also be found in Butzer 1982, Schiffer 1987, and Wood and Johnson 1978.

Cryoturbation

Cryoturbation is the disturbance of archaeological remains in a matrix that undergoes periodic freezing and thawing (Butzer 1982; Johnson and Hansen

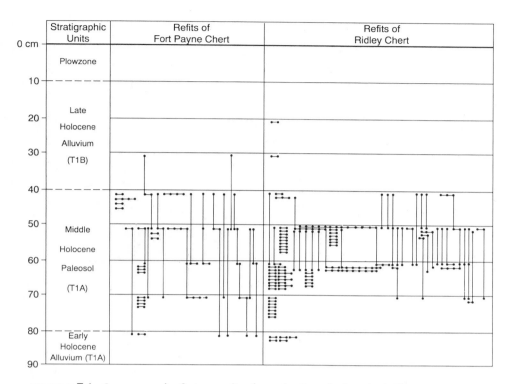

FIGURE 7.1. Summary of refitting studies from the Cave Spring site in Tennessee. The stratigraphy and age of the site deposits are shown to the left. Each dot represents the location of an artifact or flake within the stratigraphy, and a line connects those artifacts and flakes that could be refitted. This refitting study showed that, as a result of postdepositional alterations to the site matrix, artifacts that had originally rested on the surface of the paleosol or in it became displaced vertically and are now found in three different stratigraphic units (early and late Holocene alluvium and a middle Holocene paleosol). Disturbance processes at this site included burrowing animals, root growth, tree fall, and heaving associated with freezing and thawing, and wetting and drying, of the ground. (Modified from Hofman 1986)

1974; Johnson et al. 1977; Rolfsen 1980; Schiffer 1987; Schweger 1985; Strauss 1985; Thorson 1990; Wood and Johnson 1978). Freezing of the ground begins at the surface and progresses downward into the soil when surface temperatures drop below freezing. As freezing temperatures penetrate the ground, moisture in the voids between the sediment particles freezes. Capillary forces in the soil pull additional moisture to the freezing front, where it freezes into segregated lenses of ice that lie parallel to the ground

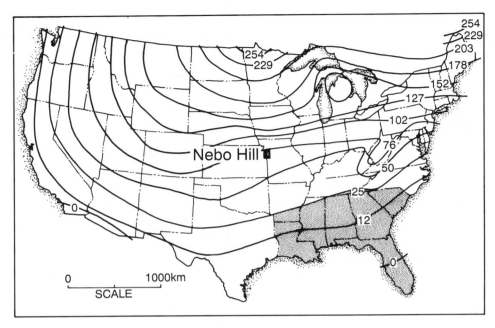

FIGURE 7.2. The maximum potential depth of soil freezing in the United States. The lines are isotherms of equal frost penetration, in centimeters. The shaded area shows the distribution of fiber-tempered pottery. Note that it is concentrated below the 25 cm isotherm, though such pottery has also been recovered from the Nebo Hill site in Missouri. (Modified from Reid 1984)

surface. As a result, the soil matrix is heaved toward the surface. A matrix undergoing freezing typically expands more than 9%, because numerous ice lenses form in the matrix. In extreme cases, the volume of the matrix may increase by 70%. The depth and rate of freezing varies with annual temperature conditions (especially the duration of freezing temperatures), soil texture, and moisture availability. The depth and rate of freezing are maximized in areas where (1) annual temperatures are below freezing for long periods, (2) the matrix is composed of fine-grained particles such as silt, and (3) abundant moisture is present in the soil to enhance ice lens formation. The depth of maximum freezing across North America is illustrated in Figure 7.2, and as would be expected, potential maximum freezing depths increase with increasing latitude.

In parts of Alaska and Canada where the winters are long and average annual temperatures are below freezing, the ground is permanently frozen and does not thaw during the summer. This perennially frozen ground is called permafrost (Péwé 1975; Washburn 1980). Much of the permafrost that exists today is a relic of the Pleistocene, created when temperatures were below freezing for thousands of years. Temperatures have never risen enough during the Holocene to melt this ground ice. Because permafrost is relatively stable, anything in it undergoes little degradation or movement (e.g., frozen mammoth carcasses).

In that portion of the ground that undergoes seasonal freezing and thaw-ing, however, small particles comprising the matrix, and any objects in it undergo degradation and are physically rotated and moved slightly upward during periods of freezing and settle slightly back into the matrix during periods of thawing. Two processes are at work: frost heave and frost pull (Fig. 7.3). Frost pull occurs when freezing does not penetrate deeply enough to cover the entire artifact, leaving the base of the artifact in an unfrozen matrix. As the matrix expands, the artifact is pulled upward toward the surface. Frost heave occurs when freezing engulfs the entire artifact-bearing matrix. In this case, ice lenses form directly under artifacts and push them toward the surface. In both cases, soil particles settle back to nearly their original position when the matrix thaws, but artifacts remain displaced in the matrix because the void space under the artifact becomes distorted so that it does not mirror the original shape of the stone and because the void becomes filled with sediment derived from the sides of the void before the artifact can resettle into its former position. As a result, the artifact is perma-nently displaced upward. The effects of freezing and thawing are cumulative; eventually, after repeated cycles of freezing and thawing, buried objects find their way to the surface.

The major effects of freezing and thawing are (1) destruction of the spatial relationships between temporally related artifacts (the systemic con-text) on a single occupation surface; (2) homogenization of the site matrix (i.e., destruction of sediment layers and soil horizons and the contacts be-tween them); (3) mixing of temporally discrete archaeological occupation debris that may be spatially separated in the matrix; and (4) damage to, or even destruction of, the archaeological remains themselves.

At a site where the temperature and composition of the matrix are simi-lar, artifacts are differentially heaved to the surface depending on their size, orientation, material composition, and depth of burial. In general, artifacts with long vertical dimensions and large surface areas are ejected to the sur-face more rapidly than smaller artifacts. This is well illustrated at the Hungry Whistler site (Benedict and Olson 1978), a 5800-year-old hunting and butch-ering site located above the timberline in the Rocky Mountains of Colorado, where the mean air temperature is −2°C. Benedict and Olson studied the size differences of artifacts from the surface to the base of the site matrix (at

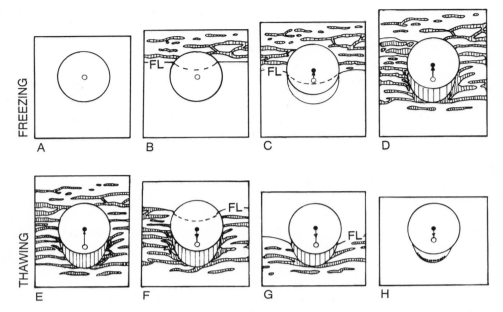

FIGURE 7.3. The processes associated with freezing (A–D) and thawing (E–H) of the ground and the movement of an object within the affected ground. The frost line (FL) dips where it comes into contact with the stone because of the stone's higher thermal conductivity. The hatched areas represent segregated ice lenses. Note that the ground is heaved upward as ice lenses form. As the stone becomes frozen to the upper soil, it is pulled upward, and as an ice lens forms beneath the stone, it is also pushed upward. Soil material that falls into the void beneath the stone and distortion of the void prevent the stone from falling back into its original position after the ground thaws. Thus the object is permanently displaced upward. The open circle indicates the original position of the center of the stone before freezing and thawing of the ground occur. The black circle indicates the displaced position of the center of the stone during and after freezing and thawing. The arrows indicate the direction in which the stone is moving. (Modified from Rolfsen 1980)

a depth of 20 cm) and discovered that larger artifacts had heaved to the surface more rapidly than artifacts with a smaller surface area (Fig. 7.4). Of all the debitage recovered at the site (maximum diameter: 9 mm) only 13.7% of it occurred at the surface, while 68.2% of the groundstone tools (maximum diameter: 83 mm) were recovered from the surface. Most hearths at the site were modified so extensively by cryoturbation that their original characteristics could not be discerned, and the charcoal they contained was dispersed in the matrix. Cryoturbation has also disturbed other archaeological sites above timberline in the Colorado Front Range (Benedict 1981, 1985).

The orientation of an artifact in the deposit also affects its movement to the surface. Artifacts that are oriented with their longest axis perpendicular to the ground surface are heaved to the surface faster than those lying parallel to it. Those with their long axis lying parallel to the ground surface must first be rotated vertically before they can be heaved upwards. For example, at the late Archaic Nebo Hill site in Missouri, many artifacts were oriented vertically in the site matrix as a result of cryoturbation (Reid 1983, 1984). Projectile points were inclined at angles of up to 85°, nearly perpendicular to the occupation surface. Even a quartzite anvil weighing 15.2 kg was positioned on edge, rather than on the flat plane opposite the worked surface (its behavior position).

The composition of objects also affects the process of heaving. Because of differences in thermal conductivity, some artifact materials promote the formation of segregated ice lenses and thus are more rapidly heaved out of the ground.

The depth of burial in relation to the depth of freezing and thawing also influences the intensity of frost heaving experienced by artifacts. Sites and their components closest to the surface undergo more freeze-thaw cycles.

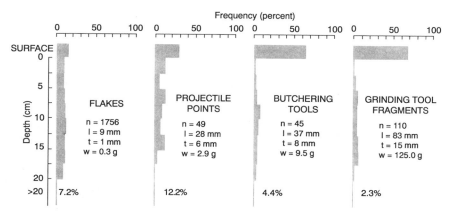

FIGURE 7.4. Vertical distribution of artifacts of different sizes at the Hungry Whistler site in Colorado. Four artifact classes are shown, and data on the number of specimens (n), median length (l), median thickness (t), and mean weight (w), are given for each group. Clearly, the artifacts with a large vertical dimension are ejected to the surface more rapidly than smaller artifacts. Note that the zone between 0 and 5 cm, the depth most affected by diurnal freezing and thawing, has the lowest concentration of artifacts. (Modified from Benedict and Olson 1978)

Artifacts in this zone heave more rapidly than those buried at a greater depth. In addition, because the depth of freezing varies from year to year, the layers closest to the surface are most consistently affected, while more deeply buried artifacts are actively displaced only during deep freezes. At the Hungry Whistler site, artifacts were virtually absent from the upper 5 to 7.5 cm of the soil because this zone is the most strongly affected by diurnal frost-heave cycles (Fig. 7.4; Benedict and Olson 1978). As artifacts entered this zone from below, the rate of upward freezing dramatically accelerated and led to their rapid ejection at the ground surface. Sites buried for a long time may also undergo periodic episodes of more intensified freezing. For example, frost heaving at the Hungry Whistler site was intensified during several cold periods during the Little Ice Age, when the range of freezing and thawing extended to greater depths (Benedict and Olson 1978). This accelerated the heaving of all artifacts, even those buried below the zone typically affected by cycles of freezing and thawing.

Repeated freezing and thawing of the ground also contorts and destroys stratigraphic layering and pedogenic horizonation. At the Smoky site, on a terrace overlooking the Smoky River in western Alberta, Canada, radiocarbon ages suggest that the site was occupied at three discrete times between approximately 4500 and 1500 B.P. (Brink 1977). However, three corresponding vertically separated occupation surfaces were not found. Instead, cryoturbation had homogenized the stratigraphy and had mixed the artifacts into a single zone 10 to 50 cm below the surface. Flakes from one core and portions of another tool were recovered from depths ranging from 10 to 40 cm in this stratigraphic unit. In some cases, freezing and thawing is severe enough to sort the matrix particles according to size. This results in surface landforms such as patterned ground, stone nets, and stripes (Washburn 1980), which can take on the appearance of artificial features. The distribution of these periglacial features across North America has been mapped by Péwé (1983; see Fig. 5.9). However, severe destruction and mixing of the stratigraphy does not always occur. For example, the stratigraphy at the Onion Portage (Schweger 1985) and Dry Creek sites (Fig. 4.9; Thorson and Hamilton 1977) in Alaska was disturbed by freezing and thawing but is still discernible.

Frost heaving may damage or destroy artifacts while they are being pushed to the surface. Mechanical movement to the surface abrades, rounds, polishes, crushes, and nicks artifact surfaces as they pass through the matrix. Bostwick (1985) demonstrated that sherds became rounded as they moved upward through the fill of Sinagua pithouses in northern Arizona. Likewise, at the Nebo Hill site, fiber-tempered pottery sherds were mechanically disintegrated and abraded as they moved through the matrix (Reid 1983, 1984).

This differential destruction may lead to false distribution patterns of artifacts and invalid archaeological interpretations. This is well illustrated by the work of Reid (1983, 1984) on the distribution of fiber-tempered pottery. Prior to his work on the Nebo Hill phase at several sites in eastern Kansas and western Missouri (dated between 4550 and 3500 B.P.), the distribution of fiber-tempered pottery was thought to be concentrated in the southeastern portion of the United States (Fig. 7.2). However, the discovery of fiber-tempered potsherds at four Nebo Hill phase sites to the north called into question the traditional view of fiber-tempered pottery distribution. Examination of the latitudinal distribution of fiber-tempered pottery and climatic variables (frost penetration depths) showed that most sites with fiber-tempered pottery cluster south of 35° N latitude, where freezing penetrates to a maximum depth of 35 cm. In this area, destruction of sherds would be less intense. Porous fiber-tempered ceramics at sites north of 35° N latitude were more vulnerable to decomposition because more intense freezing and thawing was at work, prying the sherds apart and disintegrating them. Consequently, the preservation and distribution of fiber-tempered pottery in the southeast is not a reflection of prehistoric culture patterns but is instead a result of the intensity and distribution of freeze-thaw processes.

Argilliturbation

If the matrix surrounding archaeological remains is composed of expandable clay minerals, the spatial position of artifacts and other archaeological debris may be disturbed as the site matrix expands and contracts (Fig. 7.5; Butzer 1982; Cahen and Moeyersons 1977; Schiffer 1987; Wood and Johnson 1978). Some clays, especially smectites, permit water to enter and exit their crystalline structures easily. When the ground becomes wet, water is taken into the clay mineral structure, and the ground swells. As the ground dries, water leaves the structure, the ground shrinks, and cracks form at the surface. Dehydration cracks extend anywhere from a few centimeters to several meters below the surface. They eventually close when the ground again becomes wet, which causes the clay matrix to swell. This process occurs annually in regions with a wet and a dry season. Surficial layers of shrinking and swelling clays are often referred to as Vertisols (Soil Survey Staff 1975). A surficial microrelief of ridges and swales, known as gilgai, may form in places with extreme ground shrinking and swelling.

If a site matrix contains expandable clay minerals, repeated cycles of wetting and drying mechanically transport artifacts and other archaeological debris to the surface (Fig. 7.5). When expansion occurs, an artifact is lifted slightly from its original position, leaving a small void or cavity under the artifact. As the soil dries, the matrix around the artifact shrinks. Because the cavity under the artifact also shrinks, the artifact cannot fall back into its original position, and fine-grained particles fill the void. The net effect is the upward displacement of the artifact. After many years of expansion and contraction of the ground, an artifact is heaved to the surface. Once at the surface, it may fall into a dehydration crack that opens during the dry season if the artifact is narrower than the crack. In this way, an artifact may be recycled through the archaeological matrix several times.

Like freezing and thawing, expansion and contraction of a site matrix associated with wetting and drying distorts and in some cases totally obliterates any behavioral or temporal associations between archaeological remains. Archaeological debris of different ages may become mixed within the matrix or at the surface. This process also homogenizes the stratigraphy. Mixing caused by expanding clays is a major problem in regions where Vertisols are present, such as the Gulf Coast states of Texas, Louisiana, Mississippi, and Alabama. Here, Vertisols are well known for mixing and churning sites (Duffield 1970). Expandable clays are also present in other states. For example, artifacts from late prehistoric surface sites on San Miguel Island off the coast of California became buried in Vertisols when they fell down seasonally open dehydration cracks (Johnson and Hester 1972; Wood and Johnson 1978). At the Cherokee Sewer site in Iowa, Hoyer (1980) found that artifacts that had originally been on the surface of paleosols were vertically displaced into the montmorillonite-rich A horizons of the buried soils. Argilliturbation has also been responsible for disturbing other coastal sites in California (Erlandson and Rockwell 1987) and sites in the American Bottoms on the Mississippi River floodplain near St. Louis, Missouri (Gladfelter 1981).

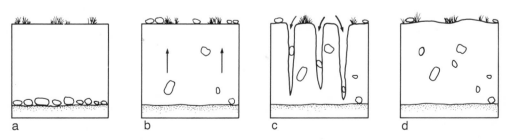

FIGURE 7.5. The upward movement of artifacts due to the expansion and contraction of a clay matrix (a and b). Note too, that artifacts can fall into open cracks created when the ground contracts (c) and again become sealed within the clay as the ground expands and the cracks close (d). These stones will eventually be heaved to the surface again. (Modified from Butzer 1982)

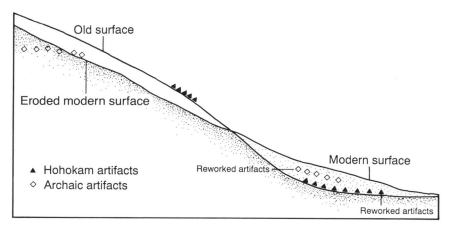

FIGURE 7.6. A hypothetical example of the way cultural stratigraphy may be reversed by slope processes. First, the younger Hohokam (ceramic period) artifacts and associated soil mantle are transported to the base of the hill by slope processes such as soil creep. Second, Archaic artifacts are eroded from a layer exposed on the slope and transported downhill. These artifacts and additional colluvium are deposited over the younger Hohokam artifacts at the base of the hill. This results in a reversed cultural stratigraphy. (Modified from Butzer 1982)

Graviturbation

Graviturbation is the mixing of artifacts and other archaeological debris by noncatastrophic mass wasting, which is the slow downslope movement of masses of loose bedrock, unconsolidated sediment, and soil under the influence of gravity and without the aid of running water, blowing wind, or other active geomorphic agents (Fig. 7.6; Young 1972).

These processes occur at rates of a few millimeters or centimeters per year. While this downslope movement is slow and almost imperceptible on an annual basis, over many years the cumulative effects of these processes are discernible and may grossly disturb the archaeological context of a site (Butzer 1982; Schiffer 1987; Wood and Johnson 1978). The slow downslope mass-wasting processes considered here include soil creep, solifluction, and gelifluction.

Soil creep is the slow downslope movement of surficial unconsolidated sediment and soil particles under the influence of gravity (Fig. 5.8). The primary mechanism responsible for displacing particles downslope is the expansion and contraction of the ground caused by surficial wetting and drying, and freezing and thawing (sometimes called frost creep). During expansion, surface particles are heaved upward; upon thawing or drying, gravity pulls them back to the surface. By repeating this process diurnally or seasonally, particles move slowly downslope. Wedging and prying caused by root growth, tree fall, swaying vegetation, burrowing soil fauna (e.g., worms, gophers, and insects), the collapse of burrows, and animals treading over the surface all cause particles to move downslope.

The upper meter of the soil is the zone primarily affected by soil creep. Because gravity is virtually uniform over the surface of the earth, the rate of soil creep is governed by (1) the slope angle; (2) the type, magnitude, and frequency of the process causing the creep; (3) vegetation; (4) particle size; and (5) moisture content. Rates of creep vary from 0.1 to 15 mm per year, with maximum rates of downslope movement reaching more than 50 cm per year (Young 1972).

Soil creep causes the downslope translocation of surficial and shallowly buried archaeological remains. This process may also result in the burial and mixing of artifacts at the base of slopes (Fig. 7.6). Rick (1976) showed that artifacts and other debris have crept 20 to 300 m on slopes varying from 10° to 44°. Bowers, Bonnichsen, and Hoch (1983) showed in an experimental study that flakes on the surface of shallow slopes in central Alaska were reoriented, inverted, and moved 4 to 20 cm per year by surficial frost action. At the Rincon Point site on the Santa Barbara coast of California, Kornfeld (1982) showed that most of the midden and archaeological material located on the middle and lower portions of the slope were redeposited from an intact midden at the top of the hill by soil creep and slopewash. Soil creep was also an important process responsible for filling abandoned house pits in California (Erlandson and Rockwell 1987; Orr 1951).

Solifluction is the slow downslope movement of water-saturated, surficial unconsolidated sediments and soils. Downslope movement occurs when the sediments on the hillslope become saturated to the point that the cohesive properties of the sediment and the frictional forces holding it on the slope are overcome by gravity. Solifluction can occur on slopes of as little as 1°, with optimum displacements occurring on slopes ranging from 5° to 20°. The surficial matrix is displaced downslope at rates of 0.5 to 5 cm per year, while the sediments below the saturated zone are not affected by solifluction processes. Cumulative downslope movement by solifluction creates bulbous sheets and lobes of debris that mantle the hillslope (Fig. 5.8). Solifluction can occur in any environment in which moisture collects in the sediment.

Solifluction is most prevalent in cold periglacial regions, where the water released in the spring during thawing of the upper frozen zone saturates the sediment. This water cannot drain into the substrate because the underlying ground is still frozen and impermeable. As the soil becomes increasingly

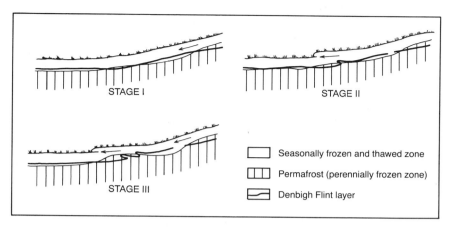

FIGURE 7.7. The creation of folds in the Denbigh culture layer at the Iyatayet site in Alaska. At Stage I, the upper portion of the ground thaws during the spring, but the deeper portions remain frozen. Portions of the Denbigh layer are within the thawed and frozen zones. At Stage II, the saturated surface layer flows downslope, forming a solifluction lobe, and the Denbigh layer is folded and overrides the portion of the Denbigh layer that is still frozen in the ground. The occupation surface is broken upslope where the thawed zone pulls away from the frozen portion of the cultural level. At Stage III, during later thawing episodes the saturated sediment continues to flow downslope, the cultural layers become more folded, and the gap between the Denbigh layer in the frozen and seasonally thawed ground widens. (Modified from Hopkins and Giddings 1953)

saturated, gravity eventually overcomes the cohesional and frictional forces holding the sediment in place on the slope. At this point, the surficial material flows downslope until it refreezes and stabilizes late in the fall. This produces huge sheets and bulbous masses of soliflucted debris on hillsides in northern latitudes. This special type of solifluction is referred to as gelifluction.

During the downslope movement of debris, the sediment and soil particles become oriented, and the stratigraphic layering and soil horizons present in the affected zone become folded. If an archaeological site is within the surficial zone affected by solifluction or gelifluction, it too becomes disturbed. At the Iyatayet site on Cape Denbigh on the west coast of Alaska, gelifluction has distorted a 10,000-year-old Denbigh Flint Complex occupation surface buried in a silt layer (Hopkins and Giddings 1953). The site matrix and the occupation zone were folded in a complex manner, and in some cases sediments and artifacts were turned completely upside down (Fig. 7.7). Part of the Denbigh layer was not contorted, however, because it was in the permafrost and was thus anchored to the slope. Gelifluction has also contorted the original stratigraphy at the Engigstciak site in the northwestern Yukon Territory in Canada (Mackay et al. 1961; MacNeish 1964). The upper 70 cm of the matrix of this multicomponent site was intensely folded, and artifacts were displaced many meters on a slope of 5° to 7°. Disturbance was so intense in places that the original stratigraphic relationships were obliterated. In some areas of the site, artifacts of different ages were mixed, while in others, older artifacts moved downslope over younger archaeological debris, reversing the original stratigraphic sequence.

Deformation

Deformation refers to any change in the orientation, shape, or volume of a layer as a result of folding (plastic deformation), faulting (rigid deformation), or compaction. Deformation of sediments and soils may occur both during and at any time after deposition (Butzer 1982; Schiffer 1987; Wood and Johnson 1978).

Plastic deformation is the plastic distortion of the matrix without rigid rupture of the strata. This usually occurs when a moist sediment is placed under compressional stresses, is affected by a sudden shock (e.g., an earthquake), or slumps. Folds (curves or bends in otherwise planar beds or horizons) are the most common expression of plastic deformation. Other types of plastic deformation structures include flame structures (tongues of mud that project upward into an overlying layer), ball-and-pillow structures (elliptical masses of sand in a fine-grained matrix), convoluted bedding (complicated folding or crumpling of laminae into irregular small-scale folds), and load structures (bulbous protrusions of sediment into underlying sediments from overlying units). For a complete list of deformation structures, including illustrations, see Collinson and Thompson 1982; Pettijohn and Potter 1964; and Reineck and Singh 1980. Many sites show evidence of plastic sediment deformation, including the Mammoth Hot Springs site in South Dakota (Laury 1980), Onion Portage in Alaska (Schweger 1985), the Wasden site in Idaho (Miller and Dort 1978), and the Dutton site in Colorado (Stanford 1979).

Rigid deformation is the rigid displacement of the matrix along a fault zone. This usually occurs when a dry or only slightly wet matrix is placed under compressional or tensional stresses. Faults are easily recognized by the offset of distinctive beds. At the Dry Creek site in Alaska, normal faults displace deposits by up to 3 m (Fig. 4.9; Thorson and Hamilton 1977). Small-scale offsets were noted along faults at the Stalker (Taber Child) site in Alberta (Wilson et al. 1983). Faulting associated with the New Madrid

FIGURE 7.8. Human leg bones offset along a fault at the Campbell site in Missouri as a result of the New Madrid earthquake. (Photograph by Carl H. Chapman, courtesy W. Raymond Wood)

earthquake in 1811 displaced the leg bones of human skeletons at a Mississippian age cemetery at the Campbell site in Pemiseot County, Missouri (Fig. 7.8; Chapman and Anderson 1955). Rapp 1986 provides a detailed discussion of the archaeological evidence for seismic catastrophes.

Compaction is the collapse of pore spaces or voids between individual particles making up a soil or sediment layer due to the weight of overlying sediments. If an archaeological site is buried in a layer or horizon undergoing compaction, small-scale vertical displacements of archaeological remains and warping and breakage of bone and artifacts (especially soft material such as ceramics) will occur.

Subsidence, the downward settling or sinking of the ground surface, often accompanies compaction, and many archaeological sites are affected by it. For example, the late prehistoric mounds and shell middens situated on natural levees at the Magnolia Mound site in Louisiana have subsided 2 to 3 m into the surrounding marsh (Gagliano 1984; Gagliano et al. 1982). Many sites on the Mississippi Delta have also sunk into the deltaic muds (Coastal Environments 1977; Gagliano 1984; McIntire 1971).

Compaction may cause cracking of the ground surface, which may allow artifacts at the surface to fall into the lower levels of a site. Water withdrawals from the aquifers in the Valley of Mexico caused subsidence and surface cracking at the Tlapacoya site. Artifacts have fallen into these cracks and have become displaced in the matrix. For example, an obsidian blade, common on late prehistoric sites in the region, was found under a buried log that dated to 27,000 B.P. (Haynes 1967; Lorenzo and Mirambell 1986; Mirambell 1978).

Other Physical Disturbance Processes

Other physical processes may also mechanically disturb the site matrix and alter the buried archaeological context. Wood and Johnson (1978) describe how air bubbles produced after rainfall move through soils in arid and semiarid regions. This process, known as aeroturbation, creates a vesicular fabric and may displace artifacts.

Another process, called crystalturbation (Butzer 1982; Wood and Johnson 1978), involves the displacement of artifacts and other archaeological remains by the growth and wasting of salt crystals in arid regions. During periods of intense evaporation, salt crystals may form around or under artifacts and displace them vertically in the matrix. Most salts, because they are soluble, dissolve when the ground becomes wet again, causing the artifact to settle. Repeated salt crystallization, solutioning, and reprecipitation cause artifacts to move within a salt-affected matrix. In some cases, such as the formation of calcic soil horizons, salt crystal growth is irreversible, and the displaced artifacts become permanently engulfed in a matrix of secondary calcium carbonate.

Floralturbation

Floralturbation is the partial or complete disturbance of the archaeological site matrix and its contents by trees, shrubs, or other types of plants (Butzer 1982; Johnson and Watson-Stegner 1990; Rolfsen 1980; Schiffer 1987; Strauss 1978, 1985; Wood and Johnson 1978). This disturbance is accomplished by four mechanical processes: (1) tree-throw, whereby surficial sediments and soils held by the roots are torn up from the substrate as a tree falls over; (2) the formation of hollows and tunnels due to root decay that may later collapse or become filled with younger sediments; (3) root growth and expansion, which exerts pressure on the soil and pushes it apart; and (4) tree-sway, which loosens and compacts the soil.

Tree-throw is the primary mechanism of floralturbation. During high wind conditions, trees commonly topple over (Fig. 7.9). When this occurs, the soil and archaeological debris entwined in the roots are pried from the substrate, leaving a shallow, craterlike depression. The soil particles and archaeological debris adhering to the root mass fall back into the depression or collect in a mound adjacent to the crater. This process creates a low-relief surface of pits and mounds known as cradle-and-knoll topography (Malde 1964). Over hundreds or thousands of years, tree-throw can significantly rework surficial sediments in forested regions.

The constant churning resulting from tree-throw can destroy the spatial patterning of archaeological debris at a site. The Debert Paleoindian site in Nova Scotia, for example, was significantly churned by tree-throw. MacDonald (1968) reports that in the upper 0.6 m of the site, the spatial relationships between artifacts were disrupted, the boundaries of hearths were blurred or obliterated beyond recognition, and living surfaces were not discernible. Below the tree-throw zone, the boundaries of features were sharp and undisturbed. Tree-throw in the forested regions of the Northeast has also caused considerable damage to shallowly buried Woodland period sites (Strauss 1978). If temporally distinct archaeological assemblages are present at a site, they may become mixed as buried remains are brought to the surface and surface materials fall into the pits and become buried. This constant churning of surface and subsurface remains may create a confusing situation. Holmes (1893) demonstrated that artifacts collected from glacial till at the Babbit site in Minnesota were actually translocated downward to a depth of more than 1.25 m into the till deposits by tree-throw.

Tree fall may also produce features that mimic human-made features. Wendorf (1982) believes that the proposed pre-Clovis firepits and hearths associated with charcoal and burned mammoth remains in the Pleistocene deposits on Santa Rosa Island off the coast of California are actually root craters created by tree-throw and that the charcoal was derived from the burning of the associated root masses. It is also true that when trees or shrubs burn at the surface, their roots may also burn and smolder for weeks after a fire. Consequently, charcoal may be found in a root structure or may even become mixed within the matrix by later tree fall or root collapse and consequently look like dispersed charcoal from hearths.

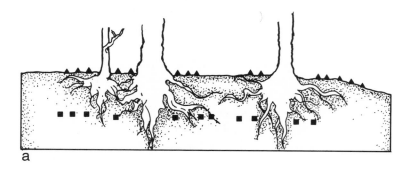

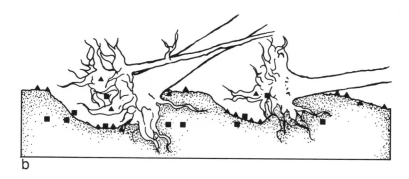

FIGURE 7.9. The disturbance of surface and buried archaeological horizons by tree fall. Diagram *c* shows the resulting crater-and-knoll topography. Note that the positions of artifacts, indicated by solid triangles and squares, have been modified by this process. (Modified from Holmes 1893)

The in-place disintegration and decay of roots after a tree or shrub dies produces hollow cavities and tunnels that may later collapse or become filled with younger sediments from above. If younger particles from overlying levels fill these cavities, a krotovina-like structure called a root cast is created (Fig. 7.10). Root casts are easily identified if the sediment filling the root void differs in color, texture, and cementation from the surrounding matrix. If, however, they become filled with material that looks similar to the host soil, they may be difficult to discern. As the root cavity fills, artifacts on the surface may fall into the root hole and become translocated and buried in the substrate. To avoid mixing of temporally different artifacts, the intrusive artifacts in the root fill must be excavated separately and not mixed with the *in situ* artifacts in the host matrix. Root casts are also created by the cementation of calcium carbonate around a root. These are created when water charged with dissolved calcium carbonate is attracted to the root. As the water is taken in by the plant, the calcium carbonate precipitates. This results in a hard, irregularly branching, tubular concretion (Fig. 7.11).

Often because of the weight of overlying sediment, the root cavity collapses before it is filled. As a result, younger sediments and artifacts contained in the collapsing sediment are translocated downward in the profile. This collapse may not be recognizable if the matrix above and below the cavity is the same texture and color. Root collapse can significantly contribute to overall site disturbance, especially considering that the volume of the root system of a typical forest tree is equal to about one-fourth to one-third of the volume of those portions of the tree exposed above ground.

As roots expand spatially and enlarge in diameter, they exert pressure on the matrix of a site. This results in the slight displacement of particles and archaeological debris as the roots push them aside. Roots may fragment an artifact if they penetrate it and expand (potsherds, for example, are easily fragmented by root expansion). Also, as trees sway in the wind, they agitate the soil and may both consolidate and loosen it.

Faunalturbation

Faunalturbation is the mixing of the site matrix and its archaeological contents by burrowing vertebrates (mammals, amphibians, birds, and reptiles) and invertebrates (insects, earthworms, and crustaceans) (see Ahlbrandt et al. 1978; Atkinson 1957; Butzer 1982; Johnson and Watson-Stegner 1990; Rolfsen 1980; Schiffer 1987; Strauss 1981, 1985; Wicksten 1989; Wilkins 1989; Wood and Johnson 1978). The nature and extent of the disturbance (e.g., the size and depth of burrows, the rate of burrowing, burrow density, and the amount and size of material brought to the surface) depends on the

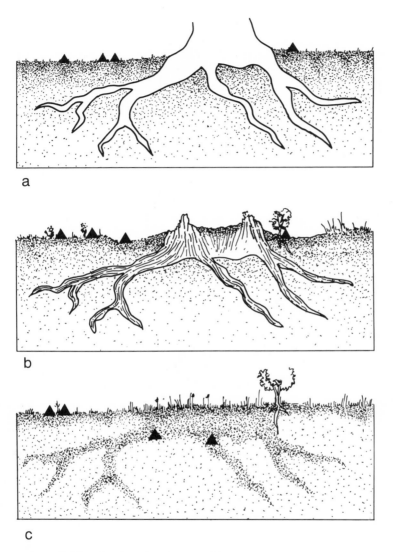

a

b

c

FIGURE 7.10. The disturbance caused by root growth while the plant is alive and the formation of root casts after it dies. As the roots grow, they push sediment particles aside (a). When the tree dies, the wood eventually rots, creating cavities (b). The root cavities then become filled with sediment derived from the surface, or they may collapse. Note that some artifacts (solid triangles) from the surface have fallen into the trunk and root cavities and have become incorporated into the krotovina fill. (Modified from Limbrey 1975)

FIGURE 7.11. A calcium carbonate root cast (note root within central channel) developed in alluvium in the Salton Basin in California.

type and density of the animals present in the matrix. The presence or absence of burrowing animals and their number depend on the characteristics of the site matrix (e.g., texture, moisture, organic matter and soil fauna, acidity, and compaction).

Burrowers, whether vertebrates or invertebrates, are categorized into two large groups: (1) those with a highly fossorial lifestyle, which spend virtually their entire life underground; or (2) those with a semifossorial lifestyle, which spend most of their life on the surface but still construct and use burrows for specific purposes (Schiffer 1987; Wilkins 1989).

Those animals with a fossorial lifestyle conduct all their daily activities of foraging, mating, raising young, and sleeping below the surface. Some of these animals (e.g., moles and pocket gophers) excavate an extensive network of tunnels and dens (Wilkins 1989). Others, such as earthworms, plow through the soil, ingesting sediment and excreting it as they go. Badgers, weasels, and ferrets are the most fossorial carnivores, digging holes in pursuit of prey. Consequently, fossorial animals are constantly digging in and churning the matrix in which they live.

Animals with a semifossorial lifestyle include amphibians (e.g., frogs, toads, and salamanders), reptiles (e.g., turtles, tortoises, and lizards), birds (e.g., cliff nesting types and burrowing owls), mammals (e.g., rabbits, some rats, ground squirrels, prairie dogs, kangaroo rats, mice, muskrats, coyotes, and foxes), insects (e.g., ants, termites), spiders, and crustaceans (e.g., crabs and crayfish). These animals conduct most of their daily activities on the surface but dig dens and tunnels for specific purposes such as shelter, hibernation, nesting, and giving birth. Ground squirrels, for instance, forage at the surface for food but go underground for shelter and protection from predators; ants live and mate underground but forage at the surface for food; owls and other birds that also forage at the surface commonly nest in burrows carved into cliff faces and riverbanks. The dens and burrows excavated by these animals range in size from shallow cavities (e.g., those of coyotes, foxes, and owls) to an extensive network of cavities and tunnels (e.g., those of prairie dogs, ground squirrels, and ants).

Whether the matrix of a site is churned by fossorial or semifossorial species, the results are similar: partial or total disturbance of the site matrix and artifact associations. Evidence of burrowing may or may not be detectable. Once excavated, burrows may collapse, may be filled with material pushed in by the burrower, or may fill with sediment from above. In the latter two cases, a krotovina is created. Krotovinas (sediment-filled burrows) may easily be distinguished in the field by differences in texture or color between the burrow fill and the surrounding matrix (Fig. 7.12). However, if the burrow collapses, it may not be recognized and the disturbance may go undetected. For example, many archaeological sites in the sand dunes of the Picacho Dune Field in Arizona were extensively bioturbated. However, be-

FIGURE 7.12. Crayfish burrows in the late Pleistocene pond sediments of the Aubrey site in Texas: (a) looking down on the top of the burrows; (b) a cross section view through a number of burrows (the dark sediments filling the burrows are krotovinas). (Photograph by C. Reid Ferring)

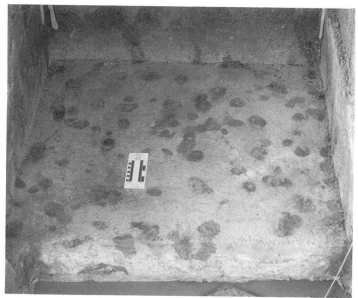

a

b

cause the sand matrix was homogeneous, collapsed burrows were not recognizable (Bayham et al. 1986; Waters 1986c).

The precise effects of burrowing animals at archaeological sites are not well documented. The specific type of disturbance varies with animal ecology and the length of time burrowing has occurred on the site. Of the studies done, those on rodents by Bocek and on earthworms by Stein illustrate the effects of burrowing organisms at specific archaeological sites.

Bocek (1986) studied the effects of burrowing animals on the Jasper Ridge site in central California, a late prehistoric midden dating to approximately A.D. 900. This midden was primarily bioturbated by pocket gophers and moles (both fossorial species), and ground squirrels (a semifossorial species). Bocek found that as a result of extensive burrowing, rodents had pushed or displaced small debris, ranging from 0.6 to 5.0 cm in maximum length, to the surface as they cleared their burrows of excavated matrix (Fig. 7.13). However, artifacts larger then 5.0 cm were too large to be moved through their burrows, so the gophers tunneled under them. As a result, larger objects were undermined and fell to the base of the burrow. As this process was repeated, the larger artifacts slowly worked their way deeper into the matrix. Most of the large artifacts and hearthstones at the site were concentrated at the base of the midden into a cobble bed that mimicked an occupation layer (Fig. 7.13). Some artifacts were even displaced below the midden to depths of 120 cm. Clearly, extreme burrowing at the Jasper Ridge site effectively segregated archaeological debris by size and concentrated small materials at the surface and larger materials at depth. Bocek also found that burrowing animals had moved archaeological remains horizontally. Artifacts from one portion of the site were moved 1.5 m laterally before they were ejected to the surface.

Johnson (1989) also found that large stones were lowered to the depth of maximum burrowing, and artificial concentrations of archaeological debris were created that had no bearing on human activity at other sites in California that had been profusely churned by pocket gophers. Taylor et al. (1986) showed how bioturbation resulted in the movement of radiocarbon samples at the Encino Village site in California, where modern dates were obtained from both the top and the base of the midden. Other radiocarbon age anomalies and reversals were also noted in the sequence. The effects of burrowing vertebrates on archaeological sites in California is also discussed in Erlandson and Rockwell 1987, Erlandson 1984, and Borst and Olmo 1985.

At the Carlston Annis Mound, an Archaic shell midden in western Kentucky, Stein (1983) documented the destructive effects of burrowing fossorial casting earthworms. These earthworms burrowed through the fine-grained matrix at the site in search of food. After they ingested and passed mineral

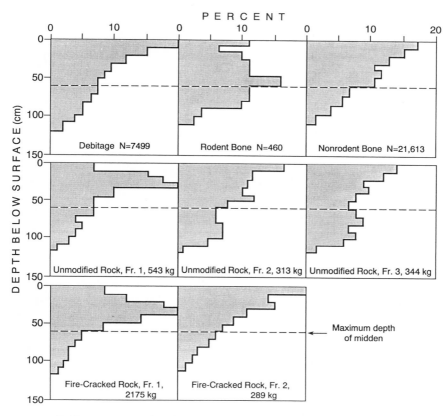

FIGURE 7.13. Frequency distributions, in percent, of the contents of the Jasper Ridge site in California. For bone and debitage, N is given in number of specimens. For fire-cracked rock and unmodified stone, N is given in kilograms. The abbreviation *Fr.* refers to the size of the unmodified rock or fire-cracked rock (Fr. 1 means larger than 3.5 cm; Fr. 2, 3.5 to 1.8 cm; Fr. 3, 1.8 to 0.6 cm). The midden occupied the zone from 0 to 60 cm. Artifacts recovered beneath 60 cm were translocated into a culturally sterile layer by rodent activity. Also note that heavier and larger artifacts are concentrated near the base of the midden, while smaller and lighter ones are concentrated near its surface. (Modified from Bocek 1986)

and organic matter (e.g., dung and leaves) through their digestive tracts, they ejected castings in the site matrix. Stein noted that these casts were common in all deposits at the site. As a result of years of earthworm activity, the deposits were mixed, and the boundaries between soil horizons and stratigraphic units were almost entirely obliterated. Feature boundaries were also blurred or absent. For example, the outlines of Archaic burial pits were not recognizable because of the severe reworking of the sediments by earthworm activity. Earthworms also altered the texture and chemistry of the deposits and destroyed all ecofacts. However, they did not affect the position of any large artifacts or stones within features. Earthworms generally only disturb sediment particles with a diameter of less than 2 mm, though they may slightly displace some small artifacts and micro-debitage.

Faunalturbation may also occur when animals scratch and root at the surface. These animals dig shallow holes to locate or cache food but do not otherwise excavate burrows or nests in the ground. For example, tree squirrels, birds, and some carnivores (e.g., foxes and bobcats) dig shallow pits in pursuit of animal prey or subterranean plant foods (e.g., roots, seeds, and bulbs). Other animals (e.g., elephants, bison, pigs, and birds) disturb the ground as they wallow in holes and cover themselves with dirt and mud.

Burrowing animals may also bury sites as sediments excavated during their burrowing accumulate on the surface. For example, some species of earthworms deposit their castings (byproducts of digestion) at the surface. These castings accumulate over time and may bury any debris lying on the surface (Butzer 1982; Limbrey 1975; Rolfsen 1980; Stein 1983; Strauss 1981). In addition, objects dropped onto a surface where surficial worm casting is ongoing will be translocated down into the zone where the earthworms are actively burrowing and may eventually come to rest at the bottom of the worm-disturbed layer to form a simulated artifact surface (Butzer 1982; Johnson et al. 1987; Limbrey 1975). For example, historic artifacts in Powissett Rockshelter in Massachusetts were buried in a 10 cm deposit of earthworm casts (Dincauze and Gramly 1973; Strauss 1981). Mounding by pocket gophers (Johnson 1989; Johnson and Watson-Stegner 1990; Johnson et al. 1987) in southern California, has buried manuports and other debris. Given enough time, ants can also bury surficial archaeological debris (Johnson et al. 1987; Petraglia and Nash 1987; Strauss 1981).

Conclusion

A number of mechanical and biological processes can alter the systemic context of a buried archaeological site. Consequently, it is necessary to determine if disturbance processes have affected a site, and if they have, to identify the types of processes and the extent of alteration. Once this is done, the limitations of the archaeological context are recognized and the accurate interpretation of human behavior is possible.

8

Geoarchaeological Research

The role of geoarchaeology is to decipher from the sediment and the soil matrix of an archaeological site the effects of earth processes on prehistoric human behavior and the archaeological debris left behind by that behavior. Depending on the goals of the archaeological research, geoarchaeological studies can range from general (e.g., determining the effect of landscape evolution on the regional archaeological record or prehistoric settlement patterns) to specific (e.g., determining the location of prehistoric agricultural fields or defining the stratigraphy at a site). Consequently, each geoarchaeological study requires a different field methodology and set of laboratory analyses. Here, I discuss general field and laboratory methods that may be used to achieve the geoarchaeological objectives discussed in this book. The general role of a geoarchaeologist is also discussed in Haynes 1964 and Rapp 1975.

Because geoarchaeologists and archaeologists collect different types of data, their field procedures and methodologies are different. Archaeologists usually focus on the contents of the site matrix, very carefully excavating and recording the position of artifacts, features, and ecofacts. Furthermore, archaeologists usually concentrate their efforts on a small area of the site, such as a house floor, living surface, or midden. The geoarchaeologist, on the other hand, must take a much broader approach to the site, examining not only the matrix of the site and its internal microstratigraphy but also the stratigraphy of the area around the site. The exposures made by archaeologists during their excavations are usually adequate for geoarchaeological analysis of the site microstratigraphy. However, exposures that extend below the depth of the archaeological stratum, and exposures that are laterally continuous and that extend beyond the limits of the site are needed for complete geoarchaeological interpretations. Therefore the geoarchaeologist must examine natural exposures adjacent to the site and in many cases employ hand augering, coring (Stein 1986), or trenching to make additional exposures.

During the study of the stratigraphy, the geoarchaeologist subdivides the sediments and soils at the site and in the surrounding exposures into different lithostratigraphic and pedostratigraphic units based on their physical characteristics and the contacts between them. Each unit is described and assigned a designation. These designations should be standardized across the site and integrated with archaeological recording. Exemplary exposures of the stratigraphy are recorded in detail to document the vertical and horizontal facies relationships between the various stratigraphic units and to show the relationship between these units and the archaeological remains. In some cases, sedimentary peels or monoliths are made as part of the documentation of a stratigraphic section (Rapp 1975). Furthermore, all the units defined at a site should also be related to surface and buried landforms (e.g., the alluvial stratigraphy of a valley may be related to the sequence of terraces along the river).

The relative sequence of stratigraphic units and landforms must be placed in absolute time for precise geoarchaeological and archaeological interpretations. The site matrix is placed in time by dating archaeological samples. However, nonarchaeological samples from the underlying and overlying units (on and off the site) must also be dated to facilitate correlations, demonstrate facies relationships, and determine the timing and duration of episodes of deposition, erosion, and stability.

In addition to recording the site and regional stratigraphy, the geoarchaeologist will construct a geomorphic map of the study area (Davidson 1985; Haynes 1964), which shows the location of all stratigraphic exposures as well as the distribution of the stratigraphic units and geomorphic landforms exposed at the surface. This is accomplished by using aerial photographs (especially black-and-white, color, and color infrared images) coupled with field investigations.

While in the field, the geoarchaeologist collects samples from the stratigraphic units and takes them back to the laboratory for analysis. Laboratory analyses are used to quantify field descriptions, identify the sedimentary processes of deposition, identify stratigraphic breaks not visible in field exposures, determine sediment origin, identify postdepositional sediment alterations, and facilitate correlations. Laboratory analyses may include (1) mechanical (particle size) analyses to determine the texture of the sediments; (2) chemical analyses to determine acidity or alkalinity (pH) or the concentrations of phosphate, calcium carbonate, and organic matter in the matrix; (3) microscopic examinations of the sediment and soil to identify mineral composition and microfabrics; and (4) X-ray diffraction and heavy mineral analyses to determine the source areas of the sediment. Other laboratory analyses might include a study of the changes in the relative proportion of stable carbon isotopes in a stratigraphic sequence. For a complete discussion of laboratory analyses, see Hassan 1978, Limbrey 1975, and Shackley 1975. The field and laboratory studies of the sediments, soils, and stratigraphy of the site and the surrounding area are the basis for geoarchaeological interpretations of site formation and landscape reconstruction.

The geoarchaeologist participating in archaeological research should have not only geological skills but also an active interest in and knowledge of archaeology. Likewise, archaeologists should have a knowledge of the potential contributions of geoarchaeological research. Furthermore, in order to achieve the best interdisciplinary cooperation, the geoarchaeologist must be involved in all aspects of the project, from planning through excavation, analysis, and final report preparation (Butzer 1982; Dincauze 1987; Gladfelter 1977, 1981; Haynes 1964; Rapp 1975; Schoenwetter 1981; Villas 1985).

Geoarchaeologists should be involved with the preparation of the archaeological research design in order to develop a mutual strategy to achieve archaeological research goals, decipher natural site formation processes, and permit synchronic and diachronic landscape reconstructions. Furthermore, a geoarchaeologist will be able to identify geological conditions that may constrain archaeological research questions or identify the need to modify archaeological methodologies. For example, if geoarchaeological studies precede an archaeological survey of a region, a model can be developed to predict where sites of certain ages might be encountered and thus help modify conventional survey methodologies to maximize site discovery.

Geoarchaeologists and archaeologists should continue to work closely together during site excavation, and they should be aware of each others' working hypotheses regarding site formation, landscape setting, and activities at the site as they develop. The geoarchaeologist should be available to work with other specialists (e.g., palynologists and malacologists) and assist with their data collecting by showing them the stratigraphic and environmental framework. Also, the geoarchaeologist should assist in deciphering complex stratigraphic situations and distinguishing natural from human-made features and objects encountered during excavation. This cooperation should continue into the analysis and final project synthesis.

In conclusion, the fundamental goals of archaeology are (1) to reconstruct culture history; (2) to reconstruct prehistoric human behavior and lifeways; and (3) to understand the processes of culture change. The resolution of these objectives can be greatly enhanced by the addition of geoarchaeological studies. Geoarchaeology contributes substantially to these broad goals of archaeological research by defining (1) the relative and absolute temporal framework of sites; (2) the way geological processes have affected the archaeological record from which human behavior is reconstructed; and (3) the way the landscape may have influenced the operation of cultural systems. Consequently, it is crucial that the close interaction between the geosciences and archaeology, fostered over a century ago, should continue to grow and that geoarchaeology should become an organized subdiscipline within archaeology, with its specialists fully integrated into archaeological research.

Appendix A

Geoarchaeological Studies Illustrating the Effects of Fluvial Landscape Evolution on the Archaeological Record

United States

Arizona

Bajadas (Brakenridge and Schuster 1986)

San Pedro Valley (Haynes 1981, 1982a)

Santa Cruz River (Haynes and Huckell 1986; Waters 1987a, 1988a, 1988b, 1988c)

Whitewater Draw (Waters 1986b)

Colorado

South Platte River (Haynes and Grey 1965; Holliday 1987b; Reider 1983)

Georgia

Savannah River (Anderson and Schuldenrein 1983a, 1983b, 1985; Brooks et al. 1986; Schuldenrein and Anderson 1988; Segovia 1985)

Illinois

Campbell Hollow site (Hajic 1985a)

Illinois River (Hajic 1985b, 1987; Schuldenrein 1976)

Koster site (Hajic 1981, 1990; Wiant et al. 1983)

Middle Mississippi River (American Bottoms) (Gladfelter 1985; Phillips and Gladfelter 1983)

Napoleon Hollow site (Styles 1985; Wiant et al. 1983)

Iowa

    Central Des Moines River (Benn and Bettis 1981; Bettis and Benn 1984; Bettis and Hoyer 1986; Schuldenrein 1987)

    Cherokee Sewer site (Hoyer 1980)

    Loess Hills (Bettis et al. 1986; Bettis and Thompson 1981, 1982, 1985; Thompson and Bettis 1980, 1982)

    Soap Creek (Bettis and Littke 1987)

Kansas

    Kansas River Basin (Johnson and Logan 1990; Johnson and Martin 1987a, 1987b; Logan and Johnson 1986)

    Neosho River (Rogers 1986, 1987a, 1987b)

Kentucky

    Cumberland River (Leach and Jackson 1987)

    Ohio River (Gray 1984)

    Tennessee River (Leach and Jackson 1987)

Mississippi

    Atchafalaya Basin (Smith et al. 1986)

    Tombigbee River (Muto and Gunn 1985)

Missouri

    Little Platte River (Gardner and Donahue 1985)

Oklahoma

    Little Caney River (Artz 1985)

    Stream valleys in the Central Plains (Ferring 1990a; Hall 1988)

Oregon

    Willamette Valley (McDowell 1984)

Texas

    Lake Creek (Mandel 1987; Mandel et al. 1987)

    Stream valleys in the Central Plains (Ferring 1990a; Hall 1988)

    Upper Trinity River (Ferring 1986c, 1990a, 1990b; Yates and Ferring 1986)

    Yellowhouse Draw (Stafford 1981)

Washington

    Lower Snake River (Hammatt 1977)

Canada

Alberta

    Bow River (Wilson 1983a, 1986, 1990)

Appendix B

Geoarchaeological Studies Illustrating Site-Specific Synchronic and Diachronic Alluvial Landscape Reconstructions

Alaska

    Onion Portage site (Hamilton 1970)

Arizona

    Lehner site (Antevs 1959; Haury et al. 1959; Haynes 1982a)

Colorado

    Jones-Miller site (Albanese 1977, 1978a)

    Olsen-Chubbock site (Malde 1972; Wheat 1972)

Illinois

    Campbell Hollow site (Hajic 1985a)

    Hill Lake site (Fortier 1985)

    Koster site (Brown and Vierra 1983; Butzer 1977, 1978b; Hajic 1981, 1990)

    Labras Lake site (Gladfelter 1981; Phillips and Gladfelter 1983)

    Napoleon Hollow site (Styles 1985; Wiant et al. 1983)

Iowa

    Cherokee Sewer site (Hoyer 1980)

Kansas

    Coffey site (Schmits 1978, 1980)

Nebraska

    Hudson-Meng site (Agenbroad 1978)

Oklahoma

    Delaware Canyon (Ferring 1986a, 1986b; Hall and Ferring 1987)

Domebo site (Albritton 1966; Ferring and Hall 1987; Leonhardy
   1966; Retallick 1966)

Dyer site (Ferring and Peter 1987)

South Carolina

Pen Point site (Brooks and Sassaman 1990)

South Dakota

Lange-Ferguson site (Hannus 1989, 1990a, 1990b)

Texas

Aubrey site (Ferring 1989, 1990b)

Bison kill site, Whiteoak Bayou (McReynolds et al. 1988; Waters
   1988d)

Lubbock Lake site (Holliday 1985a; Holliday and Allen 1987)

Washington

Hoko River site (Croes and Blinman 1980)

Wyoming

Agate Basin site (Albanese 1982; Reider 1982)

Carter/Kerr-McGee site (Frison 1984; Reider 1980)

Colby site (Albanese 1977, 1978a, 1978b, 1986)

Hanson site (Albanese 1978a)

Horner site (Albanese 1987; Reider 1987)

Mavrakis-Bentzen-Roberts site (Albanese 1978a, 1978b)

Ruby site (Albanese 1971, 1978a, 1978b)

Appendix C

Geoarchaeological Studies Illustrating Regional Synchronic and Diachronic Alluvial Landscape Reconstructions

Arizona

    Black Mesa (Gumerman 1988; Kalstrom 1983, 1986)

    Cienega Creek (Eddy and Coley 1983)

    Santa Cruz River (Waters 1987a, 1988a, 1988b)

    Whitewater Draw (Waters 1986b)

Georgia

    Savannah River (Anderson and Schuldenrein 1983a, 1983b, 1985; Brooks et al. 1986; Schuldenrein and Anderson 1988; Segovia 1985)

Illinois

    Mississippi River (American Bottoms) (Gladfelter 1981; Munson 1974; Phillips and Gladfelter 1983; White et al. 1984; Yerkes 1987)

Kentucky

    Green River (Stein 1982)

    Ohio River (Gray 1984)

Louisiana

    Red River (Pearson 1986)

Mississippi

    Mississippi River (Guccione et al. 1988)

    Swan Lake Meander (Weinstein 1981; Weinstein, Glander et al. 1979)

New Mexico

    Chaco Canyon (Bryan 1954; Hall 1977, 1990b)

    Llaues Valley (Mackey and Holbrook 1978)

Tennessee

    Tennessee River (Chapman et al. 1982)

References

Agenbroad, Larry D.
  1978   *The Hudson-Meng Site: An Alberta Bison Kill in the Nebraska High Plains.* University Press of America, Washington, D.C.
  1984   Hot Springs, South Dakota: Entrapment and Taphonomy of Columbian Mammoth. In *Quaternary Extinctions: A Prehistoric Revolution,* edited by Paul S. Martin and Richard G. Klein, pp. 113–127. University of Arizona Press, Tucson.

Ager, Derek V.
  1981   *The Nature of the Stratigraphical Record.* 2d ed. Halsted Press, New York.

Ahlbrandt, Thomas S.
  1974   Dune Stratigraphy, Archaeology, and the Chronology of the Killpecker Dune Field. In *Applied Geology and Archaeology: The Holocene History of Wyoming,* edited by Michael Wilson, pp. 51–57. Report of Investigations No. 10. Geological Survey of Wyoming, Laramie.

Ahlbrandt, Thomas S., Sarah Andrews, and Darryl T. Gwynne
  1978   Bioturbation in Eolian Deposits. *Journal of Sedimentary Petrology* 48:839–848.

Ahlbrandt, Thomas S., and Steven G. Fryberger
  1982   Introduction to Eolian Deposits. In *Sandstone Depositional Environments,* edited by Peter A. Scholle and Darwin Spearing, pp. 11–47. Memoir 31. American Association of Petroleum Geologists, Tulsa, Okla.

Ahler, Stanley A.
  1976   Sedimentary Processes at Rodgers Shelter, Missouri. In *Prehistoric Man and His Environments: A Case Study in the Ozark Highland,* edited by W. R. Wood and R. B. McMillan, pp. 123–139. Academic Press, New York.

Albanese, John P.
  1971   Geology of the Ruby Site Area, Wyoming 48 CA 302. *American Antiquity* 36:91–95.

1974a   Geology of the Casper Archeological Site. In *The Casper Site: A Hell
         Gap Bison Kill on the High Plains,* edited by George C. Frison, pp.
         173–190. Academic Press, New York.

1974b   Geology of the Casper Archaeological Site, Natrona County, Wyoming.
         In *Applied Geology and Archaeology: The Holocene History of Wyo-
         ming,* edited by Michael Wilson, pp. 46–50. Report of Investigations
         No. 10. Geological Survey of Wyoming, Laramie.

1977   Paleotopography and Paleoindian Sites in Wyoming and Colorado. In
         Paleoindian Lifeways, edited by E. Johnson, pp. 28–47. *Museum Jour-
         nal,* vol. 17. West Texas Museum Association, Texas Tech University,
         Lubbock.

1978a   Archeogeology of the Northwestern Plains. In *Prehistoric Hunters of the
         High Plains,* by George C. Frison, pp. 375–389. Academic Press, New
         York.

1978b   Paleotopography and Bison Traps. In *Bison Procurement and Utiliza-
         tion: A Symposium,* edited by Leslie B. Davis and Michael Wilson. *Plains
         Anthropologist* 23, no. 82, pt. 2 (Memoir 14): 58–62.

1982   Geologic Investigation. In *The Agate Basin Site: A Record of the Paleoin-
         dian Occupation of the Northwestern High Plains,* by George C. Frison
         and Dennis J. Stanford, pp. 309–330. Academic Press, New York.

1986   The Geology and Soils of the Colby Site. In *The Colby Mammoth Site:
         Taphonomy and Archaeology of a Clovis Kill in Northern Wyoming,* by
         George C. Frison and Lawrence C. Todd, pp. 143–163. University of
         New Mexico Press, Albuquerque.

1987   Geologic Investigations. In *The Horner Site: The Type Site of the Cody
         Cultural Complex,* edited by George C. Frison and Lawrence C. Todd,
         pp. 279–326. Academic Press, New York.

Albanese, John P., and Michael Wilson
1974   Preliminary Description of the Terraces of the North Platte River at
         Casper, Wyoming. In *Applied Geology and Archaeology: The Holocene
         History of Wyoming,* edited by Michael Wilson, pp. 8–18. Report of
         Investigations No. 10. Geological Survey of Wyoming, Laramie.

Albertson, Paul E., and Tommy C. Birchett
1990   Geotechniques in the Archeological Exploration for the U.S.S. *Eastport*
         Along the Lower Red River, Louisiana. Geological Society of America,
         Abstracts with Programs 22 (7): A121.

Albritton, Claude C., Jr.
1966   Stratigraphy of the Domebo Site. In *Domebo: A Paleo-Indian Mammoth
         Kill in the Prairie-Plains,* edited by Frank C. Leonhardy, pp. 11–13. Con-
         tributions of the Museum of the Great Plains, no. 1. Great Plains Histor-
         ical Association, Lawton, Okla.

Allen, P. A., and J. D. Collinson
1986   Lakes. In *Sedimentary Environments and Facies,* 2d ed., edited by H. G.
         Reading, pp. 63–94. Blackwell Scientific Publications, Oxford.

Anderson, David G., and Joseph W. Schuldenrein
   1983a   Early Archaic Settlement on the Southeastern Atlantic Slope: A View
            from the Rucker's Bottom Site, Elbert County, Georgia. *North American
            Archaeologist* 4:177–210.
   1983b   Mississippian Period Settlement in the Southern Piedmont: Evidence
            from the Rucker's Bottom Site, Elbert County, Georgia. *Southeastern
            Archaeology* 2 (2): 98–117.
Anderson, David G., and Joseph W. Schuldenrein (editors)
   1985   *Prehistoric Human Ecology Along the Upper Savannah River: Excava-
            tions at the Rucker's Bottom, Abbeville and Bullard Site Groups*, 2 vols.
            Gilbert-Commonwealth Associates, Inc., Jackson, Michigan.
Andrews, J. T., Robert McGhee, and Lorna McKenzie-Pollock
   1971   Comparison of Elevations of Archaeological Sites and Calculated Sea
            Levels in Arctic Canada. *Arctic* 24:210–228.
Antevs, Ernst
   1935   Age of the Clovis Lake Clays. In *The Occurrence of Flints and Extinct
            Animals in Fluvial Deposits, New Clovis, New Mexico*, pt. 2. Academy
            of Natural Sciences of Philadelphia, *Proceedings* 87:304–312.
   1937   Age of the Lake Mohave Culture. In *The Archeology of Pleistocene Lake
            Mohave*, pp. 45–49. Southwest Museum Papers, no. 11. Southwest
            Museum, Los Angeles.
   1941   Age of the Cochise Culture Stages. In *The Cochise Culture*, by E. B.
            Sayles and Ernst Antevs, pp. 31–56. Medallion Papers, no. 29. Gila
            Pueblo, Globe, Ariz.
   1949   Geology of the Clovis Sites. In *Ancient Man in North America*, 3d ed., by
            H. M. Wormington, pp. 185–192. Popular Series, no. 4. Denver Museum
            of Natural History, Denver.
   1953   Artifacts with Mammoth Remains, Naco, Arizona; II. Age of the Clovis
            Fluted Points with the Naco Mammoth. *American Antiquity* 19:15–17.
   1955   Geologic-Climatic Dating in the West. *American Antiquity* 20:317–335.
   1959   Geological Age of the Lehner Mammoth Site. *American Antiquity*
            25:31–34.
Artz, Joe A.
   1985   A Soil-Geomorphic Approach to Locating Buried Late Archaic Sites in
            Northeast Oklahoma. *American Archeology* 5:142–150.
Aten, Lawrence E.
   1983   *Indians of the Upper Texas Coast*. Academic Press, New York.
Atkinson, R.J.C.
   1957   Worms and Weathering. *Antiquity* 31:219–233.
Bagnold, R. A.
   1954   *The Physics of Blown Sand and Desert Dunes*. Methuen, London.
Bates, Robert L., and Julia A. Jackson (editors)
   1987   *Glossary of Geology*. 3d ed. American Geological Institute, Alexandria,
            Va.

Bayham, Frank E., Donald H. Morris, and M. Steven Shackley
  1986   *Prehistoric Hunter-Gatherers of South Central Arizona: The Picacho Reservoir Archaic Project.* Anthropological Field Studies, no. 13. Office of Cultural Resource Management, Department of Anthropology, Arizona State University, Tempe.

Beckett, Patrick H.
  1980   *The Ake Site: Collection and Excavation of LA 13423, Catron County, New Mexico.* Department of Sociology and Anthropology, Cultural Resources Management Division, New Mexico State University, Las Cruces.

Bedwell, Stephen F.
  1973   *Fort Rock Basin: Prehistory and Environment.* University of Oregon Books, Eugene.

Belknap, Daniel F., and John C. Kraft
  1981   Preservation Potential of Transgressive Coastal Lithosomes on the U.S. Atlantic Shelf. *Marine Geology* 42:429–442.
  1985   Influence of Antecedent Geology on Stratigraphic Preservation Potential and Evolution of Delaware's Barrier Systems. In *Barrier Islands*, edited by G. F. Oertel and S. P. Leatherman, pp. 235–262. Special issue of *Marine Geology*, vol. 63.

Benedict, James B.
  1981   *The Fourth of July Valley: Glacial Geology and Archeology of the Timberline Ecotone.* Research Report No. 2. Center for Mountain Archeology, Ward, Colo.
  1985   *Arapaho Pass: Glacial Geology and Archeology at the Crest of the Colorado Front Range.* Research Report No. 3. Center for Mountain Archeology, Ward, Colo.

Benedict, James B., and Byron L. Olson
  1978   *The Mount Albion Complex: A Study of Prehistoric Man and the Altithermal.* Research Report No. 1. Center for Mountain Archeology, Ward, Colo.

Benn, David W., and E. Arthur Bettis III
  1981   *Archaeological and Geomorphological Survey of the Downstream Corridor, Saylorville Lake, Iowa.* Archaeological Research Center, Luther College, Decorah, Ia.

Benson, Larry, and Robert S. Thompson
  1987   The Physical Record of Lakes in the Great Basin. In *North America and Adjacent Oceans During the Last Deglaciation*, edited by W. F. Ruddiman and H. E. Wright, Jr., pp. 241–260. *The Geology of North America*, vol. K-3. Geological Society of America, Boulder, Colo.

Berger, Rainer
  1983   Sea Levels and Tree-Ring Calibrated Radiocarbon Dates. In *Quaternary Coastlines and Marine Archaeology*, edited by P. M. Masters and N. C. Flemming, pp. 51–61. Academic Press, New York.

Bettis, E. Arthur, III
    1984   New Conventions for the Designation of Soil Horizons and Layers. *Plains Anthropologist* 29 (103): 57–59.
Bettis, E. Arthur, III, and David W. Benn
    1984   An Archaeological and Geomorphological Survey in the Central Des Moines River Valley, Iowa. *Plains Anthropologist* 29 (105): 211–227.
Bettis, E. Arthur, III, David W. Benn, and Michael J. O'Brien
    1985   The Interaction of Archaeology and the Earth Sciences in the American Midwest. *American Archeology* 5:120–126.
Bettis, E. Arthur, III, and Bernard E. Hoyer
    1986   *Late Wisconsinan and Holocene Landscape Evolution and Alluvial Stratigraphy in the Saylorville Lake Area, Central Des Moines River Valley, Iowa.* Iowa Geological Survey, Iowa City.
Bettis, E. Arthur, III, and John P. Littke
    1987   *Holocene Alluvial Stratigraphy and Landscape Development in Soap Creek Watershed, Appanoose, Davis, Monroe, and Wapello Counties, Iowa.* Geological Survey Bureau, Iowa Department of Natural Resources, Open File Report 87–2. Iowa City, Ia.
Bettis, E. Arthur, III, Jean C. Prior, George R. Hallberg, and Richard L. Handy
    1986   Geology of the Loess Hills Region. *Proceedings of the Iowa Academy of Science* 93 (3): 78–85.
Bettis, E. Arthur, III, and Dean M. Thompson
    1981   Holocene Landscape Evolution in Western Iowa: Concepts, Methods and Implications for Archaeology. In *Current Directions in Midwestern Archaeology: Selected Papers from the Mankato Conference*, edited by S. F. Anfinson, pp. 1–14. Occasional Publications in Minnesota Anthropology, no. 9. Minnesota Archaeological Society. St. Paul, Minn.
    1982   *Interrelations of Cultural & Fluvial Deposits in Northwest Iowa.* Association of Iowa Archaeologists, Field Trip Guidebook, Vermillion, S.D.
    1985   Gully Erosion. *Rangelands* 7 (2): 70–72.
Birkeland, Peter W.
    1984   *Soils and Geomorphology.* Oxford University Press, New York.
Black, Craig C. (editor)
    1974   *History and Prehistory of the Lubbock Lake Site. Museum Journal*, vol. 15. West Texas Museum Association, Texas Tech University, Lubbock.
Blair, Terence C., Jeffrey S. Clark, and Stephen G. Wells
    1990   Quaternary Continental Stratigraphy, Landscape Evolution, and Application to Archeology: Jarilla Piedmont and Tularosa Graben Floor, White Sands Missile Range, New Mexico. *Geological Society of America Bulletin* 102:749–759.
Blatt, Harvey, Gerard V. Middleton, and Raymond C. Murray
    1972   *Origin of Sedimentary Rocks.* Prentice-Hall, Englewood Cliffs, N.J.

Blong, R. J., and R. Gillespie
   1978   Fluvially Transported Charcoal Gives Erroneous ^{14}C Ages for Recent
             Deposits. *Nature* 271:739–741.
Bloom, Arthur L.
   1983a   Sea Level and Coastal Morphology of the United States Through the
             Late Wisconsin Glacial Maximum. In *Late-Quaternary Environments
             of the United States,* vol. 1: *The Late Pleistocene,* edited by H. E. Wright,
             Jr., and Stephen C. Porter, pp. 215–229. University of Minnesota Press,
             Minneapolis.
   1983b   Sea Level and Coastal Changes. In *Late-Quaternary Environments of
             the United States,* vol. 2: *The Holocene,* edited by H. E. Wright, Jr., pp.
             42–51. University of Minnesota Press, Minneapolis.
Bobrowsky, Peter T., Norm R. Catto, Jack W. Brink, Brian E. Spurling, Terry H.
Gibson, and Nathaniel W. Rutter
   1990   Archaeological Geology of Sites in Western and Northwestern Canada.
             In *Archaeological Geology of North America,* pp. 87–122. *See* Lasca
             and Donahue 1990.
Bocek, Barbara
   1986   Rodent Ecology and Burrowing Behavior: Predicted Effects on Archaeo-
             logical Site Formation. *American Antiquity* 51:589–603.
Boggs, Sam, Jr.
   1987   *Principles of Sedimentology and Stratigraphy.* Merrill Publishing, Co-
             lumbus, Ohio.
Boldurian, Anthony T., and George A. Agogino
   1982   A Reexamination of Spring Deposited Lithics from Blackwater Draw
             Locality No. 1. *Plains Anthropologist* 27 (97): 211–215.
Bonnichsen, Robson, George L. Jacobson, Jr., Ronald B. Davis,
and Harold W. Borns, Jr.
   1985   The Environmental Setting for Human Colonization of Northern New
             England and Adjacent Canada in Late Pleistocene Time. In *Late Pleis-
             tocene History of Northeastern New England and Adjacent Quebec,*
             edited by Harold W. Borns, Jr., Pierre LaSalle, and Woodrow B. Thomp-
             son, pp. 151–159. Geological Society of America Special Paper 197.
             Geological Society of America, Boulder, Colo.
Borden, Ferris, W.
   1971   *The Use of Surface Erosion Observations to Determine Chronological
             Sequence in Artifacts From a Mojave Desert Site.* Archaeological Survey
             Association of Southern California, Paper no. 7.
Borst, George, and Rich Olmo
   1985   Stratified Prehistoric Sites of Cismontane San Diego County: The Null
             Set. *Cultural Resources Management Casual Papers* 1 (3): 120–125. Cul-
             tural Resource Management Center, Department of Anthropology, San
             Diego State University, San Diego.

Bostwick, Todd W.
  1985   *The Wilson Project: An Inquiry into Sinagua Fieldhouses.* Master's thesis, Arizona State University. University Microfilms, Ann Arbor, Mich.
Bowers, Peter M., Robson Bonnichsen, and David M. Hoch
  1983   Flake Dispersal Experiments: Noncultural Transformation of the Archaeological Record. *American Antiquity* 48:553–572.
Bradfield, Maitland
  1971   *The Changing Pattern of Hopi Agriculture.* Occasional Paper No. 30. Royal Anthropological Institute of Great Britain and Ireland, London.
Bradley, R. S.
  1985   *Quaternary Paleoclimatology: Methods of Paleoclimatic Reconstruction.* Allen & Unwin, Boston.
Braidwood, Robert J.
  1957   Means Toward An Understanding of Human Behavior Before the Present. In *The Identification of Non-artifactual Archaeological Materials,* edited by Walter W. Taylor, pp. 14–16. National Academy of Sciences, National Research Council, Publication 565. Washington, D.C.
Brakenridge, G. Robert
  1984   Alluvial Stratigraphy and Radiocarbon Dating Along the Duck River, Tennessee: Implications Regarding Flood-Plain Origin. *Geological Society of America Bulletin* 95:9–25.
  1988   River Flood Regime and Floodplain Stratigraphy. In *Flood Geomorphology,* edited by Victor R. Baker, R. Craig Kochel, and Peter C. Patton, pp. 139–156. John Wiley & Sons, New York.
Brakenridge, G. Robert, and J. Schuster
  1986   Late Quaternary Geology and Geomorphology in Relation to Archaeological Site Locations, Southern Arizona. *Journal of Arid Environments* 10:225–239.
Brakenridge, G. Robert, Peter A. Thomas, Laura E. Conkey, and Jane C. Schiferle
  1988   Fluvial Sedimentation in Response to Postglacial Uplift and Environmental Change, Missisquoi River, Vermont. *Quaternary Research* 30:190–203.
Brink, John W.
  1977   Frost-Heaving and Archaeological Interpretation. *Western Canadian Journal of Anthropology* 7 (3): 61–73.
Britsch, L. D., and L. M. Smith
  1989   Geomorphic Investigation of the Terrebonne Marsh, Louisiana: Foundation for Cultural Resource Surveys. *Geoarchaeology* 4:229–250.
Bronger, A., and J. A. Catt
  1989   Paleosols: Problems of Definition, Recognition and Interpretation. In *Paleopedology: Nature and Application of Paleosols,* edited by A. Bronger and J. A. Catt, pp. 1–7. *Catena Supplement* 16. CATENA VERLAG, Cremlingen-Destedt, Germany.

Brookes, Ian A., Louis D. Levine, and Robin W. Dennell
  1982   Alluvial Sequence in Central West Iran and Implications for Archaeolog-
          ical Survey. *Journal of Field Archaeology* 9:285–299.
Brookfield, Michael E.
  1984   Eolian Sands. In *Facies Models,* 2d ed., edited by Roger G. Walker, pp.
          91–103. Geoscience Canada, Reprint Series 1. Geological Association
          of Canada, Toronto.
Brooks, Mark J., and Kenneth E. Sassaman
  1990   Point Bar Geoarchaeology in the Upper Coastal Plain of the Savannah
          River Valley, South Carolina: A Case Study. In *Archaeological Geology
          of North America,* pp. 183–197. *See* Lasca and Donahue 1990.
Brooks, Mark J., Peter A. Stone, Donald J. Colquhoun, Janice G. Brown,
and Kathy B. Steele
  1986   Geoarchaeological Research in the Coastal Plain Portion of the Savan-
          nah River Valley. *Geoarchaeology* 1:293–307.
Brooks, Richard H., Robert Orlins, and Pete Williams
  1967   Part 7, Locality 2 (C1-245), Tule Springs, Nevada. In *Pleistocene Studies
          in Southern Nevada,* edited by H. M. Wormington and Dorothy Ellis,
          pp. 331–351. Anthropological Papers, no. 13, Nevada State Museum,
          Carson City.
Brown, James A., and Robert K. Vierra
  1983   What Happened in the Middle Archaic? Introduction to an Ecological
          Approach to Koster Site Archaeology. In *Archaic Hunters and Gatherers
          in the American Midwest,* edited by James L. Phillips and James A.
          Brown, pp. 165–195. Academic Press, New York.
Brumley, J. H., and B. J. Dau
  1988   *Historical Resources Investigations Within the Forty Mile Coulee Reser-
          voir.* Archaeological Survey of Alberta Manuscript Series, no. 13,
          Edmonton.
Brune, Gunnar
  1981   *Springs of Texas.* Branch-Smith, Fort Worth, Tex.
Bryan, Alan L.
  1977   The Problem of Finding Early Man in the Northeast. In *Amerinds and
          Their Paleoenvironments in Northeastern North America,* edited by Wal-
          ter S. Newman and Bert Salwen, pp. 160–162. *Annals of the New York
          Academy of Sciences,* vol. 288. New York.
Bryan, Kirk
  1929a   Folsom Culture and Its Age. Discussion by K. Bryan. *Geological Society
          of America Bulletin* 40:128–129.
  1929b   Flood-Water Farming. *Geographic Review* 19:444–456.
  1937   Geology of the Folsom Deposits in New Mexico and Colorado. In *Early
          Man,* edited by George G. MacCurdy, pp. 139–152. J. B. Lippincott,
          Philadelphia.

1941   Correlation of the Deposits of Sandia Cave, New Mexico, with the Gla-
           cial Chronology. In *Evidences of Early Occupation in Sandia Cave, New
           Mexico, and Other Sites in the Sandia-Manzano Region,* by Frank C.
           Hibben, pp. 45–64. Smithsonian Miscellaneous Collections, vol. 99,
           no. 23. Smithsonian Institution, Washington, D.C.
1950   Geologic Interpretation of the Deposits. In *The Stratigraphy and Archae-
           ology of Ventana Cave,* by E. W. Haury, pp. 75–126. University of Ari-
           zona Press, Tucson.
1954   *The Geology of Chaco Canyon, New Mexico, in Relation to the Life
           and Remains of the Prehistoric Peoples of Pueblo Bonito.* Smithsonian
           Miscellaneous Collections, vol. 122, no. 7. Smithsonian Institution,
           Washington, D.C.

Bryan, Kirk, and Louis L. Ray
1940   *Geologic Antiquity of the Lindenmeier Site in Colorado.* Smithsonian
           Miscellaneous Collections, vol. 99, no. 2. Smithsonian Institution,
           Washington, D.C.

Buchner, A. P., and L. F. Pettipas
1990   The Early Occupations of the Glacial Lake Agassiz Basin in Manitoba,
           11,500 to 7,700 B.P. In *Archaeological Geology of North America,* pp.
           51–59. *See* Lasca and Donahue 1990.

Bull, William B.
1972   Recognition of Alluvial-Fan Deposits in the Stratigraphic Record. In *Rec-
           ognition of Ancient Sedimentary Environments,* edited by J. Keith Rigby
           and W. Kenneth Hamblin, pp. 63–83. Special Publications, no. 16. Soci-
           ety of Economic Paleontologists and Mineralogists, Tulsa, Okla.

Bullard, Fred M.
1979   Volcanoes and Their Activity. In *Volcanic Activity and Human Ecology,*
           edited by Payson D. Sheets and Donald K. Grayson, pp. 9–48. Academic
           Press, New York.

Buol, S. W., F. D. Hole, and R. J. McCracken
1989   *Soil Genesis and Classification.* 3d ed. Iowa State University Press,
           Ames.

Butzer, Karl W.
1971   *Environment and Archaeology: An Ecological Approach to Prehistory.*
           2d ed. Aldine, Chicago.
1976   *Geomorphology from the Earth.* Harper & Row, New York.
1977   *Geomorphology of the Lower Illinois Valley as a Spatial-Temporal Con-
           text for the Koster Archaic Site.* Reports of Investigations No. 34. Illinois
           State Museum, Springfield.
1978a   Toward an Integrated, Contextual Approach in Archaeology: A Per-
           sonal View. *Journal of Archaeological Science* 5:191–193.
1978b   Changing Holocene Environments at the Koster Site: A Geo-Archaeolog-
           ical Perspective. *American Antiquity* 43:408–413.

1980a   Context in Archaeology: An Alternative Perspective. *Journal of Field Archaeology* 7:417–422.

1980b   Holocene Alluvial Sequences: Problems of Dating and Correlation. In *Timescales in Geomorphology,* edited by R. A. Cullingford, D. A. Davidson, and J. Lewin, pp. 131–142. John Wiley & Sons, Chichester.

1982   *Archaeology as Human Ecology: Method and Theory for a Contextual Approach.* Cambridge University Press, Cambridge.

Byrd, Thomas M.

1988   Sedimentology and Geomorphology at the Seminole Sink Site. In *Seminole Sink: Excavation of a Vertical Shaft Tomb, Val Verde County, Texas,* compiled by Solveig A. Turpin. *Plains Anthropologist* 33, no. 122, pt. 2 (Memoir 22): 37–74.

Cahen, D., and J. Moeyersons

1977   Subsurface Movements of Stone Artefacts and Their Implications for the Prehistory of Central Africa. *Nature* 266:812–815.

Cant, Douglas J.

1982   Fluvial Facies Models and Their Application. In *Sandstone Depositional Environments,* edited by Peter A. Scholle and Darwin Spearing, pp. 115–137. Memoir 31. American Association of Petroleum Geologists, Tulsa, Okla.

Cassidy, M.

1987   *The Gathering Place: A History of the Wet'suwet'en Village of Tse-kya.* Hagwilget Band Council. Hagwilget, Canada.

Castetter, Edward F., and Willis H. Bell

1942   *Pima and Papago Indian Agriculture.* University of New Mexico Press, Albuquerque.

Catt, John A.

1986   *Soils and Quaternary Geology: A Handbook for Field Scientists.* Clarendon Press, Oxford.

1988   *Quaternary Geology for Scientists and Engineers.* Ellis Horwood, Chichester.

Catto, Norm, and Carole Mandryk

1990   Geology of the Postulated Ice-Free Corridor. In *Megafauna and Man: Discovery of America's Heartland,* edited by Larry D. Agenbroad, Jim I. Mead, and Lisa W. Nelson, pp. 80–85. Scientific Papers, vol. 1. The Mammoth Site of Hot Springs, South Dakota, and Northern Arizona University, Flagstaff.

Chapman, Carl H., and Leo O. Anderson

1955   The Campbell Site: A Late Mississippi Town Site and Cemetery in Southeast Missouri. *Missouri Archaeologist* 17, nos. 2–3: 1–119.

Chapman, Jefferson, Paul A. Delcourt, Patricia A. Cridlebaugh, Andrea B. Shea, and Hazel R. Delcourt

1982   Man-Land Interaction: 10,000 Years of American Indian Impact on Native Ecosystems in the Lower Little Tennessee River Valley, Eastern

Tennessee. *Southeastern Archaeology* 1 (2): 115–121.

Childers, W. Morlin, and Herbert L. Minshall
1980   Evidence of Early Man Exposed At Yuha Pinto Wash. *American Antiquity* 45:297–308.

Chomko, Stephen A.
1978   Phillips Spring, 23HI216: A Multicomponent Site in the Western Missouri Ozarks. *Plains Anthropologist* 23 (81): 235–255.

Chorley, Richard J., Stanley A. Schumm, and David E. Sugden
1985   *Geomorphology.* Methuen, New York.

Clarke, David L.
1968   *Analytical Archaeology.* Methuen, London.

Clausen, Carl J., H. K. Brooks, and Al B. Wesolowsky
1975   The Early Man Site at Warm Mineral Springs, Florida. *Journal of Field Archaeology* 2:191–213.

Clausen, C. J., A. D. Cohen, Cesare Emiliani, J. A. Holman, and J. J. Stipp
1979   Little Salt Spring, Florida: A Unique Underwater Site. *Science* 203:609–614.

Clifton, H. Edward
1982   Estuarine Deposits. In *Sandstone Depositional Environments*, edited by Peter A. Scholle and Darwin Spearing, pp. 179–189. Memoir 31. American Association of Petroleum Geologists, Tulsa, Okla.

Coastal Environments, Inc.
1977   *Cultural Resource Evaluation of the Northern Gulf of Mexico Continental Shelf.* 3 vols. Coastal Environments, Inc., Baton Rouge, La.

Cockrell, Wilburn A.
1980   Drowned Sites in North America. In *Archeology Under Water: An Atlas of the World's Submerged Sites*, edited by Keith Muckelroy, pp. 138–145. McGraw-Hill Book Co., New York.

Cockrell, W. A., and Larry Murphy
1978   Pleistocene Man in Florida. *Archaeology of Eastern North America* 6:1–13.

COHMAP Members
1988   Climatic Changes of the Last 18,000 Years: Observations and Model Simulations. *Science* 241:1043–1052.

Coleman, James M.
1988   Dynamic Changes and Processes in the Mississippi River Delta. *Geological Society of America Bulletin* 100:999–1015.

Coleman, James M., and D. B. Prior
1982   Deltaic Environments of Deposition. In *Sandstone Depositional Environments*, edited by Peter A. Scholle and Darwin Spearing, pp. 139–178. Memoir 31. American Association of Petroleum Geologists, Tulsa, Okla.

Coleman, Steven M., Kenneth L. Pierce, and Peter W. Birkeland
1987   Suggested Terminology for Quaternary Dating Methods. *Quaternary Research* 28:314–319.

Collins, Henry B.
  1937   *Archeology of St. Lawrence Island, Alaska*. Smithsonian Miscellaneous Collections, vol. 96, no. 1. Smithsonian Institution, Washington, D.C.
Collins, Michael B.
  1991   Rockshelters and the Early Archaeological Record in the Americas. In *The First Americans: Search and Research*, edited by Tom D. Dillehay and David J. Meltzer, pp. 157–182. CRC Press, Boca Raton, Fla.
Collinson, J. D.
  1986a   Alluvial Sediments. In *Sedimentary Environments and Facies*, 2d ed., edited by H. G. Reading, pp. 20–62. Blackwell Scientific Publications, Oxford.
  1986b   Deserts. In *Sedimentary Environments and Facies*, 2d ed., edited by H. G. Reading, pp. 95–112. Blackwell Scientific Publications, Oxford.
Collinson, J. D., and D. B. Thompson
  1982   *Sedimentary Structures*. George Allen & Unwin, London.
Colquhoun, Donald J., and Mark J. Brooks
  1986   New Evidence from the Southeastern U.S. for Eustatic Components in the Late Holocene Sea Levels. *Geoarchaeology* 1:275–291.
Colquhoun, Donald J., Mark J. Brooks, W. M. Abbott, F. W. Stapor, Walter S. Newman, and R. R. Pardi
  1981   Principles and Problems in Establishing a Holocene Sea-Level Curve for South Carolina. In *Excursions in Southeastern Geology: The Archaeology-Geology of the Georgia Coast*, edited by J. D. Howard, C. B. DePratter, and R. W. Frey, pp. 143–159. Guidebook 20, Geological Society of America, 1980 Annual Meeting, Atlanta, Ga.
Compton, Robert R.
  1962   *Manual of Field Geology*. John Wiley & Sons, New York.
Cook, Harold J.
  1927   New Geological and Palaeontological Evidence Bearing on the Antiquity of Mankind in America. *Natural History* 27:240–247.
Cooke, Ronald U.
  1970   Stone Pavements in Deserts. *Annals of the Association of American Geographers* 60:560–577.
Cooke, Ronald U., and Richard W. Reeves
  1976   *Arroyos and Environmental Change in the American South-West*. Clarendon Press, Oxford.
Cooke, Ronald U., and Andrew Warren
  1973   *Geomorphology in Deserts*. University of California Press, Berkeley and Los Angeles.
Cornwall, Ian W.
  1958   *Soils for the Archaeologist*. Phoenix House, London.
Courty, Marie A., Paul Goldberg, and Richard Macphail
  1989   *Soils and Micromorphology in Archaeology*. Cambridge University Press, Cambridge.

Croes, Dale R., and Eric Blinman (editors)
    1980   *Hoko River: A 2500 Year Old Fishing Camp on the Northwest Coast of North America*. Reports of Investigations, no. 58. Laboratory of Anthropology, Washington State University, Pullman.

Crusoe, Donald L., and Chester B. DePratter
    1976   A New Look at the Georgia Coastal Shell Mound Archaic. *Florida Anthropologist* 29 (1): 1–23.

Curray, Joseph R.
    1965   Late Quaternary History, Continental Shelves of the United States. In *The Quaternary of the United States,* edited by H. E. Wright, Jr., and David G. Frey, pp. 723–735. Princeton University Press, Princeton, N.J.

Curry, Dennis C.
    1980   Burial of Late Archaic Coastal Plain Sites as a Result of Aeolian Deposition. Paper presented at the Middle Atlantic Archeological Conference, Dover, Del.

Dart, Allen
    1987   *Archaeological Studies of the Avra Valley, Arizona, for the Papago Water Supply Project*. Institute for American Research Anthropological Papers, no. 9. Institute for American Research, Tucson.

Davidson, Donald A.
    1985   Geomorphology and Archaeology. In *Archaeological Geology,* edited by George Rapp, Jr., and John A. Gifford, pp. 25–55. Yale University Press, New Haven, Conn.

Davidson, Donald A., and Myra L. Shackley (editors)
    1976   *Geoarchaeology: Earth Science and the Past*. Duckworth, London.

Davis, Emma Lou
    1967   Man and Water at Pleistocene Lake Mohave. *American Antiquity* 32:345–353.

Davis, Emma Lou (editor)
    1978   *The Ancient Californians: Rancholabrean Hunters of the Mojave Lakes Country*. Natural History Museum of Los Angeles County Science Series, no. 29. Natural History Museum of Los Angeles County, Los Angeles.

Davis, Jonathan O.
    1983   Geology of Gatecliff Shelter: Sedimentary Facies and Holocene Climate. In *The Archaeology of Monitor Valley: 2. Gatecliff Shelter,* edited by David H. Thomas, pp. 64–87. Anthropological Papers of the American Museum of Natural History, vol. 59, pt. 1. American Museum of Natural History, New York.

    1985   Sediments and Geological Setting of Hidden Cave. In *The Archaeology of Hidden Cave, Nevada,* edited by David H. Thomas, pp. 80–103. Anthropological Papers of the American Museum of Natural History, vol. 61, pt. 1. American Museum of Natural History, New York.

Davis, Jonathan O., Wilton N. Melhorn, Dennis T. Trexler, and David H. Thomas
   1983   Geology of Gatecliff Shelter: Physical Stratigraphy. In *The Archaeology of Monitor Valley: 2. Gatecliff Shelter*, edited by David H. Thomas, pp. 39–63. Anthropological Papers of the American Museum of Natural History, vol. 59, pt. 1. American Museum of Natural History, New York.

Davis, Leslie B., and Michael Wilson (editors)
   1978   *Bison Procurement and Utilization: A Symposium. Plains Anthropologist* 23, no. 82, pt. 2, (Memoir 14).

Davis, Richard A., Jr.
   1983   *Depositional Systems: A Genetic Approach to Sedimentary Geology.* Prentice-Hall, Englewood Cliffs, N.J.

Davis, Richard A., Jr. (editor)
   1985   *Coastal Sedimentary Environments.* 2d ed. Springer-Verlag, New York.

Davis, Stanley D. (editor)
   1989   *The Hidden Falls Site, Baranof Island, Alaska.* Aurora Monograph Series, no. 5. Alaska Anthropological Association, Anchorage, Alaska.

Day, Kent C.
   1964   Thorne Cave, Northeastern Utah: Archaeology. *American Antiquity* 30:50–59.

Dean, Jeffrey S.
   1978   Independent Dating in Archaeological Analysis. In *Advances in Archaeological Method and Theory*, vol. 1, edited by Michael B. Schiffer, pp. 223–255. Academic Press, New York.

De Meyer, L. (editor)
   1984   *Stratigraphica Archaeologica*, vol. 1. Archaeostratigraphic Classification and Terminology Workshop, University of Ghent, Ghent, Belgium.
   1987   *Stratigraphica Archaeologica*, vol. 2. Archaeostratigraphic Classification and Terminology Workshop, University of Ghent, Ghent, Belgium.

DePratter, Chester B., and James D. Howard
   1977   History of Shoreline Changes Determined by Archaeological Dating: Georgia Coast, U.S.A. Gulf Coast Association of Geological Societies, *Transactions*, 27:252–258.
   1981   Evidence for a Sea Level Lowstand Between 4500 and 2400 Years B.P. on the Southeast Coast of the United States. *Journal of Sedimentary Petrology* 51:1287–1295.

Dick, Herbert W., and Bert Mountain
   1960   The Claypool Site: A Cody Complex Site in Northeastern Colorado. *American Antiquity* 26:223–235.

Dincauze, Dena F.
   1987   Strategies for Paleoenvironmental Reconstruction in Archaeology. In *Advances in Archaeological Method and Theory*, vol. 11, edited by Michael B. Schiffer, pp. 255–336. Academic Press, New York.

Dincauze, Dena F., and R. Michael Gramly
1973   Powissett Rockshelter: Alternative Behavior Patterns in a Simple Situation. *Pennsylvania Archaeologist* 43 (1): 43–61.

Dixon, E. James, and George S. Smith
1990   A Regional Application of Tephrochronology in Alaska. In *Archaeological Geology of North America*, pp. 383–398. *See* Lasca and Donahue 1990.

Dixon, E. James, Sam Stoker, and Ghanshyan Sharma
1986   *Alaskan Outer Continental Shelf, Cultural Resource Compendium, Final Report.* Technical Report Number 119. OCS Study MMS 86-0018. U.S. Department of the Interior, Minerals Management Service, Washington, D.C.

Doelle, William H., Allen Dart, and Henry D. Wallace
1985   *The Southern Tucson Basin Survey: Intensive Survey Along the Santa Cruz River.* Institute for American Research Technical Report 85–3. Institute for American Research, Tucson.

Donahue, Jack, and James M. Adovasio
1990   Evolution of Sandstone Rockshelters in Eastern North America: A Geoarchaeological Perspective. In *Archaeological Geology of North America*, pp. 231–251. *See* Lasca and Donahue 1990.

Donahue, Roy L., Raymond W. Miller, and John C. Shickluna
1977   *Soils: An Introduction to Soils and Plant Growth.* 4th ed. Prentice-Hall, Englewood Cliffs, N.J.

Dorn, Ronald I., and Theodore M. Oberlander
1982   Rock Varnish. *Progress in Physical Geography* 6:317–367.

Dort, Wakefield, Jr.
1975   Archaeo-geology of Jaguar Cave, Upper Birch Creek Valley, Idaho. *Tebiwa: The Journal of the Idaho Museum of Natural History* 17:33–57.

Dumond, Don E.
1979   People and Pumice on the Alaska Peninsula. In *Volcanic Activity and Human Ecology*, edited by Payson D. Sheets and Donald K. Grayson, pp. 373–392. Academic Press, New York.

Duffield, Lathel F.
1970   Vertisols and Their Implications for Archeological Research. *American Anthropologist* 72:1055–1062.

Easterbrook, Don J.
1982   Characteristic Features of Glacial Sediments. In *Sandstone Depositional Environments*, edited by Peter A. Scholle and Darwin Spearing, pp. 1–10. Memoir 31. American Association of Petroleum Geologists, Tulsa, Okla.

Eddy, Frank W., and Maurice E. Cooley
1983   *Cultural and Environmental History of Cienega Valley Southeastern Arizona.* Anthropological Papers of the University of Arizona, no. 43. University of Arizona Press, Tucson.

Edwards, M.
   1986   Glacial Environments. In *Sedimentary Environments and Facies,* 2d ed.,
             edited by H. G. Reading, pp. 445–470. Blackwell Scientific Publications,
             Oxford.
Edwards, Robert L., and K. O. Emery
   1977   Man on the Continental Shelf. In *Amerinds and Their Paleoenviron-
             ments in Northeastern North America,* edited by Walter S. Newman and
             Bert Salwen, pp. 245–256. *Annals of the New York Academy of Sci-
             ences,* vol. 288. New York.
Edwards, Robert L., and Arthur S. Merrill
   1977   A Reconstruction of the Continental Shelf Areas of Eastern North
             America for the Times 9,500 B.P. and 12,500 B.P. *Archaeology of East-
             ern North America* 5:1–43.
Eidt, Robert C.
   1985   Theoretical and Practical Considerations in the Analysis of Anthrosols.
             In *Archaeological Geology,* edited by George Rapp, Jr., and John A.
             Gifford, pp. 155–190. Yale University Press, New Haven, Conn.
Elliott, T.
   1986a   Siliciclastic Shorelines. In *Sedimentary Environments and Facies,* 2d ed.,
             edited by H. G. Reading, pp. 155–188. Blackwell Scientific Publications,
             Oxford.
   1986b   Deltas. In *Sedimentary Environments and Facies,* 2d ed., edited by H. G.
             Reading, pp. 113–154. Blackwell Scientific Publications, Oxford.
Ellis, G. Lain, and Michael R. Waters
   1991   Cultural and Landscape Influences on Tucson Basin Hohokam Settle-
             ment. *American Anthropologist* 93:125–137.
Emery, K. O., and R. L. Edwards
   1966   Archaeological Potential of the Atlantic Continental Shelf. *American
             Antiquity* 31:733–737.
Erlandson, Jon M.
   1984   A Case Study in Faunalturbation: Delineating the Effects of the Burrow-
             ing Pocket Gopher on the Distribution of Archaeological Materials.
             American Antiquity 49:785–790.
   1988   The Role of Shellfish in Prehistoric Economies: A Protein Perspective.
             American Antiquity 53:102–109.
Erlandson, Jon M., and Thomas K. Rockwell
   1987   Radiocarbon Reversals and Stratigraphic Discontinuities: The Effects of
             Natural Formation Processes on Coastal California Archaeological
             Sites. In *Natural Formation Processes and the Archaeological Record,*
             edited by D. T. Nash and M. D. Petraglia, pp. 51–73. BAR International
             Series 352. BAR, Oxford.
Evans, John G.
   1978   *An Introduction to Environmental Archaeology.* Paul Elek, London.

Eyles, Nicholas, and Andrew D. Miall
    1984   Glacial Facies. In *Facies Models*, 2d ed., edited by Roger G. Walker, pp. 15–38. Geoscience Canada, Reprint Series 1. Geological Association of Canada, Toronto.

Fairbridge, Rhodes W.
    1961   Eustatic Changes in Sea Level. In *Physics and Chemistry of the Earth 4*, edited by L. H. Ahrends, Frank Press, Kalervo Rankama, and S. K. Runcorn, pp. 99–185. Pergamon Press, New York.

Farrand, William R.
    1984a   Stratigraphic Classification: Living Within the Law. *Quarterly Review of Archaeology* 5 (1): 1, 4.
    1984b   More on Stratigraphic Practice. *Quarterly Review of Archaeology* 5 (4): 3.
    1985a   The Birth of a Discipline? *Quarterly Review of Archaeology* 6 (3): 1–2.
    1985b   Rockshelter and Cave Sediments. In *Archaeological Sediments in Context*, edited by Julie K. Stein and William R. Farrand, pp. 21–39. Center for the Study of Early Man, University of Maine, Orono.
    1990   Origins of Quaternary-Pleistocene-Holocene Stratigraphic Terminology. In *Establishment of a Geologic Framework for Paleoanthropology*, edited by Léo F. Laporte, pp. 15–22. Geological Society of America Special Paper 242. Geological Society of America, Boulder, Colo.

Fedele, F. G.
    1976   Sediments as Palaeo-land Segments: The Excavation Side of Study. In *Geoarchaeology: Earth Science and the Past*, edited by D. A. Davidson and M. L. Shackley, pp. 23–48. Duckworth, London.

Fedje, Daryl
    1986   Banff Archaeology 1983–1985. In *Eastern Slopes Prehistory: Selected Papers*, edited by Brian Ronaghan, pp. 25–62. Archaeological Survey of Alberta Occasional Paper No. 30. Archaeological Survey of Alberta, Edmonton.

Ferring, C. Reid
    1986a   Rate of Fluvial Sedimentation: Implications for Archaeological Variability. *Geoarchaeology* 1:259–274.
    1986b   Late Holocene Cultural Ecology in the Southern Plains: Perspectives from Delaware Canyon, Oklahoma. In *Current Trends in Southern Plains Archaeology*, edited by Timothy G. Baugh. *Plains Anthropologist* 31, no. 114, pt. 2 (Memoir 21): 55–82.
    1986c   Late Quaternary Geology and Environments of the Upper Trinity Basin. In *An Assessment of the Cultural Resources in the Trinity River Basin, Dallas, Tarrant, and Denton Counties, Texas*, edited by Bonnie C. Yates and C. Reid Ferring, pp. 32–112. Institute of Applied Sciences, North Texas State University, Denton.
    1987   Geoarchaeology of Site 41CO141: A Late Holocene Locality in the Upper

Trinity Basin, Cooke County, Texas. In *Test Excavations at 41CO141, Ray Roberts Reservoir, Cooke County, Texas,* edited by Daniel J. Prikryl and Bonnie C. Yates, pp. 19–52. Contributions in Archaeology, no. 4. Institute of Applied Sciences, North Texas State University, Denton.

1989   The Aubrey Clovis Site: A Paleoindian Locality in the Upper Trinity River Basin, Texas. *Current Research in the Pleistocene* 6:9–11.

1990a   Archaeological Geology of the Southern Plains. In *Archaeological Geology of North America,* pp. 253–266. *See* Lasca and Donahue 1990.

1990b   *Late Quaternary Geology and Geoarchaeology of the Upper Trinity River Drainage Basin, Texas.* Field Trip No. 11 Guidebook. Geological Society of America 1990 Annual Meeting. Dallas Geological Society.

Ferring, C. Reid, and Stephen A. Hall
1987   Domebo Canyon. In *Late Quaternary Stratigraphy, Neotectonics and Geoarchaeology of Southwestern Oklahoma,* assembled by C. Reid Ferring, pp. 56–66. Guidebook for the Fifth Annual Field Trip, Friends of the Pleistocene—South Central Cell, Institute of Applied Sciences, North Texas State University, Denton.

Ferring, C. Reid, and Duane E. Peter
1987   Geoarchaeology of the Dyer Site, a Prehistoric Occupation in the Western Ouachitas, Oklahoma. *Plains Anthropologist* 32 (118): 351–366.

Field, John J., and James P. Lombard
1987   Geomorphology as an Archaeological Tool in the Red Rock Basin, Arizona. Geological Society of America, *Abstracts with Programs* 19 (7): 662.

Figgins, J. D.
1927   The Antiquity of Man in America. *Natural History* 27:229–239.

Fish, Paul R.
1989   The Hohokam: 1,000 Years of Prehistory in the Sonoran Desert. In *Dynamics of Southwest Prehistory,* edited by Linda S. Cordell and George J. Gumerman, pp. 19–63. Smithsonian Institution Press, Washington, D.C.

Fish, Suzanne K., Paul R. Fish, Charles Miksicek, and John Madsen
1985   Prehistoric Age Cultivation in Southern Arizona. *Symposium on the Genus Agave,* edited by Donald J. Pinkava and Howard S. Gentry, pp. 100, 107–112. Special issue of *Desert Plants,* vol. 7.

Fitzhugh, William
1977   Population Movement and Culture Change on the Central Labrador Coast. In *Amerinds and Their Paleoenvironments in Northeastern North America,* edited by Walter S. Newman and Bert Salwen, pp. 481–497. *Annals of the New York Academy of Sciences,* vol. 288. New York.

Fladmark, Knut R.
1978   The Feasibility of the Northwest Coast as a Migration Route for Early Man. In *Early Man in America, from a Circum-Pacific Perspective,* edited

by Alan L. Bryan, pp. 119–128. Occasional Papers of the Department of Anthropology, no. 1. University of Alberta, Edmonton.

1979   Routes: Alternative Migration Corridors for Early Man in North America. *American Antiquity* 44:55–69.

1983   Times and Places: Environmental Correlates of Mid-to-Late Wisconsinan Human Population Expansion in North America. In *Early Man in the New World*, edited by Richard Shutler, Jr., pp. 13–41. Sage Publications, Beverly Hills, Calif.

Flemming, N. C.

1983   Survival of Submerged Lithic and Bronze Age Artifact Sites: A Review of Case Histories. In *Quaternary Coastlines and Marine Archaeology*, edited by P. M. Masters and N. C. Flemming, pp. 135–173. Academic Press, New York.

Flint, Richard Foster

1971   *Glacial and Quaternary Geology.* John Wiley and Sons, New York.

Folk, Robert L.

1954   The Distinction Between Grain Size and Mineral Composition in Sedimentary-Rock Nomenclature. *Journal of Geology* 62:344–359.

1974   *Petrology of Sedimentary Rocks.* Hemphill Publishing, Austin, Tex.

Ford, T. D.

1976   The Geology of Caves. In *The Science of Speleology*, edited by T. D. Ford and C.H.D. Cullingford, pp. 11–60. Academic Press, London.

Fortier, Andrew C.

1985   *Selected Sites in the Hill Lake Locality.* American Bottom Archaeology, FAI-270 Site Reports, vol. 13. University of Illinois Press, Urbana and Chicago.

Fouch, Thomas D., and Walter E. Dean

1982   Lacustrine and Associated Clastic Depositional Environments. In *Sandstone Depositional Environments*, edited by Peter A. Scholle and Darwin Spearing, pp. 87–114. American Association of Petroleum Geologists, Memoir 31. Tulsa, Okla.

Friedman, G. M., and J. E. Sanders

1978   *Principles of Sedimentology.* John Wiley & Sons, New York.

Frison, George C.

1978   *Prehistoric Hunters of the High Plains.* Academic Press, New York.

1984   The Carter/Kerr-McGee Paleoindian Site: Cultural Resourse Management and Archaeological Research. *American Antiquity* 49:288–314.

Frison, George C. (editor)

1974   *The Casper Site: A Hell Gap Bison Kill on the High Plains.* Academic Press, New York.

Frison, George C., and Lawrence C. Todd

1986   *The Colby Mammoth Site: Taphonomy and Archaeology of a Clovis Kill in Northern Wyoming.* University of New Mexico Press, Albuquerque.

Fulton, R. J. (editor)
  1989   *Quaternary Geology of Canada and Greenland. The Geology of North America*, vol. K-1. Geological Society of America, Boulder, Colo.
Gagliano, Sherwood M.
  1967   *Occupation Sequence at Avery Island.* Coastal Studies Series No. 22. Louisiana State University Press, Baton Rouge.
  1970   *Archaeological and Geological Studies at Avery Island, 1968–1970.* Coastal Studies Institute, Louisiana State University, Baton Rouge.
  1984   Geoarchaeology of the Northern Gulf Shore. In *Perspectives on Gulf Coast Prehistory,* edited by Dave Davis, pp. 1–40. Ripley P. Bullen Monographs in Anthropology and History, no. 5. University of Florida Press and the Florida State Museum, Gainesville.
Gagliano, Sherwood M. (editor)
  1979   *A Cultural Resources Survey of the Empire to the Gulf of Mexico Waterway.* Coastal Environments, Inc., Baton Rouge, La.
Gagliano, Sherwood M., Charles E. Pearson, Richard A. Weinstein, Diane E. Wiseman, and Christopher M. McClendon
  1982   *Sedimentary Studies of Prehistoric Archaeological Sites: Criteria for the Identification of Submerged Archaeological Sites of the Northern Gulf of Mexico Continental Shelf.* Coastal Environments, Inc., Baton Rouge, La.
Gagliano, Sherwood M., and Roger T. Saucier
  1963   Poverty Point Sites in Southeastern Louisiana. *American Antiquity* 28:320–327.
Gagliano, Sherwood M., Richard A. Weinstein, and Eileen K. Burden
  1975   *Archeological Investigations Along the Gulf Intracoastal Waterway: Coastal Louisiana Area.* Coastal Environments, Inc., Baton Rouge, La.
Gagliano, Sherwood M., Richard A. Weinstein, Eileen K. Burden, Katherine L. Brooks, and Wayne P. Glander
  1979   *Cultural Resources Survey of the Barataria, Segnette, and Rigaud Waterways, Jefferson Parish, Louisiana.* Coastal Environments, Inc., Baton Rouge, La.
Gallegos, Dennis R.
  1985   *A Review and Synthesis of Environmental and Cultural Material for the Batiquitos Lagoon Region.* Paper presented at the Society for California Archaeology, San Diego, California, March 30, 1985.
  1986   *Lake Cahuilla Prehistoric Occupation at IMP-4434 and IMP-5167, Imperial Valley, California.* Submitted to Ryerson Concrete. WESTEC Services, Inc., San Diego.
Gallegos, Dennis R., and Richard L. Carrico
  1985   *The La Costa Site SDi-4405 (W-945) 7000 Years Before Present, Carlsbad, California.* WESTEC Services, Inc., San Diego.
Galloway, W. E., and David K. Hobday
  1983   *Terrigenous Clastic Depositional Systems: Applications to Petroleum, Coal, and Uranium Exploration.* Springer-Verlag, New York.

Gardner, George D., and Jack Donahue
  1985   The Little Platte Drainage, Missouri: A Model for Locating Temporal Surfaces in a Fluvial Environment. In *Archaeological Sediments in Context*, edited by Julie K. Stein and William R. Farrand, pp. 69–89. Center for the Study of Early Man, University of Maine, Orono.
Garrett, Susan E.
  1983   *Coastal Erosion and Archeological Resources on National Wildlife Refuges in the Southeast.* Archaeological Services Branch, National Park Service, Atlanta.
Gasche, Hermann, and Önhan Tunca
  1983   Guide to Archaeostratigraphic Classification and Terminology: Definitions and Principles. *Journal of Field Archaeology* 10:325–335.
Giddings, J. L.
  1966   Cross-Dating the Archeology of Northwestern Alaska. *Science* 153:127–135.
Gifford, Diane P.
  1978   Ethnoarchaeological Observations of Natural Processes Affecting Cultural Materials. In *Explorations in Ethnoarchaeology*, edited by Richard A. Gould, pp. 77–101. University of New Mexico Press, Albuquerque.
Gifford, John A., and George Rapp, Jr.
  1985a   History, Philosophy and Perspectives. In *Archaeological Geology*, edited by George Rapp, Jr., and John A. Gifford, pp. 1–23. Yale University Press, New Haven, Conn.
  1985b   The Early Development of Archaeological Geology in North America. In *Geologists and Ideas: A History of North American Geology*, edited by E. T. Drake and W. M. Jordan, pp. 409–421. Centennial Special Volume 1. Geological Society of America, Boulder, Colo.
Gifford-Gonzalez, Diane P., David B. Damrosch, Debra R. Damrosch, John Pryor, and Robert L. Thunen
  1985   The Third Dimension in Site Structure: An Experiment in Trampling and Vertical Dispersal. *American Antiquity* 50:803–818.
Gladfelter, Bruce G.
  1977   Geoarchaeology: The Geomorphologist and Archaeology. *American Antiquity* 42:519–538.
  1981   Developments and Directions in Geoarchaeology. In *Advances in Archaeological Method and Theory*, vol. 4, edited by Michael B. Schiffer, pp. 343–364. Academic Press, New York.
  1985   On the Interpretation of Archaeological Sites in Alluvial Settings. In *Archaeological Sediments in Context*, edited by Julie K. Stein and William R. Farrand, pp. 41–52. Center for the Study of Early Man, University of Maine, Orono.
Goodyear, Albert C., Sam B. Upchurch, and Mark J. Brooks
  1980   Turtlecrawl Point: An Inundated Early Holocene Archeological Site on the West Coast of Florida. In *Holocene Geology and Man in Pinellas*

and Hillsborough Counties, Florida, assembled by Sam B. Upchurch, pp. 24–33. Southeastern Geological Society, Guidebook 22. Southeastern Geological Society, Tallahassee, Fla.

Goodyear, Albert C., and Lyman O. Warren
1972   Further Observations on the Submarine Oyster Shell Deposits of Tampa Bay. *Florida Anthropologist* 25 (2), pt. 1: 52–66.

Graf, William L.
1988   *Fluvial Processes in Dryland Rivers.* Springer-Verlag, New York.

Gray, Henry H.
1984   Archaeological Sedimentology of Overbank Silt Deposits on the Floodplain of the Ohio River Near Louisville, Kentucky. *Journal of Archaeological Science* 11:421–432.

Grayson, Donald K.
1979   Mount Mazama, Climatic Change, and Fort Rock Basin Archaeofaunas. In *Volcanic Activity and Human Ecology,* edited by Payson D. Sheets and Donald K. Grayson, pp. 427–457. Academic Press, New York.

Grayson, Donald K., and Payson D. Sheets
1979   Volcanic Disasters and the Archaeological Record. In *Volcanic Activity and Human Ecology,* edited by Payson D. Sheets and Donald K. Grayson, pp. 623–632. Academic Press, New York.

Greeley, Ronald, and James D. Iversen
1985   *Wind as a Geological Process: On Earth, Mars, Venus and Titan.* Cambridge University Press, Cambridge.

Guccione, M. J., R. H. Lafferty III, and L. Scott Cummings
1988   Environmental Constraints of Human Settlement in an Evolving Holocene Alluvial System, The Lower Mississippi Valley. *Geoarchaeology* 3:65–84.

Gumerman, George J. (editor)
1988   *The Anasazi in a Changing Environment.* Cambridge University Press, Cambridge.

Hack, John T.
1942   *The Changing Physical Environment of the Hopi Indians of Arizona.* Papers of the Peabody Museum of American Archaeology and Ethnology, vol. 35, no. 1. Harvard University, Cambridge, Mass.

1943   The Finley Site: Antiquity of the Finley Site. *American Antiquity* 8:235–241.

Hajic, Edwin R.
1981   *Geology and Paleopedology of the Koster Archeological Site, Greene County, Illinois.* Master's thesis, University of Iowa. University Microfilms, Ann Arbor, Mich.

1985a   Geomorphic and Stratigraphic Investigations at Campbell Hollow. In *The Campbell Hollow Archaic Occupations,* edited by C. Russell Stafford, pp. 53–81. Kampsville Archeological Center Research Series, vol. 4. Center for American Archeology, Kampsville, Ill.

1985b   Landscape Evolution and Archeological Contexts in the Lower Illinois River Valley. *American Archeology* 5:127–136.

1987   *Geoenvironmental Context for Archeological Sites in the Lower Illinois River Valley.* St. Louis District Historic Properties Management Report No. 34. U.S. Army Corps of Engineers, St. Louis.

1990   *Koster Site Archeology I: Stratigraphy and Landscape Evolution.* Kampsville Archeological Center Research Series, vol. 8. Center for American Archeology, Kampsville, Ill.

Hall, Stephen A.

1977   Late Quaternary Sedimentation and Paleoecologic History of Chaco Canyon, New Mexico. *Geological Society of America Bulletin* 88:1593–1618.

1988   Environment and Archaeology of the Central Osage Plains. *Plains Anthropologist* 33 (120): 203–218.

1990a   Channel Trenching and Climatic Change in the Southern U.S. Great Plains. *Geology* 18:342–345.

1990b   Holocene Landscapes of the San Juan Basin, New Mexico: Geomorphic, Climatic, and Cultural Dynamics. In *Archaeological Geology of North America*, pp. 323–334. *See* Lasca and Donahue 1990.

Hall, Stephen A., and C. Reid Ferring

1987   Delaware Canyon. In *Late Quaternary Stratigraphy, Neotectonics and Geoarchaeology of Southwest Oklahoma*, assembled by C. R. Ferring, pp. 32–55. Guidebook for the Fifth Annual Field Trip, Friends of the Pleistocene—South Central Cell. Institute of Applied Sciences, North Texas State University, Denton.

Hallam, A.

1981   *Facies Interpretation and the Stratigraphic Record.* W. H. Freeman, San Francisco.

Hamblin, W. Kenneth

1989   *The Earth's Dynamic Systems: A Textbook in Physical Geology.* 5th ed. MacMillan, New York.

Hamilton, Thomas D.

1970   Geologic Relations of the Akmak Assemblage, Onion Portage Area. In *Akmak: An Early Archeological Assemblage from Onion Portage, Northwest Alaska*, by Douglas D. Anderson. *Acta Arctica* [Copenhagen] 16:71–78.

Hammatt, Hallett H.

1977   *Late Quaternary Stratigraphy and Archaeological Chronology in the Lower Granite Reservoir Area, Lower Snake River, Washington.* Ph.D. diss., Washington State University. University Microfilms, Ann Arbor, Mich.

Hannus, L. Adrien

1989   Flaked Mammoth Bone from the Lange/Ferguson Site, White River Badlands Area, South Dakota. In *Bone Modification*, edited by Robson Bonnichsen and Marcella H. Sorg, pp. 395–412. Center for the Study of the First Americans, University of Maine, Orono.

1990a   The Lange-Ferguson Site: A Case for Mammoth Bone-Butchering Tools. In *Megafauna and Man: Discovery of America's Heartland,* edited by Larry D. Agenbroad, Jim I. Mead, and Lisa W. Nelson, pp. 86–99. Scientific Papers, vol. 1. The Mammoth Site of Hot Springs, South Dakota, and Northern Arizona University, Flagstaff.

1990b   Mammoth Hunting in the New World. In *Hunters of the Recent Past,* edited by Leslie B. Davis and Brian O.K. Reeves, pp. 47–67. Unwin Hyman, London.

Harrington, Mark Raymond

1933   *Gypsum Cave, Nevada.* Southwest Museum Papers, no. 8. Southwest Museum, Los Angeles.

1948   *An Ancient Site at Borax Lake, California.* Southwest Museum Papers, no. 16. Southwest Museum, Los Angeles.

Harris, Edward C.

1975   The Stratigraphic Sequence: A Question of Time. *World Archaeology* 7:109–121.

1977   Units of Archaeological Stratification. *Norwegian Archaeological Review* 10:84–94.

1979a   The Laws of Archaeological Stratigraphy. *World Archaeology* 11:111–117.

1979b   *Principles of Archaeological Stratigraphy.* Academic Press, London.

Harris, R. Cole (editor)

1987   *Historical Atlas of Canada.* Vol. 1: *From the Beginning to 1800.* University of Toronto Press, Toronto.

Harvard University

1979   *A Summary of Analysis of Cultural Resources Information on the Continental Shelf from the Bay of Fundy to Cape Hatteras.* 4 vols. National Technical Information Service, Springfield, Va.

Hassan, Fekri A.

1978   Sediments in Archaeology: Methods and Implications for Palaeoenvironmental and Cultural Analysis. *Journal of Field Archaeology* 5:197–213.

1979   Geoarchaeology: The Geologist and Archaeology. *American Antiquity* 44:267–270.

1985a   Paleoenvironments and Contemporary Archaeology: A Geoarchaeological Approach. In *Archaeological Geology,* edited by George Rapp, Jr., and John A. Gifford, pp. 85–102. Yale University Press, New Haven, Conn.

1985b   Fluvial Systems and Geoarchaeology in Arid Lands: With Examples from North Africa, the Near East, and the American Southwest. In *Archaeological Sediments in Context,* edited by Julie K. Stein and William

R. Farrand, pp. 53–68. Center for the Study of Early Man, University of Maine, Orono.

Haury, Emil W.
  1950   *The Stratigraphy and Archaeology of Ventana Cave*. University of Arizona Press, Tucson.
  1953   Artifacts with Mammoth Remains, Naco, Arizona: I. Discovery of the Naco Mammoth and the Associated Projectile Points. *American Antiquity* 19:1–14.
  1976   *The Hohokam: Desert Farmers and Craftsmen*. University of Arizona Press, Tucson.
  1983   Concluding Remarks. In *The Cochise Cultural Sequence in Southeastern Arizona*, by E. B. Sayles, pp. 158–166. Anthropological Papers of the University of Arizona, no. 42. University of Arizona Press, Tucson.

Haury, Emil W., E. B. Sayles, and William W. Wasley
  1959   The Lehner Mammoth Site, Southeastern Arizona. *American Antiquity* 25:2–30.

Hayden, Brian, and June M. Ryder
  1991   Prehistoric Cultural Collapse in the Lillooet Area. *American Antiquity* 56:50–65.

Hayden, Julian D.
  1965   Fragile-Pattern Areas. *American Antiquity* 31:272–276.
  1967   A Summary Prehistory and History of the Sierra Pinacate, Sonora. *American Antiquity* 32:335–344.
  1976   Pre-Altithermal Archaeology in the Sierra Pinacate, Sonora, Mexico. *American Antiquity* 41:274–289.
  1982   Ground Figures of the Sierra Pinacate, Sonora, Mexico. In *Hohokam and Patayan: Prehistory of Southwestern Arizona*, edited by Randall H. McGuire and Michael B. Schiffer, pp. 581–588. Academic Press, New York.

Haynes, C. Vance, Jr.
  1964   The Geologist's Role in Pleistocene Paleoecology and Archaeology. In *The Reconstruction of Past Environments*, assembled by James J. Hester and James Schoenwetter, pp. 61–64. Publication of the Fort Burgwin Research Center, no. 3. Taos, N.M.
  1967   Part 1. Quaternary Geology of the Tule Springs Area, Clark County, Nevada. In *Pleistocene Studies in Southern Nevada*, edited by H. M. Wormington and Dorothy Ellis, pp. 15–104. Nevada State Museum Anthropological Papers, no. 13. Nevada State Museum, Carson City.
  1968   Geochronology of Late-Quaternary Alluvium. In *Means of Correlation of Quaternary Successions*, Proceedings VII Congress, International Association for Quaternary Research, vol. 8, edited by Roger B. Morrison and Herbert E. Wright, Jr., pp. 591–631. University of Utah Press, Salt Lake City.

1973   The Calico Site: Artifacts or Geofacts? *Science* 181:305–310.

1981   Geochronology and Paleoenvironments of the Murray Springs Clovis Site, Arizona. *National Geographic Society Research Reports* 13:243–251.

1982a   Archeological Investigations at the Lehner Site, Arizona, 1974–1975. *National Geographic Society Research Reports* 14:325–334.

1982b   Were Clovis Progenitors in Beringia? In *Paleoecology of Beringia*, edited by David M. Hopkins, John V. Matthews, Jr., Charles E. Schweger, and Steven B. Young, pp. 383–398. Academic Press, New York.

1985   *Mastodon-Bearing Springs and Late Quaternary Geochronology of the Lower Pomme de Terre Valley, Missouri.* Geological Society of America Special Paper 204. Geological Society of America, Boulder, Colo.

1989   Archaeological Geology of Deep Ravine, Custer Battlefield National Monument. In *Archaeological Perspectives on the Battle of the Little Bighorn*, edited by Douglas D. Scott, Richard A. Fox, Jr., Melissa A. Connor and Dick Harmon, pp. 224–242. University of Oklahoma Press, Norman.

1990   The Antevs-Bryan Years and the Legacy for Paleoindian Geochronology. In *Establishment of a Geologic Framework for Paleoanthropology*, edited by Léo F. Laporte, pp. 55–68. Geological Society of America Special Paper 242. Geological Society of America, Boulder, Colo.

Haynes, C. Vance, Jr., and George A. Agogino

1966   Prehistoric Springs and Geochronology of the Clovis Site, New Mexico. *American Antiquity* 31:812–821.

1986   *Geochronology of Sandia Cave.* Smithsonian Contributions to Anthropology, no. 32. Smithsonian Institution Press, Washington, D.C.

Haynes, C. Vance, Jr., and D. C. Grey

1965   The Sister's Hill Site and Its Bearing on the Wyoming Postglacial Alluvial Chronology. *Plains Anthropologist* 10 (29): 196–217.

Haynes, C. Vance, Jr., and Bruce B. Huckell

1986   *Sedimentary Successions of the Prehistoric Santa Cruz River, Tucson, Arizona.* Arizona Bureau of Mines and Geology, Open File Report. Tucson.

Hedberg, Hollis D. (editor)

1976   *International Stratigraphic Guide: A Guide to Stratigraphic Classification, Terminology, and Procedure.* John Wiley and Sons, New York.

Hendrickson, Dean A., and W. L. Minckley

1984   Ciénegas: Vanishing Climax Communities of the American Southwest. *Desert Plants* 6:131–175.

Hester, James J.

1972   *Blackwater Locality No. 1: A Stratified, Early Man Site in Eastern New Mexico.* Publication of the Fort Burgwin Research Center, no. 8. Fort Burgwin Research Center, Taos, N.M.

Hevly, Richard H., Roger E. Kelly, Glenn A. Anderson, and Stanley J. Olsen
   1979   Comparative Effects of Climatic Change, Cultural Impact, and Volcan-
             ism in the Paleoecology of Flagstaff, Arizona, A.D. 900–1300. In *Vol-
             canic Activity and Human Ecology*, edited by Payson D. Sheets and
             Donald K. Grayson, pp. 487–523. Academic Press, New York.
Hoffecker, John F.
   1988   Applied Geomorphology and Archaeological Survey Strategy for Sites
             of Pleistocene Age: An Example from Central Alaska. *Journal of Archae-
             ological Science* 15:683–713.
Hofman, Jack L.
   1986   Vertical Movement of Artifacts in Alluvial and Stratified Deposits. *Cur-
             rent Anthropology* 27:163–171.
Hole, Francis D.
   1961   A Classification of Pedoturbations and Some Other Processes and Fac-
             tors of Soil Formation in Relation to Isotropism and Anisotropism. *Soil
             Science* 91:375–377.
Holliday, Vance T.
   1985a   Archaeological Geology of the Lubbock Lake Site, Southern High Plains
             of Texas. *Geological Society of America Bulletin* 96:1483–1492.
   1985b   Morphology of Late Holocene Soils at the Lubbock Lake Archeological
             Site, Texas. *Soil Science Society of America Journal* 49:938–946.
   1985c   Early and Middle Holocene Soils at the Lubbock Lake Archeological
             Site, Texas. *Catena* 12:61–78.
   1985d   Holocene Soil-Geomorphical Relations in a Semi-Arid Environment:
             The Southern High Plains of Texas. In *Soils and Quaternary Landscape
             Evolution*, edited by J. Boardman, pp. 325–357. John Wiley & Sons,
             New York.
   1987a   A Reexamination of Late-Pleistocene Boreal Forest Reconstructions for
             the Southern High Plains. *Quaternary Research* 28:238–244.
   1987b   Geoarchaeology and Late Quaternary Geomorphology of the Middle
             South Platte River, Northeastern Colorado. *Geoarchaeology* 2:317–329.
   1989a   Paleopedology in Archeology. In *Paleopedology: Nature and Application
             of Paleosols*, edited by A. Bronger and J. A. Catt, pp. 187–206. *Catena
             Supplement* 16. Catena Verlag, Cremlingen-Destedt, Germany.
   1989b   Middle Holocene Drought on the Southern High Plains. *Quaternary
             Research* 31:74–82.
   1990   Pedology in Archaeology. In *Archaeological Geology of North America*,
             pp. 525–540. *See* Lasca and Donahue 1990.
Holliday, Vance T. (editor)
   1986   *Guidebook to the Archaeological Geology of Classic Paleoindian Sites
             on the Southern High Plains, Texas and New Mexico*. Field Trip Guide-
             book. Geological Society of America, Annual Meeting, 1986. Depart-
             ment of Geography, Texas A & M University, College Station.

1992   *Soils in Archaeology: Landscape Evolution and Human Occupation.*
        Smithsonian Institution Press, Washington, D.C.

Holliday, Vance T., and B. L. Allen
1987   Geology and Soils. In *Lubbock Lake: Late Quaternary Studies on the
        Southern High Plains,* edited by Eileen Johnson, pp. 14–21. Texas A & M
        University Press, College Station.

Holliday, Vance T., Eileen Johnson, Herbert Haas, and Robert Stuckenrath
1983   Radiocarbon Ages from the Lubbock Lake Site, 1950–1980: Framework
        for Cultural and Ecological Change on the Southern High Plains. *Plains
        Anthropologist* 28 (101): 165–182.

1985   Radiocarbon Ages from the Lubbock Lake Site, 1981–1984. *Plains An-
        thropologist* 30 (101), pt. 1: 277–291.

Holmes, Nicholas H., Jr., and E. Bruce Trickey
1974   Late Holocene Sea-Level Oscillation in Mobile Bay. *American Antiquity*
        39:122–124.

Holmes, W. H.
1893   Vestiges of Early Man in Minnesota. *American Geologist* 11:219–240.

Hopkins, David M.
1979   Landscape and Climate of Beringia During Late Pleistocene and
        Holocene Time. In *The First Americans: Origins, Affinities, and Adapta-
        tions,* edited by W. S. Laughlin and A. B. Harper, pp. 15–41. Gustav
        Fischer, New York.

Hopkins, David M. (editor)
1967   *The Bering Land Bridge.* Stanford University Press, Stanford, Calif.

Hopkins, David M., and J. L. Giddings, Jr.
1953   *Geological Background of the Iyatayet Archeological Site, Cape Den-
        bigh, Alaska.* Smithsonian Miscellaneous Collections, vol. 121, no. 11.
        Smithsonian Institution, Washington, D.C.

Hopkins, David M., John V. Matthews, Jr., Charles E. Schweger,
and Steven B. Young (editors)
1982   *Paleoecology of Beringia.* Academic Press, New York.

Howard, Edgar B.
1943   The Finley Site: Discovery of Yuma Points, in Situ, Near Eden, Wyoming.
        American Antiquity 8:224–234.

Hoyer, Bernard E.
1980   The Geology of the Cherokee Sewer Site. In *The Cherokee Excavations:
        Holocene Ecology and Human Adaptations in Northwestern Iowa,*
        edited by Duane C. Anderson and Holmes A. Semken, Jr., pp. 21–66.
        Academic Press, New York.

Hoyt, William H., John C. Kraft, and Michael J. Chrzastowski
1990   Prospecting for Submerged Archaeological Sites on the Continental
        Shelf: Southern Mid-Atlantic Bight of North America. In *Archaeologi-
        cal Geology of North America,* pp. 147–160. *See* Lasca and Donahue
        1990.

Hughes, P. J., and M. E. Sullivan
   1974   The Re-Deposition of Midden Material by Storm Waves. Royal Society
           of New South Wales, *Journal and Proceedings* 107:6–10.
Ingram, R. L.
   1954   Terminology for the Thickness of Stratification and Parting Units in Sedi-
           mentary Rocks. *Bulletin of the Geological Society of America* 65:937–
           938.
Inman, Douglas L.
   1983   Application of Coastal Dynamics to the Reconstruction of Paleocoast-
           lines in the Vicinity of La Jolla, California. In *Quaternary Coastlines
           and Marine Archaeology,* edited by P. M. Masters and N. C. Flemming,
           pp. 1–49. Academic Press, New York.
Irwin-Williams, Cynthia
   1979   Post-Pleistocene Archeology, 7000–2000 B.C. In *Handbook of North
           American Indians,* William G. Sturtevant, general editor, vol. 9: *South-
           west,* edited by Alfonso Ortiz, pp. 31–42. Smithsonian Institution,
           Washington, D.C.
Isaac, Glynn Ll.
   1967   Towards the Interpretation of Occupation Debris: Some Experiments
           and Observations. *Kroeber Anthropological Society Papers,* no. 37, pp.
           31–57.
Jelgersma, S.
   1966   Sea-Level Changes During the Last 10,000 Years. In *International
           Symposium on World Climates from 8000 B.C. to 0 B.C.,* pp. 54–71.
           Proceedings of the Royal Meteorological Society, London.
Jennings, Jesse D.
   1957   *Danger Cave.* University of Utah Anthropological Papers, no. 27. Uni-
           versity of Utah Press, Salt Lake City. Also published as *American An-
           tiquity* 23 (2), pt. 2 (Memoir 14).
   1978   *Prehistory of Utah and the Eastern Great Basin.* University of Utah
           Anthropological Papers, no. 98. University of Utah Press, Salt Lake City.
Johnson, Charles
   1974   Geologic Investigations at the Lubbock Lake Site. In *History and Prehis-
           tory of the Lubbock Lake Site,* edited by Craig C. Black, pp. 79–105.
           Museum Journal, vol. 15. West Texas Museum Association, Texas Tech
           University, Lubbock.
Johnson, Donald L.
   1978   The Origin of Island Mammoths and the Quaternary Land Bridge His-
           tory of the Northern Channel Islands, California. *Quaternary Research*
           10:204–225.
   1983   The California Continental Borderland: Landbridges, Watergaps and
           Biotic Dispersals. In *Quaternary Coastlines and Marine Archaeology,*
           edited by P. M. Masters and N. C. Flemming, pp. 481–527. Academic
           Press, New York.

1989   Subsurface Stone Lines, Stone Zones, Artifact-Manuport Layers, And Biomantles Produced by Bioturbation via Pocket Gophers (*Thomomys Bottae*). *American Antiquity* 54:370–389.

Johnson, Donald L., and Kenneth L. Hansen

1974   The Effects of Frost-Heaving on Objects in Soils. *Plains Anthropologist* 19 (64): 81–98.

Johnson, Donald L., and Norman C. Hester

1972   Origin of Stone Pavements on Pleistocene Marine Terraces in California. In *Proceedings of the Association of American Geographers* 4:50–53.

Johnson, Donald L., Daniel R. Muhs, and Michael L. Barnhardt

1977   The Effect of Frost Heaving on Objects in Soils, II: Laboratory Experiments. *Plains Anthropologist* 22 (76), pt. 1: 133–147.

Johnson, Donald L., and Donna Watson-Stegner

1990   The Soil-Evolution Model as a Framework for Evaluating Pedoturbation in Archaeological Site Formation. In *Archaeological Geology of North America*, pp. 541–560. *See* Lasca and Donahue 1990.

Johnson, Donald L., Donna Watson-Stegner, Diana N. Johnson, and Randall J. Schaetzl

1987   Proisotropic and Proanisotropic Processes of Pedoturbation. *Soil Science* 143: 278–292.

Johnson, Eileen (editor)

1987   *Lubbock Lake: Late Quaternary Studies on the Southern High Plains.* Texas A & M University Press, College Station.

Johnson, Eileen, and Vance T. Holliday

1980   A Plainview Kill/Butchering Locale on the Llano Estacado: The Lubbock Lake Site. *Plains Anthropologist* 25 (88), pt. 1: 89–111.

1981   Late Paleo-Indian Activity at the Lubbock Lake Site. *Plains Anthropologist* 26 (93): 173–193.

1985   A Clovis-Age Megafaunal Processing Station at the Lubbock Lake Landmark. *Current Research in the Pleistocene* 2:17–19.

1986   The Archaic Record at Lubbock Lake. In *Current Trends in Southern Plains Archaeology*, edited by Timothy G. Baugh. *Plains Anthropologist* 31 (114), pt. 2 (Memoir 21): 7–54.

1989   Lubbock Lake: Late Quaternary Cultural and Environmental Change on the Southern High Plains, USA. *Journal of Quaternary Science* 4:145–165.

Johnson, William C., and Brad Logan

1990   Geoarchaeology of the Kansas River Basin, Central Great Plains. In *Archaeological Geology of North America*, pp. 267–299. *See* Lasca and Donahue 1990.

Johnson, William C., and Charles W. Martin

1987a   Emergence of an Alluvial Geoarchaeological Model for the Kansas River Basin. *Current Research in the Pleistocene* 4:130–132.

1987b   Holocene Alluvial-Stratigraphic Studies from Kansas and Adjoining
         States of the East-Central Plains. In *Quaternary Environments of Kan-
         sas*, edited by William C. Johnson, pp. 109–122. Guidebook Series 5.
         Kansas Geological Survey, Lawrence.

Jones, J. Richard, and John J. Fisher
1990   Environmental Factors Affecting Prehistoric Shellfish Utilization: Grape
         Island, Boston Harbor, Massachusetts. In *Archaeological Geology of
         North America*, pp. 137–146. *See* Lasca and Donahue 1990.

Julig, P. J., J. H. McAndrews, and William C. Mahaney
1990   Geoarchaeology of the Cummins Site on the Beach of Proglacial Lake
         Minong, Lake Superior Basin, Canada. In *Archaeological Geology of
         North America*, pp. 21–50. *See* Lasca and Donahue 1990.

Karlstrom, Erik T.
1983   Soils and Geomorphology of Northern Black Mesa. In *Excavations on
         Black Mesa, 1981: A Descriptive Report*, edited by F. E. Smiley, Deborah
         L. Nichols, and Peter E. Andrews, pp. 317–342. Center for Archaeolog-
         ical Investigations, Research Paper No. 36. Southern Illinois University,
         Carbondale.

1986   Late Quaternary Alluvial Stratigraphy and Soils of the Black Mesa–Lit-
         tle Colorado River Areas, Northern Arizona. In *Geology of Central and
         Northern Arizona*, Geological Society of America, Rocky Mountain Sec-
         tion Guidebook, edited by J. D. Nations, C. M. Conway, and G. A.
         Swann, pp. 71–92. Geological Society of America, Boulder, Colo.

Kearns, Timothy M., Ronald I. Dorn, and Dennis J. Stanford
1990   Flat Top Mountain and Initial Observations on Desert Varnish Cation
         Ratio Values from Southeastern Utah. *Current Research in the Pleis-
         tocene* 7:84–87.

Kehoe, Thomas F.
1973   *The Gull Lake Site: A Prehistoric Bison Drive Site in Southwestern Sas-
         katchewan*. Publications in Anthropology and History, no. 1. Milwaukee
         Public Museum, Milwaukee.

Kellogg, Douglas C.
1988   Problems in the Use of Sea-Level Data for Archaeological Reconstruc-
         tions. In *Holocene Human Ecology in Northeastern North America*,
         edited by George P. Nicholas, pp. 81–104. Plenum Press, New York.

Kemp, R. A.
1985   A Consideration of the Use of the Terms 'Paleosol' and 'Rubification.'
         Quaternary Research Association of Britain, *Quaternary Newsletter*, no.
         45:6–11.

King, James E.
1988   Palynology of Midcontinental Spring Deposits. In *Late Pleistocene and
         Early Holocene Paleoecology and Archeology of the Eastern Great
         Lakes Region*, edited by Richard S. Laub, Norton G. Miller, and David

W. Steadman, pp. 151–158. Bulletin of the Buffalo Society of Natural Sciences, vol. 33. Buffalo, N.Y.

Kirk, Ruth, and Richard D. Daugherty
1974   *Hunters of the Whale.* William Morrow and Co., New York.
1978   *Exploring Washington Archaeology.* University of Washington Press, Seattle.

Kirkby, A., and M. J. Kirkby
1976   Geomorphic Processes and the Surface Survey of Archaeological Sites in Semi-Arid Areas. In *Geoarchaeology: Earth Science and the Past,* edited by D. A. Davidson and M. L. Shackley, pp. 229–253. Duckworth, London.

Kittleman, Laurence R.
1977   Preliminary Report on the Geology of Dirty Shame Rockshelter, Malheur County, Oregon. *Tebiwa: The Journal of the Idaho Museum of Natural History* 5:1–22.
1979   Geologic Methods in Studies of Quaternary Tephra. In *Volcanic Activity and Human Ecology,* edited by Payson D. Sheets and Donald K. Grayson, pp. 49–82. Academic Press, New York.

Knighton, David
1984   *Fluvial Forms and Processes.* Edward Arnold, London.

Knox, J. C.
1983   Responses of River Systems to Holocene Climates. In *Late-Quaternary Environments of the United States,* vol. 2: *The Holocene,* edited by H. E. Wright, Jr., pp. 26–41. University of Minnesota Press, Minneapolis.

Kornfeld, Marcel
1982   Down the Hill Without a Site. In *Wyoming Contributions to Anthropology,* vol. 3, edited by John W. Fisher, Jr., and Carolyn Craig, pp. 91–105. Department of Anthropology, University of Wyoming, Laramie.

Kraft, John C.
1971   Sedimentary Facies Patterns and Geologic History of a Holocene Marine Transgression. *Geological Society of America Bulletin* 82:2131–2158.
1977   Late Quaternary Paleogeographic Changes in the Coastal Environments of Delaware, Middle Atlantic Bight, Related to Archaeologic Settings. In *Amerinds and Their Paleoenvironments in Northeastern North America,* edited by Walter S. Newman and Bert Salwen, pp. 35–69. *Annals of the New York Academy of Sciences,* vol. 288. New York.
1985   Marine Environments: Paleogeographic Reconstructions in the Littoral Region. In *Archaeological Sediments in Context,* edited by Julie K. Stein and William R. Farrand, pp. 111–125. Center for the Study of Early Man, University of Maine, Orono.

Kraft, John C., Elizabeth A. Allen, and Evelyn M. Maurmeyer
1978   The Geological and Paleogeomorphological Evolution of a Spit System and Its Associated Coastal Environments: Cape Henlopen Spit, Delaware. *Journal of Sedimentary Petrology* 48:211–226.

Kraft, J. C., D. F. Belknap, and J. M. Demarest
  1987   Prediction of Effects of Sea-Level Change from Paralic and Inner Shelf
          Stratigraphic Sequences. In *Climate: History, Periodicity, and Predict-*
          ability, edited by Michael R. Rampino, John E. Sanders, Walter S. New-
          man, and L. K. Königsson, pp. 166–192. Van Nostrand Reinhold, New
          York.
Kraft, J. C., D. F. Belknap, and I. Kayan
  1983   Potentials of Discovery of Human Occupation Sites on the Continental
          Shelves and Nearshore Coastal Zone. In *Quaternary Coastlines and*
          Marine Archaeology, edited by P. M. Masters and N. C. Flemming, pp.
          87–120. Academic Press, New York.
Kraft, John C., and Chacko J. John
  1978   Paleogeographic Analysis of Coastal Archaeological Settings in Dela-
          ware. *Archaeology of Eastern North America* 6:41–60.
Kraft, John C., Ilhan Kayan, and Stanley E. Aschenbrenner
  1985   Geological Studies of Coastal Change Applied to Archaeological Set-
          tings. In *Archaeological Geology*, edited by George Rapp, Jr., and John
          A. Gifford, pp. 57–84. Yale University Press, New Haven, Conn.
Kraus, Mary J., and Thomas M. Bown
  1986   Paleosols and Time Resolution in Alluvial Stratigraphy. In *Paleosols:*
          Their Recognition and Interpretation, edited by V. Paul Wright, pp. 180–
          207. Princeton University Press, Princeton, N.J.
Kreutzer, Lee Ann
  1988   Megafaunal Butchering at Lubbock Lake, Texas: A Taphonomic Re-
          analysis. *Quaternary Research* 30:221–231.
Krumbein, W. C., and L. L. Sloss
  1963   *Stratigraphy and Sedimentation*. 2d ed. W. H. Freeman, San Francisco.
Lancaster, Judith
  1986   Wind Action on Stone Artifacts: an Experiment in Site Modification.
          Journal of Field Archaeology 13:359–363.
Larsen, Curtis E.
  1985   Geoarchaeological Interpretation of Great Lakes Coastal Environments.
          In *Archaeological Sediments in Context*, edited by Julie K. Stein and
          William R. Farrand, pp. 91–110. Center for the Study of Early Man,
          University of Maine, Orono.
Larsen, Curtis E., and Joseph Schuldenrein
  1990   Depositional History of an Archaeologically Dated Flood Plain, Haw
          River, North Carolina. In *Archaeological Geology of North America*,
          pp. 161–181. *See* Lasca and Donahue 1990.
Lasca, Norman P., and Jack Donahue (editors)
  1990   *Archaeological Geology of North America*. Centennial Special Volume
          4. Geological Society of America, Boulder, Colo.
Laub, Richard S., Mary F. DeRemer, Catherine A. Dufort, and William L. Parsons
  1988   The Hiscock Site: A Rich Late Quaternary Locality in Western New

York State. In *Late Pleistocene and Early Holocene Paleoecology and Archeology of the Eastern Great Lakes Region,* edited by Richard S. Laub, Norton G. Miller, and David W. Steadman, pp. 67–81. Bulletin of the Buffalo Society of Natural Sciences, vol. 33. Buffalo, N.Y.

Laury, Robert L.

1980   Paleoenvironment of a Late Quaternary Mammoth-Bearing Sinkhole Deposit, Hot Springs, South Dakota. *Geological Society of America Bulletin,* 91, pt. 1:465–475.

1990   Geologic History of the Mammoth Site and Surrounding Region, Hot Springs Area, Fall River and Custer Counties, South Dakota: An Overview. In *Megafauna and Man: Discovery of America's Heartland,* edited by Larry D. Agenbroad, Jim I. Mead, and Lisa W. Nelson, pp. 15–21. Scientific Papers, vol. 1. The Mammoth Site of Hot Springs, South Dakota, and Northern Arizona Univerity, Flagstaff.

Laville, Henri

1976   Deposits in Calcareous Rock Shelters: Analytical Methods and Climatic Interpretation. In *Geoarchaeology: Earth Science and the Past,* edited by D. A. Davidson and M. L. Shackley, pp. 137–155. Duckworth, London.

Laville, Henri, Jean-Philippe Rigaud, and James Sackett

1980   *Rock Shelters of the Perigord: Geological Stratigraphy and Archaeological Succession.* Academic Press, New York.

Leach, Elizabeth K., and Michael J. Jackson

1987   Geomorphic History of the Lower Cumberland and Tennessee Valleys and Implications for Regional Archaeology. *Southeastern Archaeology* 6 (2): 100–107.

Leeder, M. R.

1982   *Sedimentology: Process and Product.* George Allen & Unwin, London.

Leonhardy, Frank C. (editor)

1966   *Domebo: A Paleo-Indian Mammoth Kill in the Prairie-Plains.* Contributions of the Museum of the Great Plains, no. 1. Great Plains Historical Association, Lawton, Okla.

Leopold, Luna B., M. Gordon Wolman, and John P. Miller

1964   *Fluvial Processes in Geomorphology.* W. H. Freeman, San Francisco.

Leute, Ulrich

1987   *Archaeometry: An Introduction to Physical Methods in Archaeology and the History of Art.* VCH Publishers, Weinheim, Germany.

Limbrey, Susan

1983   Archaeology and Paleohydrology. In *Background to Paleohydrology,* edited by K. J. Gregory, pp. 189–212. John Wiley & Sons, New York.

1975   *Soil Science and Archaeology.* Academic Press, London.

Logan, Brad, and William C. Johnson

1986   Geoarchaeological Investigations in the Lower Kansas River Basin. *Current Research in the Pleistocene* 3:84–85.

Long, Russell J.
  1977   *McFaddin Beach*. The Pattillo Higgins Series of Natural History and
          Anthropology, no. 1. Spindletop Museum, Lamar University, Beaumont,
          Tex.
Lorenzo, José Luis, and Lorena Mirambell (editors)
  1986   *Tlapacoya: 35,000 años de historia del Lago de Chalco*. Instituto Na-
          cional de Antropologia e Historia, Mexico City.
Lowe, J. J., and M.J.C. Walker
  1984   *Reconstructing Quaternary Environments*. Longman, New York.
Luternauer, J. L., John J. Clague, K. W. Conway, I. V. Barrie, B. Blaise,
and R. W. Mathewes
  1989   Late Pleistocene Terrestrial Deposits on the Continental Shelf of Western
          Canada: Evidence for Rapid Sea-Level Change at the End of the Last
          Glaciation. *Geology* 17:357–360.
Lyell, Charles
  1863   *The Geological Evidence of the Antiquity of Man, with Remarks on
          Theories of the Origin of Species by Variation*. John Murray, London.
McCubbin, Donald G.
  1982   Barrier-Island and Strand-Plain Facies. In *Sandstone Depositional En-
          vironments,* edited by Peter A. Scholle and Darwin Spearing, pp. 247–
          279. Memoir 31. American Association of Petroleum Geologists, Tulsa,
          Okla.
MacDonald, George F.
  1968   *Debert: A Paleo-Indian Site in Central Nova Scotia*. Anthropology Paper
          No. 16. National Museums of Canada, Ottawa.
McDowell, Patricia F.
  1984   Geomorphic Setting of Archaeological Sites, Southern Willamette Valley,
          Oregon. In *Geoarchaeology in the Northwest: Recent Applications and
          Contributions,* edited by Judith A. Willig, pp. 35–44. Special issue of
          Tebiwa: The Journal of the Idaho Museum of Natural History, vol. 21.
McFadden, Leslie D., Stephen G. Wells, and Michael J. Jercinovich
  1987   Influences of Eolian and Pedogenic Processes on the Origin and Evolu-
          tion of Desert Pavements. *Geology* 15:504–508.
McIntire, William G.
  1958   *Prehistoric Indian Settlements of the Changing Mississippi River Delta*.
          Louisiana State University Studies, Coastal Studies Series No. 1. Louisi-
          ana State University Press, Baton Rouge.
  1971   Methods of Correlating Cultural Remains with Stages of Coastal Devel-
          opment. In *Introduction to Coastline Development,* edited by J. A.
          Steers, pp. 188–203. MIT Press, Cambridge, Mass.
Mackay, J. R., W. H. Mathews, and R. S. MacNeish
  1961   Geology of the Engigstciak Archaeological Site, Yukon Territory. *Arctic*
          14:25–52.

McKee, Edwin D. (editor)
 1979   *A Study of Global Sand Seas.* U.S. Geological Survey Professional Paper 1052. USGPO, Washington, D.C.

McKee, Edwin D., and Gordon W. Weir
 1953   Terminology for Stratification and Cross-Stratification in Sedimentary Rocks. *Bulletin of the Geological Society of America* 64:381–390.

Mackey, James C., and Sally J. Holbrook
 1978   Environmental Reconstruction and the Abandonment of the Largo-Gallina Area, New Mexico. *Journal of Field Archaeology* 5:29–49.

MacNeish, Richard S.
 1964   *Investigations in the Southwest Yukon: Archaeological Excavations, Comparisons, and Speculations.* Papers of the Robert S. Peabody Foundation for Archaeology, vol. 6, no. 2. Phillips Academy, Andover, Mass.

McReynolds, Mary Jane, Randy Korgel and H. Blaine Ensor
 1988   *Archeological Investigations at a Late Ceramic Bison Kill Site, (41HR541), Whiteoak Bayou, Harris County, Texas.* Reports of Investigations, no. 7. Archeological Research Laboratory, Texas A & M University, College Station.

Mahaney, William C. (editor)
 1984   *Quaternary Dating Methods.* Elsevier, New York.

Malde, Harold E.
 1960   Geological Age of the Claypool Site, Northeastern Colorado. *American Antiquity* 26:236–243.
 1964   The Ecologic Significance of Some Unfamiliar Geologic Processes. In *The Reconstruction of Past Environments,* assembled by James J. Hester and James Schoenwetter, pp. 7–13. Publication of the Fort Burgwin Research Center, no. 3. Taos, N.M.
 1972   Geology of the Olsen-Chubbuck Site. In *The Olsen-Chubbuck Site: A Paleo-Indian Bison Kill,* by Joe Ben Wheat, pp. 171–177. *American Antiquity* 37 (1), pt. 2 (Memoir 26).

Malde, Harold E., and Asher P. Schick
 1964   Thorne Cave, Northeastern Utah: Geology. *American Antiquity* 30:60–73.

Mandel, Rolfe D.
 1987   Geomorphological Investigations. In *Buried in the Bottoms: The Archeology of Lake Creek Reservoir, Montgomery County, Texas,* edited by Leland C. Bement, Rolfe D. Mandel, Jesus F. de la Teja, Dan K. Utley, and Solveig A. Turpin, pp. 4.1–4.41. Texas Archeological Survey Research Report 97, Texas Archeological Survey, University of Texas, Austin.

Mandel, Rolfe D., Leland Bement, and S. Christopher Caran
 1987   Geoarchaeological Investigations at Lake Creek Valley, Southeastern Texas. *Current Research in the Pleistocene* 4:132–134.

Marsh, William M.
 1987   *Earthscape: A Physical Geography.* John Wiley & Sons, New York.

Martin, Paul S., and Fred Plog
1973   *The Archaeology of Arizona: A Study of the Southwest Region*. Double-
        day/Natural History Press, Garden City, New York.
Mason, Owen K., and Stefanie L. Ludwig
1990   Resurrecting Beach Ridge Archaeology: Parallel Depositional Records
        from St. Lawrence Island and Cape Krusenstern, Western Alaska. *Geoar-
        chaeology* 5:349–373.
Mason, Ronald J.
1981   *Great Lakes Archaeology*. Academic Press, New York.
Masters, Patricia M.
1983   Detection and Assessment of Prehistoric Artifact Sites off the Coast of
        Southern California. In *Quaternary Coastlines and Marine Archaeology*,
        edited by P. M. Masters and N. C. Flemming, pp. 189–213. Academic
        Press, New York.
Masters, Patricia M., and N. C. Flemming
1983   Summary and Conclusions. In *Quaternary Coastlines and Marine Ar-
        chaeology*, edited by P. M. Masters and N. C. Flemming, pp. 601–629.
        Academic Press, New York.
Mehringer, Peter J., Jr., and Claude N. Warren
1976   Marsh, Dune and Archaeological Chronology, Ash Meadows, Amar-
        gosa Desert, Nevada. In *Holocene Environmental Change in the Great
        Basin*, edited by Robert Elston, pp. 120–150. Research Paper No. 6.
        Nevada Archeological Survey, University of Nevada, Reno.
Mehringer, Peter J., Jr., and P. E. Wigand
1986   Holocene History of Skull Creek Dunes, Catlow Valley, Southeastern
        Oregon, U.S.A. *Journal of Arid Environments* 11:117–138.
Meighan, Clement W., and C. Vance Haynes
1970   The Borax Lake Site Revisited. *Science* 167:1213–1221.
Meinzer, Oscar E.
1923   *Outline of Ground-Water Hydrology with Definitions*. U.S. Geological
        Survey, Water-Supply Paper 494. USGPO, Washington, D.C.
1927   *Large Springs in the United States*. U.S. Geological Survey, Water-Supply
        Paper 557. USGPO, Washington, D.C.
1939   *Ground Water in the United States*. U.S. Geological Survey, Water-Supply
        Paper 836–D. USGPO, Washington, D.C.
Melhorn, Wilton N., and Dennis T. Trexler
1983a   Geology and Geomorphology of Mill Canyon. In *The Archaeology of
        Monitor Valley: 2. Gatecliff Shelter*, edited by David H. Thomas, pp.
        29–38. Anthropological Papers of the American Museum of Natural
        History, vol. 59, pt. 1. American Museum of Natural History, New
        York.
1983b   Geology of Gatecliff Shelter: Stratigraphic and Climatic Interpretations.
        In *The Archaeology of Monitor Valley: 2 Gatecliff Shelter*, edited by
        David H. Thomas, pp. 88–98. Anthropological Papers of the American

Museum of Natural History, vol. 59, pt 1. American Museum of Natural History, New York.

Melton, Mark A.
1965   The Geomorphic and Paleoclimatic Significance of Alluvial Deposits in Southern Arizona. *Journal of Geology* 73:1–38.

Meltzer, David J.
1991a   On "Paradigms" and "Paradigm Bias" in Controversies Over Human Antiquity in America. In *The First Americans: Search and Research*, edited by Tom D. Dillehay and David J. Meltzer, pp. 13–49. CRC Press, Boca Raton, Fla.

1991b   Altithermal Archaeology and Paleoecology at Mustang Springs, on the Southern High Plains of Texas. *American Antiquity* 56:236–267.

Meltzer, David J., and Michael B. Collins
1987   Prehistoric Water Wells on the Southern High Plains: Clues to Altithermal Climate. *Journal of Field Archaeology* 14:9–28.

Miall, Andrew D.
1977   A Review of the Braided-River Depositional Environment. *Earth-Science Reviews* 13:1–62.

1984   Deltas. In *Facies Models*, 2d ed., edited by Roger G. Walker, pp. 105–118. Geoscience Canada, Reprint Series 1. Geological Association of Canada, Toronto.

Michels, Joseph W.
1973   *Dating Methods in Archaeology.* Seminar Press, New York.

Milanich, Jerald T., and Charles M. Fairbanks
1980   *Florida Archaeology.* Academic Press, New York.

Miller, E. Willard
1985   *Physical Geography: Earth Systems and Human Interactions.* Charles E. Merrill Publishing, Columbus, Ohio.

Miller, Susanne J., and Wakefield Dort, Jr.
1978   Early Man At Owl Cave: Current Investigations at the Wasden Site, Eastern Snake River Plain, Idaho. In *Early Man in America, From a Circum-Pacific Perspective*, edited by Alan L. Bryan, pp. 129–139. Occasional Papers No. 1 of the Department of Anthropology, University of Alberta, Edmonton.

Milliman, John D., and K. O. Emery
1968   Sea Levels During the Past 35,000 Years. *Science* 162:1121–1123.

Mirambell, Lorena
1978   Tlapacoya: a Late Pleistocene Site in Central Mexico. In *Early Man in America, From a Circum-Pacific Perspective*, edited by Alan L. Bryan, pp. 221–230. Occasional Papers No. 1 of the Department of Anthropology, University of Alberta, Edmonton.

Mitchell, Douglas R.
1986   Adaptations on the Georgia Coast During the Early Prehistoric Period. *Florida Anthropologist* 39 (1–2): 57–67.

Moody, Ula L., and Wakefield Dort, Jr.
1990   Microstratigraphic Analysis of Sediments and Soils: Wasden Archaeo-
        logical Site, Eastern Snake River Plain, Idaho. In *Archaeological Geol-
        ogy of North America*, pp. 361–382. *See* Lasca and Donahue 1990.

Mook, W. G., and H. T. Waterbolk (editors)
1983   Proceedings of the First International Symposium: [14]C and Archaeology,
        Groningen, 1981. *PACT: Journal of the European Study Group on Phys-
        ical, Chemical, Biological and Mathematical Techniques Applied to Ar-
        chaeology* [Council of Europe, Strasbourg] 8.

Moore, Raymond C.
1949   Meaning of Facies. In *Sedimentary Facies in Geologic History*, edited by
        Chester R. Longwell, pp. 1–34. Geological Society of America, Memoir
        39. Geological Society of America, New York.

Morgan, James P. (editor)
1970   *Deltaic Sedimentation: Modern and Ancient*. Special Publication No.
        15. Society of Economic Paleontologists and Mineralogists, Tulsa,
        Okla.

Morice, A. G.
1906   *The History of the Northern Interior of British Columbia*. John Lane,
        Bodley Head, London.

Morisawa, Marie
1985   *Rivers: Form and Process*. Longman, London.

Morlan, Richard E.
1978   Early Man in Northern Yukon Territory: Perspectives as of 1977. In
        Early Man in America, From a Circum-Pacific Perspective, edited by
        Alan L. Bryan, pp. 78–95. Occasional Papers No. 1 of the Department
        of Anthropology, University of Alberta, Edmonton.
1979   A Stratigraphic Framework for Pleistocene Artifacts from Old Crow
        River, Northern Yukon Territory. In *Pre-Llano Cultures of the Americas:
        Paradoxes and Possibilities*, edited by Robert L. Humphrey and Dennis
        Stanford, pp. 125–145. Anthropological Society of Washington, Wash-
        ington, D.C.
1986   Pleistocene Archaeology in Old Crow Basin: A Critical Reappraisal. In
        New Evidence for the Pleistocene Peopling of the Americas, edited by
        Alan L. Bryan, pp. 27–48. Center for the Study of Early Man, University
        of Maine, Orono.

Mörner, N. A.
1969   The Late Quaternary History of the Kattegatt Sea and the Swedish West
        Coast. *Sveriges Geologiska Undersoekning*. Arsbok, Serie C. Avhand-
        lingar och Uppsatser, no. 640.

Morrison, Roger B.
1967   Principles of Quaternary Soil Stratigraphy. In *Quaternary Soils*, edited
        by Roger B. Morrison and Herbert E. Wright, Jr., pp. 1–69. Proceedings
        of the 7th Congress of the International Association for Quaternary Re-

search, vol. 9. Center for Water Resources Research, Desert Research Institute, University of Nevada, Reno.

1978   Quaternary Soil Stratigraphy: Concepts, Methods, and Problems. In *Quaternary Soils*, edited by W. C. Mahaney, pp. 77–108. Geo. Abstracts, Norwich, England.

Moss, John H.

1951   *Early Man in the Eden Valley*. Museum Monographs. University Museum, University of Pennsylvania, Philadelphia.

Muller, Ernest H., and Parker E. Calkin

1988   Late Pleistocene and Holocene Geology of the Eastern Great Lakes Region: Geologic Setting of the Hiscock Paleontological Site, Western New York. In *Late Pleistocene and Early Holocene Paleoecology and Archeology of the Eastern Great Lakes Region*, edited by Richard S. Laub, Norton G. Miller, and David W. Steadman, pp. 53–63. Bulletin of the Buffalo Society of Natural Sciences, vol. 33. Buffalo, New York.

Muller, Robert A., and Theodore M. Oberlander

1984   *Physical Geography Today: A Portrait of a Planet*. 3d ed. Random House, New York.

Munson, Patrick J.

1974   Terraces, Meander Loops, and Archaeology in the American Bottoms, Illinois. Illinois State Academy of Science, *Transactions* 67:384–392.

Muto, Guy R., and Joel Gunn

1985   *A Study of Late-Quaternary Environments and Early Man Along the Tombigbee River, Alabama and Mississippi: Phase I Final Report*. 4 vols. Benham Blair & Affiliates, Oklahoma City.

Nabhan, Gary P.

1979   The Ecology of Floodwater Farming in Arid Southwestern North America. *Agro-Ecosystems* 5:245–255.

1986a   'Ak-ciñ "Arroyo Mouth" and the Environmental Setting of the Papago Indian Fields in the Sonoran Desert. *Applied Geography* 6:61–75.

1986b   Papago Indian Desert Agriculture and Water Control in the Sonoran Desert, 1697–1934. *Applied Geography* 6:43–59.

Nash, David T., and Michael D. Petraglia

1984   Natural Disturbance Processes: A Preliminary Report on Experiments in Jemez Canyon, New Mexico. *Haliksa'I: University of New Mexico Contributions to Anthropology* 3:129–147. University of New Mexico Press for the University of New Mexico Anthropology Society, Albuquerque.

1987   Natural Formation Processes and the Archaeological Record: Present Problems and Future Requisites. In *Natural Formation Processes and the Archaeological Record*, edited by D. T. Nash and M. D. Petraglia, pp. 186–204. BAR International Series 352. BAR, Oxford.

Neumann, Thomas W.

1978   A Model for the Vertical Distribution of Flotation-Size Particles. *Plains Anthropologist* 23 (80): 85–101.

Nilsen, Tor H.
1982   Alluvial Fan Deposits. In *Sandstone Depositional Environments*, edited by Peter A. Scholle and Darwin Spearing, pp. 49–86. Memoir 31. American Association of Petroleum Geologists, Tulsa, Okla.

Nilsson, Tage
1983   *The Pleistocene: Geology and Life in the Quaternary Ice Age.* D. Reidel Publishing, Dordrecht, Holland.

North American Commission on Stratigraphic Nomenclature (NACOSN)
1983   North American Stratigraphic Code. *American Association of Petroleum Geologists Bulletin* 67:841–875.

Ollier, Cliff D.
1969   *Weathering.* American Elsevier, New York.

Orr, Phil C.
1951   What Significance Depth? *Bulletin of the Southern California Academy of Sciences* 50 (3): 167–171.

Otto, George H.
1938   The Sedimentation Unit and Its Use in Field Sampling. *Journal of Geology* 46:569–582.

Parkes, P. A.
1987   *Current Scientific Techniques in Archaeology.* St. Martin's Press, New York.

Patton, Peter C., and Stanley A. Schumm
1981   Ephemeral-Stream Processes: Implications for Studies of Quaternary Valley Fills. *Quaternary Research* 15:24–43.

Pearson, Charles E.
1986   Dating the Course of the Lower Red River in Louisiana: The Archaeological Evidence. *Geoarchaeology* 1:39–43.

Pearson, Charles E., David B. Kelley, Richard A. Weinstein, and Sherwood Gagliano
1986   *Archaeological Investigations on the Outer Continental Shelf: A Study Within the Sabine River Valley, Offshore Louisiana and Texas.* Prepared for the U.S. Department of the Interior, Minerals Management Services. OCS Study, MMS 86-0119. Coastal Environments, Inc., Baton Rouge, La.

Petraglia, Michael D., and David T. Nash
1987   The Impact of Fluvial Processes on Experimental Sites. In *Natural Formation Processes and the Archaeological Record*, edited by D. T. Nash and M. D. Petraglia, pp. 108–130. BAR International Series 352. BAR, Oxford.

Petsche, Jerome E.
1974   *The Steamboat Bertrand.* National Park Service Publications in Archeology 11. USGPO, Washington, D.C.

Pettijohn, F. J.
1975   *Sedimentary Rocks.* 3d ed. Harper & Row, New York.

Pettijohn, F. J., and Paul E. Potter
1964   *Atlas and Glossary of Primary Sedimentary Structures.* Springer-Verlag, New York.

Pettijohn, F. J., Paul E. Potter, and Raymond Siever
1972   *Sand and Sandstone.* Springer-Verlag, New York.
Péwé, Troy L.
1975   *Quaternary Geology of Alaska.* U.S. Geological Survey Professional
        Paper 835. USGPO, Washington, D.C.
1978   Terraces of the Lower Salt River Valley in Relation to the Late Cenozoic
        History of the Phoenix Basin, Arizona. In *Guidebook to the Geology of
        Central Arizona,* Special Paper No. 2, edited by Donald M. Burt and
        Troy L. Péwé, pp. 1–45. State of Arizona, Bureau of Geology and Min-
        eral Technology. Tucson, Ariz.
1983   The Periglacial Environment in North America During Wisconsin Time.
        In *Late-Quaternary Environments of the United States,* vol. 1: *The Late
        Pleistocene,* edited by H. E. Wright, Jr., and Stephen C. Porter, pp. 157–
        189. University of Minnesota Press, Minneapolis.
Péwé, Troy L. (editor)
1981   *Desert Dust: Origin, Characteristics, and Effect on Man.* Geological
        Society of America Special Paper 186. Geological Society of America,
        Boulder, Colo.
Phillips, Brian A. M.
1988   Paleogeographic Reconstruction of Shoreline Archaeological Sites
        Around Thunder Bay, Ontario. *Geoarchaeology* 3:127–138.
Phillips, James L., and Bruce G. Gladfelter
1983   The Labras Lake Site and the Paleogeographic Setting of the Late Ar-
        chaic in the American Bottom. In *Archaic Hunters and Gatherers in the
        American Midwest,* edited by James L. Phillips and James A. Brown, pp.
        197–218. Academic Press, New York.
Picard, M. Dane, and Lee R. High, Jr.
1972   Criteria for Recognizing Lacustrine Rocks. In *Recognition of Ancient
        Sedimentary Environments,* edited by J. Keith Rigby and W. K. Hamblin,
        pp. 108–145. Special Publication, no. 16. Society of Economic Paleon-
        tologists and Mineralogists, Tulsa, Okla.
Pierson, Larry J., Gerald I. Shiller, and Richard A. Slater
1987   *Archaeological Resource Study: Morro Bay to Mexican Border.* Prepared
        for the U.S. Department of the Interior, Minerals Management Service,
        Washington, D.C. OCS Study, MMS 87-0025. PS Associates, Cardiff,
        Calif.
Pilles, Peter J., Jr.
1979   Sunset Crater and the Sinagua: A New Interpretation. In *Volcanic Activ-
        ity and Human Ecology,* edited by Payson D. Sheets and Donald K.
        Grayson, pp. 459–485. Academic Press, New York.
Pinter, Nicholas, and Thomas W. Gardner
1989   Construction of a Polynominal Model of Glacio-Eustatic Fluctuation:
        Estimating Paleo–Sea Levels Continuously Through Time. *Geology*
        17:295–298.

Porter, Stephen C.
1988   Landscapes of the Last Ice Age in North America. In *Americans Before Columbus: Ice-Age Origins,* edited by Ronald C. Carlisle, pp. 1–24. Ethnology Monographs, no. 12. Department of Anthropology, University of Pittsburgh, Pittsburgh, Pa.

Powers, M. C.
1953   A New Roundness Scale for Sedimentary Particles. *Journal of Sedimentary Petrology* 23:117–119.

Powers, William R., and John F. Hoffecker
1989   Late Pleistocene Settlement in the Nenana Valley, Central Alaska. *American Antiquity* 54:263–287.

Prikryl, Daniel J., and Bonnie C. Yates (editors)
1987   *Test Excavations at 41CO141, Ray Roberts Reservoir, Cooke County Texas.* Contributions in Archaeology, no. 4. Institute of Applied Sciences, North Texas State University, Denton.

Pyddoke, Edward
1961   *Stratification for the Archaeologist.* Phoenix House, London.

Pye, Kenneth
1987   *Aeolian Dust and Dust Deposits.* Academic Press, London.

Quigg, J. M.
1977   1976 Field Investigations in the Neutral Hills Region. In *Archaeology in Alberta 1976,* compiled by J. M. Quigg, pp. 54–73. Archaeological Survey of Alberta Occasional Paper No. 4. Edmonton.

Rampino, Michael R., and John E. Sanders
1980   Holocene Transgression in South-Central Long Island, New York. *Journal of Sedimentary Petrology,* 50:1063–1080.

Rapp, George, Jr.
1975   The Archaeological Field Staff: The Geologist. *Journal of Field Archaeology* 2:229–237.

1986   Assessing Archaeological Evidence for Seismic Catastrophies. *Geoarchaeology* 1:365–379.

Rapp, George, Jr., and John A. Gifford
1982   Archaeological Geology. *American Scientist* 70:45–53.

Rapp, George, Jr., and John A. Gifford (editors)
1985   *Archaeological Geology.* Yale University Press, New Haven, Conn.

Ravesloot, John C. (editor)
1987   *The Archaeology of the San Xavier Bridge Site (AZ BB:13:14) Tucson Basin, Southern Arizona.* Archaeological Series 171, 3 parts. Cultural Resource Management Division, Arizona State Museum, University of Arizona, Tucson.

Reading, H. G.
1986   Facies. In *Sedimentary Environments and Facies,* 2d ed., edited by H. G. Reading, pp. 4–19. Blackwell Scientific Publications, Oxford.

Reid, Kenneth C.

   1983   The Nebo Hill Phase: Late Archaic Prehistory in the Lower Missouri
            Valley. In *Archaic Hunters and Gatherers in the American Midwest*,
            edited by James L. Phillips and James A. Brown, pp. 11–39. Academic
            Press, New York.

   1984   Fire and Ice: New Evidence for the Production and Preservation of Late
            Archaic Fiber-Tempered Pottery in the Middle-Latitude Lowlands.
            American Antiquity 49:55–76.

Reider, Richard G.

   1980   Late Pleistocene and Holocene Soils of the Carter/Kerr-McGee Ar-
            cheological Site, Powder River Basin, Wyoming. *Catena* 7:301–315.

   1982   Soil Development and Paleoenvironments. In *The Agate Basin Site: A
            Record of the Paleoindian Occupation of the Northwestern High Plains*,
            by George C. Frison and Dennis J. Stanford, pp. 331–344. Academic
            Press, New York.

   1983   Soils and Late Pleistocene-Holocene Environments of the Sister's Hill
            Archeological Site near Buffalo, Wyoming. *Contributions to Geology* 22
            (2): 117–127. University of Wyoming, Laramie.

   1987   Soil Formation and Paleoenvironmental Interpretation at the Horner
            Site, Park County, Wyoming. In *The Horner Site: The Type Site of the
            Cody Cultural Complex*, edited by George C. Frison and Lawrence C.
            Todd, pp. 347–360. Academic Press, New York.

   1990   Late Pleistocene and Holocene Pedogenic and Environmental Trends at
            Archaeological Sites in Plains and Mountain Areas of Colorado and
            Wyoming. In *Archaeological Geology of North America*, pp. 335–360.
            See Lasca and Donahue 1990.

Reineck, H.-E., and I. B. Singh

   1980   *Depositional Sedimentary Environments: With Reference to Terrigenous
            Clastics*. 2d ed. Springer-Verlag, New York.

Reinson, G. E.

   1984   Barrier-Island and Associated Strand-Plain Systems. In *Facies Models*,
            2d ed., edited by Roger G. Walker, pp. 119–140. Geoscience Canada,
            Reprint Series 1. Geological Association of Canada, Toronto.

Renfrew, Colin

   1976   Archaeology and the Earth Sciences. In *Geoarchaeology: Earth Science
            and the Past*, edited by D. A. Davidson and M. L. Shackley, pp. 1–5.
            Duckworth, London.

Retallack, Greg J.

   1988   Field Recognition of Paleosols. In *Paleosols and Weathering Through
            Geologic Time: Principles and Applications*, edited by Juergen Rein-
            hardt and Wayne R. Sigleo, pp. 1–20. Geological Society of America
            Special Paper 216. Geological Society of America, Boulder, Colo.

Retallick, Harold J.

   1966   Geomorphology of the Domebo Site. In *Domebo: A Paleo-Indian Mam-*

moth Kill in the Prairie-Plains, edited by Frank C. Leonhardy, pp. 3–9. Contributions of the Museum of the Great Plains, no. 1. Great Plains Historical Association, Lawton, Okla.

Rice, Glen E. (editor)
1987   *Studies in the Hohokam Community of Marana*. Anthropological Field Studies, no. 15. Office of Cultural Resource Management, Department of Anthropology, Arizona State University, Tempe.

Richards, Keith
1982   *Rivers: Form and Process in Alluvial Channels*. Methuen, London.

Rick, John W.
1976   Downslope Movement and Archaeological Intrasite Spatial Analysis. *American Antiquity* 41:133–144.

Ritter, Dale F.
1986   *Process Geomorphology*. 2d ed. W. C. Brown, Dubuque, Ia.

Rogers, Malcolm J.
1939   *Early Lithic Industries of the Lower Basin of the Colorado River and Adjacent Desert Areas*. San Diego Museum Papers, no. 3. San Diego.
1966   *Ancient Hunters of the Far West*. Copley Press, San Diego.

Rogers, Richard A.
1986   Spurred End Scrapers as Diagnostic Paleoindian Artifacts: A Distributional Analysis on Stream Terraces. *American Antiquity* 51:338–341.
1987a   Stream Terraces and Surface Derived Paleoindian Material on the Neosho River Drainage. *Current Research in the Pleistocene* 4:136–137.
1987b   Frequency of Occurrence of Paleoindian Sites in the Neosho River Drainage of Kansas: A Geomorphological Analysis. In *Quaternary Environments of Kansas*, edited by William C. Johnson, pp. 197–199. Guidebook Series 5. Kansas Geological Society, Lawrence.

Rolfsen, Perry
1980   Disturbance of Archaeological Layers by Processes in the Soil. *Norwegian Archaeological Review* 13:110–118.

Rosen, Arlene M.
1986   *Cities of Clay: The Geoarchaeology of Tells*. University of Chicago Press, Chicago.

Ruddiman, W. F., and H. E. Wright, Jr. (editors)
1987   *North America and Adjacent Oceans During the Last Deglaciation. The Geology of North America*, vol. K-3. Geological Society of America, Boulder, Colo.

Ruhe, Robert V.
1975   *Geomorphology: Geomorphic Processes and Surficial Geology*. Houghton Miffin, Boston.

Ruppé, Reynold J.
1980   *The Archaeology of Drowned Terrestrial Sites: A Preliminary Report*. In Bureau of Historic Sites and Properties, Bulletin No. 6, pp. 35–45. Tallahassee, Fla.

1988   The Location and Assessment of Underwater Archaeological Sites. In *Wet Site Archaeology*, edited by Barbara A. Purdy, pp. 55–68. Telford Press, N.J.

Rust, Brian R.
1978   Depositional Models for Braided Alluvium. In *Fluvial Sedimentology*, edited by Andrew D. Miall, pp. 605–625. Canadian Society of Petroleum Geologists, Calgary.

Rust, Brian R., and Emlyn H. Koster
1984   Coarse Alluvial Deposits. In *Facies Models*, 2d ed., edited by Roger G. Walker, pp. 53–69. Geoscience Canada, Reprint Series 1. Geological Association of Canada, Toronto.

Rutter, Nathaniel W. (editor)
1985   *Dating Methods of Pleistocene Deposits and Their Problems*. Geoscience Canada, Reprint Series 2. Geological Association of Canada, Toronto.

Rutter, N. W., and C. E. Schweger (editors)
1980   *The Ice-Free Corridor and Peopling of the New World*. Proceedings of the 5th Biennial Conference of the American Quaternary Association. *Canadian Journal of Anthropology* 1 (1). Special AMQUA issue.

Sadler, Peter M.
1981   Sediment Accumulation Rates and the Completeness of Stratigraphic Sections. *Journal of Geology* 89:569–584.

Salwen, Bert
1967   A Comment on Emery and Edwards' "Archaeological Potential of the Atlantic Continental Shelf." *American Antiquity* 32:546–547.

Sanders, John E., and Naresh Kumar
1975a   Evidence of Shoreface Retreat and In-place "Drowning" During Holocene Submergence of Barriers, Shelf off Fire Island, New York. *Geological Society of America Bulletin* 86:65–76.

1975b   Holocene Shoestring Sand on Inner Continental Shelf off Long Island, New York. *American Association of Petroleum Geologists Bulletin* 59:997–1009.

Sanger, David
1967   Prehistory of the Pacific Northwest Plateau as Seen from the Interior of British Columbia. *American Antiquity* 32:186–197.

Sarna-Wojcicki, Andrei M., Duane E. Champion, and Jonathan O. Davis
1983   Holocene Volcanism in the Conterminous United States and the Role of Silicic Volcanic Ash Layers in Correlation of Latest-Pleistocene and Holocene Deposits. In *Late-Quaternary Environments of the United States*, vol. 2: *The Holocene*, edited by H. E. Wright, Jr., pp. 52–77. University of Minnesota Press, Minneapolis.

Saunders, Jeffrey J.
1988   Fossiliferous Spring Sites in Southwestern Missouri. In *Late Pleistocene and Early Holocene Paleoecology and Archeology of the Eastern Great Lakes Region*, edited by Richard S. Laub, Norton G. Miller, and David

W. Steadman, pp. 127–149. Bulletin of the Buffalo Society of Natural Sciences, vol. 33. Buffalo, N.Y.

Savelle, James M.
1984   Cultural and Natural Formation Processes of a Historic Inuit Snow Dwelling Site, Somerset Island, Arctic Canada. *American Antiquity* 49:508–524.
1987   Natural Formation Processes and Snow-Based Sites: Examples for Arctic Canada. In *National Formation Processes and the Archaeological Record*, edited by D. T. Nash and M. D. Petraglia, pp. 30–50. BAR International Series 352. BAR, Oxford.

Sayles, E. B.
1983   *The Cochise Cultural Sequence in Southeastern Arizona*. Anthropological Papers of the University of Arizona, no. 42. University of Arizona Press, Tucson.

Sayles, E. B., and Ernst Antevs
1941   *The Cochise Culture*. Medallion Papers, no. 29. Gila Pueblo, Globe, Arizona.

Schaefer, Jerry
1986   *Late Prehistoric Adaptations During the Final Recessions of Lake Cahuilla: Fish Camps and Quarries on West Mesa, Imperial County, California*. Mooney-Levine and Associates, San Diego.

Schick, Kathy D.
1986   *Stone Age Sites in the Making: Experiments in the Formation and Transformation of Archaeological Occurrences*. BAR International Series 319. BAR, Oxford.
1987   Experimentally-Derived Criteria for Assessing Hydrologic Disturbance of Archaeological Sites. In *Natural Formation Processes and the Archaeological Record*, edited by D. T. Nash and M. D. Petraglia, pp. 86–107. BAR International Series 352. BAR, Oxford.

Schiffer, Michael B.
1972   Archaeological Context and Systemic Context. *American Antiquity* 37:156–165.
1975   Archaeology as Behavioral Science. *American Anthropologist* 77:836–848.
1976   *Behavioral Archeology*. Academic Press, New York.
1983   Toward the Identification of Formation Processes. *American Antiquity* 48:675–706.
1987   *Formation Processes of the Archaeological Record*. University of New Mexico Press, Albuquerque.

Schmid, Elisabeth
1969   Cave Sediments and Prehistory. In *Science in Archaeology: A Survey of Progress and Research*, 2d ed., edited by Don Brothwell and Eric S. Higgs, pp. 151–166. Thames and Hudson, London.

Schmits, Larry J.
1978   *The Coffey Site: Environment and Cultural Adaptation at a Prairie Plains Archaic Site. Mid-Continental Journal of Archaeology,* vol. 3, no. 1, Special Paper No. 1. Kent State University Press, Kent, Ohio.

1980   Holocene Fluvial History and Depositional Environments at the Coffey Site, Kansas. In *Archaic Prehistory on the Prairie-Plains Border,* edited by A. E. Johnson, pp. 79–105. Publication in Anthropology No. 12. University of Kansas, Lawrence.

Schoch, Robert M.
1989   *Stratigraphy: Principles and Methods.* Van Nostrand Reinhold, New York.

Schoenwetter, James
1981   Prologue to a Contextual Archaeology. *Journal of Archaeological Science* 8:367–379.

Scholle, Peter A., and Darwin Spearing (editors)
1982   *Sandstone Depositional Environments.* Memoir 31. American Association of Petroleum Geologists, Tulsa.

Schuldenrein, Joseph
1976   Occupation and Natural Stratigraphy in the Central Illinois River Valley: The Beardstown Terrace Complex. Illinois State Academy of Science, *Transactions* 69:122–144.

1987   *Late Quaternary Landscape Evolution and the Geoarcheology of Lake Red Rock.* Gilbert/Commonwealth Associates, Inc., Jackson, Mich.

Schuldenrein, Joseph, and David G. Anderson
1988   Paleoenvironmental History and Archaeology in the Russell Lake Area. In *Prehistory and History Along the Upper Savannah River,* edited by David G. Anderson and J. W. Joseph, pp. 56–93. Garrow & Associates, Atlanta, Ga.

Schumm, Stanley A.
1977   *The Fluvial System.* John Wiley & Sons, New York.

Schumm, Stanley A., and G. Robert Brakenridge
1987   River Responses. In *North America and Adjacent Oceans During the Last Deglaciation,* edited by W. F. Ruddiman and H. E. Wright, Jr., pp. 221–240. *The Geology of North America,* vol. K-3. Geological Society of America, Boulder, Colo.

Schumm, S. A., and R. S. Parker
1973   Implications of Complex Response of Drainage Systems for Quaternary Alluvial Stratigraphy. *Nature* 243:99–100.

Schwartz, Maurice L., and Garland F. Grabert
1973   Coastal Processes and Prehistoric Maritime Cultures. In *Coastal Geomorphology,* edited by Donald R. Coates, pp. 303–320. Proceedings of the Third Annual Geomorphology Symposium, Binghamton, New York, 1972. Publications in Geomorphology, State University of New York, Binghamton.

Schweger, Charles
1985   Geoarchaeology of Northern Regions: Lessons from Cryoturbation at
        Onion Portage, Alaska. In *Archaeological Sediments in Context*, edited
        by Julie K. Stein and William R. Farrand, pp. 127–141. Center for the
        Study of Early Man, University of Maine, Orono.
Segovia, Antonio V.
1985   *Archeological Geology of the Savannah River Valley and Main
        Tributaries in the Richard B. Russell Multiple Resource Area*. Thunder-
        bird Research Corp., Front Royal, Va.
Shackley, Myra L.
1974   Stream Abrasion of Flint Implements. *Nature* 248:501–502.
1975   *Archaeological Sediments:A Survey of Analytical Methods*. John Wiley
        & Sons/Halsted Press, New York.
1978   The Behaviour of Artefacts as Sedimentary Particles in a Fluviatile Envi-
        ronment. *Archaeometry* 20:55–61.
1979   Geoarchaeology: Polemic on a Progressive Relationship. *Die Natur-
        wissenschaften* 66:429–432.
1981   *Environmental Archaeology*. George Allen and Unwin, London.
Sheets, Payson D.
1979   Environmental and Cultural Effects of the Ilopango Eruption in Central
        America. In *Volcanic Activity and Human Ecology*, edited by Payson D.
        Sheets and Donald K. Grayson, pp. 525–564. Academic Press, New
        York.
Sheets, Payson D., and Donald K. Grayson (editors)
1979   *Volcanic Activity and Human Ecology*. Academic Press, New York.
Shepard, F. P.
1963   Thirty-Five Thousand Years of Sea Level. In *Essays in Marine Geology*,
        edited by T. Clements, pp. 1–10. University of Southern California Press,
        Los Angeles.
Sheppard, John C., Peter Wigand, and Meyer Rubin
1984   The Marmes Site Revisited: Dating and Stratigraphy. In *Geoarchaeology
        in the Northwest: Recent Applications and Contributions*, edited by
        Judith A. Willig, pp. 45–49. Special issue of *Tebiwa: The Journal of the
        Idaho Museum of Natural History*, vol. 21.
Shlemon, Roy J.
1978   Quaternary Soil-Geomorphic Relationships, Southeastern Mojave
        Desert, California and Arizona. In *Quaternary Soils*, edited by W. C.
        Mahaney, pp. 187–207. Geo Abstracts, Norwich, England.
Shlemon, Roy J., and Fred E. Budinger, Jr.
1990   The Archaeological Geology of the Calico Site, Mojave Desert, Califor-
        nia. In *Archaeological Geology of North America*, pp. 301–313. *See*
        Lasca and Donahue 1990.
Simpson, Ruth D.
1978   The Calico Mountains Archaeological Site. In *Early Man in America*,

From a Circum-Pacific Perspective, edited by Alan L. Bryan, pp. 218–220. Occasional Papers No. 1 of the Department of Anthropology, University of Alberta, Edmonton.

Simpson, Ruth D., Leland W. Patterson, and Clay A. Singer

1986   Lithic Technology of the Calico Mountains Site, Southern California. In *New Evidence for the Pleistocene Peopling of the Americas,* edited by Alan L. Bryan, pp. 89–105. Center for the Study of Early Man, University of Maine, Orono.

Sjöberg, Alf

1976   Phosphate Analysis of Anthropic Soils. *Journal of Field Archaeology* 3:447–454.

Smith, Derald G.

1983   Anastomosed Fluvial Deposits: Modern Examples from Western Canada. In *Modern and Ancient Fluvial Systems,* edited by J. D. Collinson and J. Lewin, pp. 155–168. International Association of Sedimentologists, Special Publication No. 6, Oxford, Blackwell Scientific.

Smith, George I., and F. Alayne Street-Perrott

1983   Pluvial Lakes of the Western United States. In *Late-Quaternary Environments of the United States,* vol. 1: *The Late Pleistocene,* edited by H. E. Wright, Jr., and Stephen C. Porter, pp. 190–212. University of Minnesota Press, Minneapolis.

Smith, Lawson M., Joseph B. Dunbar, and Louis D. Britsch

1986   *Geomorphological Investigation of the Atchafalaya Basin, Area West, Atchafalaya Delta, and Terrebonne Marsh.* Vol. 1. Technical Report GL-86-3. U.S. Army Corps of Engineers, Waterways Experiment Station, Vicksburg, Miss.

Soil Survey Staff

1951   *Soil Survey Manual.* U.S. Department of Agriculture Handbook No. 18. USGPO, Washington, D.C.

1975   *Soil Taxonomy: A Basic System of Soil Classification for Making and Interpreting Soil Surveys.* Agriculture Handbook No. 436. U.S. Department of Agriculture, Soil Conservation Service, Washington, D.C.

1990   *Keys to Soil Taxonomy.* 4th ed. U.S. Department of Agriculture, Soil Management Support Services Technical Monograph, no. 19. Blacksburg, Va.

Sorenson, Curtis J., James C. Knox, James A. Larsen, and Reid A. Bryson

1971   Paleosols and the Forest Border in Keewatin, N.W.T. *Quaternary Research* 1:468–473.

Springer, M. E.

1958   Desert Pavement and Vesicular Layer of Some Desert Soils in the Desert of the Lahontan Basin, Nevada. *Proceedings of the Soil Science Society of America* 22:63–66.

Stafford, Thomas, Jr.

1981   Alluvial Geology and Archaeological Potential of the Texas Southern

High Plains. *American Antiquity* 46:548–565.

Stanford, Dennis

1979   The Selby and Dutton Sites: Evidence for a Possible Pre-Clovis Occupation of the High Plains. In *Pre-Llano Cultures of the Americas: Paradoxes
and Possibilities*, edited by Robert L. Humphrey and Dennis Stanford,
pp. 101–123. Anthropological Society of Washington, Washington,
D.C.

Steen-McIntyre, Virginia

1985   Tephrochronology and Its Application to Archaeology. In *Archaeological Geology*, edited by George Rapp, Jr., and John A. Gifford, pp. 265–
302. Yale University Press, New Haven, Conn.

Stein, Julie K.

1982   Geologic Analysis of the Green River Shell Middens. *Southeastern Archaeology* 1 (1): 22–39.

1983   Earthworm Activity: A Source of Potential Disturbance of Archaeological Sediments. *American Antiquity* 48:277–289.

1985   Interpreting Sediments in Cultural Settings. In *Archaeological Sediments
in Context*, edited by Julie K. Stein and William R. Farrand, pp. 5–19.
Center for the Study of Early Man, University of Maine, Orono.

1986   Coring Archaeological Sites. *American Antiquity* 51:505–527.

1987   Deposits for Archaeologists. In *Advances in Archaeological Method and
Theory*, vol. 11, edited by Michael B. Schiffer, pp. 337–395. Academic
Press, New York.

1990   Archaeological Stratigraphy. In *Archaeological Geology of North
America*, pp. 513–523. *See* Lasca and Donahue 1990.

Stein, Julie K., and William R. Farrand

1985   Context and Geoarchaeology: An Introduction. In *Archaeological Sediments in Context*, edited by Julie K. Stein and William R. Farrand, pp.
1–3. Center for the Study of Early Man, University of Maine, Orono.

Stein, Julie K., and William R. Farrand (editors)

1985   *Archaeological Sediments in Context*. Center for the Study of Early
Man. University of Maine, Orono.

Stein, Julie K., and George Rapp, Jr.

1985   Archaeological Sediments: A Largely Untapped Reservoir of Information.
In *Contributions to Aegean Archaeology: Studies in Honor of William
A. McDonald*, edited by Nancy C. Wilkie and William D. E. Coulson,
pp. 143–159. University of Minnesota Publications in Ancient Studies.
University of Minnesota, Center for Ancient Studies, Minneapolis.

Stevenson, Marc G.

1985   The Formation of Artifact Assemblages at Workshop/Habitation Sites:
Models from Peace Point in Northern Alberta. *American Antiquity*
50:63–81.

1986   *Window on the Past: Archaeological Assessment of the Peace Point Site,
Wood Buffalo National Park, Alberta*. Studies in Archaeology, Architec-

ture and History. Parks Canada, National Historic Parks and Sites Branch, Ottawa.

Storck, Peter L.
    1982   Palaeo-Indian Settlement Patterns Associated with the Strandline of Glacial Lake Algonquin in Southcentral Ontario. *Canadian Journal of Archaeology* 6:1–31.
    1984   Glacial Lake Algonquin and Early Paleo-Indian Settlement Patterns in Southcentral Ontario. *Archaeology of Eastern North America* 12:286–298.

Strahler, Arthur N., and Alan H. Strahler
    1989   *Elements of Physical Geography.* 4th ed. John Wiley & Sons, New York.

Straus, Lawrence Guy
    1990   Underground Archaeology: Perspectives on Caves and Rockshelters. In *Archaeological Method and Theory,* vol. 2, edited by Michael B. Schiffer, pp. 255–304. University of Arizona Press, Tucson.

Strauss, Alan E.
    1978   Nature's Transformations and Other Pitfalls: Toward a Better Understanding of Post-Occupational Changes in Archaeological Site Morphology in the Northeast. Part I: Vegetation. *Bulletin of the Massachusetts Archaeological Society* 39 (2): 47–64.
    1981   Nature's Transformations and Other Pitfalls: Toward a Better Understanding of Post-Occupational Changes in Archaeological Site Morphology in the Northeast. Part II: Invertebrates. *Bulletin of the Massachusetts Archaeological Society* 42 (1): 2–11.
    1985   Nature's Transformations and Other Pitfalls: Toward a Better Understanding of Post-Occupational Changes in Archaeological Site Morphology in the Northeast. Part III: Animal Activity and Frost Action. *Bulletin of the Massachusetts Archaeological Society* 46 (2): 65–72.

Stright, Melanie J.
    1986a   Evaluation of Archaeological Site Potential on the Gulf of Mexico Continental Shelf Using High-Resolution Seismic Data. *Geophysics* 51:605–622.
    1986b   Human Occupation of the Continental Shelf During the Late Pleistocene/Early Holocene: Methods for Site Location. *Geoarchaeology* 1:347–364.
    1990   Archaeological Sites on the North American Continental Shelf. In *Archaeological Geology of North America,* pp. 439–465. *See* Lasca and Donahue 1990.

Styles, Bonnie W., Steven R. Ahler, and Melvin L. Fowler
    1983   Modoc Rock Shelter Revisited. In *Archaic Hunters and Gatherers in the American Midwest,* edited by James L. Phillips and James A. Brown, pp. 261–297. Academic Press, New York.

Styles, Thomas R.
    1985   *Holocene and Late Pleistocene Geology of the Napoleon Hollow Site in*

the Lower Illinois Valley. Kampsville Archeological Center Research
Series, vol. 5. Center for American Archeology, Kampsville, Ill.

Swanston, Douglas N.
1989   Glacial Stratigraphic Correlations and Late Quaternary Chronology. In
Hidden Falls Site, Baranof Island, Alaska, edited by Stanley D. Davis,
pp. 47–60. Aurora Monograph Series 5. Alaska Anthropological Association, Anchorage.

Swift, Donald, Daniel J. Stanley, and Joseph R. Curray
1971   Relict Sediments on Continental Shelves: A Reconsideration. *Journal of
Geology* 79:322–346.

Tamplin, M. J.
1969   The Application of Pedology to Archaeological Research. In *Pedology
and Quaternary Research,* edited by S. Pawluk, pp. 153–161. National
Research Council of Canada, University of Alberta, Edmonton.

Taylor, R. E.
1987   *Radiocarbon Dating: An Archaeological Perspective.* Academic Press,
Orlando, Fla.

Taylor, R. E, Paul J. Ennis, Louis A. Payen, Christine A. Prior, and Peter J. Slota, Jr.
1986   Encino Village (CA-LAN-43) Site Radiocarbon Determinations: Geo-
physical/Geochemical Considerations. *Pacific Coast Archaeological Society Quarterly* 22 (3): 35–48.

Ters, M.
1973   Les Variations du Niveau Marin Depuis 10,000 ans le Long du Littoral
Atlantique Francais, Le Quatermaire: Géodynamique, Stratigraphie et
Environment, Travaux Français Recents, International Quaternary Asso-
ciation. *Proceedings of the International Quaternary Association, 9th
International Congress,* pp. 114–135 Christchurch, New Zealand.

Thomas, David H. (editor)
1983   *The Archaeology of Monitor Valley: 2. Gatecliff Shelter.* Anthropological Papers of the American Museum of Natural History, vol. 59, pt. 1.
American Museum of Natural History, New York.

1985   *The Archaeology of Hidden Cave, Nevada.* Anthropological Papers of
the American Museum of Natural History, vol. 61, pt. 1. American
Museum of Natural History, New York.

Thompson, Dean M., and E. Arthur Bettis III
1980   Archeology and Holocene Landscape Evolution in the Missouri Drainage of Iowa. *Journal of the Iowa Archaeological Society* 27:1–60.

1982   Out of Sight, Out of Planning: Assessing and Protecting Cultural Resources in Evolving Landscapes. *Contract Abstracts and CRM Archeology* 2 (3): 16–22.

Thorson, Robert M.
1990   Geologic Contexts of Archaeological Sites in Beringia. In *Archaeological Geology of North America,* pp. 399–420. *See* Lasca and Donahue
1990.

Thorson, Robert M., and Gary Bender
   1985   Eolian Deflation by Ancient Katabatic Winds: A Late Quaternary Exam-
             ple from the North Alaska Range. *Geological Society of America Bulle-
             tin* 96:702–709.
Thorson, Robert M., and Thomas D. Hamilton
   1977   Geology of the Dry Creek Site, A Stratified Early Man Site in Interior
             Alaska. *Quaternary Research* 7:149–176.
Thorson, Robert M., and Vance T. Holliday
   1990   Just What is Geoarchaeology? *Geotimes* 35 (7): 19–20.
Timlin, Joseph P., and B. E. Raemsch
   1971   *Pleistocene Tools from the Northeast of North America: The Timlin Site.*
             Yager Museum Publications in Anthropology, Bulletin No. 3. Yager
             Museum, Hartwick College, Oneonta, New York.
Tippitt, V. Ann, and William H. Marquardt
   1984   *The Gregg Shoals and Clyde Gulley Sites: Archaeological and Geolog-
             ical Investigations at Two Piedmont Sites on the Savannah River.* Insti-
             tute of Archeology and Anthropology, University of South Carolina,
             Columbia.
Titiev, Mischa
   1944   *Old Oraibi: A Study of the Hopi Indians of Third Mesa.* Papers of the
             Peabody Museum of American Archaeology and Ethnology, Harvard
             University, vol. 22, no. 1. Cambridge, Mass.
Turnbaugh, William A.
   1978   Floods and Archaeology. *American Antiquity* 43:593–607.
Turner, William B., and Walter E. Klippel
   1989   Hunter-Gatherers in the Nashville Basin: Archaeological and Geological
             Evidence for Variability in Prehistoric Land Use. *Geoarchaeology* 4:43–
             67.
Turpin, Solveig A. (compiler)
   1988   *Seminole Sink: Excavation of a Vertical Shaft Tomb, Val Verde County,
             Texas. Plains Anthropologist* 33 (122), pt. 2 (Memoir 22).
Upchurch, Sam D.
   1984   Geoarchaeology of the Gregg Shoals–Clyde Gulley Group. In *The Gregg
             Shoals and Clyde Gulley Sites: Archaeological and Geological Investiga-
             tions at Two Piedmont Sites on the Savannah River,* edited by V. Ann
             Tippett and William H. Marquardt, pp. A.1–A.69. Institute of Archeol-
             ogy and Anthropology, University of South Carolina, Columbia.
Valentine, K.W.G., and J. B. Dalrymple
   1976   Quaternary Buried Paleosols: A Critical Review. *Quaternary Research*
             6:209–222.
Villa, Paola
   1982   Conjoinable Pieces and Site Formation Processes. *American Antiquity*
             47:276–290.

Villa, Paola, and Jean Courtin
  1983   The Interpretation of Stratified Sites: A View from Underground. *Journal of Archaeological Science* 10:267–281.
Villas, Cathleen A.
  1985   Tapping the Subsurface to Unearth the Paleogeomorphology of an Archaeological Site. In *Contributions to Aegean Archaeology: Studies in Honor of William A. MacDonald*, edited by Nancy C. Wilkie and William D. E. Coulson, pp. 161–169. University of Minnesota Publications in Ancient Studies. University of Minnesota, Center for Ancient Studies, Minneapolis.
Vita-Finzi, Claudio
  1978   *Archaeological Sites in Their Setting.* Thames and Hudson, London.
Vreeken, W. J.
  1984   Relative Dating of Soils and Paleosols. In *Quaternary Dating Methods*, edited by William C. Mahaney, pp. 269–281. Elsevier, Amsterdam.
Walker, Roger G.
  1984   General Introduction: Facies, Facies Sequences and Facies Models. In *Facies Models*, 2d ed., edited by Roger G. Walker, pp. 1–9. Geoscience Canada, Reprint Series 1. Geological Association of Canada, Toronto.
Walker, Roger G. (editor)
  1984   *Facies Models.* 2d ed. Geoscience Canada, Reprint Series 1. Geological Association of Canada, Toronto.
Walker, Roger G., and Douglas J. Cant
  1984   Sandy Fluvial Systems. In *Facies Models*, 2d ed., edited by Roger G. Walker, pp. 71–89. Geoscience Canada, Reprint Series 1. Geological Association of Canada, Toronto.
Wandsnider, LuAnn
  1984   Geomorphological Processes and the Integrity of Archaeological Remains in Dune Fields. Paper presented at the 50th Annual Meeting of the Society for American Archaeology, Denver.
  1987   Natural Formation Process Experimentation and Archaeological Analysis. In *Natural Formation Processes and the Archaeological Record*, edited by D. T. Nash and M. D. Petraglia, pp. 150–185. BAR International Series 352. BAR, Oxford.
  1988   Experimental Investigation of the Effect of Dune Processes on Archeological Remains. *American Archeology* 7:18–28.
Warren, Claude N.
  1967   The San Dieguito Complex: A Review and Hypothesis. *American Antiquity* 32:168–185.
Warren, Claude N. (editor)
  1966   *The San Dieguito Type Site: M. J. Rogers' 1938 Excavation on the San Dieguito River.* San Diego Museum Papers, no. 5. San Diego Museum of Man, San Diego.

Warren, Claude N., and D. L. True
  1961   The San Dieguito Complex and Its Place in California Prehistory. *UCLA Archaeological Survey Annual Report, 1960–1961,* pp. 246–338. Department of Anthropology and Sociology, University of California, Los Angeles.
Warren, Lyman O.
  1964   Possibly Submerged Oyster Shell Middens of Upper Tampa Bay. *Florida Anthropologist* 17 (4): 227–230.
Washburn, A. L.
  1980   *Geocryology: A Survey of Periglacial Processes and Environments.* 2d ed. John Wiley & Sons, New York.
Waters, Michael R.
  1983   Late Holocene Lacustrine Chronology and Archaeology of Ancient Lake Cahuilla, California. *Quaternary Research* 19:373–387.
  1985   Late Quaternary Alluvial Stratigraphy of Whitewater Draw, Arizona: Implications for Regional Correlation of Fluvial Deposits in the America Southwest. *Geology* 13:705–708.
  1986a   The Sulphur Spring Stage and Its Place in New World Prehistory. *Quaternary Research* 25:251–256.
  1986b   *The Geoarchaeology of Whitewater Draw, Arizona.* Anthropological Papers of the University of Arizona, no. 45. University of Arizona Press, Tucson.
  1986c   Geoarchaeological Investigations of the Picacho Study Area. In *Prehistoric Hunter-Gatherers of South Central Arizona: The Picacho Reservoir Archaic Project,* edited by Frank E. Bayham, Donald H. Morris, and M. Steven Shackley, pp. 17–35. Anthropological Field Studies, no. 13. Office of Cultural Resource Management, Department of Anthropology, Arizona State University, Tempe.
  1987a   Holocene Alluvial Geology and Geoarchaeology of AZ BB:13:14 and the San Xavier Reach of the Santa Cruz River, Arizona. In *The Archaeology of the San Xavier Bridge Site (AZ BB:13:14), Tucson Basin, Southern Arizona,* edited by John C. Ravesloot, pp. 39–60. Archaeological Series, no. 171. Cultural Resource Management Division, Arizona State Museum, University of Arizona, Tucson.
  1987b   Geomorphic Analysis of Hohokam Settlement Patterns on Alluvial Fans Along the Western Flank of the Tortolita Mountains, Arizona. In *Studies in the Hohokam Community of Marana,* edited by Glen E. Rice, pp. 31–48. Anthropological Field Studies, no. 15. Office of Cultural Resource Management, Department of Anthropology, Arizona State University, Tempe.
  1987c   Geoarchaeological Investigations of the Schuk Toak and San Xavier Study Areas. In *Archaeological Studies of the Avra Valley, Arizona, For the Papago Water Supply Project,* edited by Allen Dart, pp. 207–220.

Anthropological Papers, no. 9. Institute for American Research, Tucson.

1988a   The Impact of Fluvial Processes and Landscape Evolution on Archaeological Sites and Settlement Patterns Along the San Xavier Reach of the Santa Cruz River, Arizona. *Geoarchaeology* 3:205–219.

1988b   Holocene Alluvial Geology and Geoarchaeology of the San Xavier Reach of the Santa Cruz River, Arizona. *Geological Society of America Bulletin* 100:479–491.

1988c   Implications of the Alluvial Record of the Santa Cruz River to the Discovery of Paleoindian and Early Archaic Sites in the Tucson Basin, Arizona. *Current Research in the Pleistocene* 5:98–99.

1988d   Geoarcheological Investigations at 41HR541, Harris County, Texas. In *Archeological Investigations at a Late Ceramic Bison Kill Site, (41HR541), Whiteoak Bayou, Harris County, Texas,* edited by Mary J. McReynolds, Randy Korgel, and H. Blaine Ensor, pp. 93–103. Reports of Investigations, no. 7. Archeological Research Laboratory, Texas A & M University, College Station.

1989   Late Quaternary Lacustrine History and Paleoclimatic Significance of Pluvial Lake Cochise, Southeastern Arizona. *Quaternary Research* 32:1–11.

1990   Late Quaternary Alluvial Stratigraphy and Early Holocene Archaeology of Whitewater Draw, Arizona. In *Archaeological Geology of North America,* pp. 315–322. *See* Lasca and Donahue 1990.

1991   The Geoarchaeology of Gullies and Arroyos in Southern Arizona. *Journal of Field Archaeology* 18:141–159.

Waters, Michael R., and John J. Field

1986   Geomorphic Analysis of Hohokam Settlement Patterns on Alluvial Fans Along the Western Flank of the Tortolita Mountains, Arizona. *Geoarchaeology* 1:329–345.

Waters, Michael R., and Anne I. Woosley

1990   The Geoarchaeology and Preceramic Prehistory of the Willcox Basin, SE Arizona. *Journal of Field Archaeology* 17:163–175.

Weber, Robert H.

1980   Geology of the Ake Site. In *The Ake Site: Collection and Excavation of LA 13423, Catron County, New Mexico,* edited by Patrick H. Beckett, pp. 223–238. Cultural Resources Management Division, Department of Sociology and Anthropology, New Mexico State University, Las Cruces.

Weide, Margaret L.

1976   A Cultural Sequence for the Yuha Desert. In *Background to Prehistory of the Yuha Desert Region,* edited by Philip J. Wilke, pp. 81–94. Ballena Press Anthropological Papers, no. 5. Ballena Press, Ramona, Calif.

Weimer, Robert J., James D. Howard, and Donald R. Lindsay

1982   Tidal Flats and Associated Tidal Channels. In *Sandstone Depositional*

Environments, edited by Peter A. Scholle and Darwin Spearing, pp. 191–245. Memoir 31. American Association of Petroleum Geologists, Tulsa, Okla.

Weinstein, Richard A.
 1981 Meandering Rivers and Shifting Villages: A Prehistoric Settlement Model in the Upper Steele Bayou Basin, Mississippi. *Southeastern Archaeological Conference Bulletin* 24:37–41.

Weinstein, Richard A., Wayne P. Glander, Sherwood M. Gagliano, Eileen K. Burden, and Kathleen G. McCloskey
 1979a *Cultural Resources Survey of the Upper Steele Bayou Basin, West-Central Mississippi.* 3 vols. Coastal Environments, Inc., Baton Rouge, La.

Weinstein, Richard A., Diane E. Wiseman, Laura A. Landry, and Wayne P. Glander
 1979b *Environment and Settlement on the Southwestern Louisiana Prairies: A Cultural Resources Survey in the Bayou Mallet Watershed.* Coastal Environments, Inc., Baton Rouge, La.

Wendorf, Michael
 1982 The Fire Areas of Santa Rosa Island: An Interpretation. *North American Archaeologist* 3:173–180.

Whalen, Norman B.
 1971 *Cochise Culture Sites in the Central San Pedro Drainage, Arizona.* Ph.D. diss., University of Arizona. University Microfilms, Ann Arbor, Mich.

Wheat, Joe Ben
 1972 *The Olsen-Chubbuck Site: A Paleo-Indian Bison Kill.* Society for American Archaeology, Washington, D.C. *American Antiquity* 37 no. 1, pt. 2 (Memoir 26).

Wheeler, Harry E.
 1958 Time-Stratigraphy. *Bulletin of the American Association of Petroleum Geologists* 42:1047–1063.

White, William P., and Thomas E. Emerson
 1983 Site Geomorphology. In *The Florence Street Site,* by Thomas E. Emerson, George R. Milner, and Douglas K. Jackson. American Bottom Archaeology FAI-270 Site Reports, 2:13–18. University of Illinois Press, Urbana and Chicago.

White, William P., Sissel Johannessen, Paula G. Cross, and Lucretia S. Kelly
 1984 Environmental Setting. In *American Bottom Archaeology: A Summary of the FAI-270 Project Contribution to the Culture History of the Mississippi River Valley,* edited by Charles J. Bareis and James W. Porter, pp. 15–33. University of Illinois Press, Urbana and Chicago.

Whittlesey, Stephanie M., Eric J. Arnould, and William E. Reynolds
 1982 Archaeological Sediments: Discourse, Experiment, and Application. In *Multidisciplinary Research at Grasshopper Pueblo Arizona,* edited by William A. Longacre, Sally J. Holbrook, and Michael W. Graves, pp. 28–35. Anthropological Papers of the University of Arizona, no. 40. University of Arizona Press, Tucson.

Wiant, Michael D., Edwin R. Hajic, and Thomas R. Styles
1983   Napoleon Hollow and Koster Site Stratigraphy: Implications for Holocene Landscape Evolution and Studies of Archaic Period Settlement Patterns in the Lower Illinois River Valley. In *Archaic Hunters and Gatherers in the American Midwest,* edited by James C. Phillips and James A. Brown, pp. 147–164. Academic Press, New York.

Wicksten, Mary K.
1989   Invertebrates that Disturb Archaeological Materials. In *Interdisciplinary Workshop on the Physical-Chemical-Biological Processes Affecting Archeological Sites,* edited by Christopher C. Mathewson, pp. 181–194. Contract Report EL-89-1. U.S. Army Corps of Engineers, Waterways Experiment Station, Vicksburg, Miss.

Wilke, Philip J.
1978   *Late Prehistoric Human Ecology at Lake Cahuilla, Coachella Valley, California.* Contributions of the University of California Archaeological Research Facility, no. 38. University of California, Berkeley.

Wilkins, Kenneth T.
1989   Burrowing Vertebrates and Their Role in Archaeological Site Decay. In *Interdisciplinary Workshop on the Physical-Chemical-Biological Processes Affecting Archeological Sites,* edited by Christopher C. Mathewson, pp. 195–217. Contract Report EL-89-1. U.S. Army Corps of Engineers, Waterways Experiment Station, Vicksburg, Miss.

Willey, G. R., and Philip Phillips
1958   *Method and Theory in American Archaeology.* University of Chicago Press, Chicago.

Williams, Pete A., and Robert I. Orlins
1963   *The Corn Creek Dunes Site: A Dated Surface Site in Southern Nevada.* Nevada State Museum Anthropological Papers, no. 10. Nevada State Museum, Carson City.

Willig, Judith A.
1984   Geoarchaeological Research at the Dietz Site and the Question of Clovis Lake/Marsh Adaptation in the Northern Great Basin. In *Geoarchaeology in the Northwest: Recent Applications and Contributions,* edited by Judith A. Willig, pp. 56–69. Special issue of *Tebiwa: The Journal of the Idaho Museum of Natural History,* vol. 21.
1988   Paleo-Archaic Adaptations and Lakeside Settlement Patterns in the Northern Alkali Basin. In *Early Human Occupation in Far Western North America: The Clovis-Archaic Interface,* edited by Judith A. Willig, C. Melvin Aikens, and John L. Fagan, pp. 417–482. Nevada State Museum Anthropological Papers, no. 21. Nevada State Museum, Carson City.

Wilson, Michael C.
1983a   *Once Upon A River: Archaeology and Geology of the Bow River Valley at Calgary, Alberta, Canada.* National Museum of Man, Mercury Series.

Archaeological Survey of Canada, Paper No. 114. National Museums of Canada, Ottawa.

1983b   On the Threshold of Archaeological Visibility. *Alberta Archaeological Review* 6:9–20.

1983c   *Geological Influences on Archaeological Visibility in the Forty Mile Coulee Area, Alberta, Calgary.* Report prepared for Ethos Consultants, Ltd., and Alberta Environment.

1986   Late Quaternary Landscape Modification in the Cochrane-Calgary Area of the Bow Valley and Its Influence on Archaeological Visibility. In *Eastern Slopes Prehistory: Selected Papers,* edited by B. Ronaghan, pp. 63–90. Occasional Paper No. 30. Archaeological Survey of Alberta, Edmonton.

1990   Archaeological Geology in Western Canada: Techniques, Approaches, and Integrative Themes. In *Archaeological Geology of North America,* pp. 61–86. *See* Lasca and Donahue 1990.

Wilson, Michael C., David W. Harvey, and Richard G. Forbis

1983   Geoarchaeological Investigations of the Age and Context of the Stalker (Taber Child) Site, DIPa 4, Alberta. *Canadian Journal of Archaeology* 7:179–207.

Wood, W. Raymond, and Donald L. Johnson

1978   A Survey of Disturbance Processes in Archaeological Site Formation. In *Advances in Archaeological Method and Theory,* vol. 1, edited by Michael B. Schiffer, pp. 315–381. Academic Press, New York.

Workman, William B.

1979   The Significance of Volcanism in the Prehistory of Subarctic Northwest North America. In *Volcanic Activity and Human Ecology,* edited by Payson D. Sheets and Donald K. Grayson, pp. 339–392. Academic Press, New York.

Wright, H. E., Jr., and Stephen C. Porter (editors)

1983   *Late-Quaternary Environments of the United States.* Vol. 1: *The Late Pleistocene.* University of Minnesota Press, Minneapolis.

Wright, V. Paul (editor)

1986   *Paleosols: Their Recognition and Interpretation.* Princeton University Press, Princeton, N.J.

Wymer, J. J.

1976   The Interpretation of Palaeolithic Cultural and Faunal Material Found in Pleistocene Sediments. In *Geoarchaeology: Earth Science and the Past,* edited by D. A. Davidson and M. L. Shackley, pp. 327–334. Duckworth, London.

Yaalon, Dan H. (editor)

1971   *Paleopedology: Origin, Nature, and Dating of Paleosols.* International Society of Soil Sciences and Israel University Press, Jerusalem.

Yates, Bonnie C., and C. Reid Ferring (editors)

1986   *An Assessment of Cultural Resources in the Trinity River Basin: Dallas,*

Tarrand, and Denton Counties, Texas. Institute of Applied Sciences, North Texas State University, Denton.

Yerkes, Richard W.

1987   *Prehistoric Life on the Mississippi Floodplain.* University of Chicago Press, Chicago.

Young, Anthony

1972   *Slopes.* Oliver and Boyd, Edinburgh.

Zingg, T.

1935   Beitrage zur Schatteranalyse. *Schweizerische Mineralogische und Petrographische Mitteilungen* 15:39–140.

Index

Note: Figures referenced independently of text are given in italics. Additional figures related to a topic may also be found on the pages cited for text.

Ablation till, 237
Accretion (eolian) deposits, 189
Accretionary soil, 43. *See also* Cumulative soil
Aeroturbation, 306
Aggradation (deposition), 60. *See also* Lithostratigraphic units; Lithostratigraphy; Sediments
A horizon, *41, 45,* 46, 49
Ak-Chin, *145,* 171–75
Ake site (N.M.), 196–97
Albic horizon, 50, 52–53
Alluvial environments, 37, 115–84; alluvial fans, *39,* 154–57, *158;* anastomosing rivers, *123,* 143–44; archaeological record in, *84,* 89, 157–63, 321–22; arroyos, 145–49; braided rivers, *123,* 124–28; gullies, 145–49; landscape reconstruction in, 163–83, 323–25; meandering rivers, *38, 123,* 128–43; sedimentary processes of, 116–22; site formation in, 126–28, *129,* 138–43, 144, 148–49, 151–54, 156–57, *158;* terraces, 149–54

Alluvial fans, *39,* 154–57, *158;* geology of, 154–56; site formation in, 156–57, *158*
Alluvial piedmont, 154. *See also* Bajada
Alluvium, 122
Anastomosing rivers, *123,* 143–44; geology of, 143–44; site formation in, 144
Antevs, Ernst, 8, *10*
Anthrogenic sediments, 33
Anthropic epipedon, 50, 52
Anthropic sediments and soils, 33
Anthropogenic sediments and soils, 32
Aquifer, 215, *218*
Archaeobotany, 3, 11–13
Archaeological context, 11
Archaeological geology, 4, 7
Archaeological record, 11, *84,* 89, 92–103; in alluvial environments, *84,* 89, 157–63, 321–22; in coastal environments, 262–66, *267, 268, 269,* 275–80; creation of, 89, 92–100, 102–3; detection of, 100; erosion and, 83–85, 89, 97–100, 159–65; stability and, *84,*

94, 95–96, 97; modeling of, 100–
102; site context preservation,
102, 103–5; site preservation,
92–103. See also Site formation
Archaeological stratigraphic code, 62
Archaeometry, xix–xx, 3
Archaeosediments, 16, 32–33
Argillic horizon, 50, 52
Argilliturbation, 104, 299–300
Arroyo, 145–149; archaeological
record in, 89, 97–100; geology
of, 145–48; landscape
reconstruction in, 175–79; site
formation in, 64, 148–49
Arroyo-mouth fan, 90, 145, 147
Artesian spring, 215–20
Articlasts, 126
Ash, 31, 32. See also Volcanic ash
Aubrey site (Tex.), 100, 313
Avalanche deposits, 188, 189
Avulsion, 137–38

Backshore, 256, 257
Bajada, 90, 146, 154, 171–75
Ball-and-pillow structures, 304
Barchan dunes, 190–92
Barchanoid dunes, 191, 192
Barrier islands, 257–58
Bars. See Channel bars
Baseflow, 118, 119
Batiquitos Lagoon (Calif.), 283–85
Beach drift, 250, 251
Beaches, 256, 257
Beachface, 256, 257
Beds, lithostratigraphic, 68
Beds, sedimentary: boundaries of, 34;
thickness of, 34, 35; types of, 34–
36
Bedload, 122
Bering Land Bridge, 235, 289
Berm, 257
B horizon, 41, 45, 47, 49
Bioturbation, 104. See also
Floralturbation; Faunalturbation

Blocks (volcanic), 30–31
Blocky structure (soil), 44–45
Blowouts, 191, 193
Bombs (volcanic), 31
Boney Springs (Mo.), 218
Borax Lake site (Calif.), 156
Braided rivers, 123, 124–28; geology
of, 124–26; site formation in,
126–28, 129
Breaker zone, 250, 256, 257
Breccia, 242
Bryan, Kirk, 8, 9
Buried Dune site (Ariz.), 198
Buried paleosol, 57–58, 59, 72

C. W. Harris site (Calif.), 128, 129
Calcic horizon, 51, 53
Cambic horizon, 50, 52
Campbell site (Mo.), 305
Cape Henlopen (Del.), 281–83,
284
Carbonaceous (organic) sediments, 16,
31
Carbonate sediments, 29–30
Carlston Annis Mound (Ky.), 314–16
Casper site (Wyo.), 198–99, 200–202
Caves, 240–41
Cave Spring site (Tenn.), 291–92, 293
Channel abandonment, 135–38
Channel bars: chute, 38, 133–34;
lateral, 124, 126; longitudinal,
124, 125; point, 38, 130–31,
132–33; transverse, 124, 125–26
Channel lag, 124, 131, 132, 133
Chemical sediments, 16, 28–30
Chemical weathering, 16–19
Chenier plain, 260
Cheniers, 259–260
Cherokee Sewer site (Ia.), 157, 158
China Lake (Calif.), 210
C horizon, 41, 45, 47, 49
Chronostratigraphy, 77–86;
completeness and structure of the
stratigraphic record, 79, 83–86,

97–100; dating episodes of
deposition, erosion, or stability,
78, 79, 82
Chute, 38, 133–34
Chute bar, 38, 133–34
Chute cut-off, 135–36
Cienegas, 147
Cinders, 31
Clastic sediments, 16, 19–28;
classification of, 22–24; fabric of,
27–28; mineralogy of, 28;
morphology (shape) of, 26–27,
28, origin of, 16–19; roundness
of, 26–27, 28; size of, 20–22;
sorting of, 24–26; sphericity of,
26, 28
Claypool site (Colo.), 197–98
Climbing dune, 194
Coastal environments, 37, 249–90;
archaeological record in, 262–66,
267, 268, 269, 275–80; barrier
islands, 257–58; beaches, 256,
257; cheniers, 259–60; deltas,
261–62; depositional coastlines,
256–62; emergent coastlines,
274–75; erosional coastlines,
254, 255; landscape
reconstruction in, 280–90;
preservation of submerged sites,
275–80; sea level changes, 251–
54; sedimentary processes of,
249–51; site formation (extant
coastline), 270–75; submerged
coastlines, 255; submerged sites,
263–66, 268, 269, 278–81, 282,
tidal flats, 258–59
Coffey site (Kans.), 142–43, 168–70
Colby site (Wyo.), 164–67
Colluvial (slope) environments. See
Slope (colluvial) environments
Colluvium, 232
Columnar structure (soil), 44–45
Compaction, 305–6
Complex dunes, 190

Composite (polygenetic) soils, 59
Compound dunes, 189–90
Conformable contacts and sequences,
64, 69–71. See also Contacts
Constant elements of the landscape,
88, 90, 91. See also Landscape
Contacts (lithostratigraphic), 68–74;
conformable, 64, 69–71; lateral,
73–74; unconformable, 64, 68–
69, 71–73. See also
Unconformities
Context (site), 11, 102, 103–5;
archaeological, 11; primary, 105;
secondary, 105; systemic, 11, 102,
103–5
Contextual archaeology, 4–7, 11–13
Continental shelf, 252
Convoluted bedding, 304
Coppice dune, 194
Cordilleran ice sheet, 234, 235
Correlation, 86–88, 89
Cradle-and-knoll topography, 307,
308
Creep: eolian, 186, 188; slope, 231,
232, 301–2
Crevasse channel, 134–35
Crevasse splay, 38, 134–35
Cross-bedding, 34–35, 189
Cross-lamination, 34, 35
Crumb structure (soil), 44–45
Cryoturbation, 104, 292–99
Crystalturbation, 104, 306
Cultural processes of site formation
(cultural transformation), 11, 102
Cumulative (cumulic) soil, 43, 58, 72,
95, 140
Cut terraces, 149–151. See also
Terraces

Dating methods, 77–79, 80–81
Debert site (Nova Scotia), 307
Debris flows, 155, 231
Deflation, 205, 206
Deformation, 34, 36, 304–6

Degradation (erosion), 60–61. *See also* Erosional unconformity
Degradational vacuity, *78, 82*
Delaware Canyon (Okla.), *72, 93*
Deltas: in glaciolacustrine environments, *236, 239*; in lacustrine environments, *221, 222*; landscape reconstruction in, *285–87, 288, 289*; in marine environments, *261–62*
Deposition (aggradation), 60. *See also* Lithostratigraphic units; Lithostratigraphy; Sediments
Deposition (environments), 16, 36–38. *See also* Facies
Depositional terraces, 149, *150*. See also Terraces
Desert pavements, 204–8; formation of, 204–7; site formation in, *206*, 207–8
Desert varnish, 207
Des Moines River Valley (Ia.), 152–54
Diagnostic soil horizons: subsurface, 50–53; surface, 50, 51–52
Diastems, 34, 70
Diatomite, 30
Dietz site (Oreg.), 227–29
Disconformities, 71
Dissolved load, 122
Dome dunes, *191*, 192
Double Adobe site (Ariz.), *10*, 127–28
Drainage basin, 116, *117*
Drift, 234–37
Dripline, 241
Dripstones, *241*, 242
Dry Creek site (Alaska), 203, *204*
Duripan, 51, 53
Dust: eolian, 202; volcanic, 31
Dynamic elements of the landscape, 88, *90*, 91. *See also* Landscape

Éboulis, *241*, 242
Echo dunes, 194

Effluent (perennial) streams, 119
E horizon, 45, 46, 49
Eluvial horizon, 42
Eluviation, 42
Endogenous sediments, *241, 242*
Eolian environments, 37, 185–213; desert pavements, 204–8; erosion in, 208–10; interdune areas, *189*, 195; landscape reconstruction in, 200–202; loess, 202–4, *235*; sand dunes, 187–202; sand sheets, 195; sedimentary processes of, 185–87; site formation in, 195–200; 203–4; 207–8; 209–10
Ephemeral streams, 120
Epilimnion, 221–22
Epipedons, 50, 51–52
Erosion (degradation), 60–61. *See also* Erosional unconformity
Erosional terraces, 149–51. *See also* Terraces
Erosional unconformity, *25, 64, 67, 68–69, 71–73, 78, 82, 84. See also* Unconformities
Eskers, *236, 239*
Estuaries, 255
Evaporites, 30
Event age, 77
Exhumed paleosol, 58, *59*
Exogenous sediments, *241*, 242–43

Facies, 38–40, 74, *75*, 86. *See also* Sedimentary environments
Falls, 230, *231*
Falling dune, 194
Fan. *See* Alluvial fans
Faults, 34, 304–5
Faunalturbation, 104, 309–16
Fill terraces, 149, *150*. *See also* Terraces
Fining-upward (sedimentary) sequence, *38, 131*, 133
Fjords, 255

Flame structures, 304
Floodbasins, *38*, 135
Floodplains, 66, 132
Floralturbation, 104, 306–9, *310*, *311*
Flows, 231–32
Flowstones, *241*, 242
Fluvial environments, 115. *See also* Alluvial environments
Folds, *34*, 304
Folk classification of sediments, 22–23, *24*
Folsom site (N.M.), 8
Foreshore, 256, *257*
Formation, *64*, 66–68
Formation processes. *See* Site formation processes
Fragipans, 51, 53
Frost: creep, 301; heave, 295, *296*; pull, 295, *296*

Gelifluction, 302–3
Geoarchaeology, 3–13, 317–20; definition of, xix, 3–4; history of, 7–12; methodologies of, 317–19; objectives of, 7–13, 317
Geochronology, 4
Geomorphology, 3–4
Geosols, 75
Gilgai, 299
Glacial environments, 37, 234–40; effects on people, 240; geology of, 234–38; during the Pleistocene, 234, *235*; site formation in, 239–40
Glaciolacustrine environments, *236*, 239
Glaciomarine environments, 239
Gleyed soils, 48
Graded bedding, *34*, 36
Grain size nomenclature and classification, 20–26
Grain-supported fabric, 28
Granular structure (soil), 44–45

Gravelly braided rivers, 125
Graviturbation, 301–4
Gravity springs, 215, *217*
Groundwater, 117, *118*
Growth bedding, 36
Gullies, 145–49; geology of, 145–46; landscape reconstruction in, 171–75; site formation in, 148
Gully-mouth fan, 145–46, 172–75
Gypsic horizon, 51, 53

Halocline, 222
Harris, C. W., site (Calif.), 128, *129*
Helical flow, 130–31
Hiatus, 69
Hidden Falls site (Alaska), *238*, 239–40
Histic epipedon, 50, 52
Hjulstrom diagram, 120–21
Holocene epoch, 86
Horizons, soil, *41*, 45–51
Hot Springs site (S.D.), 220
Human ecosystem, 4–7, 11–13
Hungry Whistler site (Colo.), 295–96, *297*, 298
Hydrograph, 118, *119*
Hypolimnion, 221–22

Ice-free corridor, *235*, 240
Ice sheets, 134, *235*, *236*
Illuvial horizon, 42
Illuviation, 42
Imbrication, 27
Influent streams, 119–20
Interdune areas, *189*, 195
Interflow: in alluvial environments, 117–18; in lacustrine environments, *221*, 222–23
Intermittent streams, 120
Island Field site (Del.), 266, *267*
Iyatayet site (Alaska), 303–4

Jasper Ridge site (Calif.), 314, *315*

Kames, 239
Kettles, *236*, 239
Krotovina, 312, *313*

Lacuna, 78, 82
Lacustrine environments, 37, 219–30;
    geology of, 219–23; landscape
    reconstruction in, 225–30;
    playas, 223–25; pluvial lakes,
    225, *226*; site formation in, 225–
    27, *228*
Lag (channel), *124*, *131*, 132, *133*
Lag pavements. *See* Desert pavements
Lagoon, 257–58
Lake environments. *See* Lacustrine
    environments
Lake Bonneville (Utah), 225, *226*
Lake Cahuilla (Calif.), *29*, 226, 227,
    228, 229
Lake Cochise (Ariz.), *226*, 230
Lake Lahontan (Nev.), 225, *226*
Laminae, *34*, *35*
Landscape, 12, 88; constant elements
    of, 88, *90*, 91; dynamic elements
    of, 88, *90*, 91
Landscape evolution. *See* Landscape
    reconstruction
Landscape reconstruction, 11–12, 88–
    92; in alluvial environments,
    163–83, 323–25; in coastal
    environments, 280–90; in eolian
    environments, 200–202; in
    glacial environments, 239–40; in
    lacustrine environments, 225–30;
    regional diachronic, 92, 170–71,
    175–83; regional synchronic, 91–
    92, 170–75; in rockshelter
    environments, 246–47; site-
    specific diachronic, 92, 164, 168–
    70; site-specific synchronic, 91–
    92, 164–67; in slope
    environments, 232–33; in spring
    environments, 219, *220*
Landslides. *See* Slides

Lapilli, 31
Lateral accretion, *38*, *66*, *130*, 131–34
Lateral bars, *124*, 126
Laurentide ice sheet, 234, *235*
Lee dunes, 194
Lens, *34*, 36
Levees, 38, *131*, 134
Linear dunes, *191*, 193
Lithostratigraphic units, 62–74;
    burial of artifacts in, 93, 95;
    contacts between, *64*, 68–74;
    dating of, 78, 79; definition of,
    62–63; vs. pedostratigraphic
    units, 76–77; time transgressive
    nature of, 63–66; types of, *64*,
    66–68
Lithostratigraphy, 62–74
Load structures, *34*, 304
Lodgement till, 237
Loess, 202–4; geology of, 202–3,
    235, site formation in, 203–4
Loess Hills (Ia.), 159–63
Longitudinal bars, *124*, 125
Longitudinal dunes, 193
Longshore currents, 250, *252*
Lubbock Lake site (Tex.), *75*, 76–77,
    105–14

Marker horizon, *34*, 36, 68, *101*
Marls, 30
Massive bedding, *34*, 35
Massive structure (soil), *44*, 45
Mass wasting, 230–32; catastrophic,
    154–55, 230–31; non-
    catastrophic, 230, 231–32, 301–
    4. *See also* Slope environments
Matrix-supported fabric, 28
Mazama Ash, *32*, 211–12
Mean-residence ages (soil), 79
Meander belt, 137
Meandering rivers, *38*, *66*, *123*, 128–
    43; geology of, *38*, *66*, 128–38;
    landscape reconstruction in, 179–
    83; lateral accretion, *38*, *66*, *130*,

131–34; site formation in, 138–43; vertical accretion, *38*, *66*, 132, 134–35

Member, *64*, 68

Mineral soil horizons, 48

Mississippi River Delta, 285–87, *288*, *289*

Mollic epipedon, 50, *52*

Moraines, *236*, 237–38

Mudflows, 155, *156*, 231

Murray Springs site (Ariz.), *101*, 102

Natric horizon, 50, *52*

Natural levees, *38*, *131*, 134

Natural processes of site formation (natural transformations), 11, *102*; preservation of site context, 102, 103–5; and the archaeological record, *84*, 92–103. *See also* Site formation

Nebo Hill site (Mo.), *294*, 297, 298–99

Neck cut-off, 135, *136*

Ochric epipedon, 50, *52*

O horizon, 45, *46*, 49

Oraibi site (Ariz.), 5–6

Organic (carbonaceous) sediments, 16, 31

Organic soil horizons, 48

Outwash plains, *236*, 239

Overbank flooding, *119*, 129, 132, 134–35

Overflow (lake), *221*, 222

Overland flow, 116, *118*

Overturn (lake), 222

Oxbow lake, *38*, 135–37

Oxic horizon, 51, *52*

Paired terraces, *150*, 151. *See also* Terraces

Paleosols, 57–60; as unconformities, *59*, 68–69, 71, 74, *75*, 78, *79*, 82,

84; buried, 57–58, *59*, *72*; dating of, *78*, *79*, 82; exhumed, 58, *59*; relationship to pedostratigraphic units, 74–76; relict, 58–59. *See also* Pedostratigraphic units; Pedostratigraphy; Soils

Palimpsest sediments, 277

Parabolic dunes, *191*, 192

Parent material, 40, *41*, 53, 56

Peace Point site (Canada), 139–40

Peat, 31

Pedology, 4, 40

Pedostratigraphic units, 74–77; dating of, *78*, *79*, 82; definition of, 75; deposition of archaeological debris onto, 94, 95–96; incorporation of archaeological debris into, 93–95; vs. lithostratigraphic units, 76–77. *See also* Paleosols

Pedostratigraphy, 74–77

Peds, 44

Pen Point site (S.C.), 140, *141*

Perennial (effluent) streams, 119

Permafrost, *235*, 294–95

Permeability, 28

Petrocalcic horizon, 51, *53*

Petrogypsic horizon, 51, *53*

Phi (ϕ) scale, 20–21, 22

Physical weathering, 16–19

Piedmont, 154. *See also* Bajada

Piedmont glaciers, 234

Pinchout, 73–74

Plaggen epipedon, 50, *52*

Plastic deformation, 304

Platy structure (soil), 44

Playas, 223–25

Pleistocene epoch, 86

Pluvial lakes, 225, *226*

Point bars, *38*, 130–31, 132–33

Polygenetic (composite) soils, 59

Porosity, 28

Precipitation dunes, 195

Primary context, 105

Prismatic structure (soil), 44
Pyroclastic sediments, 16, 30–31, *32*

Quaternary period, 86

Rates of sedimentation, 79, 93, *96*
Ravinement surface, *276, 277*
Recessional moraine, *236,* 237–38
Relict paleosols, 58–59
Retention ridges, 195
Reversing dunes, *190,* 193
R horizon, 45, 48, 49
Rigid deformation, 304–5
Rip currents, 250, *252*
Riser, 149, *150*
Rockshelters, 37, 240–47; evolution
    of, 246–47; geology of, 240–44;
    site formation in, 244–47
Root casts, 309, *310, 311*
Roundness, 26–27, *28*

Sabine River, 278–79, 280–81, *282*
Salic horizon, 51, 53
Saltation: in alluvial environments,
    121–22; in eolian environments,
    186, *188*
Sample age, 77
Sandblasting, 208
Sand dunes, 187–202; geology of,
    187–89; landscape reconstruction
    in, 200–202; site formation in,
    195–200; types of, 189–95
Sand sheets, 195
Sandy braided rivers, 125
Santa Cruz River (Ariz.), *64,* 83–85,
    89, 90, 97, 98–100, *147,* 175–
    79
San Xavier Bridge site (Ariz.), *64,*
    148–49
Sapropel, 31
Scree, 156, 230
Sea level: changes in, 251–54; land
    connections created by, *235,* 289–
    90

Searles Lake system (Calif.), 225, *226*
Secondary context, 105
Sedimentary environments, 16, 36–38.
    See also Facies
Sedimentary structures, 33–36
Sedimentation rates, 79, 93, *96*
Sedimentation units, 34
Sedimentology, 4
Sediments, 15–40; archaeosediments,
    16, 32–33; burial of sites by, 93,
    94, carbonaceous (organic), 16,
    31; chemical, 16, 28–30;
    classification of, 16; clastic, 16,
    19–28; definition of, 15; facies,
    38–40; origin of, 16–19;
    pyroclastic, 16, 30–31, *32;* and
    lithostratigraphic units, 62–63,
    76; sedimentary (depositional)
    environments, 16, 36–38;
    sedimentary structures, 33–36;
    vs. soils, 15, 40, *41;*
    volcaniclastic, 31. *See also* Facies;
    Lithostratigraphic units;
    Lithostratigraphy
Seeps, 215, *217. See also* Spring
    environments
Shadow dunes, 194
Shoaling zone, 250, *257*
Shoreface, 256, *257*
Shoreface retreat, 275–77
Shrub-coppice dunes, 194
Sief dunes, 193
Sinter, 30
Site disturbance: aeroturbation, 306;
    argilliturbation, 104, 299–300;
    bioturbation, 104; before burial,
    102, 103–4; during burial, *102,*
    104; after burial, *102,* 104–5,
    291–316; cryoturbation, 104,
    292–99; crystalturbation, 104,
    306; deformation, 304–6;
    faunalturbation, 104, 309–16;
    floralturbation, 104, 306–9, *310,*
    311; graviturbation, 301–4

Site formation, 11, 92–105; in alluvial environments, 126–28, *129, 138–43, 144, 148–49, 151–54, 156–57, 158*; in coastal environments, 270–75; cultural processes of, 11, *102*; in eolian environments, 195–200, 203–4, 207–8, 209–10; in glacial environments, 239–40; in lacustrine environments, 225–27, *228*; natural processes in, 11, 92–105; in rockshelter environments, 244–47; in slope (colluvial) environments, 156–57, 232, 301–4; in spring environments, 216–20. *See also* Archaeological record; Systemic context

Site matrix, 15, *17. See also* Sediments; Soils; Site disturbance

Site prediction models, 100–102, 319

Slides, 230, *231*

Slipface, 187, *189*

Slope (colluvial) environments, 37, 230–33; geology of, 154–55, 230–32, 301–3; landscape reconstruction in, 232–33; site formation in, 156–57, 232, 301–4

Slumps, 230–31

Soil, 15, 40–60; archaeological debris in, 93–95; chronosequence, 55; classification, 53, *54*; creep, *231*, 232, 301–2; definition of, 40; diagnostic horizons, 50–53; formation of, 41–43; 53–57; horizon nomenclature, *41*, 45–51; orders, 52, *54, 56*; paleosols, 57–60; and pedostratigraphic units, 74–76; properties of, 43–45; structure of, 44–45; texture of, 23–24, 44; vs. sediments, 15, 40, *41. See also* Paleosols; Pedostratigraphic units; Pedostratigraphy

Solifluction, 302–4

Solum, 49

Sorting, 24–26

Spelothems, 242

Sphericity, 26, *28*

Spit, 257

Spodic horizon, 50, 52

Spring environments, 37, 215–20; artesian, 215–16, *218, 220*; gravity (seeps), 215, *217*; landscape reconstruction in, 219, *220*; site formation in, 216–20

Stability, landscape, 60. *See also* Paleosols; Pedostratigraphic units; Pedostratigraphy; Unconformities

Stalactites, *241*, 242

Stalagmites, 242

Star dunes, *190*, 192

Stepwise retreat, *276, 277*

Stone pavements. *See* Desert pavements

Stormflow, 118, *119*

Straight rivers, 123

Strandplains, 257

Strath terraces, 151

Stratification, 33–36

Stratigraphy, 4, 60–88; chronostratigraphy, 77–86; lithostratigraphy, 62–74; pedostratigraphy, 74–77

Stratum, 33–34

Stream: discharge, 116, 118–19; flow, 116–20; ordering, 116, *117*

Subsidence, 270, 306

Surf zone, 250, 256, *257*

Suspended load: in alluvial environments, 121, *122*; in eolian environments, 186, *188*

Swan Lake Meander (Miss.), 179–83

Swash zone, 250, *251, 256, 257*

Systemic context, 11, *102, 103*; disturbance of, *102*, 103–5. *See also* Context

Talus, 230, *231*

Talus cones, 156

Tephra, 30
Terminal moraine, *236*, 237
Terraces, 149–54; depositional (fill),
        149, *150*; erosional (cut), 149–
        51; paired, *150*, 151; site
        formation in, 151–54; strath,
        151; unpaired, *150*, 151
Thermocline, 221
Thorne Cave (Utah), 243, *245*, 246
Tidal channels, 258–59
Tidal flats, 258–59
Tides, 251
Till, 234–38; ablation, 237;
        lodgement, 237
Topographic dunes, 193–95
Traction, 122
Transgression, 275–77
Transverse bars, *124*, 125–26
Transverse dunes, *191*, 192
Travertine, 29–30
Tread, 149, *150*
Tree-sway, 307
Tree-throw, 307, *308*
Tufa, 29
Tuffs, 31
Turbidites, *221*, 223
Turbidity flows, 223

Umbric epipedon, 50, 52
Unconformable contacts and
        sequences, *64*, 68–69, 71–73. *See
        also* Contacts
Unconformities, 68–69, 71–73; and
        the archaeological record, 83–85,
        89, *94*, 95–100, 159–63; dating
        of (erosional), 78, 82; dating of
        (stable), 78, 79, 82; caused by
        erosion, 25, *64*, 67, 68–69, 71–

73, *78*, 82, *84*; caused by
        stability, *59*, 68–69, 71, 74, *75*,
        78, 79, 82, *84*
Underflow (lake), *221*, 223
Unpaired terraces, *150*, 151
USDA textural classification of soils,
        23–34

Valley glaciers, 234
Varves, *221*, 223
Ventifacts, 208–9
Vertical accretion, *38*, *66*, *132*,
        134–35
Vertisols, 299–300
Volcanic ash, 31, *32*; effects on people,
        212–13; use as marker bed, 210–
        12
Volcaniclastic sediment, 31

Walther's Law, 40
Washover fans, 257–58
Watershed, 116
Water table, 117, *118*
Wave-cut cliffs, notches, and
        platforms, 254, *255*
Waves, 249, *250*; form, 249, *250*;
        wave base, 249–50, 251
Weathering, 16–19
Welded soil profile, 58, *59*
Wentworth grain-size classification,
        20–22
Whitewater Draw (Ariz.), *10*, *67*,
        127–28
Wisconsin Glaciation, 234, *235*

Yardangs, 209

Zooarchaeology, 3, 11–13

About the Author

Michael R. Waters is an Associate Professor of Anthropology and Geography at Texas A & M University, where he has been teaching since 1985. He received his doctorate from the Department of Geosciences at the University of Arizona in 1983. His research interests include geoarchaeology, the geological and archaeological problems concerned with the peopling of the Americas, and late Quaternary geology. Dr. Waters has conducted research in the western United States and Jamaica. He has published articles on the late Quaternary lacustrine history and geoarchaeology of Paleolake Cahuilla in California and Paleolake Cochise in Arizona; the late Quaternary alluvial history and geoarchaeology of Whitewater Draw, the Santa Cruz River, and Tonto Creek, all in Arizona; and the late Holocene geology and geoarchaeology of St. Ann's Bay in Jamaica.